S0-AIU-016

SURVEY OF

American Industry and Careers

SURVEY OF

American Industry and Careers

Volume 5

Printing Industry—
Telecommunications Infrastructure Industry

The Editors of Salem Press

SALEM PRESS
Pasadena, California   Hackensack, New Jersey

WEST BEND LIBRARY

Editorial Director: Christina J. Moose
Project Editor: Rowena Wildin
Manuscript Editors: Stacy Cole, Andy Perry
Acquisitions Manager: Mark Rehn
Administrative Assistant: Paul Tifford, Jr.

Research Supervisor: Jeffry Jensen
Photo Editor: Cynthia Breslin Beres
Design and Layout: James Hutson
Additional Layout: William Zimmerman

Cover photo: ©Jose Luis Pelaez Inc./Blend Images/CORBIS

Copyright ©2012, by Salem Press, A Division of EBSCO Publishing, Inc.
All rights in this book are reserved. No part of this work may be used or reproduced in any manner whatsoever or transmitted in any form or by any means, electronic or mechanical, including photocopy, recording, or any information storage and retrieval system, without written permission from the copyright owner except in the case of brief quotations embodied in critical articles and reviews or in the copying of images deemed to be freely licensed or in the public domain. For information, address the publisher, Salem Press, at csr@salemspress.com.

∞ The paper used in these volumes conforms to the American National Standard for Permanence of Paper for Printed Library Materials, X39.48-1992 (R1997).

Library of Congress Cataloging-in-Publication Data

Survey of American industry and careers / The Editors of Salem Press.
    v.   cm.
    Includes bibliographical references and indexes.
    ISBN 978-1-58765-768-9 (set : alk. paper) — ISBN 978-1-58765-769-6 (vol. 1 : alk. paper) — ISBN 978-1-58765-770-2 (vol. 2 : alk. paper) — ISBN 978-1-58765-771-9 (vol. 3 : alk. paper) — ISBN 978-1-58765-772-6 (vol. 4 : alk. paper) — ISBN 978-1-58765-773-3 (vol. 5 : alk. paper) — ISBN 978-1-58765-774-0 (vol. 6 : alk. paper) 1. Business—Vocational guidance—United States. 2. Industries—United States. 3. Occupations—United States. 4. Vocational guidance—United States. I. Salem Press.
    HF5382.5.U5S87 2012
    331.7020973—dc23
                                                                    2011019601

First Printing

PRINTED IN THE UNITED STATES OF AMERICA

REF
331.702
SU79
v. 5

Contents

Complete List of Contents

VOLUME 4

VOLUME 5

VOLUME 6

List of Tables and Sidebars

SURVEY OF
American Industry and Careers

Printing Industry

©Dreamstime.com

INDUSTRY SNAPSHOT

General Industry: Manufacturing

Career Cluster: Manufacturing

Subcategory Industries: Book Printing; Bookbinding and Repair; Calendar Printing; Card Printing; Commercial Flexographic Printing; Commercial Gravure Printing; Commercial Lithographic Printing; Commercial Screen Printing; Digital Printing; Directory and Database Printing; Magazine and Periodical Printing; Manifold Business Form Printing; Music Printing; Postpress Services; Prepress Services; Quick Printing; Sign and Poster Printing

Related Industries: Advertising and Marketing Industry; Computer Hardware and Peripherals Industry; Heavy Machines Industry; Libraries and Archives Industry; Paper Manufacturing and Products Industry; Publishing and Information Industry

Annual Domestic Revenues: $166.6 billion USD (Printing Industries of America, 2009)

Annual International Revenues: $234.5 billion USD (Datamonitor USA, Global Commercial Printing Industry Profile, 2009)

Annual Global Revenues: $401.1 billion USD (Datamonitor USA, Global Commercial Printing Industry Profile, 2009)

NAICS Number: 323

INDUSTRY DEFINITION

Summary

The printing industry produces printed materials on a variety of substrates, including paper, plastic, metal, and fabric. These products range from books and magazines to forms, labels, packaging, and signage. Printing is divided into three areas: prepress, press, and finishing. Prepress entails preparing materials and client electronic files for reproduction. Press is the actual reproduction stage, where ink is married to the substrate. Finishing includes cutting, folding, and binding. Related companies produce equipment and consumables for the industry, such as printing presses and bindery equipment, ink, paper, chemicals, and printing plates.

History of the Industry

Printing dates back to around 200 B.C.E., during the Han Dynasty in China. The Chinese used carved wooden blocks coated with ink to apply an image to paper. This woodblock printing was widely used both for artistic prints and for

The blue rollers of an offset printing machine. (©Boris Fojtik/Dreamstime.com)

text. Woodblock printing probably arrived in Europe in the late fourteenth century.

The Chinese developed moveable type around 1000 C.E., using porcelain, tin, and wood as type materials. Around 1403, King Taejong of Korea established a type foundry that made type from bronze. The complexity of the Chinese writing system, which was used in China, Korea, and Japan, made it economically prohibitive to produce a complete set of type.

In Europe, around 1450, Johann Gutenberg created moveable type for the Latin alphabet. His type was made by using a mold to cast individual metal type pieces that consisted of an alloy of lead, tin, and antimony. This metal did not expand or contract, so it could produce letters of uniform size. Gutenberg also designed a composing stick and a flat-bed press, which was modeled after wine presses of the era. His press used a flat metal plate to press paper or vellum against the inked type, while a screw mechanism adjusted the position and amount of pressure of the platen.

The wooden printing press produced one page at a time and remained largely unchanged for three hundred years. In 1800, Lord Stanhope developed a cast-iron press, and the first steam-powered press was patented by Friedrich Koenig in 1810. Koenig produced machines with the assistance of Andreas Friedrich Bauer. The first steam presses were purchased by *The Times* newspaper of London.

The rotary printing press was introduced in 1843 by Richard March Hoe. This press passed paper around a cylinder and could handle both rolls and individual sheets of paper. Flexography was invented in 1890 and could handle a wide range of substrate materials. The lithographic offset press was invented in 1903 by Ira W. Rubel. This press used flat metal sheets called "plates," which transfered an inked image first to a rubber impression cylinder and then to paper. This process produced a clearer image than printing directly from a metal plate to paper.

Screen printing was developed in China around

1000 and was introduced to Europe around 1700. In 1907, Samuel Simon patented the process in England. Because the printing screen was made from silk, the process became known as "silk screening." Silk screening was originally used to produce wallpapers, but today it is widely used in printing fabrics, metals, and even compact discs (CDs).

In the late 1880's, hot metal type replaced foundry type. Two kinds of typesetting machines emerged: monotype, which made individual letters from lead, and linotype, which formed an entire line of type in one pass. Cold type, or phototypesetting, emerged in the 1940's but did not become widely popular until the late 1970's. Early machines produced a punched paper tape that was fed into a mechanical typesetting device, which in turn used a negative filmstrip to expose photographic paper. Later models dispensed with the filmstrip and used lasers to expose the photographic paper.

Personal computers entered the printing industry in the early 1980's as front-end word processing stations. In the mid-1980's, graphical user interfaces (GUIs) and page-layout software ushered in the age of desktop publishing. As prepress became computerized, so did presses. By the end of the twentieth century, desktop publishing had replaced manual prepress work. By 2009, digital printing represented about 12 percent of commercial printing products.

The Industry Today

The printing industry today is divided into two main categories: traditional and digital. Traditional printing companies use printing methods—such as offset lithography, flexography, or gravure—in which printing plates carry ink onto a substrate material, such as paper, plastic, metal, or fabric. Digital printing may be toner- or ink-based, and it does not require printing plates.

Offset lithography constitutes the largest segment of the printing industry. Nearly one-third of today's commercial printing establishments are lithographers. More commonly called offset print-

In the computer-to-plate process, a desktop publishing application is output directly to a printing plate. (©Moreno Soppelsa/ Dreamstime.com)

ing, lithography uses smooth printing plates that carry ink images onto carrier rollers, and these images are then offset to paper and other substrate materials. The printing plates may be made from metal or plastic and are coated with photosensitive emulsions that are exposed to produce right-reading plates.

Offset printers account for approximately 39 percent of the jobs in the printing industry. This does not include newspaper-press jobs, which are considered to be part of the publishing industry. Offset presses range from small, sheet-fed machines that can print only one or two colors of ink at a time to large presses that can handle both sheets and rolls of paper and can print in six or even eight colors in one pass. Small quick-print shops typically operate two-color offset presses.

Flexography is similar to offset printing, but it uses flexible printing plates made from plastic or rubber. These flexible plates allow presses to print on a wide range of substrates. Flexographic printing companies generally print consumer goods, such as shopping bags, packaging materials, cartons, and labels.

Digital printing is the fastest-growing portion of the printing industry. Digital printing technologies are used for photocopying and duplicating

services, as well as for short-run printing, and they include electronic, inkjet, and electrostatic printing. Because digital printing equipment requires no printing plates, it involves lower material costs, which makes it more economical to own and operate than a traditional press. Digital printing presses are therefore very attractive to smaller companies that do not have the financial resources needed to invest in large presses and the accompanying platemaking equipment. Increasingly, graphic design firms are investing in digital presses as a way of offering more in-house services to their clients.

Quick printing is the second-largest segment of the printing industry. Unlike other forms of commercial printing, quick-printing establishments are most likely to be found in shopping centers or office buildings, where their storefronts are easily reached by customers. Quick printers are able to attract walk-in business, and they appeal to individuals because they generally produce wedding invitations and other custom-printed products for nonbusiness use.

Small businesses make extensive use of quick-print shops for printed materials such as stationery and forms, as well as for many types of photocopying and bindery services that are not easily handled in a small office. Additionally, many quick-print shops have expanded their operations to offer other business-related services, including packaging, mailing, and shipping. Because they are stores, many quick printers also sell a small range of office supplies, including postage. Variable-data printing has also been widely accepted in the quick-printing segment of the industry because it is very economical for short-run and personalized orders.

Letterpress printing, which uses raised metal type, is a traditional printing method that dates back to the fourteenth century. Although high-speed offset presses have replaced letterpresses as the primary means of commercial printing, letterpresses continue to be used in the industry for specialty printing needs. Foil stamp-

This digital four-color press does not need printing plates. (©Moreno Soppelsa/ Dreamstime.com)

Letterpresses continue to be used in the industry for specialty printing needs. (©Dreamstime.com)

Inputs Consumed by the Printing Industry

Input	Value
Energy	$2.0 billion
Materials	$37.1 billion
Purchased services	$25.1 billion
Total	$64.2 billion

Source: U.S. Bureau of Economic Analysis. Data are for 2008.

ing, embossing, and die cutting are all accomplished using letterpresses. Because of its unique nature, letterpress printing is widely used by graphic artists who seek to achieve a "retro" look to their work, and it is also used for custom invitations and specialty books.

The printing industry as a whole is moving away from traditional ink-on-paper methods and toward digital methods of printing. Additionally, printers are offering more ancillary services to maintain their competitiveness within the industry. Many now offer variable-data printing (personalization), short-run printing, and warehousing. Some printers are even positioning themselves to be complete communications service providers. In addition to printing, these companies offer graphic design, Web-site creation and management, database management, and marketing services. They may also offer complete distribution services, including mailing-list management, inventory control, and fulfillment services.

Screen printers continue to carve out a niche for themselves in the industry, and screen printing is the one area of commercial printing that is not predicted to decline during the 2010's. Screen printers produce printed textile products, signage, promotional goods, and display items. As digital methods continue to improve and replace earlier technologies used to create screens, screen printing will become more efficient and profitable.

Print shops have increased the amount of green materials and supplies that they use in the production of printed goods. Soy inks, which were problematic when they were first introduced to the market, are now widely used in printing. These inks do not give off volatile organic compounds as oil-based inks do, and they are easier on humans as well as the environment. Additionally, water-based cleaning solvents can be used on plates and presses that use soy inks. Recycled paper stock has become more common as client demand

The Printing Industry's Contribution to the U.S. Economy

Value Added	Amount
Gross domestic product	$37.1 billion
Gross domestic product	0.3%
Persons employed	596,000
Total employee compensation	$32.4 billion

Source: U.S. Bureau of Economic Analysis. Data are for 2008.

has increased for it, and print shops also recycle their paper trimmings and waste. Shops that still use photochemical processes for developing plates or negatives recover and recycle the silver from the photographic chemicals they use.

INDUSTRY MARKET SEGMENTS

The printing industry is extremely diverse. It includes small, quick-print shops that may have only one or two employees, midsize companies of up to one hundred employees, and large multinational corporations with more than one hundred employees. The following sections describe the different segments of the printing industry in more detail.

Small Businesses

Small print shops offer a range of printing services that are geared toward small businesses and individuals, including printing business cards, stationery, resumes, and wedding invitations. Typically located within urban areas, such as shopping centers or office buildings, they are often accessible to walk-in customers. Small print shops may be sole proprietorships, limited liability companies, or corporations.

Potential Annual Earnings Scale. The chief executive officer (CEO) or president of a small print shop is usually also the owner of the company. According to the Printing Industries of America's *Compensation and Benefits Report*, during the 2009-2010 period persons in these positions generally earned between $26,000 and $150,000 per year. The mean annual salary was $65,443, and the median was $60,500.

Salaries for vice presidents and general managers of small print shops averaged $65,659 and $57,057, respectively. Sales managers earned an average of $54,372, and customer service representatives earned an average of $47,763. Production planners averaged $53,531 per year. Department supervisors' salaries averaged $44,880 for bindery supervisors, $43,542 for sheetfed pressroom supervisors, and $46,666 for prepress supervisors. Office and administrative positions averaged $27,306 for human resources assistants, $36,296 for accounting managers, $35,386 for office managers, and $38,612 for estimators.

Clientele Interaction. Many quick-print shops occupy storefronts or office space, and they provide excellent opportunities for employees to interact closely with customers. Walk-in customers often need help with photocopying tasks and rely on the experience of shop employees to help them. Customers who are purchasing printing services frequently want advice on design, especially with regard to choice of paper stock and ink colors. Press operators may even come out to the front counter to speak with clients.

Small shops that are not quick printers are usually located in light industrial parks, where walk-in business is not common. They may have reception areas for clients, but usually their sales representatives call on clients at their workplaces. There is little interaction between production employees and customers in these businesses, as most customer service is handled outside of the shop by salespersons, or over the telephone or through e-mail by customer service representatives and receptionists.

Amenities, Atmosphere, and Physical Grounds. Quick-print shops constitute the printing industry's second-largest segment in number of establishments. Many quick-print shops have storefronts that include one or two small printing presses, bindery equipment, and storage space for paper and ink in the back, which also serves as the pressroom. The atmosphere of a quick-print shop is generally relaxed and friendly. The front of the store generally houses a counter, one or more photocopy machines, bookracks with wedding invitation books, and a seating area for clients that includes chairs and a table large enough to accommodate the invitation catalogs.

Often, quick-print shops offer a small assortment of office supplies for sale, and they can function as stationery stores for everyday office needs. Quick-print shops that are located in office buildings or office parks are most likely to have these amenities. The physical grounds are usually part of a commercial office building or a shopping center and are usually well groomed. There is usually parking for customers at the front of the building.

Typical Number of Employees. Small print shops generally employ between one and fifteen people, usually fewer than ten. The owner of a business often doubles as sales representative and customer service representative and may also handle human resources and accounting. Often, small quick-print shops are family businesses whose administrative functions are divided so that one person focuses on staffing the front counter and conducting sales while another handles the administrative part of the business.

Traditional Geographic Locations. The ten states with the most graphic communications jobs are California, Illinois, New York, Pennsylvania, Texas, Ohio, Wisconsin, Minnesota, New Jersey, and Michigan. However, quick-print and small print shops are located in every state and are usually located in urban and suburban areas. They tend to be very close to commercial businesses, and small print shops are most likely to solicit work from businesses in their local geographic area.

Pros of Working for a Small Printing Business. Owners of small printing companies generally have complete control over the kinds of printing services they offer, as well as over the marketing, purchasing, and hiring processes. Small shops are often family businesses and, as such, offer an intimate working atmosphere for both owners and employees. Quick-print franchises often provide training and support services to help owners establish prices and market their services. Franchise owners may group together to purchase materials at reduced rates, so they can price their printing competitively within the local market. Owners do not need to have formal business school training.

A small print shop generally operates during regular business hours, especially if it is located within an office building or shopping center. As a consequence, little or no overtime is required of employees. A small print shop's limited employee base requires each worker to perform a variety of tasks, which keeps the work from becoming repetitive or boring. Employees who enjoy learning new skills will find that they are not blocked from advancing their skill sets within small printing companies. Front-counter employees also have the opportunity to interact directly with customers.

Cons of Working for a Small Printing Business. Because they usually have fewer than fifteen employees, small shops may sometimes be stressful places to work. It is not possible to move to a different department to avoid working alongside another employee, for example, and if someone is sick or otherwise absent, another employee must be found to cover for him or her.

Small printing companies do not pay as well as do midsize and large printing companies. They provide little or no room for advancement and no way to avoid unpleasant tasks. Small shops may not provide health care coverage or disability insurance, and they may offer only a minimum amount of vacation and holiday time. Often, no one on staff has the technical expertise to solve problems or answer questions that may arise about software or equipment. Employees and owners must figure out solutions for themselves or pay consultants or information technology workers, decreasing profits.

For employees, dealing with customers is not ideal because it takes away from the production time needed to complete assignments. Although managers and owners typically deal with customer-related problems, some employees do not like a working atmosphere where they feel exposed to the public.

Costs

Payroll and Benefits: Small print shops generally hire just a few workers, but they pay more than minimum wage. Small shops are not mandated by the government to provide benefits, although many offer some vacation and sick leave to their employees.

Supplies: Small print shops require standard office supplies and cleaning materials, as well as printing machinery, computer hardware and software, and specific cleaning materials for pressrooms. An assortment of ink and bindery supplies must be kept on hand. Paper is a large portion of any print shop's budget and typically represents just about one-tenth of all expenses.

External Services: Most small print shops rely on their landlords to supply landscaping and snow removal. Routine cleaning services may be taken care of by the shop staff or contracted out to a janitorial service. Small print shops generally lease space from office buildings or shopping centers. They carry property and casualty insurance to cover theft and damage, as well as liability insurance to cover personal injury. Small print shops may ship their finished products directly to customers and may use local couriers or delivery services. Occasionally, they may use a nationwide service such as FedEx or DHL.

Utilities: Typical utilities for a small print shop include electricity, telephone, and Internet services. Water and sewage expenses may be included in a lease or paid separately.

Taxes: Small print shops must pay federal, state, and local income taxes. They are also responsible for collecting sales taxes on their sales.

Midsize Businesses

Midsize print shops offer a wide range of printing services. The majority of their customers are business clients. Midsize print shops are generally located in office parks or light industrial parks and have few walk-in customers. Most employ dedicated sales representatives. They are most likely to be limited liability companies or corporations.

Potential Annual Earnings Scale. Midsize print shops have a wider range of job titles than smaller shops, and owners are not necessarily plant managers. A CEO or president of a midsize printing company may see a salary as low as $45,000 or as high as $300,000, according to the Printing Industries of America's 2009-2010 *Compensation and Benefits Report*. The average annual take-home pay for a chief executive in those years was just over $136,000. The salaries for chief operating officers, vice presidents, and general managers ranged between $32,400 and roughly $190,000, with an average of just over $103,000. Salaries for plant managers, vice presidents for operations, and production managers ranged from $32,000 to $189,987, and salaries for financial managers ranged from $31,800 to $143,688.

Sales manager positions at midsize printing businesses varied widely but averaged just over $92,000. Marketing and business development managers earned average salaries of $66,228, and human resources managers and directors averaged $52,500. Environmental health and safety managers averaged $66,859, while quality managers averaged $57,603. Bindery supervisors earned an average of $49,412; sheetfed pressroom supervisors earned $60,015; web-fed pressroom supervisors earned $52,323; and prepress supervisors earned $58,056 on average. Office managers averaged $44,000; human resources workers and administrators averaged $36,000; bookkeepers averaged $42,800; customer service representatives averaged $40,000; and cost estimators averaged just over $45,000.

Clientele Interaction. Employees at most midsize shops have fairly limited exposure to customers. Typically, a company's salespeople and customer service representatives handle contact with the clients on a day-to-day basis. Shops that offer design services may invite customers to meet and work with their in-house design staffs on their premises.

Amenities, Atmosphere, and Physical Grounds. Midsize print shops are generally situated in office parks or light industrial areas and are most likely in suburban areas rather than downtown city locations. They are typically not located close to restaurants and often provide food-vending machines for their employees' convenience. They also generally provide refrigerators, microwave ovens, water fountains, and coffee service, and some offer small dining areas.

The atmosphere of a midsize print shop is that of a manufacturing plant. A plant's front office generally houses sales, administrative, and managerial staff. Its prepress department is also typically found in the front office area, so the department's computers may be kept in a climate-controlled environment. The back of a typical printing shop includes presses, bindery equipment, a warehouse, and loading docks. Shops' physical grounds are usually office parks, which are generally maintained by management companies. A printing plant may be in its own separate building or may occupy a portion of a larger warehouse. Free parking is typically available and is shared by all the companies within a given office park.

Typical Number of Employees. Midsize print shops employ between sixteen and one hundred people. A typical staff includes a general manager, a production manager, a sales manager, a human resources manager, and several department supervisors, including prepress, press, and bindery supervisors. Employees typically perform one or two tasks each and tend to specialize more than workers in small print shops. Larger midsize shops may also employ quality managers. Additionally, midsize plants may have more than one work shift, and some are unionized. Employees may be required to work overtime in order to meet printing deadlines.

Traditional Geographic Locations. Midsize print shops are located throughout the country, within suburban office parks and light industrial regions of most major cities. The top ten states for printing are California, Illinois, New York, Pennsylvania, Texas, Ohio, Wisconsin, Minnesota, New

Jersey, and Michigan. Large metropolitan areas, such as Washington, D.C., are also home to a large number of midsize print shops.

Pros of Working for a Midsize Printing Business. Midsize printing companies are usually large enough to employ general managers and department supervisors to oversee daily plant operations. Owners maintain control over their businesses, but these managers relieve them of many of the chores associated with running a business. They can focus on marketing their businesses, usually through networking, while purchasing and hiring decisions are made by the management staff.

Midsize print shops are also usually large enough to support several workers in each department, so the working atmosphere for employees is somewhat more professional and less intimate than that of small shops. These companies may offer their employees uniforms at no expense, saving them the costs of purchasing and laundering work clothes. Midsize shops may be unionized. Many employees consider this to be an advantage in dealing with their employers. Typically, unions offer pension plans and some kind of disability insurance, while companies offer health care packages, as well as holiday and vacation pay. Some unions offer their members training programs on specific software packages and equipment.

Midsize companies may run several shifts and require some overtime. Front office staffs, which include human resources, accounting, sales, and support personnel, work normal business hours, while production employees work in multiple shifts. Second- and third-shift workers earn slightly higher wages than first-shift workers.

Teamwork is a part of everyday operations at midsize print shops. With several workers per department, it is easier for an employee to get help with problems from other employees. While there is some variety to the work being done, the kinds of tasks that each employee performs are limited. Production employees are typically isolated from having to deal with customer problems, which allows them to focus on the tasks at hand.

Cons of Working for a Midsize Printing Business. Because owners do not need to be involved in the daily task of running midsize businesses, there may be poor communication between an owner and his or her managers. This type of situation can lead to poor working relationships among the managers, which may also affect the working atmosphere of the entire shop.

Employees may have fewer opportunities for advancement within departments than they would have at larger businesses: Several other employees may perform the same job duties, and lateral movement from one department to another is rare. Some employees or owners consider unions to be a drawback instead of a benefit. Union dues are not optional for employees of union shops, and employees typically have little or no ability to negotiate pay or other employment benefits for themselves: They are bound by the terms of collective-bargaining contracts.

Shift work is often undesirable for employees, particularly those with young children. A company may require only a "reasonable" amount of overtime, but what constitutes a reasonable amount is open to interpretation and, often, dispute. Thus, working hours tend to be somewhat unpredictable for production workers. Employees usually have little or no contact with customers and must receive their instructions indirectly, from sales or customer service representatives. Often, breakdowns in communication cause quality problems or prevent work from being completed on time, which usually reflects badly on the production staff and can be a cause for resentment between production and customer relations personnel, as well as harming their companies' profits.

Costs

Payroll and Benefits: Midsize print shops have enough employees that they must pay for government-mandated benefits for their workers. Employees are paid more than minimum wage. Vacation, sick time, and holidays are offered to full-time employees and sometimes to part-time employees. A company may offer health care, insurance, and retirement plans.

Supplies: Midsize print shops require standard office supplies, kitchen supplies, and cleaning materials. Pressrooms and binderies need heavy machinery and cleaning materials for that equipment. Pressrooms require printing plates, blanket rollers, developing chemicals for the printing plates, ink, and drying powder. Binderies need staples, comb bindings, and other supplies. Mail rooms and warehouses need containers, tape, and packaging materials. Paper costs are a major portion of a midsize print shop's budget and represent an average of 8.5 percent of expenses.

External Services: Landscaping, parking lot maintenance, and snow removal are usually included in a company's lease. Midsize companies typically hire janitorial services to clean common areas and office areas, while equipment areas and equipment are maintained by shop employees. Midsize print shops typically lease their space in an office park or industrial center. They carry property and casualty insurance to cover damage to equipment from theft or natural disaster and liability insurance to cover injury to employees or visitors. Insurance represents only about 2 percent of expenses.

Most midsize print shops have at least one truck or van for local pickup and delivery needs. They may use nationwide shipping and delivery services for customers outside their local areas.

Utilities: Typical utilities costs include electricity, telephone, and Internet services. These costs average about 7 percent of a print shop's expenses. Some utilities, such as water and sewage expenses, may be included in a company's lease.

Taxes: Federal, state, and local income taxes are required. Midsize shops are also responsible for state and local sales taxes. If they work with out-of-state customers, they may be required to collect sales taxes for other locales.

Large Businesses

Large print shops offer the widest selection of printing processes to their customers. They are most likely to attract prestigious clients who want high-quality printing or customers who need large quantities and quick turnaround time. Large shops are almost always located in industrial parks and have dedicated sales representatives.

Potential Annual Earnings Scale. Large print shops' employees have a range of job titles similar to those of midsize shops, but each department tends to have a larger number of nonmanagement positions. Managers supervise more employees and consequently have greater responsibilities and receive increased compensation.

As with midsize companies, owners may not be the managers of their plants. The average annual take-home pay for a large printing company's chief executive was just over $192,000 for 2009-2010. The salaries of chief operating officers, vice presidents, and general managers at such companies averaged $133,907. Salaries for plant managers, vice president of operations, and production managers averaged $99,922. Chief financial officers, controllers, and financial managers were paid an average of $108,699.

Sales managers received $123,126, on average. Marketing and business development managers earned $93,958, and customer service managers earned $66,828. Human resources managers, directors, and personnel managers earned an average of $64,598; environmental health and safety managers were paid an average of $55,734; and quality managers received an average of $66,575. Information technology managers averaged $81,744, while prepress supervisors averaged $67,515. Sheetfed pressroom supervisors averaged $69,038, and web-fed pressroom supervisors averaged $67,738. Bindery supervisors averaged $61,765; mail room and fulfillment managers averaged $54,254; and warehouse supervisors averaged $55,837.

Office managers received average salaries of $50,966. Receptionists earned $28,467 on average. Human resources and administrative assistants earned $35,125; bookkeepers earned $43,288; purchasing agents earned $48,789; customer service representatives earned $43,517; and cost estimators earned $47,526.

Clientele Interaction. Large print shops rarely host customers on site. There is almost no interaction between production employees and customers. Salespeople and customer service representatives handle contact with clients on a day-to-day basis. Companies that offer design services, whether print or Web design, may invite their customers into the shop to meet and work with their in-house design staff. Most clients will never see the pressroom, bindery, or warehouse areas of the shop unless they are on a tour, as allowing nonemployees in such areas is disruptive to the production workflow and represents a safety concern.

Amenities, Atmosphere, and Physical Grounds. Large print shops may be situated in office parks, but they are more likely to be found in suburban industrial areas, where they typically occupy single buildings. Amenities for employees include one or more dining areas with refrigerators, microwave ovens, water fountains, coffee service, and vending machines. There may be a waiting area in the front office for customers and at least one conference room.

The atmosphere of a large print shop is that of a manufacturing plant. The front office is usually much smaller than the production area and houses sales, administrative, managerial, prepress, and information technology (IT) staff offices. The front office is climate controlled and generally resembles an ordinary office environment. The back of the printing shop houses the presses, bindery equipment, warehouse, and loading docks. The press and bindery areas are usually noisy, and safety regulations require workers to wear hearing protection. The physical grounds are usually industrial areas that have little or no landscaping. There is usually ample parking for employees and access to the loading dock large enough to accommodate tractor trailers.

Typical Number of Employees. Large print shops employ more than one hundred people. These companies have a wider range of management functions, including presidents, vice presidents, plant managers, production managers, sales managers, human resources managers, customer service managers, production planners or schedulers, quality managers, and environmental health and safety managers. Department supervisors are responsible for several employees each, and these jobs include IT managers, prepress supervisors, sheetfed press and web-fed press supervisors, bindery supervisors, mail room supervisors, and warehouse supervisors.

Employees typically are highly specialized and may be trained to operate one specific piece of equipment each. Usually, more than one employee is able to perform each job. Shift work is the norm, and employees may be required to work overtime in order to meet printing deadlines. Large print shops are very likely to be unionized.

Traditional Geographic Locations. Large printing companies can be found in most large metropolitan areas. They often conduct business nationally instead of relying solely on local businesses for their customer base. Because they often ship their products nationwide, they tend to be situated where there is good access for truck traffic, often just off of main roads or interstates.

Pros of Working for a Large Printing Business. Large printing companies' daily operations are handled by plant managers. They are likely to be incorporated and have stockholders. They have several employees per department, and, because departments are large, there is more room for possible advancement within a department. Department supervisors can earn good incomes because they are responsible for large crews.

Large print shops may offer uniforms to their production-line employees. They are likely to be unionized. Unions may offer pension plans, disability insurance, and training programs to their members. Large print shops nearly always run three shifts and may require some overtime. Second- and third-shift workers earn night differential or shift differential, which typically amounts to a 3 to 5 percent pay increase. Nonproduction employees work standard business hours.

Production employees almost never have to deal with customer problems, since customer service representatives, department supervisors, and sales representatives act as intermediaries between clients and production staff. Thus, production employees can focus on the jobs at hand.

Cons of Working for a Large Printing Business. Owners of large businesses are often absent, leaving management on its own to conduct business. This sometimes leads to a poor working relationship between an owner and management, which may also affect the entire shop.

The higher number of employees at a large firm reduces the chances of any given employee being promoted to a management position. If such an opportunity does arise, there will be competition for the job, based upon seniority. Lateral movement within a shop is relatively rare.

Some employees consider unions to be a drawback, since they are required to join the union to work in a union shop in most states. Union dues are not optional, and employees typically have little or no ability to negotiate pay or other employment benefits outside of their union contracts. Shift work is often undesirable for employees, but it is often the only option for a new hire. Also, some overtime is generally required of production-line employees. Thus, the work tends to be hectic and often tiring, and working hours are unpredictable. Large printing shops tend to have a number of presses and bindery equipment, which makes the working environment very noisy. Employees in large print shops usually have no contact with customers, which may make it difficult to solve problems. Breakdowns in communication occur and can cause stress.

Costs

Payroll and Benefits: Large print shops must pay for government-mandated benefits for their workers. Vacation time, sick time, and holidays are offered to full-time employees and sometimes to part-time employees. Retirement plans may be offered, with or without company contributions.

Supplies: Standard office and kitchen supplies are needed. Pressrooms require heavy machinery, printing plates, blanket rollers, developing chemicals, ink, drying powder, and cleaners. Binderies require staples and other supplies. Mail rooms and warehouses need containers, tape, labels, and packaging materials. Paper costs are a major expense, representing an average of 8.5 percent of total costs.

External Services: If there is a lease, it may include landscaping, property and parking lot maintenance, and snow removal. Otherwise, a large printing shop may employ a landscaping service. Facilities maintenance may be a separate job role at the plant and include janitorial service. Equipment is maintained by press workers and other equipment operators.

Large print shops may lease warehouse space or own their own building. Large print shops purchase property and casualty insurance to cover damage to equipment from theft or natural disaster and liability insurance to cover injury to employees or visitors. They may have their own fleets of trucks or vans for local pickup and delivery needs. They may use nationwide shipping and delivery services for customers outside their local areas.

Utilities: Typical utilities costs include electricity, telephone, and Internet services. These costs average about 7 percent of a print shop's expenses. If there is a lease, water and sewage utilities may be included in the lease.

Taxes: Federal, state, and local income taxes are required, as well as any state and local sales taxes. Companies may be required to collect sales taxes for other states if they work with out-of-state customers.

ORGANIZATIONAL STRUCTURE AND JOB ROLES

Most print shops are organized in a similar fashion, with production workers accounting for over half of the jobs in the industry. Printing machine operators alone make up 17 percent of the workforce. Other occupations in the industry include administrative functions, such as accounting and bookkeeping, office support, and sales staff.

In large plants, jobs tend to be more compartmentalized. Employees typically handle one or just a few duties, and their tasks tend to be more highly specialized. Midsize companies have fewer departments and more streamlined management systems, with management employees often performing production tasks in addition to their management duties. Production personnel are typically asked to perform more than one task each.

Small shops make up about 70 percent of the printing industry. They require workers who are versatile and willing to perform a variety of tasks. These shops generally employ fewer than ten people and are often owner-operated or family businesses.

The following umbrella categories apply to the organizational structure of businesses in the printing industry:

- Business Management
- Office and Administrative Support
- Human Resources
- Sales and Customer Service
- Information Technology
- Desktop Publishing and Graphics
- Production
- Facilities and Distribution

Business Management

Management roles in the printing industry vary widely according to the size of each business. At a small print shop, the owner is usually also the manager and oversees the entire operation of the shop, including production, inventory control, accounting and bookkeeping, customer service, and sales. The owner-manager may also be able to step in and perform production tasks when necessary.

In midsize and large printing operations, general managers usually oversee all aspects of printing plants. The general manager position is usually

OCCUPATION SPECIALTIES

Cost Estimators

Specialty	Responsibilities
Printing estimators	Estimate labor and material costs of printing and binding books, pamphlets, periodicals, and other printed matter, based on outlined specifications.

a nontechnical one that does not require the ability to perform production tasks. All other department supervisors report to general managers. Large companies may have fairly large accounting departments, which are usually headed by chief financial officers who oversee the financial operations of entire businesses. This job may involve supervising the accounting or bookkeeping department.

At midsize and large printing companies, production is overseen by shop foremen or supervisors. They inspect all aspects of prepress, press, and bindery work; help train apprentices; and are able to step in and perform production tasks as necessary. This position requires extensive knowledge and experience of printing processes. Supervisors schedule and assign jobs and overtime, perform inventories, order materials, and schedule equipment maintenance. They have usually ascended through the ranks and have vocational school or on-the-job training rather than management degrees.

At any printing company, at least one employee must function as a cost estimator. Cost estimators are responsible for determining the costs of materials, labor, time on press, delivery charges, warehousing fees, and any other business expenses involved in production. They add markup charges to these amounts and use them to determine the price for each job. In some smaller printing companies, salespeople may do their own cost estimating.

Business management occupations may include the following:

- Owner
- President/Chief Executive Officer (CEO)
- General Manager
- Chief Financial Officer (CFO)
- Vice President of Sales and Marketing
- Comptroller
- Shop Foreman
- Shop Supervisor
- Cost Estimator

Office and Administrative Support

Office and administrative support personnel manage the daily operations of printing companies. They do not need any specialized training within the printing field but must be competent within their fields of expertise. Secretaries and administrative assistants perform a wide range of clerical duties within printing plants. They handle routine office tasks, manage reception areas, and greet clients. They order office supplies and handle mail and shipping tasks.

Accountants analyze financial information and prepare financial reports. Most accountants have some formal training, and they must be familiar with financial and accounting software. They also need a firm grasp of federal, state, and local financial regulations. Accountants prepare tax forms and work closely with auditors to make sure that company financial records are complete and accurate.

Office and administrative support occupations may include the following:

- Secretary
- Administrative Assistant
- Office Clerk
- Accounting Manager
- Accountant
- Bookkeeper
- Auditor

Human Resources

Human resources personnel recruit, hire, and fire employees; administer payrolls and benefits, including insurance; grant promotions; and ensure that companies adhere to a wide range of federal, state, and local employment regulations. In union shops, human resources managers facilitate relations between unions and upper management and may participate directly in collective-bargaining negotiations. Small and some midsize printing companies may not have dedicated human resources directors.

The department is responsible not only for placing job advertisements but also for ensuring that those advertisements comply with equal employment opportunity laws. Human resources directors and managers screen resumes, conduct initial job interviews, and administer any tests that may be required of applicants. One of the more important requirements of a human resources manager's job is to stay abreast of the many state and federal regulations that cover employee relations and to enforce hiring and promotion policies that are in accordance with these regulations.

Human resources occupations may include the following:

- Human Resources Director
- Human Resources Manager
- Human Resources Coordinator
- Human Resources Generalist
- Benefits Specialist
- Payroll Clerk

Sales and Customer Service

Sales representatives solicit work from clients and potential clients. They need to have general knowledge about the printing industry because they must understand what services their company has to offer and why those particular services are valuable to clients. Representatives identify potential clients, follow up on leads and referrals, and make client presentations. They often take paper samples, ink-swatch books, and finished printed materials to show to clients. Sales representatives are essential to the success of any printing plant, and clients often change printers in order to follow sales representatives who are sensitive and responsive to their business printing needs.

Customer service representatives work closely with sales departments. As soon as sales representatives bring in new jobs, customer service representatives take over the management of those projects.

They write up job orders, pass financial information to the accounting department, and put jobs into production. Customer service representatives order material and supplies for jobs and coordinate with subcontractors for finishing, shipping, or warehousing needs. They must have excellent organizational and communication skills and be able to work in high-pressure environments.

Sales and customer service occupations may include the following:

- Customer Service Representative
- Customer Service Manager
- Sales Manager
- Printing Sales Executive
- Printing Sales Representative
- Sales Account Representative

Information Technology

The printing industry is highly computerized, yet only the largest plants may employ full-time information technology (IT) specialists. Small quick-print shops may have a few desktop computers in the production department. Production-department computers may or may not be networked, although office computers generally have Internet access and e-mail capability. Midsize and large companies often have at least one dedicated IT staffer, and this employee is responsible for maintaining both a company's computer hardware and its software.

Database managers compile and maintain company databases. They may also create and maintain databases for customers, particularly for variable-printing projects. Database managers usually have some college or formal computer training.

IT occupations may include the following:

- Computer Specialist
- Help Desk Specialist
- Information Technology Specialist
- Database Administrator

Desktop Publishing and Graphics

Desktop publishers and graphic artists typically work in an office environment. Desktop publishers must be able to work on the PC and Macintosh computer platforms and be fluent with page-layout and graphics software. They also commonly work with word processing software, database files, and presentation software and must know how to extract data from these files if necessary. Desktop publishers may on occasion also do some writing and editing of materials. While desktop publishing has largely replaced typesetting and paste-up, true typesetting is still performed by artisan letterpress companies.

Graphic artists design and create the artwork for a wide variety of items, from books and newspapers to advertising, packaging, and Web sites. They usually have bachelor's degrees or design school experience, and they must understand the printing process. Graphic artists also meet with clients to discuss projects and make sure that designs stay on target and within clients' budgets. Desktop publishing and graphic arts careers are likely to appeal to freelance workers, who often work at home on their own equipment. They often work irregular hours, including shift work and weekends.

Desktop publishing and graphics occupations may include the following:

- Desktop Publisher
- Graphic Artist
- Graphic Designer
- Typesetter

Production

Production is the largest labor segment of the printing industry, accounting for 53 percent of total employment. Printing-machine operators alone account for 17 percent of industry employment. Production roles within the industry fall into three broad categories: prepress, press, and postpress (also called bindery or finishing).

Prepress technicians prepare materials to go on press. A prepress technician takes a customer's electronic files and checks them for problems before outputting them to printing plates. In small shops, prepress technicians may also do graphic design work. In midsize and large print shops, one prepress technician may do mostly layout and graphic-related work, while others specialize in color separations or imposition.

OCCUPATION PROFILE

Compositor and Typesetter

Considerations	Qualifications
Description	Using mostly computers, puts written text into a form that printers can use to produce printed matter.
Career clusters	Arts, A/V Technology, and Communications; Manufacturing
Interests	Data; things
Working conditions	Work inside
Minimum education level	On-the-job training; high school diploma/technical training; apprenticeship
Physical exertion	Light work
Physical abilities	Unexceptional/basic fitness
Opportunities for experience	Apprenticeship; part-time work
Licensure and certification	Usually not required
Employment outlook	Decline expected
Holland interest score	CRE; RCE; RCS

Note: See volume 1, "Publisher's Note," for an explanation of the Holland interest score.

In some shops, dedicated preflight technicians make sure that all of a customer's files are present and are ready to go into production. Preflight technicians use software to scan files for problems and act as intermediaries between customer service representatives or salespeople and the prepress department. They are sometimes responsible for scheduling work.

Printing-machine operators run presses and are responsible for routine equipment maintenance. They review materials coming from the prepress department and inspect printing plates for damage or problems. Presspersons or assistant presspersons deliver final printed materials to paper cutters, bindery departments, or warehouses as appropriate.

Bindery workers assemble trimmed printed sheets into magazines, newsletters, or other finished products. They operate bindery equipment such as stitchers, folders, and other finishing equipment. Bindery work is highly automated.

Bookbinders finish printed pages into books. They cut, fold, and glue paper to create finished books. Bookbinders may produce perfect-bound paperback books, or they may work in hand binderies, creating specialty bindings for limited-edition books. Bookbinders may also repair and restore books.

Production occupations may include the following:

- Preflight Technician
- Prepress Technician
- Pressperson
- Assistant Pressperson
- Cutter
- Folder Operator
- Platemaker
- Bindery Worker
- Bookbinder

Facilities and Distribution

Small print shops are often located in office buildings or shopping centers and do not employ their own facilities managers. Typically, building and property maintenance is taken care of by a property's owner. Print shop employees or owners clean their shops themselves, or the shops may employ independent cleaning companies.

Midsize printing companies are often located in office parks that provide building and property maintenance. Large printing companies are most

OCCUPATION SPECIALTIES

Bindery Workers

Specialty	Responsibilities
Bindery machine setters	Set up machines that perform one or more bindery operations, such as folding, cutting, gathering, stitching, or gluing, following blueprint or job specifications. They gather signatures (pages) and form book bodies for binding.
Book-sewing machine operators	Tend machines that sew sheets of gathered and collated signatures (pages) into book form preparatory to binding.
Bookbinders	Cut, assemble, sew, and glue components to bind books according to specifications, using sewing machines, hand presses, and handcutters.
Case-making machine operators	Tend machines that glue covering material to cover boards to assemble covers.
Casing-in-line setters	Set up machines that convert signatures (pages) into a finished book.

likely to employ full-time workers to provide building maintenance and to take care of routine tasks such as trash removal. Facilities managers also supervise the recycling of paper and chemicals.

Warehouse employees unload raw materials from delivery trucks and store them or deliver them to the proper departments. They must perform routine lifting of materials and be trained in the use of forklifts. The job requires the use of safety equipment, such as steel-toed work books, hardhats, and hearing protection.

Warehouse managers oversee the packaging of finished printed products and their preparation for shipment to clients. Boxed products may be loaded onto company vans or trucks for local delivery, or they may be held in warehouses to be picked up by third-party delivery services. Drivers deliver printed materials to clients or to other companies for finishing. They may also perform errands, such as picking up supplies for the front office or materials for the shop floor.

Facilities and distribution occupations may include the following:

- Facility Manager
- Warehouse Manager
- Warehouse Worker
- Shipping and Receiving Clerk
- Driver

INDUSTRY OUTLOOK

Overview

The outlook for this industry shows it to be on the rise, although growth is projected to be modest, averaging about 2 percent. The growth rate for domestic commercial conventional printing is expected to be less than 1 percent through 2020, while the growth rate for digital printing is expected to reach 7 percent or more. Ancillary services are expected to grow at a rate of about 4.5 percent.

Printing is a major American industry, representing 1.2 percent of the total annual economic output of the United States. There are more than 36,500 printing plants within the United States, employing more than 965,000 people. This makes printing the second-largest manufacturing industry by number of plants and the third-largest manufacturing industry by number of employees. However, as printing processes have become more automated, fewer employees have been needed to perform tasks that used to be done by hand. Within the first decade of the twenty-first century, the number of employees in the domestic printing industry declined by approximately 300,000, or about 37 percent.

The U.S. Bureau of Labor Statistics (BLS) forecasts that jobs in the printing industry and its associated support businesses will continue to decrease, and it expects that approximately 95,000 jobs will be lost between 2008 and 2018. Overall, this represents an approximate 16 percent employment decline within the industry. Bindery jobs are expected to decrease by 19 percent.

Much of the projected decrease in industry jobs will result from reductions in the amount of advertising supplements being printed, as businesses continue to transition away from physical advertising and toward electronic advertising methods. On the other hand, U.S. printing demand is likely to continue to be satisfied domestically. The need for quick turnaround times make it difficult to outsource most printing tasks overseas. Thus, much bindery work will continue to be handled by domestic printers. Job prospects are best for experienced bindery workers and those who have certification or experience in related production tasks.

Jobs for printing-press operators are expected to decline by 5 percent through 2018, mainly because fewer operators will be required to operate each of the newer, more efficient presses now in use. In particular, the newspaper industry should expect to see a loss of press operator jobs, while the continued growth of digital printing will result in ample job opportunities for workers who can operate digital presses. Also, as the current workforce ages, retiring employees will leave room for new workers to enter the industry.

Prepress technician jobs are expected to decline by 13 percent through 2018. As is true of bindery jobs, most of the decrease is projected to result from continued automation within the industry, which will reduce the need for large numbers of workers. This is often referred to in the industry as "lights-out prepress." Prepress technicians who have good customer service skills will continue to remain in demand, and those who can expand their skill base to include Web design, database

PROJECTED EMPLOYMENT FOR SELECTED OCCUPATIONS

Printing and Related Support Activities

Employment		
2009	Projected 2018	Occupation
44,470	37,200	Bindery workers
23,470	20,900	First-line supervisors/ managers of production and operating workers
25,130	22,800	Job printers
32,210	27,400	Prepress technicians and workers
95,830	96,300	Printing machine operators

Source: U.S. Bureau of Labor Statistics, Industries at a Glance, Occupational Employment Statistics and Employment Projections Program.

management, or other IT functions will have the best job opportunities.

Globally, the printing industry is predicted to grow from its 2008 value of $401.1 billion to $455.5 billion in 2013, representing an annual growth rate of 2.6 percent. Commercial printing represents 47 percent of the global industry's revenue, while newspapers account for 29.7 percent of revenue. Book printing represents 7.4 percent of global revenue, and magazine printing represents just 4.9 percent.

The Americas and the Asia-Pacific region each account for roughly 35 percent of global commercial printing volume. Europe represents 27.7 percent, and the rest of the world accounts for less than 2 percent. The outlook for the global print market is expected to remain good. Despite fears of outsourcing jobs, most of the printing consumed in the United States is produced domestically. Print buyers tend to be less sensitive to printing costs and instead value quick turnaround times and quality above price.

Employment Advantages

Careers in the printing industry appeal to people who enjoy working as part of a team in order to produce finished products. Print production workers generally have a realistic outlook, like to work with machinery and computer equipment, and enjoy problem solving.

A college degree is not necessary to begin a career in the printing industry. Entry-level jobs, especially those in the postpress segment of the industry, often require only a high school diploma or the equivalent. Most press operators have some technical training, and they may get their education through a technical college. However, many press operators gain experience by working as pressroom assistants and receive on-the-job training. Many have a combination of formal schooling and experience. Prepress operators may have formal graphic arts training from community colleges, technical colleges, or associate's or bachelor's degree programs, although their jobs do not typically require such degrees.

Wages in the printing industry are very good. For instance, prepress technicians earn a median salary of just over $19 per hour, while press operators earn $22 or more per hour, depending on the equipment being used and the skill of the operator. Even bindery workers usually earn more than minimum wage, starting around $12 per hour.

Annual Earnings

The domestic printing industry as a whole has remained fairly strong, even through the recession of 2007-2009. According to a 2009 report by the Printing Industry of America, the domestic industry is expected to grow by an average of 2 percent per year through 2020.

In 2008, domestic revenues for the printing industry were $166.6 billion. This number represents both conventional and digital printing, as well as printer's ancillary services (desktop publishing, Web production, database management, and other information services). Conventional ink-on-paper printing represented 76 percent of the total revenue, digital printing represented 12 percent, and ancillary services represented 12 percent. The global printing industry is similarly robust. Its global revenues in 2008 were $401.1 billion, and it grew at a rate of 2.4 percent per year from 2004 to 2008. The global financial crisis is not expected to prevent this rate from reaching an average of 2.6 percent per year between 2008 and 2013.

RELATED RESOURCES FOR FURTHER RESEARCH

GRAPHIC ARTS EDUCATION AND RESEARCH
    FOUNDATION
1899 Preston White Dr.
Reston, VA 20191
Tel: (703) 264-7200
Fax: (703) 620-3165
http://www.gaerf.org

NATIONAL ASSOCIATION FOR PRINTING
    LEADERSHIP
75 W Century Rd., Suite 100
Paramus, NJ 07652
Tel: (201) 634-9600
Fax: (201) 634-0324
http://www.napl.org

NATIONAL ASSOCIATION OF PRINTING INK
    MANUFACTURERS
581 Main St., Suite 520
Woodbridge, NJ 07095
Tel: (732) 855-1525
Fax: (732) 855-1838
http://www.napim.org

PRINTING INDUSTRIES OF AMERICA
200 Deer Run Rd.
Sewickley, PA 15143
Tel: (412) 741-6860
Fax: (412) 741-2311
http://www.printing.org

SEYBOLD REPORT, BEARD GROUP
P.O. Box 4250
Frederick, MD 21705-4250
Tel: (240) 629-3300
Fax: (240) 629-3360
http://www.seyboldreport.com

ABOUT THE AUTHOR

Karen S. Garvin has more than thirty years of experience in the printing industry. She has set type by hand, operated a Linotype machine, and run a letterpress. She has worked as a typesetter, graphic artist, paste-up artist, prepress technician, and production manager. Witnessing firsthand the digital revolution in the printing industry, including the advent of desktop publishing and digital printing, she has run her own graphic design business for fifteen years and has also taught classes in desktop publishing and word processing. She holds a bachelor's degree in communications from the University of Maryland University College.

FURTHER READING

Career Overview. "Prepress Technician Careers, Jobs, and Employment Information." http://www.careeroverview.com/prepress-technician-careers.html.
_____. "Printing Machine Operator Careers, Jobs, and Employment Information." http://www.careeroverview.com/printing-machine-operator-careers.html.
Casals, Ricard. *The Future of Printed Signage: Market Opportunities.* Leatherhead, Surrey, England: Pira International, 2008.
Clark, Richard P., and Pamela Fehl. *Career Opportunities in the Visual Arts.* New York: Checkmark, 2006.
Davis, Ronnie H. *Beyond the Horizon: Key Dynamics Shaping Print Markets and Printers over the Next Decade.* Sewickley, Pa.: Printing Industries of America, 2009.
_____. *Profiling the Economy and Print Markets, 2009-2010.* Sewickley, Pa.: Printing Industries of America, 2009.
Febvre, Lucien, and Henri-Jean Martin. *The Coming of the Book: The Impact of Printing, 1450-1800.* 3d ed. New York: Verso, 2010.
Flecker, Sally Ann, and Deanna M. Gentile. *Careers in Printing: The Original Information Media.* Sewickley, Pa.: Graphic Arts Technical Foundation, 2002.
MacDougall, Andy. *Screen Printing Today.* Cincinnati: ST Books, 2005.

Parker, Philip M. *The 2009-2014 World Outlook for Printing and Binding of General and Trade Books*. San Diego, Calif.: ICON Group, 2008.

Rose, David S. *Introduction to Letterpress Printing in the Twenty-first Century*. http://www.fiveroses.org/intro.htm.

U.S. Bureau of Labor Statistics. *Career Guide to Industries*, 2010-2011 ed. http://www.bls.gov/oco/cg.

_____. *Occupational Outlook Handbook*, 2010-2011 ed. http://www.bls.gov/oco.

U.S. Census Bureau. North American Industry Classification System (NAICS), 2007. http://www.census.gov/cgi-bin/sssd/naics/naicsrch?chart=2007.

U.S. Department of Commerce. International Trade Administration. Office of Trade and Industry Information. Industry Trade Data and Analysis. http://ita.doc.gov/td/industry/otea/OTII/OTII-index.html.

Webb, Joe. "How Printing Industry Employment Has Changed Since 2000." WhatTheyThink?, February 10, 2010. http://blogs.whattheythink.com/economics/2010/02/how-printing-industry-employment-has-changed-since-2000.

Private Education Industry

©Monkey Business Images/Dreamstime.com

INDUSTRY SNAPSHOT

General Industry: Education and Training
Career Cluster: Education and Training
Subcategory Industries: Elementary and Secondary Schools; Exam Preparation and Tutoring; Fine Arts Schools; Language Schools; Sports and Recreation Instruction; Technical and Trade Schools
Related Industries: Higher Education Industry; Public Elementary and Secondary Education Industry
Annual Domestic Revenues: $25 billion USD (First Research, 2009)
NAICS Numbers: 6111, 6115-6116

INDUSTRY DEFINITION

Summary

The private education industry includes all jobs associated with providing educational services through private entities, rather than through public institutions. Thus, it includes private, religious, and parochial elementary and high schools, vocational schools, test-preparation service providers, private tutors, group instruction programs (such as language schools), and, to some degree, charter schools. The private education industry differs from the public education system in that its primary sources of funding are student tuition, endowments, and private investments, rather than government grants and tax funds. There are some exceptions to this rule, however (most notably charter schools and some for-profit degree-granting higher education institutes). By the same token, whereas public schools are ultimately answerable to the entire electorate of their jurisdiction—which elects and holds accountable the government officials who oversee them—private schools are accountable primarily to those who give them money, including tuition payers and donors. Private schools may be for profit or nonprofit. The industry offers many teaching opportunities, and it also includes numerous supporting occupations such as administration, management, marketing, and finance.

History of the Industry

While Massachusetts is often considered the birthplace of formal education in America, there is evidence that the first private schools were actually established by Catholic missionaries in what eventually became Florida and Louisiana during the seventeenth century. These schools served the dual purpose of teaching basic skills and instilling

A gym is set up for students taking a standardized admission test. Private schools offer classes to help students prepare. (©Betty Copeland/Dreamstime.com)

specific religious values in their students. Throughout the eighteenth century and into the nineteenth, the line between public and private schools was not especially clear. Most schools received their funding from a mixture of private and public sources, but there was not a comprehensive system of public education in place. Without specific government oversight, most schools operated in a way that more closely followed a private education model. Many of these schools focused on a particular specialty, such as religious education, reading and writing, or vocational skills.

By the early nineteenth century, a variety of school programs were available, but there was still no comprehensive oversight. The programs generally operated independently of one another and without any mandates from the government as to admissions or curriculum requirements. By the middle of the nineteenth century, factors such as industrialization, urbanization, and immigration led to a need to establish regulated, publicly funded schools to provide education for individuals who were unable to attend private institutions.

Government regulation of school programs increased markedly following the Civil War, and the availability of public schools at all levels brought a dramatic decline in the popularity of private learning institutions.

Since the advent of public schools, private schools have found themselves at the center of numerous debates concerning their curriculum choices and funding sources. For example, as World War I unfolded, private schools that taught foreign languages and adhered to particular ethnic customs (especially German) were often accused of promoting American disloyalty. Several state legislatures attempted to pass laws outlawing certain private school practices, but these laws were generally struck down by the courts. Private schools experienced a surge in popularity following World War II but ended up in the middle of another debate in the mid-twentieth century. This debate concerned whether it was appropriate for private schools, particularly those with religious affiliations, to receive public funding of any kind.

Debates about funding and revenue are not uncommon in the academic world. While many private schools are operated on a nonprofit basis, the concept of for-profit educational institutes has been around since ancient Greece. This concept lost favor during the Middle Ages but rose in popularity once again during the fifteenth century Renaissance. It has continued to grow and evolve since that time.

Within the United States, for-profit educational programs gained popularity with the founding of private business and accounting schools during the nineteenth century. This popularity was relatively short-lived, however, because public secondary and vocational schools were established during the late nineteenth and early twentieth centuries. For much of the twentieth century, private for-profit educational programs saw their enrollment numbers dwindle, as students favored public institutions for their educational needs.

Since the 1970's, however, for-profit educational programs have seen a significant resurgence. Part of this growth is due to the renewal of the Higher Education Act in 1972, which increased the amount of federal student aid available to students at private, for-profit schools. Additionally, for-profit education programs have become adept at identifying gaps in the availability of educational opportunities in specific subject areas or for specific students and then creating programs designed to fill those gaps.

The Industry Today

The contemporary private education industry is enormous and includes many different types of programs. These can include private, religious, parochial, or charter elementary and secondary schools; vocational high schools and postsecondary programs; courses to prepare for various school entrance exams or licensing exams; and private tutoring in a wide variety of subjects. As many public schools experience increased enrollment and decreased funding, some parents are turning to

As many public schools experience increased enrollment and decreased funding, some parents are turning to private or religious schools to provide for their children's education. (©Monkey Business Images/Dreamstime.com)

private or religious schools to provide for their children's education. Many towns are also experiencing a growth in the number of charter schools establishing themselves within their school districts.

Charter schools are publicly funded schools that are operated by private organizations under contracts or charters with the state. These schools obtain a significant portion of their revenue directly from the city or state in which they operate, and they are exempt from certain state and local rules and regulations that usually govern public schools. A school's charter is reviewed every three to five years to ensure that minimum standards of educational quality are being met. Despite the controversial nature of this arrangement, the number of charter schools continues to increase in the early twenty-first century, particularly in urban school districts. As of the 2004-2005 school year, according to the U.S. Department of Education, approximately 4 percent of publicly funded schools were privately operated charter schools.

Some private schools are specifically designed to serve the needs of children with special needs. These special needs may include language-based learning difficulties, dyslexia, attention or hyperactive disorders, autism, and hearing impairments, as well as more severe learning disorders or complex medical conditions. Parents, knowing that their children require specific services and accommodations, may choose to place them in one of these private schools. Further, in some states, state law allows public school systems and parents to place those students who are not adequately served in the public school system at one of these private special-needs schools, and local and state public school funds are allocated for part or all of this expenditure.

As many public schools reduce funding for academic enrichment programs, students are engaging in enrichment activities at private learning centers. Additionally, as classrooms become more crowded and teachers have less time to spend with individual students, parents are obtaining private tutoring services for their children to assist them

Large private schools may have facilities such as computer rooms. (©Dreamstime.com)

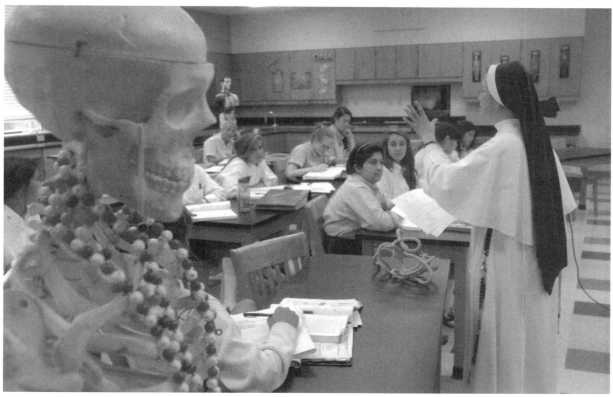

A nun teaches at St. Cecilia Academy in Nashville, Tennessee, a Catholic high school. (AP/Wide World Photos)

in their academic development. These services were traditionally provided by individuals or small groups, but they are increasingly the domain of large regional and national companies that provide a variety of tutoring programs and other educational services.

Students of all ages attend private test-preparation programs to help them prepare for the standardized admissions tests for high school, college, professional schools, and licensing exams. As school admission at all levels has become more competitive, enrollment in private test-preparation programs has increased. Students are also engaging in test preparation earlier than ever before, because standardized tests are growing steadily in importance. For example, scores on the early high school Preliminary SAT (PSAT) are now very important for obtaining financial aid awards to attend college. The Secondary School Admission Test (SSAT), administered to middle-school students, has also become extremely important to students seeking admission into competitive private high schools.

For students who choose not to attend a traditional four-year college program, private postsecondary vocational education is growing in popularity. These types of programs educate students for particular fields, such as automotive repair, medical technical support, business administration, and computer network administration. Many of these private schools offer two-year associate's degrees or other formal certification in particular fields, and they may offer job-placement assistance, making them an attractive and affordable alternative to four-year colleges.

INDUSTRY MARKET SEGMENTS

The private education industry encompasses many different types of programs. The following sections provide details on different sized programs within the industry. Even within a particular size range, the specifics of a program will be influenced by the type of education it provides and whether it operates on a nonprofit or for-profit basis.

Small Programs

A typical small educational program serves about one hundred students or fewer. The smallest type of business within the industry can be as simple as one individual offering private tutoring for an hourly rate. The most common small businesses are groups of tutors offering private instruction and small test-preparation companies offering small group classes. Some very small schools may also qualify as a small program, although most are considered midsize because of their larger staffs and facilities. Small programs offer more personalized attention than larger programs, and they may be better equipped to provide specialized training or to handle students with special needs, but they will likely not have the same resources and amenities as larger programs.

Potential Annual Earnings Scale. Instructors in small programs are likely to earn less than the industry average salary. The U.S. Bureau of Labor Statistics (BLS) reports that, in general, private elementary and middle school teachers earn about 30 percent less than their counterparts in public schools. Secondary and postsecondary teachers' wages, by contrast, are on par with those of their public school colleagues. Overall, the average hourly wage for an education, training, or library employee in the private education industry is $26.51, or $29.33 for those in nonprofit schools. Elementary and middle school teachers average $25.34 per hour in private schools or $25.32 per hour in nonprofit schools. Secondary school teachers average $32.47 per hour in private schools or $33.99 per hour in nonprofit schools. Educational administrators average $29.20 per hour in private schools, or $31.39 per hour in nonprofit schools. Various school counselor positions average $20.80 per hour in private schools, or $21.02 per hour in nonprofit schools. Pay scales for ancillary positions, such as maintenance and clerical workers, are similar to those for other employees in their respective industries.

Clientele Interaction. The clientele of a business in the private education industry are its students and, often, their parents. Most employees in small companies within the private education in-

dustry have plenty of opportunity to interact with the students, although the nature of this interaction will vary depending on the position held and the type of school or program. Individuals in positions such as teacher, instructor, tutor, and coach have frequent interactions with students, and the qualifications and abilities of these individuals are often the reason why the students (and their parents) choose to participate in a particular program. Individuals in administrative positions may not need to interact with students as frequently, but they will often have the opportunity if they choose to do so.

This frequent interaction is one of the primary benefits of small private education programs, for both the employees and the students. Small programs can be a good fit for students looking for specialized instruction in a particular subject area or for students who have special learning needs. Small programs have small staffs, who can work together closely to ensure that their students' needs are met.

Amenities, Atmosphere, and Physical Grounds. A small company that focuses primarily on tutoring may not have any facilities at all; instead, the tutors may travel to the students' homes. Other small companies might have offices with a few rooms, including space for an administrator, an area for tutors to meet with students, and classrooms for group instruction.

Small private, religious, parochial, charter, and vocational schools usually have dedicated buildings, much like small public schools. The buildings have classrooms and administrative offices and some have cafeterias, libraries, and facilities such as gyms with locker rooms, auditoriums, music rooms, computer labs, and science labs. Specific amenities depend on the size of the school, the grade levels taught, and any specific areas of focus. Additionally, most schools employ some type of security personnel, even if it is only a single hall monitor, to ensure that no one gains unauthorized entry to the building.

Vocational schools have facilities similar to those of a high school or junior college, with added facilities as needed for the school's specific programs (for example, an automotive shop or medical equipment). Typical vocational schools have classrooms and administrative offices, and some provide cafeterias, auditoriums, large lecture halls, computer labs, science labs, and athletic facilities such as gyms or pools. These schools also have some security personnel to ensure no one gains unauthorized access to the building and to keep track of any expensive equipment on the premises.

Typical Number of Employees. A typical small education program will have between one and thirty employees, including instructors and teachers, managers, administrators, and support staff. It may also employ additional support positions, such as maintenance or cafeteria workers, but these services could also be provided by an outside company.

Traditional Geographic Locations. Private educational programs can be found all over the country, in towns and cities of all sizes, including rural, suburban, and urban locations. Religious schools are likely to be located next to the religious institutions with which they are affiliated. The physical size of an institution can vary considerably. The smallest programs, particularly those that specialize in private tutoring, might not have any facilities at all, or might have a small suite of offices and small classrooms. Other programs, such as private, religious, charter, or vocational schools, will have their own dedicated buildings containing classrooms, administrative offices, computer and science labs, libraries, and athletic facilities.

A program that resides in its own dedicated space will have a more cohesive feel than one with just a few administrative offices for its staff. If the students have a place to congregate, they will feel like they are part of a greater whole, which fosters a more cooperative learning atmosphere. This is particularly important for any group instruction program, including private elementary, secondary, postsecondary, and vocational schools.

Pros of Working for a Small Education Program. Small private education programs generally offer excellent opportunities to interact with students on an individual basis. This is a benefit to both the staff and the students, who often value smaller programs for this reason. With fewer employees, there are fewer layers of management and thus less bureaucracy when seeking to implement a new idea or to make changes to a program to meet the needs of a particular student. This may lead to greater flexibility in the programs offered, which will allow for more tailored instruction. This flexibility can be of great benefit to students seeking specialized instruction in a specific subject area or those with specific learning needs.

Cons of Working for a Small Education Program. Many small programs operate with a small staff, so instructors may frequently need to perform administrative and maintenance tasks. Their smaller infrastructures may provide fewer opportunities for advancement than would be available in a larger program. Smaller operating budgets may also limit opportunities to develop new programs or courses, as well as the resources from which to draw when creating such courses and programs for students, particularly those with special needs. Smaller companies may also pay lower salaries than larger institutions pay employees with comparable positions.

Costs

Payroll and Benefits: Tutors and instructors at test-preparation programs are typically paid by the hour. Instructors at full-time programs, such as small schools, usually earn annual salaries, although some are paid only during the nine or ten months per year that school is in session. Benefit packages can be quite generous or nonexistent, depending on position and employment status (full- versus part-time). Potential benefits include health insurance, retirement packages or pension plans, paid time off, and reduced or free tuition for the institute's programs.

Supplies: Education programs require standard office supplies, telecommunication equipment, computer hardware and software, networking equipment, and audiovisual equipment. Programs with classrooms require desks, chairs, and chalk- or white boards. Many programs provide common areas, which require items such as study carrels, couches, tables, chairs, refrigerators, and microwave ovens. Libraries require a variety of books, journals, and other research materials, as well as subscriptions to computer-based academic research databases. Schools that offer laboratory facilities require benches and stools, fume hoods, glassware, chemicals, storage cabinets, and safety equipment, such as laboratory coats, gloves, and eye protection. Schools that offer athletic facilities require cleaning and maintenance supplies, sporting and exercise equipment, and shower facilities, and they may provide some basic amenities for spectators.

External Services: Education programs may contract landscaping of outdoor facilities, maintenance of athletic facilities, cleaning and janitorial services, and security services. Some small programs may also contract telecommunication and computer networking services.

Utilities: Common utility costs include electricity, heat, air-conditioning, water, telephone, and Internet access for classrooms, administrative offices, and common spaces.

Taxes: Applicability of state and local taxes depends on many factors, including whether the institution is designated as a nonprofit or for-profit corporation, whether it is affiliated with a religious organization, and whether there is some specific state or federal program affecting taxation. Regardless of tax-exempt status, all institutions must pay payroll taxes on employee salaries.

Midsize Programs

A midsize education program serves between two hundred and one thousand students. These programs include private, religious, parochial, and charter elementary and secondary schools; secondary and postsecondary vocational schools; and small chains of private tutoring, group instruction, and test-preparation centers. Midsize private schools operate very much like their public counterparts and generally have the same management structure and basic amenities as would a public school of similar size. The differences can include factors such as religious affiliation, educational background of instructors, the possibility for specialization (in the case of a vocational school), and the school's ability to assist students with special needs in a way that might not be practical in a public school setting. Midsize test-preparation and other group instruction programs are likely to operate more like similarly sized corporations, with a similar management structure.

Potential Annual Earnings Scale. Instructors in midsize programs are likely to earn salaries in line with the industry averages. The BLS reports that, in general, private elementary and middle school teachers earn about 30 percent less than their counterparts in public schools. Secondary and postsecondary teachers' wages, by contrast, are on par with those of their public school colleagues. Overall, the average hourly wage for an education, training, or library employee in the private education industry is $26.51, or $29.33 for those in nonprofit schools. Elementary and middle school teachers average $25.34 per hour in private schools or $25.32 per hour in nonprofit schools. Secondary school teachers average $32.47 per hour in private schools or $33.99 per hour in nonprofit schools. Educational administrators average $29.20 per hour in private schools, or $31.39 per hour in nonprofit schools. Various school counselor positions average $20.80 per hour in private schools, or $21.02 per hour in nonprofit schools. Pay scales for ancillary positions, such as maintenance and clerical workers, are similar to those for other employees in their respective industries.

Clientele Interaction. As is true in small programs, most employees of a midsize education program have plenty of opportunities to interact with students, although the nature of this interaction will vary depending on the position held and the type of school or program. Individuals in positions such as teacher, instructor, tutor, and coach have frequent interactions with students; individuals in administrative positions may not interact with students as frequently, but they often have the opportunity to do so if they choose.

A midsize private education program often represents a good compromise between the personalized attention students receive from small private school programs and the amenities offered by large programs. Midsize programs are valued by many families because of the high academic standards and individualized attention afforded students. Many private schools, designated as college preparatory schools, are valued for the high caliber of their college placements, and the competition between these institutions and their students for spots in top colleges and universities can be fierce.

Midsize schools can also be a good fit for students with special needs, as they are small enough to give individualized attention to particular students but have large enough student populations to provide the necessary student services, amenities, and equipment for particular learning needs.

Amenities, Atmosphere, and Physical Grounds. A midsize company that focuses on tutoring, test preparation, and other group instruction will have classrooms, administrative offices, and student lounge areas. It may have an auditorium, computer labs, a library, and a cafeteria, but it is unlikely to have athletic facilities or science laboratories, unless they are necessary for the specific type of instruction offered.

Midsize private, religious, parochial, and charter schools have dedicated buildings, much like similarly sized public schools. They have classrooms, administrative offices, cafeterias, auditoriums, music rooms, computer labs, science labs, and facilities such as gyms with locker rooms, athletic fields, and possibly swimming pools. Some midsize private schools also provide room and board for students. In these cases, dormitories with resident advisor (staff) housing are provided. Cafeterias provide three meals each day for these students, and on-campus housing for all staff is often the norm.

Some midsize private high schools have very competitive sports teams and may have significant athletic facilities devoted to these teams, including special fields, stadiums, and amenities for spectators. The specific amenities depend on the size of the school, the grade levels taught, and any specialty the school might have. These schools can be located in a rural area, town, or city; a religious school is likely to be located next to the religious institution with which it is affiliated. Additionally, most schools employ security personnel to ensure that no one gains unauthorized entry to the campus.

Midsize vocational schools can also be located in any town or city and have facilities similar to a high school or junior college, with added equipment as needed for the school's specific programs (for example, an automotive shop or medical training facilities). Vocational schools generally include classrooms and administrative offices, cafeterias, auditoriums or large lecture halls, computer labs, science labs, and possibly some athletic facilities such as gyms or pools. These schools also employ security personnel to ensure no one gains unauthorized access and to keep track of any expensive equipment on the premises.

Typical Number of Employees. A typical midsize private education program has between thirty and one hundred employees, including full- and part-time staff, such as instructors, principals and assistant principals, managers, directors, and ad-

ministrators. This number may include additional support positions such as maintenance or cafeteria workers, but it is also possible that those services may be contracted through outside companies.

Traditional Geographic Locations. Midsize private education programs can be found all over the country in a variety of geographic areas, but they are most often found in suburban or urban locations, with boarding schools often located in more rural areas. The physical size of the institution can vary considerably. Midsize tutoring, test-preparation, and group instruction programs might still reside in a small office building or a single floor in a larger building, as they do not require as many additional facilities. Midsize private, religious, charter, and vocational schools often have many additional facilities, including outdoor sports fields and recreation areas, and will accordingly require more space.

Regardless of the type, programs that offer common meeting and recreation areas for students and staff foster a more cooperative learning atmosphere than programs that do not have such spaces. This is particularly important for programs such as private, religious, parochial, charter, and vocational schools, as well as other group instruction programs.

Pros of Working for a Midsize Education Program. Many midsize private education programs offer a satisfying balance between the individualized student interaction of small programs and the greater amenities of large programs. The greater numbers of staff, enrollment, and revenue may provide more opportunities to create or expand programs and course offerings. Larger staffs result in more hierarchical business structures, which may provide greater opportunities for advancement or for lateral moves between instruction and administration. Additionally, some private schools offer discounted or free tuition to their employees' children.

Cons of Working for a Midsize Education Program. Since midsize schools employ more people, the hierarchical management structure may create more bureaucracy, making it logistically more difficult to implement new ideas than one might find in a smaller school. There may also be greater competition between instructors for funds for academic programs, extracurricular activities, and classroom supplies. Additionally, many private schools do not pay as well as their similarly sized public counterparts, and they may not offer perks such as tenure or benefit and pension plans comparable to those offered by public schools.

Costs

Payroll and Benefits: Teachers and instructors in schools generally earn salaries. Instructors in midsize test-preparation programs and tutoring companies are often paid hourly wages. Those wages may include travel time for tutors who drive to their students' homes. Benefit packages range from generous to nonexistent, depending on position and employment status (full-versus part-time). Potential benefits include health insurance, retirement packages or pension plans, paid time off, and reduced or free tuition.

Supplies: Supplies include all standard office supplies, plus telecommunication equipment, computer hardware and software, networking equipment, and audiovisual equipment. Programs with classrooms require desks, chairs, and chalk- or white boards. Programs that provide common areas require items such as study carrels, couches, tables, chairs, refrigerators, and microwave ovens. Libraries require a variety of books, journals, and other research materials, as well as subscriptions to computer-based academic research databases. Laboratory facilities require benches and stools, fume hoods, glassware, chemicals, storage cabinets, and safety equipment, such as laboratory coats, gloves, and eye protection. Dormitories are required for boarding schools. Schools that offer athletic facilities require cleaning and maintenance supplies, sporting and exercise equipment, and shower facilities, and they may provide some amenities for spectators.

External Services: External services commonly contracted by midsize education programs include landscaping, maintenance of athletic facilities, cleaning and janitorial services, and security services. Some programs may contract out telecommunication and computer networking services.

Utilities: Common utility costs include electricity, heat, air-conditioning, water, telephone, and Internet access for classrooms, administrative offices, and common spaces.

Taxes: Applicability of state and local taxes depends on many factors, including whether the institution is designated as a nonprofit or for-profit corporation, whether it is affiliated with a religious organization, and whether there is some specific state or federal program affecting taxation.

Large Programs

A large program within the private education industry will generally serve more than one thousand students. These programs include private, religious, parochial, and charter elementary and secondary schools; secondary and postsecondary vocational schools; and large chains of private tutoring, group instruction, and test-preparation centers. Large schools operate very much as do their public school counterparts and generally have the same management structures and basic amenities as public schools of similar size. The differences can include factors such as religious affiliation, quality of instructors, possibility for specialization (in the case of vocational schools), and ability to assist students with special needs in a way that might not be practical in a public school setting.

Potential Annual Earnings Scale. Instructors in large programs are likely to earn salaries slightly above industry averages. The BLS reports that, in general, private elementary and middle school teachers earn about 30 percent less than their counterparts in public schools. Secondary and postsecondary teachers' wages, by contrast, are on par with those of their public school colleagues. Overall, the average hourly wage for an education, training, or library employee in the private education industry is $26.51, or $29.33 for those in non-profit schools. Elementary and middle school teachers average $25.34 per hour in private schools or $25.32 per hour in nonprofit schools. Secondary school teachers average $32.47 per hour in private schools or $33.99 per hour in nonprofit schools. Educational administrators average $29.20 per hour in private schools, or $31.39 per hour in nonprofit schools. Various school counselor positions average $20.80 per hour in private schools, or $21.02 per hour in nonprofit schools. Pay scales for ancillary positions, such as maintenance and clerical workers, are similar to those for other employees in their respective industries.

Clientele Interaction. Within a large private school, there is generally still much opportunity to interact with students. Employees in positions such as teacher, instructor, tutor, and coach do so frequently, and administrators often have the opportunity for student interaction if they so desire. Large tutoring, test-preparation, and group instruction programs are likely to have more corporate structures than their smaller competitors, and administrative staff members may have fewer opportunities for student interaction.

Large private education programs have more students, staff, and revenue and can provide more amenities to the students. As a result, many of these programs provide excellent facilities for students seeking specialized instruction in particular subjects or for students with special needs. As in midsize schools, some college preparatory schools are extremely competitive in the area of college admissions, and their reputation depends heavily on the caliber of schools to which their students are accepted. Large programs that follow a more corporate model may have less opportunity for student interaction and less program flexibility, so they may not be able to provide the individualized attention to these students that a smaller program might provide.

Amenities, Atmosphere, and Physical Grounds. Large companies that focus on tutoring, test preparation, and other group instruction have dedicated buildings, or occupy several floors of large buildings. These buildings house classrooms, administrative offices, and student lounge areas. They may have auditoriums, computer labs, libraries, and cafeterias, but they are unlikely to have athletic facilities and science laboratories unless they are necessary for the specific type of instruction offered.

Large private, religious, parochial, and charter schools have dedicated buildings, much like similarly sized public schools. These buildings have classrooms, administrative offices, cafeterias, auditoriums, music rooms, computer labs, science labs, and facilities such as gyms with locker rooms, athletic fields, and possibly swimming pools. Again, these schools may board students, requiring dormitories with resident staff housing.

Many large private high schools have very competitive sports teams and may have significant athletic facilities devoted to these teams, including special fields, stadiums, and amenities for spectators. The specific amenities depend on the size of the school, the grade levels taught, and any specialty the school might have. These schools can be located in any town, city, or rural area; a religious school is likely to be located next to the religious organization with which it is affiliated. Additionally, most schools employ security personnel to ensure that no one gains unauthorized entry to their buildings.

Large vocational schools can also be located in any town or city and have facilities similar to a high school or junior college, with added equipment as needed for the school's specific programs (for example, an automotive shop or medical training facilities). Vocational schools generally include classrooms and administrative offices, cafeterias, auditoriums or large lecture halls, computer labs, science labs, and possibly some athletic facilities such as gyms or pools. These schools also hire security personnel to ensure that no one gains unauthorized access to the building and to keep track of any expensive equipment on the premises.

Typical Number of Employees. A typical large private education company has more than one hundred employees. This number includes full- and part-time staff, such as teachers, instructors, principals and assistant principals, directors, managers, administrators, and numerous support staff positions. Some large companies may contract out maintenance, janitorial, cafeteria, or security work, while others have their own in-house staff to fill these positions.

Traditional Geographic Locations. Large private education programs can be found all over the country in a variety of geographic areas, but they are most often found in suburban or urban locations. Large tutoring, test preparation, and group instruction programs may have dedicated office buildings, or they may occupy several floors inside a larger building. Often, these companies are chains and will have facilities in multiple locations, as well as a central office located in a major city. Large private, religious, parochial, charter, and vocational schools often have many additional facilities, some in a campus setting that includes outdoor sports fields and recreation areas that require more space.

Pros of Working for a Large Education Program. Large private education companies usually have more amenities and more funding than their smaller counterparts. Accordingly, they provide a greater variety of programs and more opportunities to create and expand programs for students. Because of their larger staffs, the hierarchical management system may provide greater opportunities for career advancement than are to be had in smaller programs. Increased funding and availability of support staff may create more opportunities to establish or expand programs to better serve students. Larger programs, particularly private for-profit companies, may provide higher salaries and more comprehensive benefits packages than do smaller programs of a similar kind. Some offer discounted or free tuition for their employees' children.

Cons of Working for a Large Education Program. The hierarchical management structure within a large school creates more bureaucracy, which may make the implementation of new ideas logistically difficult. There will also be more departments competing for funds and other resources. Large programs in the tutoring, test-preparation, and group instruction business may also operate more like large corporations, which does not always mesh well with educational ideals. While the salary and benefits available at a large private education company may be better than those offered at smaller companies, they may still not be as good as what one could obtain from a similarly sized public school.

Costs

Payroll and Benefits: Teachers and instructors in schools generally earn salaries. Instructors in midsize test-preparation programs and tutoring companies are often paid hourly wages. Those wages may include travel time for tutors who drive to their students' homes. Benefit packages range from generous to nonexistent, depending on position and employment status (full-versus part-time). Potential benefits include health insurance, retirement packages or pension plans, paid time off, and reduced or free tuition.

Supplies: Supplies include all standard office supplies, plus telecommunication equipment, computer hardware and software, networking equipment, and audiovisual equipment. Programs with classrooms require desks, chairs, and chalk-or white boards. Programs that provide common areas require items such as study carrels, couches, tables, chairs, refrigerators, and microwave ovens. Libraries require a variety of books, journals, and other research materials, as well as subscriptions to computer-based academic research databases. Laboratory facilities require benches and stools, fume hoods, glassware, chemicals, storage cabinets, and safety equipment, such as laboratory coats, gloves, and eye protection. Dormitories are required for boarding schools. Schools that offer athletic facilities require cleaning and maintenance supplies, sporting and exercise equipment, and shower facilities, and they may provide some amenities for spectators.

External Services: External services commonly contracted by large education programs include landscaping, maintenance of athletic facilities, cleaning and janitorial services, and security services. Some programs may contract out telecommunication and computer networking services.

Utilities: Common utility costs include electricity, heat, air-conditioning, water, telephone, and Internet access for classrooms, administrative offices, and common spaces.

Taxes: Applicability of state and local taxes depends on many factors, including whether the institution is designated as a nonprofit or for-profit corporation, whether it is affiliated with a religious organization, and whether there is some specific program affecting taxation.

ORGANIZATIONAL STRUCTURE AND JOB ROLES

Because of the wide variety of programs that fall within the private education industry, any particular company may or may not have specific individuals or departments fulfilling all of these positions. However, all of these different areas represent vital functions for a private education company of any type or size. Some of the smaller organizations may simply combine multiple functions into a single position or department.

The following umbrella categories apply to the organizational structure of businesses in the private education industry:

- Business Management
- Customer Service
- Sales and Marketing
- Facilities and Security
- Technology, Research, Design, and Development
- Operations
- Human Resources

Business Management

Many private education companies employ a staff dedicated to performing a variety of occupations, both academic and administrative. The business structure of a private, religious, parochial, charter, or vocational school is likely to differ from that of a tutoring, test-preparation, or group instruction company. The former will have a more academic-oriented structure, while the latter will have a more corporate structure. Regardless of type, all private education companies have one or more individuals who fill important managerial roles.

Schools are generally led by principals or headmasters and possibly several assistant principals. The principal or headmaster is in charge of setting the overall vision and direction for the school, as well as for providing general oversight to all departments. He or she may also have significant decision-making power concerning academic program

development and budgets. Large schools may employ one or more assistant principals to assist with this task. These individuals have at least four-year degrees and usually have master's degrees or doctorates in education or educational administration.

Within a school, individual departments are led by department chairs, who are often also teachers within those departments. These chairs are responsible for guiding the overall direction of their departments and may have significant decision-making power with regard to setting curricula, choosing textbooks, and allocating funding. They have four-year degrees, often in their areas of interest or in education, and often have significant teaching and management or administrative experience as well.

Programs with more corporate structures are generally led by presidents, who are in charge of making top-level decisions governing their companies. The largest companies may have boards of directors, who are responsible for setting broad policies and directions for their companies and answering to the companies' private investors and shareholders. In such a case, the president is responsible for making decisions that execute the board's policies.

The president may be assisted by one or more vice presidents, who are each in charge of specific

OCCUPATION SPECIALTIES

Education Administrators

Specialty	Responsibilities
Education supervisors	Develop program curriculum, evaluate teaching techniques, and supervise and assist in the hiring and in-service training of teachers.
Principals	Direct and coordinate the educational, administrative, and counseling activities of elementary, junior high, or high schools.
School superintendents	Direct and coordinate activities concerned with the administration of city, county, or other school systems in accordance with board of education standards.
Vocational training directors	Supervise and coordinate vocational training programs according to board of education policies and state education code.

business functions (for example, finance or marketing). These vice presidents each supervise several department managers, who are responsible for making and executing decisions with respect to their specific departments and managing the employees within those departments. Employees in these various management positions generally have four-year degrees and may have graduate degrees in business or finance, as well as backgrounds in education.

Business management occupations may include the following:

- Principal
- Headmaster
- Assistant Principal
- Department Chair
- Facility Manager
- President
- Vice President
- Department Manager

Customer Service

The customers of private education companies are students and sometimes the students' parents. Depending on the size of a given program, many administrative support services may be required to help students make the most of their experience. There are many positions within private education companies that involve direct interaction with students, but some positions are more customer service oriented than others.

Within a private school, many administrative assistants act as gatekeepers to the higher-level managers, such as the principal or headmaster. Employees in these positions frequently interact with students and are responsible for deciding which higher-level administrator should address a particular student's question or concern. This role is best suited for individuals who are highly organized and extremely patient and who work well with young people. Employees in these positions may have two- or four-year degrees in business administration or another liberal arts field.

Additional customer-service positions within schools include those that help students make the most of their education. These include such positions as guidance counselors, psychologists, social service providers, and nurses. Often, those serving in guidance positions in private schools are under pressure to place students in top academic colleges and universities. These individuals often build strong networks with college and university recruiters and often can expect a high level of parent involvement and interaction related to this process. All of these support positions require individuals who have a great deal of patience and enjoy working with young people. Many, particularly counselors and nurses, require specialized degrees and licenses related to their specific fields.

In a company with a more traditional corporate structure, customer service positions usually include receptionists and telephone support staff. Individuals in these positions may have two- or four-year degrees in business, educational administration, or a liberal arts field. They need to have a friendly, helpful, service-oriented demeanor, as well as a great deal of knowledge about their companies and the programs they offer.

Customer service occupations may include the following:

- Administrative Assistant
- Guidance Counselor
- Career Development Counselor
- School Psychologist
- School Nurse
- Social Service Provider
- Social Worker
- Receptionist
- Telephone Support Staff

Sales and Marketing

Any institution in the private education industry is ultimately a business and must attract new students each year in order to remain in business. The details of how a sales and marketing department operates vary depending on the specific program of which it is a part, but its basic responsibility is always to bring in new students to keep the program alive.

In a typical private, religious, parochial, charter, or vocational school, there are several different departments that can be described as sales and marketing. First, the admissions department is responsible for attracting new students by developing promotional materials for the program and sending representatives out to meet prospective students. Second, the external relations department is responsible for interacting with the community as a whole to maintain a positive image for the school and, in some cases, to seek outside funding sources. Finally, the alumni relations department is responsible for maintaining strong ties between alumni and the school, in order to foster positive networking connections and raise revenue in the form of donations and scholarship funds. Individuals who work in these positions generally have four-year degrees in education, communication, marketing, or public relations.

The admissions department is also responsible for selecting which students to admit to the school. This requires reviewing application materials and conducting interviews with individual students. Employees who serve this function in the admissions department generally have degrees in education or educational administration and often have either teaching or school administration experience at the appropriate level.

In corporate private educational programs, the sales and marketing department more closely resembles that of a traditional company. It prepares promotional materials explaining the program's details and benefits, and publicizes the program to the larger community. In addition to advertising, this publicity may be accomplished by attending events such as career fairs and trade shows. The purpose of a sales and marketing department is to attract new students and to make enrollment a quick and easy process. Employees of such departments generally have four-year degrees in communications, marketing, or public relations and may have some experience in the education field as an instructor or administrator.

Sales and marketing occupations may include the following:

- Admissions Director
- Community Relations Director
- Alumni Relations Director
- Public Relations Director
- Marketing Director
- Sales Director
- Graphic Designer
- Copywriter
- Photographer

Facilities and Security

Any private education company with physical facilities requires maintenance and security services.

Smaller programs require less maintenance, and they often contract most of the necessary services from external vendors. Even very small programs require security to ensure that only authorized individuals have access to their facilities, for the safety of the students and staff. They either assign this task to a permanent staff member or hire an outside company to provide security personnel.

Midsize programs with larger facilities require more maintenance of both indoor and outdoor facilities. They are likely to maintain at least a small staff of permanent workers to fulfill this need. Other services may be provided by outside contractors. Midsize schools require more security staff to monitor access to buildings. This function also may be served by permanent staff members or by outside security firms. Many midsize programs—particularly private, religious, parochial, and charter secondary schools—have athletic programs that require additional maintenance for their physical facilities and corresponding equipment. Depending on the facilities, these needs may be addressed by staff members or by outside companies.

Large programs with extensive facilities require a great deal of maintenance, both indoors and out, and they often maintain a significant staff of permanent workers in addition to contracted labor. All programs and companies require janitorial services for classrooms and administrative offices and a staff of individuals ready to make small and moderate repairs quickly. Programs with athletic facilities (generally large private, religious, and charter schools) require maintenance for their fields, gyms, and pools; these services may be provided by full-time dedicated staff members or by outside contractors.

Employment requirements vary depending on position. Basic maintenance or janitorial positions may require no advanced education or experience, while more specialized facilities positions may require both special licenses and relevant experience. Qualifications for security positions vary but likely include at least some level of education or certification beyond a high school diploma.

Facilities and security occupations may include the following:

- Building and Grounds Facility Manager
- Building Maintenance and Repair Worker

- Building Security Manager
- Security Guard
- Athletic Director

Technology, Research, Design, and Development

Many private education companies rely heavily on technology to support their programs. The type of technology employed varies depending on the type of program and the size of the company. Most programs have computers for use by students and staff and maintain local-area networks as well as Internet connections. The more extensive the network (and the more that students and staff rely on it), the more support and assistance are required to keep it functioning at all times. This task may require a dedicated staff of network administrators to keep the system functioning, as well as a help desk available to answer questions. Since most schools and companies maintain all of their records on computers, this is an extremely important function. Information technology (IT) jobs are well suited for people who enjoy problem solving and are willing to work under time constraints when network repairs are needed. Employees in these occupations often have two- or four-year degrees in computer programming, computer systems engineering, or information technology, with concentrations in network systems.

Many classrooms are now equipped with audiovisual equipment such as SMART Boards, projectors, televisions, and digital video disc (DVD) players to allow instructors to make multimedia presentations in their classes. This equipment can require a great deal of support and maintenance to ensure that instructors know how to use it properly and to keep it in good working order. The presence of this equipment may require additional security personnel and precautions to ensure its safety from theft. Employees in audiovisual departments may have two- or four-year degrees in computer programming, electrical engineering, or information technology.

Private education companies are always working on research and development to ensure that their products provide the greatest possible benefit to their students, the companies, and their investors. As a result, tutoring, test-preparation, and group instruction companies, as well as private schools of all kinds, employ curriculum development professionals to regularly review and update the programs offered. Employees in these positions generally have four-year degrees in education and sometimes in the specific subject they are teaching, and they may have additional certification or graduate-level training, such as doctorates in education or curriculum development.

In more corporate environments, particularly in for-profit education companies, there may be a research and development team that includes individuals trained in market research. The role of this team is to determine what kind of programs potential students are looking for and what changes they might want to see in currently available programs. This is a very important function, because private for-profit companies need to maximize the value of their programs to students, themselves, and their shareholders in order to maintain a viable business model. Researchers generally have backgrounds in communications and statistical analysis, as well as in education.

Technology, research, design, and development occupations may include the following:

- Information Technology Manager
- Network Specialist
- Computer Support Specialist
- Audiovisual Support Specialist
- Curriculum Development Specialist
- Research and Development Director
- Market Research Analyst

Operations

Since the customer of a private education company is the student and sometimes his or her parents, the "operations" role is that of the educators, including teachers, researchers, and librarians. Qualifications for teachers vary considerably in different private education companies. In private, religious, parochial, and charter schools, teachers are generally expected to have four-year degrees in education or in their specific subjects (particularly in high school). In most states, elementary and secondary school teachers are required to pass licensing exams to teach in public schools, but many states do not require this certification for private school teachers. Vocational schools that are also secondary schools have the same academic and licensing requirements as other high schools, but those that are postsecondary institutions do not. In

OCCUPATION PROFILE

Secondary School Teacher

Considerations	Qualifications
Description	Instructs students at the secondary level and creates instructional plans.
Career clusters	Education and Training
Interests	Data; people
Working conditions	Work inside
Minimum education level	Bachelor's degree; master's degree
Physical exertion	Light work
Physical abilities	Unexceptional/basic fitness
Opportunities for experience	Internship; volunteer work; part-time work
Licensure and certification	Required
Employment outlook	Average growth expected
Holland interest score	SAE

Note: See volume 1, "Publisher's Note," for an explanation of the Holland interest score.

either case, vocational instructors are expected to have any necessary degrees and qualifications for the specific programs they teach, as well as experience working in the relevant fields and prior teaching experience.

In tutoring and group instruction programs, instructors are generally expected to have degrees in the appropriate subject area, and often some prior teaching experience is preferred. There usually is not a licensing requirement to teach in these types of private programs.

Librarians and library staff play a very important role in the academic experience at private elementary and secondary schools. Librarians are in charge of selecting library materials, maintaining organized facilities, and helping students find the materials they need for their research and projects, as well as teaching students how to use library resources to conduct research. Librarians usually have master's degrees in library science, while library support staff may have bachelor's degrees in related fields.

Operations occupations may include the following:

- Teacher
- Instructor
- Teaching Aide/Assistant Teacher
- Tutor
- Librarian
- Library Support Staff

Human Resources

Regardless of size, any private education company is likely to employ at least one individual in a human resources role. The responsibility of such employees is to hire new employees, handle the necessary paperwork, and ensure that the needs of the current staff are being met. This can include anything from processing benefits paperwork to resolving disputes between employees and supervisors.

The smallest of programs, such as a small tutoring company, may have a single person (sometimes

OCCUPATION PROFILE

Teacher Assistant

Considerations	Qualifications
Description	Helps teachers maintain order in classrooms, assists students with tasks, and helps with instruction.
Career clusters	Education and Training; Human Services
Interests	Data; people
Working conditions	Work inside
Minimum education level	High school diploma or GED; high school diploma/ technical training; junior/technical/community college; apprenticeship
Physical exertion	Light work
Physical abilities	Unexceptional/basic fitness
Opportunities for experience	Apprenticeship; volunteer work
Licensure and certification	Usually not required
Employment outlook	Average growth expected
Holland interest score	ESC; SCE

Note: See volume 1, "Publisher's Note," for an explanation of the Holland interest score.

the company owner or president) serving as the human resources manager, as well as fulfilling many other unrelated roles. Other small or midsize programs may have one or two individuals dedicated to human resources. These employees are required to fill a variety of roles within the department. Larger programs have entire, fully staffed departments dedicated to human resources and are able to hire individuals to specialize in specific areas.

Human resources staff members often have four-year degrees in business administration or management, possibly with a concentration or emphasis on higher-education administration. Department managers may also have M.B.A.s and significant related experience. Within larger institutions, individuals who specialize in benefits management may have backgrounds in finance, while those who specialize in handling employee complaints and disputes may have backgrounds in me-

diation or dispute resolution. The largest institutions may also have in-house employment-law attorneys to ensure that all policies and procedures meet legal requirements.

Human resources occupations may include the following:

- Human Resources Manager
- Human Resources Generalist
- Benefits Specialist
- Mediation/Dispute Resolution Specialist
- Employment Attorney

INDUSTRY OUTLOOK

Overview

The U.S. Department of Education projects an increase of 9 percent in total elementary and secondary education enrollment (both private and public) between 2004 and 2016. A significant portion of this growth is expected in the private education industry, particularly in early childhood and postsecondary programs, and is largely attributed to population changes (migration, immigration, and increased births), as opposed to attendance rates.

As enrollment increases, there will be an increased demand for individuals to work in private education companies of all kinds and in all occupations within the industry. There will be an increased need for teachers and instructors, particularly those who have credentials and experience in popular industries and trades. There will also be a greater demand for administrators at all levels to help oversee these programs as they expand. Demand for the highest-level managerial positions, such as school principals, corporate directors, presidents, and vice presidents, may grow somewhat, but the growth will not be as dramatic since fewer positions exist at this level within each institution.

Many of these anticipated opportunities will come in alternative education programs, such as vocational training institutes, online and correspondence courses, and group instruction programs in specialized subjects such as computer skills, languages, and professional certification. Many private education companies are looking toward the large pool of working adults who are seeking to advance or change their careers as a source of new students and new income streams. These programs will present many opportunities for individuals with specialized experience and an interest in teaching and will also provide many administrative positions for those with strong backgrounds in computers and technology.

Employment Advantages

Most people choose to work in the private education industry because of the enjoyment and satisfaction of teaching and working with students. This field can be incredibly rewarding, as there are many opportunities to help individuals make a difference in their own lives through education. It can be easier to get a job in the private education industry than in a public school, as hiring decisions may be less influenced by local politics. Additionally, some people find that there is less bureaucracy in private schools of all sizes than one might find in a comparably sized public school.

Individuals who enjoy working with young people and who are willing to provide a high level of personalized service are likely to succeed in this industry, and they will find they are able to make satisfying and lasting interpersonal connections with the students whose lives they influence in a positive way. Even those who choose to fill administrative roles within the industry often find the work to be satisfying, because their efforts to maintain the required infrastructure ultimately support students as they strive to meet their goals.

Annual Earnings

The most common sources of revenue for private education companies include student tuition, private gifts, endowments, and contracts with other private companies. Many private education companies are operated on a for-profit basis and generate billions of dollars in revenues every year.

There are some exceptions to this model. Many private elementary and secondary schools, particularly schools with religious affiliations, operate as nonprofits. They still receive funding primarily from sources other than the government, but they do not have the same objective of generating profits for shareholders as the for-profit companies within the education industry. It is difficult to track revenue numbers for these schools, as they are not subject to the same reporting requirements as for-profit institutes, and the Department of Education has only recently begun tracking data for private schools.

Charter schools present an interesting model. These schools receive most of their funding from state and local governments, but they are run by private organizations. They receive a charter to operate from the state in which they are located, but they are exempt from certain rules and regulations ordinarily governing publicly funded schools. In exchange, the charter must be reviewed and renewed every three to five years. This arrangement generates a great deal of controversy, as some argue that it takes away much-needed funds from local public schools and only benefits the few children who are able to attend the charter schools. However, others argue that, because charter schools are operated by private companies rather than by the government, they tend to be more efficient than public schools, benefiting their students and raising standards across the board. There is so far very little objective evidence that charter schools provide better educations than public schools.

For-profit institutions of any level operate explicitly to make money for their shareholders, and they are treated as businesses by the government. They are generally subject to corporate taxation and oversight by regulatory bodies such as the Federal Trade Commission (FTC) and the Securities and Exchange Commission (SEC). These institutes include two-year, four-year, and graduate-level degree programs, as well as a variety of certification programs and other courses that require less than two years to complete. This last category has been a source of significant growth in the for-profit education industry in the past few decades, as public institutions have been slow to fill the demand for these types of programs. However, they have also become controversial, because some programs misrepresent both the likelihood of employment for, and the likely salaries commanded by, their graduates.

According to the Center for College Affordability and Productivity, for-profit schools in the United States receive an average of $15,063 in revenue per student. As of 2006, there were approximately 1 million students enrolled in for-profit schools, making the total revenue more than $15 billion annually. This number represents for-profit higher-education programs, including two-year, four-year, and graduate programs, as well as certification and vocational programs. Approximately 90 percent of this revenue comes from student tuition and fees.

SBOMAG claims that nondegree-granting programs, commonly referred to as the "supplemental education market," are a $102 billion industry in the United States. These programs generate big business. The private tutoring market alone generated approximately $2.7 billion in revenue in 2001 alone.

In 2006, the Department of Labor reported that there were approximately 13.2 million individuals employed in the educational services industry generally, of whom approximately 63 percent (8.3 million) were employed in both public and private elementary and secondary education. While data were not provided relating to the breakdown between public and private school employees, the Department of Labor reported that private schools made up approximately 25 percent of all schools and educated approximately 10 percent of students. Around 4.5 percent of the sector's employees were employed in other private educational programs, such as test-preparation and certification programs. These statistics include instructors, administrators, and office staff.

The Department of Labor predicts wage and salary employment growth of 11 percent across the entire educational services sector over the 2006-2016 period, with much of this growth occurring in early childhood education, postsecondary education, English as a second language (ESL) instruction, and special education. Slightly less growth is expected in elementary and secondary schools.

RELATED RESOURCES FOR FURTHER RESEARCH

ASSOCIATION OF PRIVATE ENTERPRISE
  EDUCATION
  313 Fletcher Hall, Dept. 6106
  615 McCallie Ave.
  Chattanooga, TN 37403-2598
  http://www.apee.org

CENTER FOR TEACHING EXCELLENCE, UNIVERSITY
  OF DENTISTRY AND MEDICINE OF NEW JERSEY,
  SCHOOL OF HEALTH RELATED PROFESSIONS
  65 Bergen St.
  Newark, NJ 07107
  Tel: (973) 972-8576
  http://cte.umdnj.edu

COLLEGE BOARD
  45 Columbus Ave.
  New York, NY 10023
  Tel: (212) 713-8000
  http://www.collegeboard.com

NATIONAL EDUCATION ASSOCIATION
  1201 16th St. NW
  Washington, DC 20036-3290
  Tel: (202) 833-4000
  http://www.nea.org

NATIONAL INDEPENDENT PRIVATE SCHOOLS
  ASSOCIATION
  10134 SW 78th Ct.

Miami, FL 33156
Phone: (305) 630-2557
http://www.nipsa.org

U.S. DEPARTMENT OF EDUCATION
400 Maryland Ave. SW
Washington, DC 20202
Tel: (800) 872-5327
http://www.ed.gov

ABOUT THE AUTHOR

Tracey M. DiLascio is a practicing small business and intellectual property attorney in Newton, Massachusetts. Prior to establishing her practice, DiLascio taught writing and social science courses in Massachusetts and New Jersey colleges and served as a judicial clerk in the New Jersey Superior Court. She is a graduate of Boston University School of Law.

FURTHER READING

Associated Press. "Career Education 4Q Profit Up, Revenue Down." Boston.com, February 19, 2009. http://www.boston.com/business/articles/2009/02/19/career_education_4q _profit_up_revenue_down.

Bailey, Thomas, Norena Badway, and Patricia J. Gumport. *For-Profit Higher Education and Community Colleges.* Stanford, Calif.: National Center for Postsecondary Improvement, 2001. Available at http://www.stanford.edu/group/ncpi/documents/pdfs/forprofitandcc.pdf.

Bensinger, Greg. "Washington Post Reports Profit on Education Revenue." Bloomberg.com, July 31, 2009. http://www.bloomberg.com/apps/news?pid =20601204&sid=a99eeXcdQ4Z4.

Burch, Patricia. *Hidden Markets: The New Education Privatization.* New York: Routledge, 2009.

Butler, Amy. *Wages in the Nonprofit Sector: Occupations Typically Found in Educational and Research Institutions.* Washington, D.C.: U.S. Bureau of Labor and Statistics, 2009. Available at http://www.bls.gov/opub/cwc/cm20081124ar01p1.htm.

Coleman, James, and Richard Vedder. *For Profit Education in the United States: A Primer.* Washington, D.C.: Center for College Affordability and Productivity, 2008. Available at http://www.centerforcollegeaffordability.org/uploads/For-Profit_corr_2.pdf.

Hallinan, Maureen T. *Handbook of the Sociology of Education.* New York: Springer Press, 2006.

The Handbook of Private Schools: An Annual Descriptive Survey of Independent Education. Boston: Porter Sargent Handbooks, 2009.

Herrera, Debbi. *Resource Guide for Private School Administrators.* Danvers, Mass.: LRP Publications, 2007.

"Institutional Eligibility Under the Higher Education Act of 1965, as Amended, and the Secretary's Recognition of Accrediting Agencies; Proposed Rule." *Federal Register* 74, no. 150 (August 6, 2009). http://edocket.access.gpo.gov/2009/pdf/E9-18368.pdf.

Jones, Steven L. *Religious Schooling in America: Private Education and Public Life.* Westport, Conn.: Praeger, 2008.

Morphew, Christopher C., and Peter D. Eckel. *Privatizing the Public University: Perspectives from Across the Academy.* Baltimore: The Johns Hopkins University Press, 2009.

Sandler, Michael R. *Social Entrepreneurship in Education: Private Ventures for the Public Good.* Lanham, Md.: Rowman & Littlefield Education, 2010.

StateUniversity.com. "Private Schooling: What Is a Private School? History of Private Schools in the United States." http://education.stateuniversity.com/pages/2334/Private-Schooling.html.

U.S. Bureau of Labor Statistics. *Career Guide to Industries,* 2010-2011 ed. http://www.bls.gov/oco/cg.

_____. *Occupational Outlook Handbook,* 2010-2011 ed. http://www.bls.gov/oco.

U.S. Census Bureau. North American Industry Classification System (NAICS), 2007. http://www.census.gov/cgi-bin/sssd/naics/naicsrch?chart=2007.

U.S. Department of Commerce. International Trade Administration. Office of Trade and Industry Information. Industry Trade Data and Analysis. http://ita.doc.gov/td/industry/otea/OTII/OTII-index.html.

1536   Private Education Industry

U.S. Department of Education. Institute of Education Sciences. National Center for Education Statistics. "The Condition of Education." 2007. http://nces.ed.gov/programs/coe/2007/section4/indicator32.asp.

———. "Private School Universe Survey." 2007-2008 ed. http://nces.ed.gov/surveys/pss/index.asp.

———. "Projections of Education Statistics to 2016." 2007. http://nces.ed.gov/programs/projections/projections2016/sec1a.asp.

Public Elementary and Secondary Education Industry

©Kristin Schmidt/Dreamstine.com

INDUSTRY SNAPSHOT

General Industry: Education and Training

Career Cluster: Education and Training

Subcategory Industries: Disabled Education; Elementary School Education; High School Education; Kindergarten Education; Middle School and Junior High School Education

Related Industries: Corporate Education Services; Day-Care Services; Higher Education Industry; Private Education Industry

Annual Domestic Revenues: $631 billion USD (National Center for Education Statistics, 2009)

Annual International Revenues: $15.4 trillion USD (National Center for Education Statistics, 2009)

Annual Global Revenues: $16.1 trillion USD (National Center for Education Statistics, 2009)

NAICS Number: 61

INDUSTRY DEFINITION

Summary

The public elementary and secondary education industry exists worldwide and is the cornerstone of most countries' formal education structure, fulfilling a commitment to provide youths with the skills and knowledge necessary for fully functional members of society. Elementary school is the first formal stage of public education, where children are introduced to core skills of literacy and computation, such as reading, writing, and mathematics. Secondary education follows elementary studies and often is split between middle school and high school study levels. Secondary education provides general, technical, and professional curricula and also prepares the higher-achieving students for postsecondary, or "higher," education.

History of the Industry

American formal education has its roots in the British educational tradition. The curriculum applied in American public schools is derived from ancient ideas about education, dating back to the philosophies of Plato and Aristotle in the fourth century B.C.E. and to the medieval schools of the Catholic tradition, grounded in Aristotelian philosophy. The fundamental areas of educational concern today match the liberal arts that ancient and medieval scholars believed to be fundamental to the life of the mind and necessary to full human intellectual development.

American secondary education has its origin in the *artes liberales* of the Middle Ages. These comprise the seven liberal arts, which include the trivium (grammar, logic or dialectic, and rhetoric) and the quadrivium (arithmetic, geometry, astronomy, and music). In the earliest public schools in America, children began their formal education with grammar, considered the "lowliest of the seven arts," and later advanced to the more difficult subjects and ultimately the quadrivium. Sometimes religion was added to the curriculum to provide a moral component to the educational agenda. Religious teachings at the elementary level traditionally focused on moral teachings and biblical study.

In the tradition of European schools, which channeled education through grammar schools, gymnasia, and university colleges, the North American system offered grammar schools, academies, and liberal arts colleges. Given the religious component of public education in the United States and the fact that public schools also could be counted on to produce religious professionals such as priests as well as counselors, diplomats, physicians, and teachers, it is hardly surprising that churches were from the outset allied with the government in the sponsorship of secondary education. Families tended to seek the highest available education for their children, as a means of improving the living standards of the family, but it was not until the mid-nineteenth century that Americans began to acknowledge a distinction between secondary and higher education. This distinction marked the beginning of the modern era in education.

In the early 1820's, free urban public high schools emerged in the United States to provide alternatives to Latin grammar schools and other private and fee-charging schools. These schools were fostered with the expectation that the secondary education of the country's youths would promote economic development. The first public high school opened in Boston in 1821. Other major cities in the Northeast soon followed the example; by 1839, twenty-six high schools had been established in Boston, and the trend had spread to Philadelphia and Baltimore. Before long, Latin grammar schools were well established throughout Massachusetts, New York, Pennsylvania, New Jersey, and Maryland. The teachers in these early schools usually were ministers with dedicated teaching mis-

In elementary school, children are introduced to core skills of literacy and computation, such as reading, writing, and mathematics. (©Andres Rodriguez/Dreamstime.com)

sions. These earliest schools were aimed primarily at preparing students to enter colleges, which were strictly for men. By 1851, an estimated eighty cities had established high schools. The curriculum of the Boston schools was typical, encompassing subjects such as English, geography, history, arithmetic, algebra, geometry, trigonometry, navigation, surveying, and natural and moral philosophy.

After the United States gained independence in 1776, new educational movements arose. Most notably, monitorial schools, an educational tradition imported from England, were opened to provide inexpensive general education for the masses. However, these monitorial schools did not last. By 1840, they had all been closed because they had not produced the results to justify their existence. Another educational innovation of the time was the Sunday School, through which churches aimed at providing rudimentary academic and moral education to the poor. Its pioneer, Robert Raikes of Gloucester, wanted to "rescue children of factory workers from their filth, ignorance and sin." Free School Societies organized and developed monitorial schools, Sunday Schools, and free public schools in Connecticut and New York, and again, the trend soon spread to other areas of the country.

The Industry Today

By the final decade of the twentieth century, the enrollment rate in American public schools had reached overwhelming numbers. In 2006, about 49.3 million students were enrolled in public elementary and secondary schools. Of this number, 34.2 million were enrolled in prekindergarten through eighth grade, while 15.1 million were enrolled in grades nine through twelve. These numbers are projected to increase each year. It is estimated that by 2018, the number of students enrolled in public schools will be 53.9 million.

Between 1985 and 2007, enrollment in public elementary and secondary schools rose by 26 percent, with the fastest growth occurring in elementary levels (prekindergarten through eighth grade). This increase was matched by an increase in teachers. About 3.7 million full-time-equivalent (FTE) elementary and secondary school teachers were engaged in classroom instruction in the fall of 2007. The average salary for teachers in 2005-2006 was $49,109. About 3 million high school students were expected to graduate during the 2007-2008 school year.

Another important development in modern American schools is their initiation into the electronic age. The number of computers in public schools has increased dramatically in recent years. In 2005, the average public school contained 154 instructional computers, compared with 90 in 1998. The important technological advance that spurred that use of computers in the classroom is the introduction of the Internet. The percentage of instructional rooms with access to the Internet increased from 51 percent in 1998 to 94 percent in 2005, and nearly all schools had access to the Internet in 2005.

Today, elementary and secondary public schools continue to expand to accommodate the fast-growing American population. Demographic reports indicate that, nationwide, 1.3 percent of U.S. public school students are American Indian/Alaska natives, 3.9 percent are Asian/Pacific Islanders, 16.8 percent are African American, 17.7 percent are Hispanic, and 60.3 percent are white. The racial makeup of public schools varies from region to region. For example, in 2007, the West was reported to have the highest enrollment of African American, Hispanic, Asian/Pacific Islander, and American Indian/Alaska native students compared with other regions. In the South, enrollment of African Americans remained around 25 percent between 1972 and 2007, while Hispanic enrollment increased from 5 percent to 19 percent. White enrollment in public schools decreased from 70 percent to 51 percent.

Several laws have had, and continue to have, an enormous impact on American educational practices and policies. Among these laws is the Equal Protection Law, the Fourteenth Amendment to the Constitution, which guarantees that "no State shall . . . deny to any person within its jurisdiction the equal protection of the laws." This federal law protects the rights of students in the United States. An important legal milestone in education history was the Supreme Court's decision in *Brown v. Board of Education of Topeka, Kansas* (1954), which outlawed institutionalized segregation. As a result, schools sought to balance the quality of education for students of all races by integrating African Americans into public schools previously restricted to white students. Another critical law affecting education is the Equal Access to Federal Financial Assistance Law, or Title VI of the Civil Rights Act of 1964, which outlawed discrimination in financial assistance on the basis of race, gender, or ethnicity. This law continues to guarantee universal financial access to Department of Education funding in all educational settings. Another important law is the Bilingual Education Act of 1968. This law requires that programs for English language learners (ELLs) be held to high standards and meet special needs of the broad cultural and linguistic diversity of American students. This law continues to play a crucial role in the United States' linguistically diverse student population.

The most recent law to have an important (and highly controversial) impact on American education is the No Child Left Behind Act (NCLB), which President George W. Bush signed in 2001 in an effort to improve the educational standards of

America's public schools. This law is the key conduit through which federal funds are directed to state departments of education for operations and administration of schools. NCLB holds schools and states accountable for students' academic performance by requiring the public reporting of students' scores known as Adequate Yearly Progress (AYP) reports. The objectives of NCLB are to make schools accountable for results, to give states and communities freedom in distributing federal funds, to use effective educational methods, and to provide parents with informed options regarding school choice for their children. With the passage of the federal NCLB Act, all states are now expected to publicly announce standards, standardized tests, and accountability methods. Standardized tests are to be conducted in reading and mathematics from grades three through eight. Science was added to the list in 2008, from grades nine through twelve.

Since testing has become standardized, accountability has come under harsh criticism from parents and educators. Corporate and political leaders have defended the current program of standardized tests, arguing that this is the only way that students and the nation can monitor educational quality and student performance. The NCLB additionally requires that a school failing to meet AYP goals must provide students with options for seeking supplemental instructions, such as tutoring, after-school programs, remedial classes, or summer school. These programs should be provided by nonprofit agencies or for-profit agencies funded by the students' schools. Schools failing to meet AYP goals for four years must take drastic corrective measures that involve replacing school faculty, introducing new curricula, and appointing an expert to advise the school.

The current student assessment requirements under Elementary and Secondary Act (ESEA) Title 1-A began with the Improving America's Schools Act (IASA) of 1994, which required "contributing states to adopt curriculum content standards, pupil performance standards, and assessment" for subjects like mathematics and reading/language arts. The NCLB Act expanded these requirements and demanded that contributing states implement assessments relative to state content and align academic achievement standards for every student in every state. Furthermore, the participating states were required to develop and implement assessments at three grade levels for science by the 2007-2008 school year.

Special education programs form a crucial element of elementary and high school education in the United States. The Individuals with Disabilities Education Act (IDEA), enacted in 1975, mandates that children and young people with disabilities be provided public education. The number of students receiving special education services increased between 2004 and 2005, but again declined between 2006 and 2007.

The current economic downturn has since taken its toll on education, and curriculum restrictions tend to be the first signs of fiscal cutbacks. Curriculum often is vulnerable as well to the vicissitudes of public opinion. For example, art, music, and physical education often are the

Public high schools provide opportunities for teenagers to participate in sports. (AP/Wide World Photos)

first programs to be cut during budget shortfalls, despite evidence that student performance in mathematics has been shown to be improved by exposure to music instruction. Social studies now receives more attention in many public schools than does spelling. Physical education enjoys fluctuating popularity; at the present time, the addition of physical health components to the curriculum, whether in the form of structured sporting activities or simple free play during recess, are receiving renewed attention, and efforts are currently being made to recruit instructors in the area. New subjects have been added to the curriculum as society recognized growing needs; these include sex and health education, conflict resolution, and multicultural studies, among others.

The structure, administration, and curricula in American schools evolve with changing times and societal needs. Teachers are increasingly becoming specialized experts in their fields, especially in the subject areas of art, speech correction, and counseling, among others. Public schools also are being used as a venue for addressing diverse societal problems, such as poverty and child hunger. Programs that provide federally subsidized or free lunches are available in most public schools. Furthermore, a great variety of extracurricular activities have been introduced in the majority of elementary and secondary schools.

INDUSTRY MARKET SEGMENTS

Elementary and secondary schools in the United States serve a broad multicultural student population from rural, urban, and suburban areas. The following sections provide a comprehensive breakdown of each of these different educational venues.

Small Schools

This sector includes traditionally small public schools ranging from elementary to high school. Charter schools, which are supported by public funds, fall in this category. Currently there are few definitive research definitions of a "small" school; typically, they are defined variously by each state based on the number of students in the school. For example, in Chicago, small schools are those hav-

ing fewer than four hundred students. The number of supervisors and faculty are concomitantly low, with one to two administrators and five to eight faculty members.

Potential Annual Earnings Scale. Because there are educators and administrators at all levels of public school systems, pay for those who work in the public education industry is wide ranging. Average earnings for school principals vary from one region to another, with some states paying more than others. In North Carolina, a principal's salary is determined by the number of students and teachers the principal oversees. In general across the United States, the smaller the school, the more modest the principal's salary. The average salary in the United States for a principal in an elementary school is $85,907; for an assistant principal, the average salary is $71,192 per year. The national average salary for a secondary school teacher is $51,230 per year, with special and vocational education teachers earning $49,740 per year (at the middle school level) and $49,370 per year (at the elementary school level).

Clientele Interaction. Small schools offer students and parents a more personalized learning environment and greater opportunities for interaction. Teachers in small classrooms, as well as principals in smaller schools, are more capable of maintaining personal relationships with their students, enhancing their capacity to address individual student problems that might impede learning. Teachers share the goal of meeting individual student needs, counseling students and parents about a variety of problems, and recommending strategies and counselors who may be of use to families in need. However, this goal is best served when the teacher is not overstretched in her or his duties; that is, the smaller the class, the more effective the teacher can be. When teachers have adequate time and energy to devote to each student, students' motivation level is increased, academic results tend to improve, and dropout rates are reduced.

Amenities, Atmosphere, and Physical Grounds. Many schools are equipped with a wide range of structural amenities that include swimming pools, tennis courts, athletic tracks, football and soccer fields, and gymnasiums. However, these amenities vary greatly with the school size and local economy. Small schools generally lack many amenities, including basic "green space" or lawns and fields for physical education, although often districts share resources with neighboring schools.

Typical Number of Employees. The number of employees in a public school depends on its size, neighborhood, and state. As in any other industry, mushrooming costs constitute one of the key challenges for public education and can cause fluctuations in staffing levels. Small schools have an average of one administrator, five to eight administrative staff members, one janitor, and one secretary. Other staff, such as school nurses and psychologists, often are shared among schools in a district, appearing on site once or twice a week. In districts where there is a growing population of linguistically and culturally diverse students, bilingual teachers often are hired to cater to the needs of these students.

Traditional Geographic Locations. Except in a few big cities, small public schools generally are found in suburban neighborhoods or rural areas. The majority of the student population of suburban schools is generally white, while small urban high schools enroll mostly minority students. Alternative high schools are small public schools of choice enrolling mainly white students. Some small urban schools have been created to serve the specific needs of children from lower economic backgrounds, and part of the mission of these special schools is to fight the violence prevalent in these poor neighborhoods.

Pros of Working for a Small School. Small schools enhance the capacity for interpersonal relations among students and between staff and students. Small class sizes allow teachers to pay more individual attention to students. Smaller schools encourage stronger bonds among principals, teachers, students, and parents, and promote a level of mutual caring that is often lacking in larger schools. In small schools, students tend to demonstrate healthier attitudes toward school, and they have higher attendance rates. Students in small schools often report feeling safer and more secure, partially because the smaller environment replicates the more intimate conditions of home and community life. Moreover, smaller schools tend to command a higher level of parent and community involvement. In the best cases, parents and teachers become allies in fostering students' academic achievement. Local businesses and community organizations also find it easier to collabo-

rate with small schools, providing internships and other collaborative projects. In smaller schools, teachers more often report positive teacher working conditions and greater job satisfaction.

Cons of Working for a Small School. Small schools have greater restrictions on budget and fewer faculty and thus must limit their study offerings to a constricted curriculum, often offering only academic courses geared to the midlevel student, with few opportunities to tailor their programs or curricula to meet the special needs of their gifted or academically challenged students. Often, courses such as music and art must be cut and services for students with disabilities are limited or lacking. Because the staff is limited, each will take on multiple roles. For instance, some teachers may be required to take on administrative duties, serve on school committees, and administer extracurricular activities. Resources and technical assistance are often limited or lacking at small schools.

Costs

Payroll and Benefits: Salaries in small schools are determined by the state legislature and the amount of available district funds. Thus, salaries vary greatly by state. Licensed personnel, such as teachers, are paid monthly salaries, and nonlicensed personnel, such as janitors, are paid hourly wages. Benefits such as health and dental insurance, paid vacation time, and sick leave vary by state.

Supplies: Small schools require instructional supplies that include books, papers, pens, markers, erasers, and other office supplies. Technological equipment such as computers, calculators, television sets, and telephones, as well as the supplies to maintain them, also are necessary.

External Services: Small schools contract outside services for maintenance work and professional development. Other professional workers who may be contracted are nurses, social workers, psychologists, and tutors for after-school programs.

Utilities: Typical utilities for a small school include water and sewer, electricity, gas/oil service, telephone, and Internet.

Taxes: Small public schools do not pay taxes because they are supported by federal and state taxes. However, in many states they are required to pay sales taxes on construction materials and other supplies. Arizona, California, Hawaii, North Carolina, South Carolina, and Washington are some of the states that require their public schools to pay sales taxes.

Midsize Schools

Midsize schools are determined by the number of students enrolled, although the designation varies by each region. For example, Telecommunication Arts High School in Brooklyn, whose enrollment of 1,250 students and 80 teachers would make it a large school in most cities, is considered a midsize school by New York standards. Typically, schools that are considered midsize have between 500 and 900 students and 50 to 100 employees.

Potential Annual Earnings Scale. In general, public schoolteachers' earnings are not determined by the school size, but by experience and level of academic degree. The salary is therefore determined by the state and district and is relatively standard according to experience and academic degree across the state. Nationally, the average salary of a teacher is $50,000 per year but varies from one state to the other. Teacher assistants earn an average of $22,700 per year. These are national averages; teacher salaries vary by state and region. For example between 2004 and 2005, teachers' beginning salary in Alabama was $31,368 while average salary was $38,186. In California, teachers' beginning salary was $35,760 while average salary was $57,604.

Clientele Interaction. While educators in small schools have close interactions with students and parents, this interaction lessens in midsize schools. Teachers' and administrators' interaction with parents will not be as frequent or personal as in smaller schools.

Amenities, Atmosphere, and Physical Grounds. At midsize schools, students have access to more space, and the buildings are relatively large and spacious. These schools exist at both elementary and secondary levels. They typically have athletic fields, theaters or auditoriums, and cafeterias. Typically, the physical grounds of these schools depend on the neighborhoods. Some midsize schools, especially in affluent neighborhoods, are beautiful, sprawling sites with gymnasiums, swimming pools, and the latest technology. On the other hand, midsize schools in low-income neigh-

borhoods lack expansive facilities; the buildings may be run-down and the grounds poorly kept.

Typical Number of Employees. Midsize schools typically have fifty to one hundred teachers and an average of forty administrative employees. Some temporary employees may be contracted from time to time to engage in maintenance work and other menial jobs.

Traditional Geographic Locations. Midsize schools are found mainly in cities. While some are found in suburban areas, the majority of these schools exist in the inner cities, where infrastructure and communication systems are well developed. Many midsize schools serve students from diverse backgrounds, especially those from low socioeconomic backgrounds. These schools are found in urban areas where poverty and unemployment are endemic. For example, many midsize schools in New York and Los Angeles are found in heavily populated ethnic neighborhoods.

Pros of Working for a Midsize School. While small schools might have limited staff, such as only one special education teacher, midsize schools have extensive programs and adequate personnel to cater to a diverse student population. For example, Telecommunication Arts High School in New York has fifteen full-time special education teachers, an on-site staff psychologist, an assistant principal in charge of budgets and security, and services such as occupational and physical therapy for disabled students as of 2010. Foreign-language classes, Advanced Placement courses, and other programs typically lacking in small schools are available in midsize schools. Midsize high schools have much higher graduation rates than large high schools. A 2010 analysis conducted by Center for New York City Affairs concluded that "on average, the city's forty high schools with enrollments between six hundred and fourteen hundred are just as good as or better than smaller schools in terms of graduation rates, attendance and the ability to serve struggling students."

Cons of Working for a Midsize School. Many midsize schools are located in poor, inner-city areas and tend to be underfunded in comparison with larger schools. In 2005, the Kansas Supreme Court ordered the state to spend $285 million more on schools after midsize school districts sued the state for underfunding. Another challenge that midsize schools face is the limited interaction between teachers and students and their parents. Teachers do not get to know all their students well because of the greater student population. Also, not all students know one another in a midsize school.

Costs

Payroll and Benefits: Full-time teachers and other employees of midsize schools are paid monthly or bimonthly. Other temporary or part-time workers are paid hourly wages. Benefits such as vacation and sick days are provided to full-time employees.

Supplies: Midsize schools require stationery, textbooks, and technological and audio-visual equipment such as computers, calculators, projectors, and television sets. Other supplies for extracurricular activities and physical education programs are needed. Assistive technology to cater to a diverse student population, especially those with special needs, also is required. Office and classroom supplies include telephones, furniture, and filing cabinets.

External Services: While external services are not common in midsize schools, any that are needed are contracted and paid for by the school district. Some of these services may include professional development, interpreters, computer maintenance, vending machines, landscaping, and construction services.

Utilities: Typical utilities for these schools include water and sewer, electricity, gas/oil service, telephone, and Internet service. Because of the size of the school, utility bills tend to be higher in midsize schools than in their smaller counterparts.

Taxes: Unlike for-profit organizations that are required to pay taxes to the government, midsize schools do not pay taxes. However, they pay sales taxes, which are eventually returned to them.

Large Schools

Typically, large public schools have student populations of more than 900. While some large schools are found at the elementary level, most schools in this class are high schools. The number of teaching staff and other employees varies accordingly, usually between 150 and 250.

Potential Annual Earnings Scale. Teachers' salaries typically are based on experience and level of academic achievement. A principal, who is the instructional leader and chief administrator of the school, is paid according to the school size, number of students, and the number of employees in the school. According to *Education Week*, as of 2005 the average salary for the principal of a large elementary school was $82,283; principals of large high schools made an average of $93,749. Assistant principals of large elementary schools earn average salaries of $64,587, $68,608 for junior high schools or middle schools, and $72,868 for high schools. Salaries for permanent employees such as school nurses, counselors, secretaries, and library clerks range from $17,000 to more than $50,000.

Clientele Interaction. Teachers' interaction with students is limited compared with that at small and midsize schools. Most of their attention often focuses on the highest- and lowest-performing students, leaving those in the middle in danger of being overlooked or neglected. Large schools also make it difficult for teachers to connect with the parents of many students.

Amenities, Atmosphere, and Physical Grounds. Large schools often offer a wide range of amenities that include gymnasiums, athletic fields, swimming pools, tennis and other ball courts, libraries, and auditoriums that support a range of extracurricular activities. Physical grounds vary by school, although larger schools generally offer larger and greener playing grounds. For example, large elementary schools in affluent neighborhoods are equipped with outdoor playground equipment and sport courts. While smaller schools may have only one building, large schools have multiple buildings. These buildings are further subdivided into segments based on grade level, subject taught there, or other functions.

Some large schools are known to host small schools, creating "schools-within-schools," to achieve a distinctive curricular focus. For example, Henrico County in Virginia has a "center of excellence," a specialty school-within-a-school that attracts students from neighboring high schools as well as the host school. Other schools-within-schools are alternative schools, which are mainly for students who have been expelled or suspended from regular schools or who experience academic challenges such as learning disabilities. A large high school may house an alternative school, which can operate either during regular school hours or as an after-school program.

Typical Number of Employees. The number of employees in large schools varies by region. In large cities such as New York or Los Angeles, large schools can have 2,500 students or more, while large schools in the rural areas have an average of 1,500 students. The number of employees in large schools is determined by the number of students in the school. However, the typical number of employees in a large school ranges from 150 to 250.

Traditional Geographic Locations. Large schools traditionally are found in big cities. Some occupy multistory buildings in metropolitan centers, whereas others are constructed near airports and other major transit centers. Many are situated at, or are part of, convention centers, located outside downtown areas but still connected near them.

Pros of Working for a Large School. Large schools provide a more vibrant school atmosphere. Many of these schools are found in larger cities where they attract students from diverse backgrounds. Large schools provide more academic clubs, after-school programs, special education programs, foreign-language classes, and a host of extracurricular activities. Large schools, especially those in the wealthy neighborhoods, often are well equipped with advanced technology.

Cons of Working for a Large School. Larger schools tend to have larger classes, which in turn affect the degree of interaction and teacher attention that can be afforded to each student. Because of large student populations, some students are likely to miss out on opportunities to develop their leadership skills and participate in school activities. In view of this, students may feel overlooked and less motivated. Safety issues often are a challenge in these large schools as well. The sheer complexity of a large institution, with its vast physical property and myriad working parts, can prove extremely difficult to manage and monitor safely.

Costs

Payroll and Benefits: The salaries of workers in large schools vary by region. A principal in a large urban elementary school earns an average salary of $85,958, while in an urban junior high school the average principal's salary is $90,133. At a large high school, the principal earns an average of $96,998. Teachers in large schools earn an average salary of $46,527. Counselors, librarians, school nurses, secretaries, and payroll clerks earn salaries ranging from $31,000 to $54,000. Benefits such as vacation and sick time vary by school district.

Supplies: Stationery and technological, communication, and fitness equipment are required. Several assistive technology supplies also are needed to cater to special-needs students. Some of these assistive technology devices include specialized keyboards, e-readers, tape recorders, magnifying glasses, books on tape, arm supports, and touch screens.

External Services: In most cases, large schools are self-sufficient in terms of professional workers such as nurses, psychologists, and special educators. External services that may be needed involve yearbook publication, senior portraits, professional development, vending machines, and general maintenance.

Utilities: Typical utilities for a large school include water and sewer, electricity, gas/oil service, telephone, cable, and Internet service.

Taxes: Large schools are nonprofit institutions; therefore they do not pay taxes. Instead they operate with federal and state funds disbursed through school districts. These schools may only pay sales taxes, but those are eventually reclaimed at the end of the year.

ORGANIZATIONAL STRUCTURE AND JOB ROLES

The organizational structure and jobs roles of elementary and secondary schools are determined by the size and needs of the individual schools. Specific job titles and descriptions vary by district and state. While public schools do have some leeway to affect decision making, they do not exist as autonomous entities but operate under the supervision of district and state-level administrations.

The following umbrella categories apply to the organizational structure of small, medium, and large elementary and secondary schools:

- District-Level Administration
- School-Based Administration
- Licensed Instructional Faculty
- Student Support Services (Licensed)

- Administrative Support
- Media and Technology Specialists
- Paraprofessionals
- Bus Drivers
- Maintenance and Custodial Services
- School Nutrition

District-Level Administration

District-level administration provides supervision of schools and support with services related to academics, transportation, discipline, technology, safety, finance, facilities, and health and nutrition. Operations such as payroll, purchasing, hiring, curriculum, and training are handled by the district office rather than at the individual school level. Employees in upper-level positions tend to have advanced degrees. The number of employees at the district administration level varies according to the size and location of the school district.

Common district-level occupations include, but are not limited to, the following:

- Superintendent
- Assistant Superintendent
- Director of Curriculum and Instruction
- Assistant Director of Curriculum and Instruction
- Director of Athletics
- Assistant Director of Athletics
- Director of Technology
- Assistant Director of Technology
- Director of Payroll
- Assistant Director of Payroll
- Academic Coach
- Chief Financial Officer (CFO)
- Budget Director
- Payroll Specialist
- Program Administrator
- Human Resources Director
- Human Resources Assistant
- Nutritional Services Personnel
- Curriculum Development Specialist

OCCUPATION PROFILE

Principal

Considerations	Qualifications
Description	Directs the activities of a school, particularly its teachers, and manages school staff.
Career cluster	Education and Training
Interests	Data; people
Working conditions	Work inside
Minimum education level	Master's degree
Physical exertion	Light work
Physical abilities	Unexceptional/basic fitness
Opportunities for experience	Internship
Licensure and certification	Required
Employment outlook	Average growth expected
Holland interest score	SEI

Note: See volume 1, "Publisher's Note," for an explanation of the Holland interest score.

OCCUPATION PROFILE

Elementary School Teacher

Considerations	Qualifications
Description	Instructs students at the elementary level and creates lesson plans.
Career cluster	Education and Training
Interests	Data; people
Working conditions	Work inside; work both inside and outside
Minimum education level	Bachelor's degree; master's degree
Physical exertion	Light work
Physical abilities	Unexceptional/basic fitness
Opportunities for experience	Volunteer work; part-time work
Licensure and certification	Required
Employment outlook	Average growth expected
Holland interest score	SEC

Note: See volume 1, "Publisher's Note," for an explanation of the Holland interest score.

School-Based Administration

School-based administrators are responsible for the day-to-day operations of individual schools. Duties include overseeing instruction, discipline, transportation (buses), and school budgets. Administrators hold advanced degrees and credentials in school administration. Salaries vary according to the size of the school and years of experience in education. The number of administrators employed at each school varies according to the school size.

Occupations in the area of school-based administration include, but are not limited to, the following:

- Principal
- Assistant Principal
- Dean of Students

Licensed Instructional Faculty

As of 2010, licensed instructors account for 47 percent of all workers in the industry, according to the U.S. Department of Labor. Licensed instructional faculty are responsible for planning, organizing, and presenting instruction that helps students learn content and skills. The major job functions licensed instructional faculty perform include management of instruction time, management of student behavior, instructional presentation, and monitoring of student performance. Instructional faculty are required to hold a bachelor's degree and state credentials (licenses or certifications). Advanced degrees are not required; however, instructional personnel routinely pursue them to enhance content knowledge and pedagogical skills. Elementary teachers do not normally specialize in a particular content area, because they teach all subjects. Middle school and high school teachers, however, specialize in a specific content area, such as English, math, a foreign language, biology, or music. Salaries of instructional personnel are set by the state department of education and are based on level of education and years of experience.

OCCUPATION SPECIALTIES

Special Education Teachers

Specialty	Responsibilities
Teachers of physically impaired students	Instruct students in the elementary and secondary levels who are physically impaired. They evaluate students' abilities to determine the best training program for each individual.
Teachers of the emotionally impaired	Teach elementary and secondary school subjects, including education on socially acceptable behavior to students with emotional impairments.
Teachers of the hearing impaired	Teach elementary and secondary school subjects and special skills to deaf or hard-of-hearing students using lip reading, manual communication, or total communication.
Teachers of the mentally impaired	Teach social skills or basic academic subjects in schools, hospitals, and other institutions to mentally impaired students.
Teachers of the visually impaired	Teach elementary and secondary school subjects to visually impaired and blind students using large-print materials or the Braille system.

Occupations in the area of licensed instructional faculty include, but are not limited to, the following:

- Elementary School Teacher
- Middle School Teacher
- Special Education Teacher
- High School Teacher (All Content Areas)
- Curriculum Facilitator
- Curriculum Coach
- Literacy Facilitator or Coach
- Teacher Mentor
- Reading Teacher

Student Support Services (Licensed)

Student support services include a variety of positions that supply direct services to students who may have special needs and difficulties that interfere with their learning. The types of services offered include training, counseling, assessment, and consultation. In addition to working closely with students, support staff offer training services to all stakeholders who impact the education of children and youths. This includes parents, teachers, and members of the community. All support personnel positions require a college degree and state licenses or certifications. Some positions require advanced degrees.

Occupations in the area of student support services include, but are not limited to, the following:

- Counselor
- Career Development Counselor
- School Psychologist
- School Social Worker
- Speech-Language Therapist
- Student Intervention Specialist
- English as a Second Language Interpreter
- School Nurse
- Physical Therapist
- Occupational Therapist

Administrative Support

Administrative support personnel perform a variety of clerical, bookkeeping, receptionist, secretarial, and general office duties. Staff members in these positions are responsible for a number of specialized tasks, including maintaining student information files, compiling and administering school financial and accounting records, purchasing office and instructional supplies, processing incoming and outgoing correspondence and telephone calls, and maintaining receipt books, school records, and inventories. While a college degree is not always required for these positions, advanced knowledge of computer-based accounting systems and word-processing, spreadsheet, and database management applications is necessary.

Occupations in the area of administrative support include the following:

- Treasurer-Data Manager
- Secretary-Treasurer
- School Treasurer
- General Office Clerk
- Office Assistant
- Receptionist
- Data Manager
- Administrative Assistant

Media and Technology Specialists

Media and other technology personnel serve a variety of functions in elementary and secondary schools. They oversee the coordination of the activities of the school library and provide technological support for students, administrators, and instructional faculty. Library media specialists are required to hold graduate degrees and licenses or certifications in library science or instructional technology. Technology assistants perform clerical and technical duties related to the maintenance of school computers while also providing support for the school library, computer labs, instructional faculty, and students.

Occupations in the area of media and technology include, but are not limited to, the following:

- Library/Media Specialist
- Library/Media Assistant
- Technology Specialist
- Technology Assistant
- Instructional Technology Specialist/ Assistant
- Audiovisual Specialist

Paraprofessionals

Paraprofessionals support teachers and students by carrying out a variety of duties in the classroom. Individuals in these support positions are not licensed to teach, but they are assigned a range of support duties, working closely with the teacher and the students. Because the specific role of the paraprofessional often is loosely defined, the individual needs of the teacher and/or school administrator can require the paraprofessional to play a multitude of roles. The No Child Left Behind Act requires that paraprofessionals be "highly qualified." The specific requirements for this distinc-

---

OCCUPATION SPECIALTIES

Educational Counselors

Specialty	Responsibilities
College career planning and placement counselors	Assist college students in examining their own interests, values, abilities, and goals in exploring career alternatives and in making career choices.
Employment counselors	Deal with career planning, placement, and adjustment to employment of youths and adults.
School counselors	Assist the personal and social development of students and help them plan and achieve their educational and vocational goals.

tion, however, have been left up to individual states and include two years of college, paraprofessional certifications, and a passing score on a paraprofessional examination.

Paraprofessional occupations in elementary and secondary education include, but are not limited to, the following:

- Teacher Assistant
- Special Education Assistant
- Student Intervention Specialist
- Counseling Assistant
- Bilingual Aide
- Tutor

Bus Drivers

Bus drivers provide transportation by operating a school bus according to a specified route and schedule. In addition to this, bus drivers are responsible for completing inspections of the school bus before and after driving their routes. Moreover, they must monitor and maintain student discipline. Bus drivers are required to know safety and traffic regulations, to complete a driver training course, and to obtain a commercial driver's license. In May, 2008, school bus drivers earned an average hourly wage of $12.79.

Occupations in the area of bus driver include, but are not limited to, the following:

- Bus Driver
- Bus Driver Trainer
- Bus Mechanic

Maintenance and Custodial Services

Maintenance and custodial staff are responsible for the general cleaning, care, maintenance, and groundskeeping of school buildings and facilities. Duties may include cleaning floors, walls, furniture, and fixtures; collecting and discarding trash and debris; performing minor repairs; securing rooms and buildings; and assisting in grounds maintenance and landscaping.

Occupations in the area of

maintenance and custodial services include, but are not limited to, the following:

- Head Custodian
- Custodian/Janitor
- Groundskeeper
- Heating, Ventilation, and Air-Conditioning (HVAC) Specialist

School Nutrition

Individuals who work with school nutrition services are responsible for preparing and serving nutritious meals and snacks and for the subsequent cleanup. Food service managers are also responsible for ordering and maintaining food and supply inventories. The number of staff members employed in each school varies according to the size of the school and the number of meals served. Food service workers normally are paid by the hour.

Occupations in the area of school nutrition include, but are not limited to, the following:

- Cafeteria Manager
- Cook
- School Nutrition Assistant
- School Nutrition Services Business Manager

The school bus is a familiar sight in the city and the country. (©Jorge Salcedo/ Dreamstime.com)

INDUSTRY OUTLOOK

Overview

This industry's history demonstrates that public education is a stable area of employment for a great variety of functionaries and experts. Although school funding varies widely and depends on many factors, including population demographics, geographical location, and the economy, teachers and other education personnel always will be needed to ensure the education of millions of youths. Government regulations and standards concerning the goals and practices of public education will be a major factor in determining the employment outlook and job security of workers in this industry. Among the major concerns in public elementary and secondary education are achievement gaps based on race, gender, and socioeconomic status; raising the achievement of students whose first language is not English; and improving literacy across the board.

With the institution of the NCLB Act, education bodies and legislators have worked tirelessly to come up with strategies for holding schools accountable for students' learning. Value-added models have been proposed as a means of establishing how much students learn in schools and classrooms throughout the year. One aspect of these models is an attempt to link teachers' salary and tenure to the performance of their students. While this issue has been widely criticized, Tennessee is the only state that has embraced the idea, although some other states are investigating and considering its use.

Current efforts in the United States to improve secondary education focus on the size and structure of large schools. With the support from the Bill and Melinda Gates Foundation, the Annenberg Foundation and other nonprofit groups, the New York City school system has completed significant experimentation with small high schools in an effort to enhance secondary education. The Los Angeles Unified School District also has executed a plan to reorganize its high schools, creating smaller "learning clusters" in an effort to provide a more intimate and supportive learning environment.

American public schools continue to suffer shortages of teachers at the primary through high school levels, especially in mathematics, sciences, and special education. The National Academy of Sciences, the National Research Council, and the U.S. Department of Education have linked mathematics and science teacher shortfalls to overall quality of education and future economic and technological development. Some states, such as Arizona, have raised math and science requirements for high school students, further increasing demand for teachers in these subjects.

Employment Advantages

Teachers and other workers in the public education industry play a critical and influential role in

PROJECTED EMPLOYMENT FOR SELECTED OCCUPATIONS

Educational Services

Employment		
2009	Projected 2018	Occupation
216,220	233,000	Education administrators, elementary and secondary school
1,532,990	1,760,800	Elementary school teachers, except special education
661,700	752,800	Middle school teachers, except special and vocational education
1,084,060	1,170,300	Secondary school teachers, except special and vocational education
1,098,920	1,195,900	Teacher assistants

Source: U.S. Bureau of Labor Statistics, Industries at a Glance, Occupational Employment Statistics and Employment Projections Program.

the intellectual and social development of young people. They have the opportunity to enrich lives, provide opportunities, and motivate children to greater achievement.

According to the U.S. Department of Education, enrollment at all levels of public education is increasing. The National Center for Education Statistics projects record increases in enrollment through 2017. With the rise in enrollment, the number of teachers will concomitantly increase. In 2008, 3.2 million public school teachers were engaged in the classroom, a 15 percent increase from 1998. However, salaries are not expected to increase in the wake of the current economic crisis.

In poverty-stricken areas such as urban and rural districts, the National Center for Education Statistics reported that more than 700,000 new teachers will be required over the next decade. Among those subject areas that are most in demand are mathematics, sciences, special education, English as a second language, and foreign languages. All states require certification of teachers, while recruitment standards vary from one state to the other. Various schools offer professional development training and other staff-related programs to ensure efficiency of their staff.

Annual Earnings

The total revenue earned in the elementary and secondary public schools combined has increased in recent years. From 1989-1990 through 2005-2006, public school revenue from federal, state, and local sources increased from $348 billion to $554 billion. Federal funding, the smallest of the three sources, increased 139 percent, state funding increased 57 percent, and local revenue increased 51 percent. Revenue and its rate of increase also varies by state.

RELATED RESOURCES FOR FURTHER RESEARCH

AMERICAN FEDERATION OF TEACHERS
555 New Jersey Ave. NW
Washington, DC 20001
Tel: (202) 879-4400
Fax: (202) 879-4406
http://www.aft.org

CENTER FOR PUBLIC EDUCATION
1680 Duke St.
Alexandria, VA 22314
Tel: (703) 838-6722
Fax: (703) 548-5613
http://www.centerforpubliceducation.org

NATIONAL CENTER FOR EDUCATION STATISTICS
1990 K St. NW
Washington, DC 20006
Tel: (202) 502-7300
http://nces.ed.gov

NATIONAL EDUCATION ASSOCIATION
1201 16th St. NW
Washington, DC 20036
Tel: (202) 833-4000
Fax: (202) 822-7170
http://www.nea.org

PUBLIC EDUCATION NETWORK
601 13th St. NW, Suite 710 South
Washington, DC 20005-3808
Tel: (202) 628-7460
Fax: (202) 628-1893
http://www.publiceducation.org

U.S. DEPARTMENT OF EDUCATION, OFFICE OF ELEMENTARY AND SECONDARY EDUCATION
400 Maryland Ave. SW
Washington, DC 20202
Tel: (202) 401-0113
Fax: (202) 205-0310
http://www2.ed.gov/oese

ABOUT THE AUTHORS

Wendy C. Hamblet is a Canadian philosopher with a specialization in conflict studies, peace education, and ethics. She is a tenured professor at North Carolina Agricultural and Technical State University in Greensboro, North Carolina, and director of Therapeia Ethics Consulting.

Ruth Omunda is a graduate student in the special education program at North Carolina Agricultural and Technical State University in Greensboro, North Carolina. She also holds a master's degree in English from the university, with a specialization in African American literature.

FURTHER READING

Caillier, James. "Paying Teachers According to Student Achievement: Questions Regarding Pay-for-Performance Models in Public Education." *The Clearing House* 83, no. 2 (2010): 58-61.

Fry, Richard. *The High Schools Hispanics Attend: Size and Other Key Characteristics.* Washington, D.C.: Pew Hispanic Center, 2005.

Gardiner, Mary E., Kathy Canfield-Davis, and Keith LeMar Anderson. "Urban School Principals and the 'No Child Left Behind' Act." *The Urban Review* 41, no. 2 (September, 2008): 141-160.

Graves, Michael F., Bonnie B. Graves, and Connie Juel. *Teaching Reading in the 21st Century.* 4th ed. Boston: Pearson/Allyn & Bacon, 2007.

Herbst, Jürgen. *The Once and Future School: Three Hundred and Fifty Years of American Secondary Education.* New York: Routledge, 1996.

Hursh, David. "The Growth of High Stakes Testing in the USA: Accountability, Markets and the Decline in Educational Equality." *British Educational Research Journal* 31, no. 5 (October, 2005): 605-622.

Johnson, James Allen, et al. *Foundations of American Education: Perspectives on Education in a Changing World.* 15th ed. Boston: Pearson/ Allyn & Bacon, 2010.

Lee, Valerie E., et al. "Inside Large and Small High Schools: Curriculum and Social Relations." *Educational Evaluation and Policy Analysis* 22, no. 2 (Summer, 2000): 147-171.

"No Child Left Behind Revisited: The New Debate on Education Reform." *Congressional Digest* 87, no. 5 (May, 2008).

Parkay, Forrest W., and Beverly Hardcastle Stanford. *Becoming a Teacher.* 3d ed. Boston: Allyn & Bacon, 1998.

Pulliam, John D., and James J. Van Patten. *The History of Education in America.* 9th ed. Upper Saddle River, N.J.: Merrill, 2007.

U.S. Bureau of Labor Statistics. *Career Guide to Industries,* 2010-2011 ed. http://www.bls.gov/ oco/cg.

U.S. Census Bureau. North American Industry Classification System (NAICS), 2007. http:// www.census.gov/cgi-bin/sssd/naics/ naicsrch?chart=2007.

U.S. Department of Commerce. International Trade Administration. Office of Trade and Industry Information. Industry Trade Data and Analysis. http://ita.doc.gov/td/industry/ otea/OTII/OTII-index.html.

Public Health Services

AP/Wide World Photos

INDUSTRY SNAPSHOT

General Industry: Health Science

Career Clusters: Health Science; Law, Public Safety, and Security

Subcategory Industries: Communicable Disease Programs; Coroners' Offices; Environmental Health Programs; Food Inspection; Health Inspection; Immunization Programs; Public and Military Hospitals

Related Industries: Civil Services; Public Safety; Federal Public Administration; Hospital Care and Services; Local Public Administration; Medicine and Health Care Industry

Annual Domestic Revenues: $2.2 trillion USD (total health care expenditures; TheMedica.com, 2009)

Annual International Revenues: $2.5 trillion USD (total health expenditures; TheMedica.com, 2009)

Annual Global Revenues: $4.5 trillion (TheMedica.com, 2009)

NAICS Numbers: 622, 923120, 926140

INDUSTRY DEFINITION

Summary

The public health industry addresses health issues that face both individuals and entire communities. The industry is multifaceted, comprising public safety officials, elected and appointed government leaders, emergency personnel, medical professionals, and scientists and researchers. The mission of this industry is threefold. First, it assesses and monitors the health of populations and groups in order to identify and gauge the extent of health problems. Second, it creates policies by which these issues may be remedied. Third, it studies and promotes the use of health systems.

History of the Industry

Public health concerns and policy have been manifest for millennia. Two thousand years before the first century C.E., ancient civilizations in northern India, and later in Egypt, built cities complete with drainage systems designed to draw away unclean water runoff and sewage from pedestrian walkways and roads. For many of these ancient civilizations, cleanliness was a religious tradition, giving rise to the expression or principle "cleanliness is next to godliness."

Still, epidemics and transmissions of communicable diseases have been prevalent throughout human history. During the great "liberation of thought" in the fourth and fifth centuries B.C.E. in Greece, considered one of the major milestones in the history of human thought, a serious study of the causes of disease and epidemics was undertaken. Prior to this, disease and epidemics were largely attributed to the meddling of otherworldly beings and gods. The new school of thought in Greece, spearheaded by great philosophers such as Hippocrates (c. 460-370 B.C.E.), sought more earthbound causes. (Hippocrates himself is often referred to as the "father of medicine.")

The collapse of the Roman Empire around 476 C.E. brought with it a corresponding collapse of public health infrastructures. The Romans, who were famous for their water management and public health systems, suffered defeats by invading forces from European and Arab nations, both in Rome and throughout their realm. Lacking attention, the aqueducts and water systems that charac-

terized the Roman Empire fell into disrepair. The Byzantine Empire, to which much of the former Roman regime migrated after Rome's fall, assimilated many of the ancient Greek and Roman writings on public health practices. Europe, however, reverted to religious-based thought, and the Dark Ages followed.

During the Dark Ages, sanitation and health issues in Europe increased, exacerbated by the development of large, crowded cities. In fact, Rome's collapse was immediately followed by a plague. In the centuries that followed the Dark Ages—from which Europe emerged in the eleventh century—European governments began implementing strict cleanliness policies. These policies were designed to keep waste off the streets and to keep markets clean, not only to protect the public health but also to attract traveling consumers.

This renewed focus on public health did not

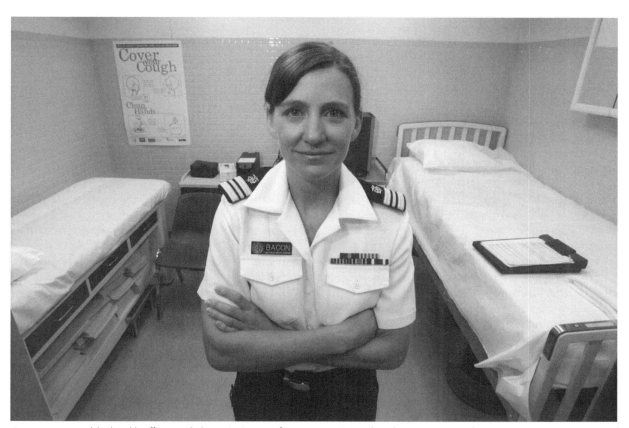

A quarantine public health officer with the U.S. Centers for Disease Control and Prevention at Chicago's O'Hare International Airport is charged with stopping infectious diseases from entering the United States. In 2007, an American with drug-resistant tuberculosis flew to several countries before being placed in isolation. (AP/Wide World Photos)

prevent devastating pandemics, particularly as humanity grew closer together through trade and exploration. In the early fourteenth century, the disease known as Black Death arrived in Italy from central Asia. This pandemic originated in China then spread to India, moving along trade routes via fleas that resided on both rats and human travelers. In only a few years, about one-third of the entire population of Europe was dead, having succumbed to the violent illness. The root causes of the illness remain shrouded in mystery. Naturalists at the time speculated that the disease was born in the swamps adjacent to large cities. Later scientists believed it was an outbreak of the bubonic plague, which had appeared on numerous occasions throughout history. Others believed it was a hemorrhagic fever akin to Ebola. The disease itself remains a mystery, as did its cessation: It abruptly disappeared in 1351.

During the era of exploration, European sailors introduced new diseases to the New World. Among these virulent strains was smallpox, a disease prevalent for millennia prior, but not present in either North nor South America. Millions of Native Americans were exposed and died as a result. It was believed that many of the items brought with these Europeans contained the agents of this disease.

In 1918, another public health crisis erupted, this time in an industrialized society. Soldiers returning from World War I had been exposed to countless contaminants and germs while living in the trenches. This exposure was due to the close quarters and unsanitary conditions of the battlefield. Veterans returned home to the United States and elsewhere with coldlike symptoms. Those symptoms erupted into a far more significant and threatening illness—influenza. Influenza would eventually affect one-fifth of the human population. Over a two-year period, 675,000 Americans died of the illness, a number that surpassed the combat deaths in World War I.

The number and severity of the pandemics and outbreaks that have occurred throughout human history have led to an evolution of public health services. Over time, medical experts and political leaders have been joined by policy makers, educators, emergency personnel, and public safety officials seeking to combat threats to public health. Agencies such as the Centers for Disease Control and Prevention (CDC) have been created not only to assess public health risks but also to trace the roots of diseases as they occur. Agencies such as the CDC work alongside the numerous local, state, and national public health departments.

The Industry Today

The public health services industry is a vast network of interconnected agencies, businesses, and institutions. According to the American Public Health Association (APHA), the industry is dedicated to meeting ten goals:

- Monitoring the public's health status to identify community health problems
- Diagnosing and investigating risks and threats
- Informing, educating, and empowering the public
- Mobilizing community partnerships
- Developing policies and plans that protect and maintain public health
- Enforcing public health laws and regulations
- Providing links and information to people with personal health needs
- Ensuring a competent public health workforce
- Evaluating and reporting on the industry's effectiveness
- Conducting research to develop new insights into public health threats and innovative solutions to those threats

Because the health of individuals is often connected to the health of others (which is the very principle behind the concept of public health), medical practitioners such as doctors, nurses, and allied personnel are but one part of the broad public health services industry. In fact, the total population of people who work in public health, either directly or indirectly, is innumerable. The APHA, for example, has 500,000 public health workers in its ranks, which does not include its local, state, and federal government partners and associated groups.

Educational opportunities for training in public health are equally innumerable, and there are dozens of major public and private universities that offer advanced degrees in public health. Harvard University, for example, offers one of the country's leading programs. The program features students from a wide range of backgrounds, including doctors, nurses, researchers, and social scientists. The field of public health entails an equally broad combination of disciplines, including epidemiology (tracing diseases to their sources), sociological analysis, statistics, environmental studies, and even history.

Although the field of public health services is broad and multifaceted, it is not without connectivity. In fact, it is designed to be a network, taking into account elements that previous fields could not because of their historical limitations. Today's public health services industry is organized in such a way that it can quickly assess public health risks and dangers, trace them back to their foundations, isolate and treat illnesses, implement protective government policies, communicate with the public on the issues at hand, and even introduce programs designed to prevent further spread of the negative agent or illness.

INDUSTRY MARKET SEGMENTS

There are several major components to the modern public health industry. Among the longest-standing members of this network are the health care provider and institution. Doctors, nurses, and other medical professionals in hospitals, community health centers, private practices, and local clinics are at the forefront in the effort to combat public health dangers. In many cases, these health care professionals treat those afflicted with disease and other health conditions before their afflictions are known to represent community-wide risks. Because of their role in public health arenas, hospitals and medical facilities have also been focal points of health care reform proposals in the United States. This is particularly true because many poor and uninsured people turn to hospital emergency rooms for treatment of ill health, rather than seeking preventive care from primary care physicians.

Another important component of the public health services industry is the government. Most political systems at their various levels (national, state, county, or municipal) have entities dedicated to initiating programs to promote good health, enforcing public health laws within their jurisdictions, and quickly assessing and reporting epidemiological risks and threats as they arise. Legislators and executive agencies are often on the tail end of public health issues, reacting to risks after the fact and issuing public policies designed to contain risks or to promote alternative behaviors that will mitigate them. The U.S. federal government has four agencies dedicated to public health, while a number of other agencies (such as the Department of Defense and the Environmental Protection Agency) also address public health as part of their functions. The military may be called in during disaster situations from which public health dangers may arise.

Additionally, the contributions of the nonprofit sector to the public health services industry are invaluable. Nonprofit organizations are myriad in nature, and many of them have access to information about their constituencies that medical practitioners and researchers (as well as sociologists) may not. Some, such as the American Red Cross, the American Diabetes Association (ADA), and the AIDS Coalition to Unleash Power (ACT UP), may have data and perspectives on their respective constituents that may suggest better vehicles for preventing public health risks.

The industry also relies heavily on the research of academic institutions. Schools of public health, medical schools, and other such programs conduct studies of existing public health systems and the dangers thereto. These studies help the industry as a whole not only address those dangers but also evolve in response to the altered conditions of an ever-changing population. Often, these schools and programs use grant monies from corporations and governments to conduct their research.

Finally, the role of the public safety agencies in public health services cannot be discounted. Paramedics, police officers, and firefighters are invaluable agents of quick containment in the event of a public health emergency. They are typically the first responders to a disaster scene, such as a fire, earthquake, or severe weather event, all of which may create peripheral health risks even after the event has ended.

The public health services industry is a vast network whose total population of workers is difficult to gauge. The constant evolution and adaptation of this industry to changing environmental conditions in the twenty-first century remain invaluable to the well-being of residents.

Medical Practitioners

Doctors and other health providers are often the first to encounter emergent public health threats. In the course of treating patients, they note patterns of illness and unusual symptoms, and they are responsible for notifying public health agencies of any worrisome anomalies. In addition, in the twenty-first century, it is possible for groups of medical practitioners to identify patterns accidentally: Reports of symptoms observed at clinics, hospitals, and other sites are aggregated and analyzed by agencies such as the CDC, so no individual frontline doctor needs to recognize an anomaly in order to sound the alarm. Conscientious reporting of seemingly innocuous data may be enough.

Potential Annual Earnings Scale. According to Allied Physicians, physicians' average annual salaries may be as low as $80,000 (for specialists in ambulatory medicine) and as high as $1.4 million (for specialists in orthopedic sports medicine or spine surgery). The U.S. Bureau of Labor Statistics (BLS) reports that, as of 2009, registered nurses earned an average of about $64,000 per year, depending on experience, education, and union contracts. Additionally, according to the BLS, medical technologists and clinical laboratory personnel earned about $54,000 per year on average, while orderlies and nursing assistants earned about $25,000.

Clientele Interaction. The relationship between medical professionals and their patients is held in the highest regard. Patients under the care of a medical professional must feel that the individuals who are caring for them are focused fully on their needs. Put simply, the medical professional's interaction with the patient is the most important part of the job.

Amenities, Atmosphere, and Physical Grounds. The environment in which a medical practitioner works is highly professional. Medical facilities, by the nature of the work performed in them, are normally impeccably clean and bound by professional protocols and rules. These rules are imposed either by the institutions themselves or by the local, state, or federal government. The environment is typically very high paced, with a great many bureaucratic systems in place to ensure that each patient is properly attended, in spite of the high volume of patients who may be on site.

Typical Number of Employees. The number of employees working in a health care institution varies. Some hospitals employ hundreds of doctors and nurses, while some smaller medical groups may employ only a dozen or fewer. These employees include doctors and nurses and may also include on-site medical technicians, such as laboratory assistants and phlebotomists (blood work specialists), as well as physician assistants.

Traditional Geographic Locations. Facilities that house medical practitioners are found in or near most cities and towns and in central locations in rural areas. They are typically situated near the highest concentrations of current and potential patients.

Pros of Working for a Medical Facility. A medical facility such as a hospital, medical practice, or physician group offers employees a fast-paced workplace with numerous challenges. There is no typical work schedule, as medical workers encounter an unpredictable environment in which the treatment required for each patient is different. Medical facilities also make available to employees a wide range of resources, such as medical labs, libraries, and medical technologies. Such facilities also present medical professionals with candidates for case studies and, as a result, opportunities to write and publish scholarly articles.

Cons of Working for a Medical Facility. Medical facilities are bound by budgetary constraints that are dictated by the revenues generated by patients and their insurance carriers. In medical facilities that administer to poor patients, reimbursement by the government is considerably less than reimbursement from insured patients. Budgets are therefore often very tight in such instances, limiting medical professionals' ability to earn higher salaries, as well as the resources available to address public health needs. Additionally, nurses are often part of a union, which means that salaries and benefits must be negotiated at the end of every contract. Medical professionals also work long hours, as patients may require around-the-clock care.

Costs

Payroll and Benefits: Doctors are generally paid either on a salary or on a fee-for-service basis. The latter requires them—or their home institutions—to navigate both private and public bureaucracies in order to receive payment, arguing with insurance claims departments and Medicare administrators, for example, over whether a given service was covered. Other medical staff may be paid annual or hourly wages, depending on the position. In many cases, they are represented by collective bargaining units.

Supplies: Medical facilities and practices require a number of supply types. For the purposes of patient recording and management, they require a number of office supplies, such as computers, paper products, and other administrative goods and hardware. They also need a great deal of medical products and hardware, ranging from stethoscopes, intravenous (IV) bags, and surgical tools to heavy machinery such as computed tomography (CT) scanners and electrocardiographs (ECGs). They must also have basic supplies for patients, such as gowns, bedding, and other materials. Finally, they must have on site a sizable volume of medications, surgical supplies (such as gloves, scrubs, and masks), and other important items.

External Services: Medical facilities may outsource security, cafeteria positions and catering, audiovisual support, and maintenance and custodial services.

Utilities: Depending on the size of the medical institution, a sizable portion of its budget may be dedicated to electricity, water, and sewage. Telephones, cable television, and Internet access are also common expenses.

Taxes: Medical professionals are subject to income taxes and sales taxes. In the United States, federal and state exemptions from commercial real estate, sales, lodging, and other taxes vary based on state law. For example, hospitals are generally exempt from local commercial real estate taxes, but private practices may not be granted similar exemptions.

Government Agencies

Federal and local governments monitor public health and formulate and implement plans to safeguard and improve health, both over the long term as a matter of policy and in response to short-term crises and disasters.

Potential Annual Earnings Scale. The pay scale for public health personnel employed by local, county, regional, state, or federal government agencies and departments varies based on the position held and the level of government, as well as the geographic location of the position. The overall average annual salary for a manager of a public health agency is $88,750, according to the BLS.

Clientele Interaction. Client interaction is extremely important to public health officials' endeavors. Departments of public health must frequently create and maintain outreach programs that provide the public with the most up-to-date information about public health risks and threats. Such programs involve frequent meetings with private citizens, in either group or individual settings, to ensure the delivery of the information. Public health departments must also enforce relevant laws and, because of this mandate, must consistently be in direct contact with individuals, businesses, and others within their jurisdictions.

Amenities, Atmosphere, and Physical Grounds. The atmosphere of a national, state, county, regional, or local department of public health is a professional one. Most are located in government buildings, either occupying space in larger office buildings or as sole tenants. Much of their work entails managing a great deal of paperwork, including research reports, program summaries, and inspection reports. Depending on the size of the organization and the project or issue with which the department is faced, the work environment may be slow- or fast-paced. Nonetheless, the environment demands a high level of clerical organization and administrative order.

Typical Number of Employees. Government agencies and departments dedicated to public health services vary in size based on the level of government, as well as the jurisdiction involved. Some local public health departments are composed of only a few employees (such as an office administrator and local inspectors), while larger departments, particularly those on the state and national levels, employ hundreds if not thousands of people to oversee their coverage areas.

Traditional Geographic Locations. Departments of public health and other government agencies dedicated to addressing public health concerns are located throughout a given political system. Federal agencies in the United States are based in Washington, D.C., but they have offices in each of the states in order to coordinate with Washington. County and regional governments usually have public health departments located in the largest city or town in the area, usually a county seat. The CDC is headquartered in Atlanta, Georgia.

Pros of Working for a Government Agency. Government agencies and public health departments have access to a wide range of resources that may be of great use to them in their pursuits. This range extends to Washington, D.C., in the case of the United States, where many of the nation's public health policies and regulations are created. This point is important, as it means that even local government employees have the same information available to them. Benefits may also be above competitive levels, since governments negotiate reasonable rates for employee insurance, investment strategies, and other benefits.

Cons of Working for a Government Agency. Because national, state, and local laws and regulations pertaining to public health are either uniform or expected to be compatible with one another, it may be a challenge to implement a new regulation in an area that may not fit the profile of the regulation. Regulations that are broadly imposed may not be easily enforced by a given local agency as a result of geography, sociological differences, or other factors. As a result, public health agents may become frustrated in their attempts to implement strategies that are not specific to their regions' demographics. Additionally, funding for programs is not always consistent or equitably distributed among agencies. Some cities receive more money from a state or national government than do others for a number of reasons, and this imbalance of distribution may affect an agency's ability to meet its goals and requirements.

Costs

Payroll and Benefits: Most public employees are paid salaries that are regulated by set pay scales and rules created and modified by legislative bodies. Public employees also tend to receive generous benefits. In some cases, much of public health policy implementation falls not to a paid staff but to a volunteer board of health (some members of which may earn small stipends for their work).

Supplies: Departments of public health and other government agencies must have the necessary supplies to operate a strong administrative system, such as office supplies, computers, copiers, and similar equipment. They may also require field supplies, including hazmat (or hazard-ous materials) suits, vehicles, and contaminant-detection hardware.

External Services: Public health agencies and departments may outsource a number of duties, including building security, transportation, printing, public relations, and custodial and maintenance services. Government agencies, particularly national agencies, may also engage private laboratories to analyze contaminants and other substances to determine their public health implications.

Utilities: Like most office environments, public health agencies pay for utilities such as telecommunications services, electricity, water, sewage, and similar services. Their rates may be less than those paid by private companies, as government agencies often negotiate lower rates directly with utility companies.

Taxes: Government agencies require their employees to pay income taxes. In many cases, however, employees on official government business are exempt from state and local sales taxes, excise taxes, and other assessments; such exemptions tend to occur on a state-by-state basis.

Nonprofit Organizations

Nonprofit organizations relating to public health range from professional advisory organizations, such as the American Heart Association, to political advocacy groups, such as ACT UP, to nongovernmental organizations, such as the Red Cross. All attempt to improve public health, whether by demanding that more public resources be spent on a particular health problem or constituency, by disseminating useful information to the public, or by administering directly to those in need.

Potential Annual Earnings Scale. Nonprofit organization salaries tend to be lower than the salaries of equivalent functions in the private and public sectors. Executive directors and association leaders tend to earn the highest salaries in such organizations, while administrative assistants and similar personnel are paid at the lower end of the organization's salary schedule. According to PayScale, as of September, 2009, the salary of a nonprofit director or president ranged from about $44,000 to $180,000 per year, depending on experience.

Clientele Interaction. Nonprofit public health organizations usually spend the bulk of their time working with clients, communicating with them directly via local or regional meetings. Such an approach gives an organization opportunities to have a more intimate relationship with the people it serves and therefore helps it increase its impact on those people. Client interaction is therefore essential for nonprofit organizations.

Amenities, Atmosphere, and Physical Grounds. Nonprofit organizations operate in professional office environments, but because of their client- and public-service-oriented missions, they may occupy smaller offices, preferring their employees to work with clients in the field. They are often less formal in terms of dress code but nonetheless remain dedicated to meeting their stated goals and benchmarks.

Typical Number of Employees. Nonprofit organizations vary in size, depending on the scope of services they provide and the number of clients served. Some are very small, employing only a handful of full-time personnel. Others, however, may be considerably larger, with subsidiary organizations serving as part of a national or international network. These organizations may employ hundreds and even thousands of people on a full-time or consultative basis, as well as engaging a large number of volunteers.

Traditional Geographic Locations. Nonprofit organizations are often located in major urban centers and capital cities, as many of them have vested interests in social and budget policy decisions at the government level. Additionally, many are found in areas heavily populated by those with whom they work, such as Native American reservations and other impoverished regions where public health issues may become manifest.

Pros of Working for a Nonprofit Organization. Individuals who work at nonprofit public health organizations enjoy an ability to interact more directly and consistently with affected clients than do the employees of hospitals and government agencies. Those with a passion for addressing a specific public health issue—such as acquired immunodeficiency syndrome (AIDS), cancer, or childhood obesity—may enjoy the one-on-one interaction with clients that nonprofits create. Additionally, the relative informality of many nonprofit organizations may appeal to those who do not wish to wear professional clothes to work or be bound by strict professional codes of conduct.

Cons of Working for a Nonprofit Organization. Nonprofit public health organizations are often hampered by a lack of donations or government grant monies, particularly during economic downturns. In the light of this fact, many of their programs may be cut short by budgetary constraints. Similarly, employees tend to have lower salaries and more limited benefits than do workers in other sectors of the industry. The relatively small size of many nonprofits limits opportunities for upward career mobility.

Costs

Payroll and Benefits: Nonprofits' employees are usually paid on a salary or contractual basis. Organizations funded primarily by grants often tie salaries to grants. That is, a grant will fund a particular position or positions for the duration of a particular project. For the position to continue beyond the term of the project, further grants must be found.

Supplies: Nonprofit public health organizations predominantly require stationery, filing materials, and related office supplies. They also need computers, telecommunications hardware, and other administrative supplies and equipment. Organizations whose personnel work in the field may also require cellular telephones, smart phones, laptop computers, and radios.

External Services: Smaller nonprofits in particular often outsource computer and networking support, publishing and copying services, and accounting and tax services. Organizations that hold large events and charitable receptions usually contract event planners, caterers, and related services.

Utilities: Nonprofit organizations are expected to pay basic utilities, such as electricity, telephones, and heat. In many cases, however, their rates are considerably lower than normal, negotiated with providers on the basis of the organization's limited budget and altruistic nature. In other situations, many of the utilities will be included in the organization's lease, creating a one-payment system.

Taxes: Nonprofit public health organizations are typically exempt from a wide range of taxes, including federal income taxes, provided they meet certain government-imposed criteria. For example, in the United States, charitable organizations that spend no more than 10 percent of their time on lobbying and that do not share profits among shareholders may qualify as 501(c)(3) groups. This status exempts them from most federal taxes and many state and local taxes, although personnel must still file personal income tax returns, and the organizations are still responsible for payroll taxes on employee salaries.

Academic Institutions

Academic institutions conduct research critical to understanding the nature of illnesses and other public health and safety threats. Like nonprofit organizations, academic institutions' activities are often funded on a project-by-project basis by specific government or private grants. Indeed, academic scholars in the sciences are expected to conduct research precisely because it brings funding into their home institutions.

Potential Annual Earnings Scale. Salaries and earnings among academic institutions dedicated to public health research vary based on the size of the university's endowments and any grants that are provided either by the university or by external sources (such as corporate groups or the government). Academic clinical researchers earn an average of about $47,000 per year, while public health researchers may earn about $46,000 per year.

Clientele Interaction. Client interaction among university-based public health researchers varies based on the requirements of the grant or program being conducted. The client of an academic researcher is usually the researcher's host university or the company or government entity providing the grant. Researchers may be required to report their findings to their clients on a quarterly or annual basis, if not upon completion of the project.

Amenities, Atmosphere, and Physical Grounds. Academic public health faculty and researchers tend to be based at larger universities, which provide them with access to a greater amount of resources. The environment of research institutions is typically professional and may or may not require business attire, depending on the nature of the work performed. Academic institutions are dynamic, and public health research departments may abut other departments that provide undergraduate and graduate education as well as research.

Typical Number of Employees. Academic institutions' public health research offices vary in size based on the scope of the work performed. Some groups are very small, composed of a single researcher and an administrative assistant, while others are much larger, as they require the analysis of a great deal of data. The amount of available grant money and other funding also contributes to an institution's ability to expand its staff to conduct larger analytical activities.

Traditional Geographic Locations. Public health departments are usually located near or within university campuses. Their geographic locations often determine the resources that are available to them, including recruiting pools and technological systems that will aid them in conducting their research. In other cases, they have smaller operations located closer to their areas of study, such as impoverished rural areas or regions affected by environmental hazards.

Pros of Working for an Academic Institution. Academic institutions offer a wide range of resources, often across the spectrum of public health (including economics, sociology, environmental engineering, and public policy, as well as medicine). Public health researchers may therefore enjoy an ability to conduct research that encompasses a broader perspective than they might find in a hospital or as part of a government agency. Many of these work environments are not as formal in terms of professional decorum, which may appeal to those who prefer to work in a less structured environment.

Cons of Working for an Academic Institution. One of the most difficult challenges of working on a public health-related project within an academic institution is the fact that such projects rely on grants, endowments, and government-imposed budget earmarks that may not be renewed from one year to the next. A team may thus go from operating with a sizable budget to working under extremely strict conditions (if its project does not lose funding altogether). Additionally, those personnel who prefer a degree of client interaction may not find a solely academic setting conducive to such interaction. Finally, those who are used to working in a corporate or government setting that establishes strict benchmarks and goals may find the flexibility and informality of academic work frustrating.

Costs

Payroll and Benefits: Academic workers are often paid salaries or contractually through project-based grants. Full-time academics earn salaries but may supplement those salaries with grants, while they are often expected to secure sufficient grant money to pay the wages of their research assistants.

Supplies: Academic institutions performing public health studies require basic office supplies, such as telecommunications equipment, computers, and basic desktop materials. In addition, they must be equipped with laboratory materials and supplies, waste-management facilities (if medical waste is produced), and the necessary computer modeling and statistical software.

External Services: Although many major universities and academic institutions are self-sufficient, a number of important external vendors may be called upon. For example, a public health department that utilizes medical samples may need a vendor that is equipped to dispose of such waste. Universities also often contract telecommunications providers.

Utilities: Universities must pay for telephone, electricity, and energy usage, as well as water and sewage. Large institutions often negotiate lower than average rates for such utilities.

Taxes: In general, institutions of higher learning are exempt from real estate taxes and federal taxes. In the United States, those exemptions require that any revenues generated from grants, philanthropic donations, and endowments be used to fund research and education and not to generate profits.

Public Safety

Public safety personnel are the first responders to any public health crisis. They rescue those in danger, treat people suffering from illness and other health defects, and protect and separate the general public from sources of danger.

Potential Annual Earnings Scale. Salaries for public safety personnel vary based on experience, geographic location of the position, seniority, and the frameworks established by collective bargaining. According to salary survey Web sites such as PayScale.com and Salary.com, the national range for police officers in the United States is between about $31,000 and $81,000 per year. The range for firefighters is about $30,000 to $78,000 per year, and the range for emergency medical technicians (EMTs) and paramedics is about $9.80 to $20.50 per hour. (Similar salary ranges are reported by the BLS.)

Clientele Interaction. Police, firefighters, paramedics, and other first responders encounter and aid people in crisis. In the event of a dangerous public health event, they are typically the first units to arrive on the scene. Client interaction is therefore a constant component of the job. Because such personnel are called upon to intervene in emergency situations, the interaction between them and private citizens can be of a confrontational nature.

Amenities, Atmosphere, and Physical Grounds. Public safety officers are usually expected to be mobile. Some work in patrols, while others stay in their headquarters until called by emergency dispatchers. All are subject to such emergency dispatch calls. When they are at headquarters, they fill out reports, conduct inventory, and perform maintenance on vehicles and equipment. Public safety is a high-stress environment, largely because it generates often confrontational relationships between officers and the many private citizens with whom they must interact.

Typical Number of Employees. Public safety departments vary in size based on the size of the jurisdiction covered. For example, major cities such as New York and Chicago each employ thousands of police officers, while many smaller communities employ only a few dozen. The number of paramedics in a particular location also depends on the size of the community, as well as the nature of the department (some are privately owned and operated, while others are publicly operated through fire departments).

Traditional Geographic Locations. Police, fire, and paramedic personnel are located in or near every municipality and county in the country. In most urban and suburban locations, there are a number of fire stations. In many cities, there are multiple police district offices in addition to the main police headquarters. In rural environments, public safety departments are usually based in county seats or larger municipalities, and personnel patrol outlying areas.

Pros of Working for a Public Safety Department. Working as a police officer, firefighter, or paramedic can involve a great deal of excitement. Such employees often place themselves at great risk to protect the lives of others. When they retire, they and their families generally receive strong retirement benefits, including insurance.

Cons of Working for a Public Safety Department. Public safety work is dangerous. In public health situations, officers may be exposed to dangerous chemicals or fumes, virulent diseases and blood, and violent patients and situations. Additionally, police and firefighters are paid by way of contracts negotiated with the cities or counties in which they operate; when budget dollars are short, they may lose pay or even their jobs as a result of budget austerity. Many officers, paramedics, EMTs, and firefighters experience trauma in their daily work that can have serious psychological repercussions over time.

Costs

Payroll and Benefits: Pay and benefits for public safety officers are dependent on the geographic location of the posting and the negotiated salary structure (unless, like many ambulance companies, the organization is private). According to the BSL and annual salary surveys such as those conducted by PayScale.com, the highest-paid leaders are chiefs of police (who earn a national average of $88,000 to $99,000 per year) and fire chiefs (who earn a national average of $73,000 to $95,000 per year).

Supplies: Public safety officials require office supplies, uniforms and protective clothing, and hardware and vehicles, including weapons, firefighting equipment, trucks, radios, and logistical systems.

External Services: Most public safety departments are self-sufficient or maintained by other government entities. However, in many cases, police, fire, and paramedic vehicles must be maintained and repaired by external mechanics. Additionally, most equipment, such as weapons, bullet-proof vests, flame-retardant suits, and medical supplies may be maintained by the private vendors from whom it is purchased.

Utilities: Public safety departments use a great deal of electricity, water, and telephone services, which come out of department or city budgets. Additionally, they use a large amount of fuel, particularly for trucks and patrol vehicles.

Taxes: Public safety departments are public, government entities and, as such, are exempt from most state and federal taxes. Personnel must, however, pay personal income taxes and other assessments. Many paramedic and ambulance organizations are privately owned and operated, and their tax-exempt status is determined on a state-by-state basis.

ORGANIZATIONAL STRUCTURE AND JOB ROLES

The organizational structure of the public health services industry is both compartmentalized and designed to interconnect its various components based on the demands of a given situation. For example, in the event of a natural disaster, emergency response, government, and health practitioners must all work in such a way that each segment is synchronized with the others. In the event of a disease outbreak or epidemic, government, health practitioners, and nonprofit organizations may work together to combat emergent illnesses, as well as to prevent dangerous behavior that might perpetuate the spread of such illnesses.

The following umbrella categories apply to the organizational structure of entities providing public health services:

- Leadership
- First Responders
- Research and Analysis
- Communications and Public Affairs
- Policy Making
- Medical Care

Leadership

Those who lead public health organizations, both public and private, are skilled administrators who are capable of organizing groups of people with diverse backgrounds and professional skills. They manage the overall operations and organizational structure of their agencies and institutions, and they oversee all aspects of an organization's endeavors. They set goals and strategies, assign tasks to personnel, draft and implement budgets, and review all data and information that is to be issued to the public.

OCCUPATION PROFILE

Firefighter

Considerations	Qualifications
Description	Controls and extinguishes fires, protects lives, and conducts rescue efforts.
Career cluster	Law, Public Safety, and Security
Interests	Data; things
Working conditions	Work both inside and outside
Minimum education level	On-the-job training; junior/technical/community college; apprenticeship
Physical exertion	Heavy work
Physical abilities	Unexceptional/basic fitness; must lift/carry heavy objects
Opportunities for experience	Apprenticeship; military service; volunteer work; part-time work
Licensure and certification	Required
Employment outlook	Faster-than-average growth expected
Holland interest score	RES

Note: See volume 1, "Publisher's Note," for an explanation of the Holland interest score.

Public health leaders generally earn higher salaries than anyone else in their organizations. Their job is to manage the overall functions of an agency or association, address systemic issues, guide any political activities when necessary, and ensure that all departments function effectively to address all relevant public health concerns. In most cases, they are also the public faces of their agencies, issuing statements and fielding questions from the media.

A public health leader is generally well educated, usually holding a master's degree in public health or business administration or a medical degree. Nonprofit leaders may not have such advanced degrees, but they often have undergraduate degrees and advanced training in organizational management. Public safety officials are also well educated in law enforcement training and disaster response.

Leadership occupations may include the following:

- President/Chief Executive Officer (CEO)
- Executive Director
- Secretary
- Board Chair
- Department Chair
- Department Chief

First Responders

Law enforcement officers, firefighters, and field medical personnel such as paramedics and EMTs are charged with intervening in situations that represent a danger to public safety. They are often the first people on the scene when an incident occurs. In the event of a public health incident—a fire, chemical spill, or terrorist attack—they must contain the incident area, redirect crowds, mitigate the incident (by extinguishing a fire, for example), and accomplish similar tasks. Law enforcement officers may have college degrees and will have graduated from a police academy, where they learn disaster preparedness and crisis intervention skills in addi-

OCCUPATION PROFILE

Medical Scientist

Considerations	Qualifications
Description	Seeks to improve human health by studying the causes of diseases and other health problems.
Career clusters	Health Science; Science, Technology, Engineering, and Math
Interests	Data; people; things
Working conditions	Work inside
Minimum education level	Doctoral degree
Physical exertion	Light work
Physical abilities	Unexceptional/basic fitness
Opportunities for experience	Military service; volunteer work; part-time work
Licensure and certification	Required
Employment outlook	Faster-than-average growth expected
Holland interest score	IRA

Note: See volume 1, "Publisher's Note," for an explanation of the Holland interest score.

tion to anticriminal actions. Firefighters, paramedics, and emergency medical technicians (EMTs) must similarly pass examinations and conduct specialized training before they can work in the field.

First response occupations may include the following:

- Police Officer
- Firefighter
- Emergency Medical Technician
- Paramedic
- Hazardous Materials Specialist
- Health Inspector
- Fire Inspector
- Detective

Research and Analysis

Public health researchers and analysts are called upon to compile and study data pertaining to public health risks and threats. They may study social behaviors and environmental conditions. In the case of epidemiologists, they may trace the occurrences of disease outbreaks back to their sources. These workers analyze the effects of treatments, outreach programs, and public policies pertaining to the cessation of a health danger, gauging their effectiveness.

Researchers, analysts, and epidemiologists are generally well educated and hold advanced degrees in public health, sociology, medicine, or a social science that entails statistical analysis. They must be able to operate across a number of disciplines in order to better understand the risks and benefits of public health issues. The average salaries for personnel working in this field are between $45,000 and $51,000 per year.

Research and analysis occupations may include the following:

- Research Director
- Research Coordinator
- Project Manager
- Researcher
- Analyst
- Epidemiologist

- Intern
- Administrative Assistant

Communications and Public Affairs

The task of issuing public statements about ongoing public health issues and risks falls to an organization's communications and public affairs staff. This group is responsible for issuing media releases, drafting and distributing public-service information (via pamphlets, brochures, e-mails, Web sites, and other media) to alert the public to threats, and helping citizens prevent the development of negative health conditions.

Communications and public affairs staff are college-educated, usually with undergraduate and graduate degrees in communications, marketing, or similar fields. They must be experienced in all forms of media, including Web-based communications and other cutting-edge technologies, as well as traditional forms such as print media, television, and radio. The U.S. average salary for a public affairs and communications specialist is about $57,000 per year.

Communications and public affairs occupations may include the following:

- Press Secretary
- Director of Communications/External Affairs
- Public Affairs Manager
- Public Relations Coordinator
- Administrative Assistant

Policy Making

The responsibility for formulating public health policy falls to government legislators and executive departments. Legislators write laws to regulate businesses, protect the environment, govern health care reporting and services, and provide emergency funds to mitigate disasters and epidemics (such as outbreaks of H1N1 and avian flu). Executive departments implement and enforce these laws by establishing oversight mechanisms and writing the regulations authorized by the laws. Lawmakers and executive department leaders are generally well educated, with advanced degrees in public policy and administration, law, business, or health care. Salaries vary widely, depending on the level of government, the individual's professional experience, and government-set pay scales.

Policy-making occupations may include the following:

- Member of Parliament
- Representative
- Senator
- Legislative Aide
- Secretary

OCCUPATION SPECIALTIES

Medical Technologists

Specialty	Responsibilities
Bacteriologists	Study growth, structure, and development of bacteria and other microorganisms. They observe action of microorganisms upon living tissues of plants and higher animals, as well as on dead organic material.
Hemotherapists	Collect blood components and provide therapeutic treatments, such as replacement of plasma or removal of white blood cells, to patients and donors.
Histotechnologists	Prepare sections of human or animal tissue for immediate examination of specimens received from surgery.
Immunohematologists	Perform tests, recommend blood problem solutions to doctors, and serve as consultants to blood banks and the community.

- Undersecretary
- Deputy Secretary
- Governor
- President
- Prime Minister

Medical Care

Hospitals, medical centers, clinics, and group practices play an integral role in the public health services sector. Doctors, nurses, and related medical staff are fully trained in the causes, transmission, and treatment of disease and other public health conditions, so they are able to work with patients to mitigate health risks. Medical professionals work as a team, caring for urgent care patients, drawing blood for tests, treating symptoms, and providing patients with information about the prevention of public health dangers.

Medical professionals have advanced degrees in their fields, such as M.D.s, nursing degrees, D.D.S.s (doctors of dental surgery), and physician assistant or master's degrees. Some have vocational training in medical assistance, such as medical technology, phlebotomy, or physician assistance. Salaries vary based on the field involved, the individual's amount of experience, collective bargaining arrangements (for those positions that are managed by unions), and the geographic location of the position.

Medical care occupations may include the following:

- Physician
- Registered Nurse
- Dentist
- Licensed Nurse Practitioner
- Nursing Assistant
- Physician Assistant
- Medical Technologist
- Phlebotomist
- Laboratory Technician

INDUSTRY OUTLOOK

Overview

The public health services industry is a diverse and complex network, composed of a number of large individual industries. Its composition is reflective of the complexity of public health itself. Public health services do not focus entirely on treating epidemics of disease or other emergencies; they also take into account lifestyle issues, such as obesity, diet, tobacco use, sexual activity, and alcohol abuse, because such issues can create social groups whose conditions affect others in the community.

Additionally, public health has a political significance. Many government social services are geared toward those with health conditions who cannot afford treatment. Increased volumes of people with tobacco-related illnesses (such as lung cancer and emphysema) who receive health care through Medicaid and other government care programs increase the financial strains on such programs. Furthermore, because public health emergencies warrant emergency money and services, political leaders have a vested interest in implementing preventative public health policies and regulatory measures.

The public health industry continues to grow. Several of its components form some of the largest industries in the world. In 2006, for example, the U.S. health care industry provided about 14 million jobs, and it is expected to add 3 million more jobs by 2016. Nonprofit organizations that focus on

A woman wears a protective mask at the Bangkok airport after an outbreak of swine flu in 2009. (©Dreamstime.com)

public health, already one of the largest sectors of the nonprofit industry, account for as much as half of the entire industry's revenue and employment, with millions of jobs and hundreds of billions of dollars in revenues for more than thirty thousand American nonprofit organizations.

In the United States, public health is expected to hold the spotlight both as a political issue and as a critical public service. In the early 1990's, the Bill Clinton administration attempted to pass comprehensive reform of the health care system, citing the need to provide affordable health care to all American citizens. The Barack Obama administration renewed this effort, successfully passing through Congress the Patient Protection and Affordable Care Act of 2010. It was repeatedly pointed out throughout the yearlong debate over this measure that total health care expenditures in the United States account for approximately one-sixth of the entire U.S. economy.

The continuing emergence of viruses and diseases in the integrated global community gives rise to a continued need for public health outreach. The so-called swine flu (also known as H1N1), eastern equine encephalitis (EEE), Creutzfeldt-Jakob disease (the human form of "mad cow disease"), and fears of transmission of avian flu to humans provide evidence of the ongoing need for active public health services in the twenty-first century. Similarly, the fact that so many developing nations are still experiencing communicable diseases in nearly epidemic proportions represents an imperative for public health services to continue to work with poor countries to combat the spread of HIV/ AIDS, tuberculosis, hemorrhagic fever, and other epidemics. These diseases, which may be treatable and curable, if left unchecked can afflict large populations and ultimately spread to the rest of the world, as residents of affected regions travel to other countries.

The public health services industry will most likely continue to remain one of the most vibrant industries, not just in the United States but also

Ear tags were used to trace the origin of a cow that came down with bovine spongiform encephalopathy (known as mad cow disease) in 2003. Canada and the United States have banned certain types of feedstuffs thought to transmit the disease. (©Dreamstime.com)

across the globe. The continuing need to protect against epidemics and outbreaks, coupled with the recognition that dangerous lifestyles have an impact on entire communities, leads to the conclusion that public health services remain an important part of the twenty-first century global community.

Employment Advantages

The diversity of the public health services industry offers potential employees an extremely broad range of subfields in which to operate. Employees in this industry may have backgrounds in politics, medicine, sociology, environmental studies, education, public relations, or law enforcement. While this diversity allows for a great deal of individual career growth, people who work within the industry are part of a network, working as an interconnected team either in the event of a public health emergency or when addressing ongoing public health issues. As was the case in both ancient Greece and Rome, this network is integral to ensuring that public systems and infrastructures do not create public health dangers.

While public health work requires a focus on the individual tasks of each component of the industry, public health services personnel also have the benefit of taking a broader view of the effects of certain conditions and behaviors on communities at large. Individual patients are important, but the systematic effects of their conditions on finances, emergency capabilities, and response times are equally critical in the eyes of public health professionals. This distinction is notable because such a broad focus can help prevent major public health crises from beginning or spreading.

Annual Earnings

The public health services industry is difficult to quantify in terms of earnings, particularly because a large percentage of it is nonprofit. Many activist organizations, community health centers, universities, and political institutions do not generate revenues or have government-initiated appropriations that mandate both public health services and extraneous activities in the same appropriation. According to the U.S. Internal Revenue Service, however, nonprofit hospitals in the United States generate about $8.3 million in excess profits after expenses. Overall, according to First Research, the U.S. hospital industry (nonprofit and for-profit) generates about $575 billion. Nonprofit health care organizations, according to a 1997 study, generated $385 billion in revenues. Around the world, the total health care expenditures of developed and developing countries amounts to $4.5 trillion, much of which is spent on public health services and programs.

Industry earnings for nonsupervisory personnel working in the public health sector are generally higher than those working in other industries. It is believed that, in times of both economic boom and stagnation, this industry will continue to expand and hire individuals at pay scales above the national average in the United States and abroad.

RELATED RESOURCES FOR FURTHER RESEARCH

AMERICAN DIABETES ASSOCIATION
1701 N Beauregard St.
Alexandria, VA 22311
Tel: (800) 342-2383
http://www.diabetes.org

AMERICAN PUBLIC HEALTH ASSOCIATION
800 I St. NW
Washington, DC 20001-3710
Tel: (202) 777-2742
Fax: (202) 777-2534
http://www.apha.org

CENTERS FOR DISEASE CONTROL AND PREVENTION
1600 Clifton Rd.
Atlanta, GA 30333
Tel: (800) 232-4636
http://www.cdc.gov

HARVARD SCHOOL OF PUBLIC HEALTH
677 Huntington Ave.
Boston, MA 02115
Tel: (617) 384-8990
Fax: (617) 384-8989
http://www.hsph.harvard.edu

U.S. DEPARTMENT OF HEALTH AND HUMAN SERVICES
200 Independence Ave. SW
Washington, DC 20201
Tel: (202) 619-0257
http://www.hhs.gov

WORLD HEALTH ORGANIZATION
Ave. Appia 20
1211 Geneva 27
Switzerland
Tel: 41-22-791-2111
Fax: 41-22-791-3111
http://www.who.int

ABOUT THE AUTHOR

Michael P. Auerbach has over sixteen years of professional experience in public policy and administration, economic development, and the hospitality industry. He is a 1993 graduate of Wittenberg University and a 1999 graduate of the Boston College Graduate School of Arts and Sciences. He is a veteran of state and federal government, having worked for seven years in the Massachusetts legislature and four years as a federal government contractor.

FURTHER READING

Allied Physicians.com. "Physician Salaries and Salary Surveys." June, 2006. http://www.allied-physicians.com/salary_surveys/physician-salaries.htm.

Bayer, Ronald, et al. *Public Health Ethics: Theory, Policy, and Practice*. Rev. ed. New York: Oxford University Press, 2007.

Billings, Molly. "The 1918 Influenza Pandemic." Palo Alto, Calif.: Human Virology at Stanford University, 1997. Available at http://virus.stanford.edu/uda/index.html.

Experience.com. "What Sectors Make Up the Nonprofit Industry?" http://www.experience.com/alumnus/article?channel_id=nonprofit&source_page=additional_articles&article_id=article_1159823736672.

First Research.com. "Hospitals Industry Profile Excerpt." June 22, 2009. http://www.firstresearch.com/Industry-Research/Hospitals.html.

Harvard School of Public Health. "About HSPH." http://www.hsph.harvard.edu/about.

Jenkins, Wiley D. *Public Health Laboratories: Analysis, Operations, and Management*. Sudbury, Mass.: Jones and Bartlett, 2011.

Loue, Sana. *Forensic Epidemiology: Integrating Public Health and Law Enforcement*. Sudbury, Mass.: Jones and Bartlett, 2010.

MedicineNet. "Definition of Public Health." October 2, 2001. http://www.medterms.com/script/main/art.asp?articlekey=5120.

PayScale.com. "Salary Snapshot for Medical and Public Health Social Worker Jobs." http://www.payscale.com/research/US/Job=Medical_and_Public_Health_Social_Worker/Salary.

Rosen, George. *A History of Public Health*. Baltimore: The Johns Hopkins University Press, 1993.

Rosner, David, and Gerald E. Markowitz. *Are We Ready? Public Health Since 9/11*. Berkeley: University of California Press, 2006.

Salary.com. http://swz.salary.com.

Schneider, Mary-Jane. *Introduction to Public Health*. 2d ed. Sudbury, Mass.: Jones and Bartlett, 2006.

Scutchfield, F. Douglas, and William Keck. *Principles of Public Health Practice*. 3d ed. Clifton Park, N.Y.: Delmar Cengage Learning, 2009.

"Statistics on Nonprofit Hospital Revenue, Expense, and Excess Revenue." *Becker's Hospital Review*, February 26, 2009. http://www.hospitalreviewmagazine.com/news-and-analysis/current-statistics-and-lists/statistics-on-nonprofit-hospital-revenue-expenses-and-excess-revenue.html.

Styles, Paula. "The Black Death, 1347-1351." http://medievalhistory.suite101.com/article.cfm/the_black_death_13471351.

Themedica.com. "Medical Industry Overview." http://www.themedica.com/industry-overview.html.

U.S. Bureau of Labor Statistics. *Career Guide to Industries*, 2010-2011 ed. http://www.bls.gov/oco/cg.

_____. *Occupational Outlook Handbook*, 2010-2011 ed. http://www.bls.gov/oco.

U.S. Census Bureau. North American Industry Classification System (NAICS), 2007. http://www.census.gov/cgi-bin/sssd/naics/naicsrch?chart=2007.

U.S. Department of Commerce. International Trade Administration. Office of Trade and Industry Information. Industry Trade Data and Analysis. http://ita.doc.gov/td/industry/otea/OTII/OTII-index.html.

U.S. Internal Revenue Service. Colleges and Universities Compliance Project. http://www.irs.gov/charities/article/0,,id=186865,00.html.

_____. Exemption Requirements. http://www.irs.gov/charities/charitable/article/0,,id=96099,00.html.

©Norman Chan/Dreamstime.com

Publishing and Information Industry

INDUSTRY SNAPSHOT

General Industry: Communications

Career Clusters: Arts, A/V Technology, and Communication; Information Technology

Subcategory Industries: Art Publishing; Book Publishing; Calendar Publishing; Directory and Mailing List Publishing; Greeting Card Publishing; News Syndicates; Newspaper Publishing; Periodical Publishing

Related Industries: Advertising and Marketing Industry; Broadcast Industry; Internet and Cyber Communications Industry; Motion Picture and Television Industry

Annual Domestic Revenues: $157.9 billion USD (SAGE Glossary of the Social and Behavioral Sciences, 2007)

Annual Global Revenues: $444.1 billion USD (Companies and Markets, 2007)

NAICS Numbers: 5111, 519110

INDUSTRY DEFINITION

Summary

The publishing and information industry mass produces and distributes written materials, including printed books, newspapers, magazines and other periodicals, as well as electronic or digital media that convey the same content, such as e-books and online full-text databases. Published works may convey information, entertain, persuade, or engage in all these activities simultaneously. Databases and guides such as telephone directories also fall within the scope of the industry, which is an important component of the overall information and communications sector.

History of the Industry

Published print was the earliest form of mass communication. Although the written word has been used since ancient times to convey messages to multiple readers or listeners, it was only after the printing press made it possible for a printed text to become standardized that print could become a mass medium. As literacy among the population grew, so did the industry.

Before the advent of the printing press, most writing was done by hand. Producing written materials was a time-consuming and difficult process completed by scribes, often in monasteries. A single copy of the Bible took up to five years to complete. The audience for these manuscripts (often religious or Latin texts) was the educated class and the clergy, as the general population was illiterate.

Publishing was revolutionized with the development of the printing press in Germany in 1450 by Johann Gutenberg. Gutenberg's press, the technology of which spread throughout Europe quickly, eliminated the need for manual transcription and made books more accessible to everyone.

In the centuries that followed, the mechanized printing press underwent many improvements, making the mass production of printed material quicker and more affordable. By the eighteenth century, books were widely available throughout the world. Regular publications such as newspapers also began to be produced. As printing technology advanced, making books easier to print, other labor-saving technologies increased the average amount of leisure time and wealth. Thus, more people had time to learn how to read and to exercise this ability once they acquired it. Both literacy and printed materials designed to be read during leisure time increased. These societal changes accompanied calls for democratic reforms within the Church and within nations. Thus, the publishing industry became inextricably tied to the democratic notions of a free press, free will, self-actualization, and autonomy.

In many ways, the twentieth century was the golden era of publishing. By the early part of the century, regular publications such as magazines and newspapers were produced in every corner of the world. Even after the advent of other modes of mass communication, such as radio and television, newspapers remained the most popular way for people to find out about current events. The second half of the twentieth century saw a strong trend toward consolidation within the industry. Smaller publishing companies, catering to local markets, increasingly came under corporate control. Part of the reason for this trend was that newer printing equipment was very expensive to purchase and maintain. Many small companies were unable to cover the high cost of equipment upgrades and were forced to sell out to large, cash-rich publishing concerns.

The Internet began to influence the publishing industry at the end of the twentieth century. Electronic rather than paper publishing presented opportunities to significantly reduce costs associated with printing and distribution. However, the fact that consumers were beginning to get information online meant decreases in sales, circulation, and advertising revenue for the paper products that had sustained the industry throughout its history.

The Industry Today

The publishing industry is facing radical challenges and poorly defined opportunities in the early twenty-first century. These challenges reflect the impact of the Internet. Reading habits are changing, and the industry has so far struggled to adjust to these changes.

Serial publications such as newspapers have suffered significant declines in both readership and revenue in the early years of the twenty-first century. One standard measurement of publication readership is circulation, or the total number of copies produced and distributed. As of 2009, newspaper circulation was down an estimated 10 percent from its peak in the early 1990's. Another measure of readership is household penetration, which is a ratio of newspapers read per household. At its peak, the household penetration of all print newspapers reached 130 percent, since many house-

Many of the publishing industry's products are sold in bookstores. (AP/Wide World Photos)

The Publishing Industry's Contribution to the U.S. Economy

Value Added	Amount
Gross domestic product	$145.5 billion
Gross domestic product	1.0%
Persons employed	957,000
Total employee compensation	$85.8 billion

Note: Includes software publishing.
Source: U.S. Bureau of Economic Analysis. Data are for 2008.

holds read multiple newspapers. In the early twenty-first century, household penetration fell to 54 percent. (This measure, however, only accounts for print readership and does not take into account Internet readership.)

Print newspaper and magazine revenue is also down significantly since the end of the twentieth century. Classified advertising, traditionally a lucrative revenue stream for newspapers, began to migrate to online venues such as Craigslist. Display advertising, the mainstay of serial publications, has also dropped. Whereas newspapers used to command profit margins of more than 20 percent, those margins fell to 6-10 percent in the early twenty-first century.

The global recession of 2007-2009 also dealt a significant blow to the publishing industry. Major market newspapers saw unprecedented drops in advertising revenue because of the recession. The largest serial publishing company in the United States, Gannett Newspapers, experienced a 60 percent decline in revenue in early 2009. The New York Times Company, as another example, saw a drop in income of more than 50 percent in the last quarter of 2008. The dramatic drop in revenues that occurred in the early twenty-first century forced a number of well-established newspa-

pers into bankruptcy. This occurred even in large cities with traditionally strong markets. For example, both of Chicago's major newspapers, the *Chicago Tribune* and the *Chicago Sun-Times*, declared insolvency in late 2008 and early 2009. Many large publishing companies opted to stop print production of their flagship products. Instead, they switched to an Internet-only format. The *Seattle Post-Intelligencer*, for instance, ceased print publication in early 2009.

While the decline of newspapers has been the development of most concern in publishing, other branches of the industry have been suffering as well. The magazine industry has suffered similar drops in circulation and advertising revenue, largely as a result of the Internet's impact. The global recession of 2007-2009 dealt a fatal blow to many magazines that had enjoyed decades of success, including Conde Nast's *Gourmet* and *Modern Bride*. Book sales also declined in the wake of the global recession, causing most of the largest book publishing firms to take austerity measures. Many companies froze salaries and hiring and cut back on development expenses.

Although publishing is in a moment of crisis in the early twenty-first century, there are many who

Newspapers have lost advertising revenue to online venues such as Craigslist. (©Norman Chan/Dreamstime.com)

The Amazon Kindle is one of several e-book reading devices on the market. (AP/Wide World Photos)

feel that the Internet will provide opportunities to rejuvenate the industry. A recent study from Scarborough Research shows that readership is actually on the rise, as many publishing concerns have made their content available through multiple online sources. A 2009 study from Scarborough also found that newspaper readership in the United States was at 74 percent. Initial attempts to move print content online have so far had mixed commercial success, however. Some media outlets receive up to 20 or 30 percent of their revenues from online products, but online revenue still only accounts for around 6 percent of revenue industrywide. What is clear is that the industry must rethink its business model, and some publishing concerns have done so with success. Some community newspapers are seeing a rise in readership. Instead of requiring their readers to pay for subscriptions, they are making their papers available to a wide range of demographics—something that advertisers appreciate.

Another threat to the publishing industry is the introduction of e-book readers such as Amazon.com's Kindle, Barnes and Noble's Nook, and Apple's iBooks application for iPad. Each e-book platform negotiates book pricing and profit share with publishers. When Amazon's Kindle dominated the market, publishers feared the power that one distribution network would have on book pric-

Inputs Consumed by the Publishing Industry

Input	Value
Energy	$1.7 billion
Materials	$27.6 billion
Purchased services	$163.4 billion
Total	$192.7 billion

Note: Includes software publishing.
Source: U.S. Bureau of Economic Analysis. Data are for 2008.

ing, marketing, and other elements. When Apple entered the market, however, contracts were renegotiated, and the prices of some e-books increased as publishers were able to use Apple's more generous terms to force Amazon to improve its terms. This event was widely covered as a rare example of a situation in which increased competition resulted in increased prices for consumers.

INDUSTRY MARKET SEGMENTS

Publishing companies range from fairly small to very large. Historically, most publishing businesses were very small and often family owned. This changed in the twentieth century, when many larger publishing corporations took over smaller concerns. The following sections give an overview of how differently sized companies operate.

Small Businesses

A small business in the publishing industry is likely to have annual revenues between $200,000 and $2 million. It will normally employ ten to fifty people, including distribution staff. Small publishing businesses are often dependent on larger companies to fulfill certain business processes, especially printing, because the costs associated with owning and maintaining modern printing presses are extremely high.

Small presses or independent publishers (known as the "indie press") also fall under this category, although they may also be considered midsize businesses. In 2005, small presses numbered sixty-three thousand and realized total sales revenues of $14 billion. Generally, small presses—as opposed to small publishing businesses that lack their own presses—have annual revenues of less than $50 million. Small presses are characterized by smaller print runs for titles and can include niche publishers, such as do-it-yourself (DIY) titles, poetry, or collectible books. Small presses typically release about twenty titles each year.

As occurs in the newspaper industry as well, there is a constant cycle of small publishing houses being purchased by larger corporations, and the same concerns about independence and maintaining local editorial control arise. In general, though, because of the opportunities available through

multiple media outlets, the publishing industry is constantly renewing itself and new, independent houses spring up when more established small houses are absorbed into larger companies.

Potential Annual Earnings Scale. According to Simply Hired, the average salary in the publishing industry in 2009 was $58,000. Individual salaries are dependent on many factors, including experience, location, and size of the publisher or company.

Clientele Interaction. Publishers generally have two types of clients: readers and advertisers. For many kinds of small publishers, advertisers are the more important—and possibly the only—source of revenue. Small publishers sometimes actively solicit subscribers and book purchasers through telemarketing and promotional events. More often, they rely on their own advertising and word of mouth to acquire new readers. They solicit advertisers far more aggressively. Even small publishing companies usually have dedicated sales staffs whose primary job is to visit potential and active clients throughout their publications' distribution areas. The sales staff is responsible for tracking clients' marketing needs and providing them with appropriate advertising programs to meet those needs. Small presses have had some success using the Internet to advertise and market their products. Additionally, they have had success developing partnerships with small independent booksellers, who both support and market their products through their stores.

Amenities, Atmosphere, and Physical Grounds. Small publishing companies may or may not have their own presses. If they do not, they require far less commercial space in which to operate: Three thousand square feet is about average. These small publishers require a space for interaction with the public, usually a reception desk and waiting area. They often display their products in these public spaces. Sales staff often have their own offices near the reception area and meeting spaces suitable for client interaction. Since there is often a fair amount of traffic into their offices, small publishing companies tend to be located in central, downtown areas.

A good deal of space in publishing firms is dedicated to the electronic production of printed products. In this space, workers create and manage written content, design ads, and electronically lay out publications. This area is generally not accessible to the public, but some clients may want to work directly with production staff to create their advertisements.

If a small publisher owns its own presses, these may be located in the same building as the offices or at a remote and more industrial location. Printing presses are very large pieces of equipment, and they increase space requirements by several thousand square feet. The printing process is messy, loud, and potentially dangerous. Therefore, the public is generally not admitted to areas dedicated to printing.

Some small presses have begun to offer print-on-demand or publish-on-demand (POD) services. With digital printing capabilities, these companies only need print the number of publications ordered, avoiding costly print runs and warehousing costs. This technology also makes it more feasible for authors to self-publish their works, footing the entire bill for printing costs and selling their publications on their own.

Typical Number of Employees. Most small publishing businesses employ between ten and fifty people, including office support and reception staff, advertising and marketing representatives, production workers, and skilled and unskilled press workers (in firms that own presses). Distribution may be conducted by dedicated employees or independent contractors.

Traditional Geographic Locations. Small publishing companies tend to be located in the largest city in a region. They typically have offices downtown to maximize accessibility to the public and potential clients. A small publishing business may also have presses at a remote location, possibly an industrial area, to mitigate space and noise concerns.

Pros of Working for a Small Publisher. Employees of a small publishing business often have opportunities to learn about all aspects of the business. Smaller companies have freedom to control the content of their products. They also have more flexibility to develop marketing strategies to suit local client needs.

Cons of Working for a Small Publisher. Small publishers have smaller cash reserves than do larger businesses, making them far more vulnerable to market fluctuations. They also have more limited access to new equipment, especially expensive printing presses and other equipment. This can put them at a major competitive disadvantage to larger businesses.

Costs

Payroll and Benefits: Small businesses generally pay employees an hourly wage or annual salary. Sales staff are often paid on a commission basis. Employees sometimes receive benefits including vacation and sick time, health insurance and 401(k) plans, though this is rarer among smaller businesses.

Supplies: Small publishing businesses require computers, printers, telephones, fax machines, and general office supplies. Those that own their own presses require paper, ink, and machine parts.

External Services: In addition to contracting printing to dedicated external presses, small publishers may contract collections and proofreading. They may also hire external cleaning, maintenance, or security companies. Post office boxes are commonly used by small businesses in this sector.

Utilities: Small publishers have typical office utility expenses, such as heat, water, electricity, telephone, and Internet access. The utility costs associated with running a press are high and can add signifcantly to overhead.

Taxes: Small publishers pay typical business taxes, including state and federal taxes on revenue, as well as payroll and property taxes.

Midsize Businesses

Midsize businesses in the publishing industry are generally defined as those with annual revenues of between $2 million and $50 million. They usually employ between 50 and 250 people, and they are likely to have multiple branches, often within a single geographic region. They generally own at least one printing press, which is sometimes shared by several publications in different communities. Some small presses fall within the category of midsize businesses. These largely independent ventures run fairly lean operations.

Potential Annual Earnings Scale. According to Simply Hired, the average salary in the publishing industry in 2009 was $58,000. All other things being equal, employees of midsize publishers can be expected to earn salaries in line with the national average.

Clientele Interaction. As is true of small publishers, midsize publishers serve both readers and advertisers. Reader relations are usually handled by a designated circulation or marketing department. Midsize publishing businesses strongly rely on local, regional, and national businesses' advertising purchases. Interaction with advertising clients is typically handled by salespeople. Off-site sales visits to client businesses are important to maintaining strong advertising revenues. Some midsize publishers may also sell a sizable portion of their advertising space to advertising firms, which then resell the space to their clients at marked up prices.

Amenities, Atmosphere, and Physical Grounds. Midsize publishing businesses are likely to have multiple locations, often in a single region. Offices range in size from modest (three thousand square feet) to large (ten thousand square feet). Offices typically include reception areas with secretarial desks and displays of print products. Advertising sales departments often have designated conference rooms for meeting with clients. These spaces are the most accessible to the public and are marked by a comfortable and inviting atmosphere.

Publishing offices usually include clusters of offices used by written content developers such as writers and editors. Separate areas are usually devoted to graphic production, and there are often circulation departments as well that oversee the distribution of print products. The public is generally not allowed in these areas, which tend to be fast-paced and deadline-driven environments.

Presses may be housed at the same location as main offices, or they may be at other sites. It is typical for a midsize publishing company to have several satellite offices that share a single press. Press areas are noisy, industrial, and potentially dangerous, and the public is usually forbidden from entering them.

Typical Number of Employees. Most midsize publishers employ between 50 and 250 people. Generally, these employees will work in specific departments, such as reception, sales, editorial, graphic production, circulation, and printing.

Traditional Geographic Locations. Midsize publishing companies often have several locations. These typically include offices in each of the larger cities in their regions. Having offices in multiple municipalities facilitates interaction with potential clients. Traditionally, publishing companies have preferred downtown locations. Being close to population centers is often helpful to sales and circulation departments. Press operations are often conducted at separate locations. Printing presses are large and noisy, so they tend to be housed in industrial areas. A single press may serve multiple offices in a region.

Pros of Working for a Midsize Publisher. Midsize publishers have a number of competitive advantages. They tend to have far higher equipment budgets than do small companies. Computer and office equipment is updated on a regular basis, boosting worker efficiency. Having the capital to own and maintain dedicated presses helps such companies control printing costs. Wider circulation in multiple markets allows midsize firms to attract regional and national advertisers in addition to their smaller local clients.

Cons of Working for a Midsize Publisher. Some clients may feel more comfortable dealing with smaller and more local publishing companies than with midsize, regional companies. Larger companies, moreover, tend to have deeper cash reserves, allowing them to weather temporary drops in revenue better than midsize companies can. Moreover, large companies command higher purchasing power with regard to supplies such as paper and ink, so they can better control these costs.

Costs

Payroll and Benefits: Midsize companies employ a mix of compensation strategies. Higher-level employees tend to be paid annual salaries with benefits such as vacation, sick days, and 401(k) plans. Lower-level workers are usually paid hourly wages without benefits. Salespeople are often paid a commission based on advertising sold. Circulation workers are compensated as individual contractors and get a flat fee per unit delivered.

Supplies: Publishers need regularly upgraded office equipment, including telephones, computers, and printers. Additionally, presses require fairly large investments in paper and ink supplies.

External Services: Midsize publishing companies require at least one post office box per location. They may contract technical consultants to maintain telecommunications infrastructure, computer networks, and press equipment. They also depend on external collection agencies to go after unpaid client bills.

Utilities: Typical utility expenses include heat, water, electricity, telephone, and Internet access. Normally, by maintaining one or more printing presses, midsize publishing companies can accrue industrial-level utility charges.

Taxes: Publishing firms must pay state and local tax on revenues. Additionally, they are liable for payroll taxes for all employees and property taxes on their offices.

Large Businesses

The publishing industry is increasingly dominated by large businesses, whose revenues range from $50 million to more than $1 billion. Large publishing houses are characterized by the great variety of publications under their control. Large newspaper publishers such as Gannett (*USA Today*) and McClatchy (*Star Tribune* of Minneapolis) publish more than twenty newspapers nationwide. Large periodicals publishers, such as Meredith (*Better Homes and Gardens* and *Family Circle*) and Time Warner (*People*, *Time*, and *Sports Illustrated*) are responsible for a similar number of major publications. Major book publishers, such as Random House and the Penguin Group, publish all over the world and in a variety of media including print, electronic, and audio. Many of these large publishing companies are divisions of even larger multimedia companies. Large publishing businesses employ more than 250 people and compete at a national and international level for revenue. They are often fragmented into regional offices, allowing sales staff to deal directly with local and regional clients.

Potential Annual Earnings Scale. According to Simply Hired, the average salary in the publishing industry in 2009 was $58,000. All other things being equal, large publishers can be expected to pay above-average salaries in order to attract and retain the most qualified possible candidates for positions.

Clientele Interaction. Large publishers deal with clients on a number of levels. Readers are usually contacted over the phone, through the mail, or on the Internet. In some ways, large publishing companies are less accessible to the public than their smaller counterparts.

Advertising clients are often the most important source of revenue for publishers. They are served by staff located at local branch offices. Meetings with important clients often involve company staff traveling around the country and internationally. Large publishing companies also do quite a bit of business with advertising firms who represent clients, rather than just the clients themselves, as these firms typically purchase advertising space in bulk, at wholesale prices, and then resell the space to individual advertisers for a profit.

Amenities, Atmosphere, and Physical Grounds. Most large publishing companies have multiple locations. These usually include several headquarters throughout the world, which tend to be fairly large buildings in excess of ten thousand square feet. Large publishing companies also often have many satellite offices, which may be as small as five thousand square feet.

There is usually a reception area at the front of each office, where the company's products are displayed. Guests are generally greeted at this reception area before being directed to the appropriate floor, office, or conference room. The headquarters of larger publishing companies tend to dedicate one or more floors to each business function or specific publication. They usually have large common conference rooms, which can be used for internal meetings or for client interaction.

Smaller satellite offices tend to be organized more like midsize companies' headquarters, with sales, editorial, and production departments for creating the print products, as well as circulation offices. They also tend to be located downtown in order to encourage interaction with local business clients. Large publishing companies own multiple, very large press operations, in excess of ten thousand square feet each. These are usually located in industrial areas, since they are massive, noisy, and must be accessible for trucks.

Typical Number of Employees. Large publishing companies have more than 250 employees. They are significant employers in the areas in which they operate. Since they usually have multiple offices located around the world, they may employ thousands of employees. Some of the largest companies employ around fifty thousand people each.

Traditional Geographic Locations. Large publishing firms are almost always headquartered in the most important cities in their areas of operation. They are typically located in the most expensive business districts of those cities, both to encourage client interaction and to bolster their prestige. Satellite offices, which typically deal with a single publication or region, are much more like the offices of midsize publishing companies. They tend to be located in the downtown areas of regional cities. Press operations, on the other hand, are housed in massive industrial buildings and tend to be located in the industrial outskirts of the cities in which their companies have offices.

Pros of Working for a Large Publisher. Larger publishing businesses are among the largest multinational companies in any sector. They are publicly traded and have access to a scale of capital not paralleled elsewhere in the industry. With such massive cash reserves, the largest publishing companies are best positioned to survive industry changes.

Cons of Working for a Large Publisher. Most of the employees of large publishing companies do not have very much decision-making power. Job functions, positions, and even regions of operation may change without local employee input. This situation translates into a kind of job insecurity that many workers find stressful.

Costs

Payroll and Benefits: Large publishing companies compensate workers in a number of different ways. Higher-level white-collar workers earn annual salaries and full benefits, such as health insurance, 401(k) plans, vacation, and sick time. Lower-level white-collar employees are normally paid an annual salary as well but may have limited benefits. Other workers are paid hourly wages with limited or no benefits. Delivery personnel are usually independent contractors paid per piece delivered.

Supplies: Large publishing companies are major purchasers of office supplies such as computers, printers, fax machines, telephones, and so forth. They are also the largest buyers of press equipment, paper, and ink.

External Services: Large publishing companies may outsource collections and press or computer maintenance, as well as legal and accounting services. Many, however, handle all these functions in-house. While they most likely have large marketing departments, it is nonetheless common for large publishers to contract external public relations and marketing firms to design major ad campaigns. These external vendors will work in cooperation with a publisher's own advertising and marketing staff.

Utilities: Since they tend to operate a number of large offices throughout the world, large publishing companies have massive utility expenses. These include heat, water, electricity, and Internet access for offices. Large presses are massive industrial operations and are extremely utility intensive.

Taxes: Large publishing companies often operate in more than one country, making their tax liabilities quite complicated. They must pay all appropriate federal, state, provincial, and local taxes on revenues. They are also responsible for payroll taxes in all areas of operation, as well as property taxes on their real estate and any applicable tariffs on imports and exports.

ORGANIZATIONAL STRUCTURE AND JOB ROLES

Regardless of size or products, all publishing companies require similar business activities to function. Division of labor becomes more specialized in larger companies, while employees in the smallest organizations have the broadest range of responsibilities. Duties are conducted on a single floor or building. At larger companies, job functions are executed in isolation from one another.

The following umbrella categories apply to the organizational structure of businesses in the publishing industry:

- Business Management
- Office Management
- Sales and Marketing
- Editorial
- Production
- Printing

Business Management

Business managers provide their companies with leadership. These white collar, salaried employees plan and implement company strategy at the executive level. Business management positions are normally filled by employees with higher-level degrees and years of experience in the industry. They have often worked in other roles within the same company.

It is typical for the majority of upper management workers to be located in their companies' main headquarters. Lower-tier business management staff are assigned to oversee operations at each location and publication. Job activities for business managers tend to be strategic, oriented toward maximizing profits for the overall company or for a specific product. Report generation is an important part of business management, and managers' reports are sent up the chain of command to inform bigger picture decisions.

The level of executive management varies with the size of a company. For example, a company that consists of a single newspaper may be overseen by the newspaper's editor in chief. By contrast, a company that publishes dozens of newspapers and magazines will include many editors in chief and will likely be overseen by a president or chief executive officer. Business managers include a number of support staff positions, such as legal and accounting services. These employees are also consulted in developing actionable business plans.

Business management occupations may include the following:

- Chief Executive Officer (CEO)
- Chief Financial Officer (CFO)
- Editor in Chief
- Managing Editor
- Regional Manager
- General Manager
- Office Manager
- Legal Counsel
- Vice President of Accounting

Office Management

Office managers include those workers who perform the functions necessary to the day-to-day operations of a specific regional branch or publication as a business. These jobs tend to be clerical in nature, including keeping records, ordering supplies, answering phones, and greeting visitors. Workers in this category usually have degrees in business administration, accounting, transcription, or related fields.

Reception workers provide the first level of interaction with the public. They act as the main telephone operators, directing calls to appropriate offices. They also greet guests to offices and are responsible for determining how best to serve each visitor's needs. Administrative staff, meanwhile, directly support their respective departments by taking messages, keeping track of schedules, and ordering necessary supplies.

There is often a subgroup of office managers dedicated to billing. These workers are responsible for all accounts receivable and accounts payable. They draft invoices and purchase orders, keep track of incoming payments, make bank deposits, and transfer funds to corporate headquarters.

Most companies have dedicated human resources staffs to handle all employee issues. These staff members hire and fire employees, administer benefits, keep employee records, make sure the company is following fair labor standards, and oversee payrolls. Some companies, especially larger ones, have specific members of the office management staff who are in charge of department payrolls.

Staff engaged in these roles at a specific location normally report to a superior, usually an office manager. These managers are ultimately responsible for all the activities having to do with the business functions of their offices or branches.

Office management occupations may include the following:

- Receptionist
- Administrative Assistant
- Billing Manager
- Human Resources Manager
- Payroll Administrator
- Benefits Specialist
- Accounts Payable Specialist
- Accounts Receivable Specialist
- Office Manager

Sales and Marketing

The revenue that sustains publishing companies comes primarily from sales of print products or advertising space. Therefore, most companies dedicate significant resources to their sales and marketing departments. These departments are the ones primarily responsible for interacting with clients.

If a publication runs classified ads (either print or online), which many newspapers and magazines do, it is likely to have a staff of inside salespeople dedicated to this revenue stream. Inside salespeople answer questions about classified ad rates, take orders, process payments, and make sure ads run correctly.

Display advertising is the primary source of revenue for many publishing businesses. Sales and marketing staffs usually include several outside salespeople who reach out to potential business clients, help these clients develop advertising strategies and ads, and facilitate payment from clients. It is common for outside sales personnel to be divided among senior executive positions and junior assistant positions.

Both inside and outside sales departments usually answer to a single manager, who is ultimately responsible for the sales revenue of one or more publications. This person works with sales staff to set advertising rates and strategic approaches in order to maximize revenue.

In the case of companies that derive their income from the sale of products such as books and calendars, marketing department staffs are responsible for facilitating sales to retail outlets. Again, divided into executive- and assistant-level positions, marketing departments work with bookstores and other outlets to maximize product sales. Marketing approaches are usually overseen by marketing managers, who work with other departments to determine the potential economic viability of prospective products.

Sales and marketing occupations may include the following:

- Sales Manager
- Inside Salesperson
- Outside Sales Executive
- Outside Sales Assistant
- Marketing Executive
- Marketing Manager
- Marketing Assistant

Editorial

An editorial department primarily determines product content. Whether working with newspapers, magazines, books, or other publications, members of editorial teams develop the specific character of their companies' products. They come up with the words and images that draw readership. Employees in this category generally have higher degrees in English, journalism, or photography.

Many publishing companies maintain staffs of reporters to investigate noteworthy events or topics. These reporters are responsible for submitting stories to run in their companies' print products. In some companies, written content is provided by contributors rather than reporters. These contributors may be company employees, or they may be freelance writers who are paid per piece. Although some reporters and contributors also take pictures, many publishing companies employ dedicated photographers. These specially trained photojournalists use their skills to capture images that complement written stories.

All potential content is screened and organized by editors. A single publication's staff usually includes a number of different editors. Some specialize in writing headlines, some in selecting photographs, and some work in a single subject area. This latter type of editor may focus on news, sports, or entertainment. All editors within a single office usually report to a chief editor, who is in charge of the day-to-day management of publication content.

All members of an editorial staff answer to a publisher, who is ultimately responsible for the overall content and layout of print products. Publishers may be removed from daily editorial operations, but they serve as conduits between the editorial department and business management staff.

Editorial occupations may include the following:

- Reporter
- Contributor
- Photographer
- Photo Editor
- Headline Editor
- Subject Area Editor
- Chief Editor
- Publisher

Production

A production department is where a given publication is electronically produced. Production workers design and coordinate all elements of a publication before it is sent to press, turning

OCCUPATION SPECIALTIES

Journalists

Specialty	Responsibilities
Columnists	Analyze news and write columns or commentaries based on personal knowledge and experience with the subject matter. They gather information through research, interviews, experience, and attendance at functions such as political conventions, news meetings, sporting events, and social activities.
Critics	Write critical reviews of literary, musical, or artistic works and performances.
Editorial writers	Write comments on topics of reader interest to stimulate or mold public opinion in accordance with the viewpoints and policies of publications.
News writers	Write news stories from notes recorded by reporters after evaluating and verifying the information, supplementing it with other material, and organizing stories to fit formats.
Reporters and correspondents	Gather and assess information, organize it, and write news stories in prescribed styles and formats. They may also take photographs for stories and give broadcast reports, or they may report live from the site of events.

unformatted text and graphic elements into fully laid out, print-ready publications. Production workers often have degrees in art, graphic design, or computer science.

A good deal of the production work that goes into serial publications involves ad design. This is usually handled by designated graphic artists, who work with sales personnel to create ads that suit client specifications. Graphic artists also create other elements of publications, including cover design. Since the advent of online publications, graphic artists have been required to be well acquainted with digital and desktop publishing applications. Layout is also a major responsibility within this department. Layout designers, usually overseen by a layout manager, coordinate with editorial staff to give publications their desired visual characteristics.

In some publishing companies, especially those that produce magazines, one person is responsible for the overall look and style of publications. This person is often called the creative director and usu-

ally answers directly to higher-level business management staff.

Production departments rely heavily on computer software to render publications suitable for printing. Since this area of a publishing company tends to use the most advanced computer technology, production departments usually include computer specialists. These computer specialists may provide support to other departments, but they are primarily responsible for maintaining the computer systems used in electronic publication development.

Production occupations may include the following:

- Graphic Artist
- Art Director
- Layout Designer
- Layout Manager
- Creative Director
- Computer Technician
- Network Administrator

OCCUPATION PROFILE

Prepress Technician

Considerations	Qualifications
Description	Prepares printed material for printing presses by transforming text and pictures into finished pages and making printing plates of those pages.
Career clusters	Arts, A/V Technology, and Communications; Manufacturing
Interests	Data; things
Working conditions	Work inside
Minimum education level	High school diploma or GED; high school diploma/technical training; apprenticeship
Physical exertion	Light work
Physical abilities	Unexceptional/basic fitness
Opportunities for experience	Apprenticeship; part-time work
Licensure and certification	Usually not required
Employment outlook	Decline expected
Holland interest score	RIE

Note: See volume 1, "Publisher's Note," for an explanation of the Holland interest score.

Printing

The printing department of a publishing company is responsible for the physical printing of all publications. It is an industrial department, using large and mechanically sophisticated pieces of press equipment. Presses are extremely expensive, starting at $1 million. Since printing departments often operate a series of presses, they are responsible for a large part of a company's monetary investment. Presses are often run twenty-four hours a day, so printing department workers are employed in multiple shifts.

Workers in printing departments vary in skill level. The less-skilled employees, who engage in more menial physical tasks such as stacking publications as they come off the press, are usually paid by the hour. Less-skilled press workers often also serve as maintenance and janitorial support staff for other departments. Other workers who are licensed to operate heavy machinery such as forklifts

may be paid by the hour or given an annual salary. Skilled press operators are usually salaried employees, as are the specialists who maintain the presses.

There are two main kinds of printing press in modern use. The older and more common is the offset-type press, which uses a reverse image on a plate or film to print on paper. The industry is now transitioning to digital presses, which print in much the same way as modern laser printers, driven by computer software that describes the image to be printed. While offset presses are still the cheapest to purchase and operate, many press workers believe that everything will be done digitally in the future. Thus, there is an emerging need for career press workers to have advanced computer skills.

Printing occupations may include the following:

- Postpress Assistant
- Assistant Press Operator

- Press Operator
- Lead Press Operator
- Platemaker
- Press Maintenance Mechanic
- Press Department Manager

INDUSTRY OUTLOOK

Overview

The outlook for print publications in this industry shows it to be in decline. By any measurement, the publishing industry is in a moment of flux, a crisis of identity that many analysts consider to be the end of traditional publishing. According to U.S. Department of Labor projections, employment in the industry will decline 7 percent between 2006 and 2016. Total employment in all industries is predicted to increase 11 percent in the same period.

Readership of serial publications has declined throughout the twentieth century. Whereas the average American household in the 1920's read 1.3 newspapers on a regular basis, now only around half of households report reading newspapers. Declining readership reflects the impact of the Internet. As the public increasingly finds its news and entertainment online, there is less demand for print publications. Younger people are more likely to use the Internet to find information, and this trend is reflected in the fact that the lowest levels of newspaper readership are in the younger demographic. The trend toward lower levels of print newspaper readership is therefore likely to continue into the future.

It is incumbent on news organizations, if they are to remain in business, to re-create the way they deliver the content they produce. Some news organizations are succeeding, although the most successful method of maintaining readership is still undetermined. Some organizations are requiring paid subscriptions for their on-line content, hoping to balance advertising revenue and reader subscriptions. Other organizations have decided to make all of their content accessible, relying most heavily on advertising revenue to maintain their positions.

Serial publications are feeling the impact of both long-term and short-term drops in revenue. Normal revenue within the industry has traditionally been around 20 percent annually. In the early twenty-first century, this figure dropped to less than 10 percent. Further, the recession of 2007-2009 did significant damage to newspaper revenues. Most of the major newspaper publishing firms reported 40 to 50 percent drops in revenue during this period.

The Department of Labor projects that book, periodical, and directory publishing will remain relatively stable. However, it notes that even these components of the publishing industry are sensitive to economic fluctuations. In the wake of the recession, book sales immediately declined 7 percent. This was a greater revenue decline than book publishing companies anticipated, and it demon-

PROJECTED EMPLOYMENT FOR SELECTED OCCUPATIONS

Publishing Industries

Employment		
2008	Projected 2018	Occupation
53,300	43,500	Advertising sales agents
69,500	88,300	Computer software engineers
4,400	5,300	Database administrators
10,300	7,000	Desktop publishers
66,100	55,300	Editors
27,010	29,000	Graphic designers
5,100	4,200	Proofreaders and copy markers
9,100	7,400	Writers and authors

Source: U.S. Bureau of Labor Statistics, Industries at a Glance, Occupational Employment Statistics and Employment Projections Program.

strated that no sector was entirely immune to the changes taking place within the industry.

Although many analysts consider the publishing industry to be in serious trouble, it is not going to vanish. Instead, it will transform. The Internet is creating information services that incorporate written articles and videos. As the Department of Labor's projections indicate, this is helping blur the traditional distinctions between media industries. Though sustainable business models that embrace the new online reality have yet to be invented, there is every reason to believe that the Internet's blurring effect will create new opportunities for many kinds of companies in the publishing industry.

Employment Advantages

The publishing industry is currently in a moment of profound change and a crisis of identity. Traditional business models are beginning to fail. However, it will survive in some form as long as the written word remains an important mode of communication.

Despite the fact that publishing careers are increasingly unstable, working in this industry is the best way to gain media experience. All forms of media and entertainment rely heavily on talented writers. Individuals with an interest in the written word can gain a level of writing experience in the publishing industry that would be hard to achieve elsewhere. The deadline-driven nature of most publishing companies teaches writers to produce quality copy in a limited time frame. This is a valuable skill for an employee in any business sector to have.

The publishing industry also remains an excellent place for people who enjoy research. Whether producing newspapers, magazines, or books, publishing businesses rely on investigative talent. Few other jobs can give an individual as many opportunities to hone qualitative research skills.

Perhaps the most attractive reason to consider a career in publishing is precisely that the industry is changing so rapidly. People entering the world of publishing now will have unparalleled opportunities to help shape the future of the industry. Pioneering sustainable business models in the age of the Internet will be an incredible challenge, and those involved will be able to define publishing for future generations. Moreover, those who are among the first to formulate successful revenue models for online publishing stand to become not only influential but also incredibly wealthy.

Annual Earnings

Rising interest in online media has led to long-term revenue stagnation throughout the print industry. Global economic woes have made it clear that publishing is very fragile. Although analysts at such organizations as the Datamonitor Group originally forecast that the $157.9 billion U.S. industry would grow at a modest rate of 3.4 percent, the global economic crisis erased that expected growth entirely.

Some sectors of the industry are in fairly dramatic decline. Publishing businesses that depend on advertising revenue are in the most serious trouble going forward, as online advertising operates largely indepently of the content in which it appears. According to respected market research firm PricewaterhouseCoopers, advertising revenue is expected to remain lower than 2008 levels through 2013. The firm's report warns that advertising revenue may remain down permanently, as advertisers reconsider their options. Newspaper companies are expected to be hurt the most by advertising losses.

Magazine advertising revenue also felt the impact of the recession. According to the industry association Magazine Publishers of America, U.S. magazine ad revenue dropped 21.2 percent in the first half of 2009. The third quarter represented a slight improvement, as losses posted in September, 2009, were only 18.6 percent, year over year.

Book publishers are also suffering drops in revenue. The recession hurt book sales in 2008. According to the Association of American Publishers, U.S. book sales fell 2.8 percent in 2008. However, this sector is expected to rebound modestly.

Although the global industry is stagnant overall, there are exceptionally robust domestic publishing industries in some countries. In India, for instance, publishing is expected to grow by 5.6 percent annually between 2009 and 2013.

RELATED RESOURCES FOR FURTHER RESEARCH

AMERICAN SOCIETY OF NEWSPAPER EDITORS
    11690-B Sunrise Valley Dr.
    Reston, VA 20191

Tel: (703) 453-1122
http://www.asne.org

ASSOCIATION OF AMERICAN PUBLISHERS
50 F St. NW, 4th Floor
Washington, DC 20001
Tel: (202) 347-3375
Fax: (202) 347-3690
http://www.publishers.org

INTERNATIONAL PUBLISHERS ASSOCIATION
3 Ave. de Miremont
1206 Geneva
Switzerland
Tel: 41-22-704-1820
Fax: 41-22-704-1821
http://www.internationalpublishers.org

MAGAZINE PUBLISHERS OF AMERICA
810 7th Ave., 24th Floor
New York, NY 10019
Tel: (212) 872-3700
http://www.magazine.org

NEWSPAPER ASSOCIATION OF AMERICA
4401 Wilson Blvd., Suite 900
Arlington, VA 22203
Tel: (517) 336-1000
Fax: (571) 366-1195
http://www.naa.org

SMALL PUBLISHERS ASSOCIATION OF NORTH
AMERICA
1618 W Colorado Ave.
Colorado Springs, CO 80904
Tel: (719) 475-1726
Fax: (719) 471-2182
http://www.spannet.org

ABOUT THE AUTHOR

Adam Berger holds a Ph.D. in social anthropology from the University of St. Andrews and maintains a strong interest in the interplay between technology and human communication. He has been working in the market research and print journalism fields for over a decade. Berger was the general manager of a small newspaper for two years, until his branch was closed by the large corporation that owned it. He is currently conducting research into the role the Internet plays in shaping future business trends in South Asia.

FURTHER READING

Burns, A. *The Power of the Written Word.* New York: Peter Lang, 1989.

"*Chicago Sun-Times* Files for Bankruptcy." *Chicago Tribune*, March 31, 2009.

"Conde Nast to Close *Gourmet* Magazine." *The Guardian*, October 5, 2009.

Henderson, J. *The World of the Ancient Maya.* Ithaca, N.Y.: Cornell University Press, 1997.

"Indian Media Industry to Outshine Global Peers." *Financial Express*, July 31, 2009.

Madigan, C. *The Collapse of the Great American Newspaper.* Chicago: Ivan R. Dee, 2007.

Martin, S., and D. Copeland. *The Function of Newspapers in Society: A Global Perspective.* Westport, Conn.: Greenwood Press, 2003.

Meyer, P. *The Vanishing Newspaper.* Columbia: University of Missouri Press, 2004.

Moorehouse, A. C. *The Triumph of the Alphabet: A History of Writing.* New York: Henry Schuman, 1953.

Moscati, S. *The Face of the Orient: A Panorama of Near Eastern Civilizations in Pre-classical Times.* Chicago: Quadrangle Books, 1960.

"The New Austerity in Publishing." *The New York Times*, January 4, 2009.

Peddie, R. A. *Printing: A Short History of the Art.* London: Grafton, 1927.

"Seattle P-I to Publish Last Edition Tuesday." *Seattle Post-Intelligencer*, March 17, 2009.

"Tribune Co. Files for Bankruptcy." *Chicago Tribune*, December 9, 2008.

U.S. Bureau of Labor Statistics. *Career Guide to Industries*, 2010-2011 ed. http://www.bls.gov/oco/cg.

U.S. Census Bureau. North American Industry Classification System (NAICS), 2007. http://www.census.gov/cgi-bin/sssd/naics/naicsrch?chart=2007.

U.S. Department of Commerce. International Trade Administration. Office of Trade and Industry Information. Industry Trade Data and Analysis. http://ita.doc.gov/td/industry/otea/OTII/OTII-index.html.

Real Estate Industry

©Dreamstime.com

INDUSTRY SNAPSHOT

General Industry: Real Estate

Career Clusters: Business, Management, and Administration; Marketing, Sales, and Service

Subcategory Industries: Escrow Agencies; Lessors of Miniwarehouses and Self-Storage Units; Lessors of Nonresidential Buildings (Except Miniwarehouses); Lessors of Other Real Estate Property; Lessors of Residential Buildings and Dwellings; Offices of Real Estate Agents and Brokers; Offices of Real Estate Appraisers; Real Estate Asset Management Services; Real Estate Property Managers

Related Industries: Banking Industry; Building Architecture Industry; Building Construction Industry; Environmental Engineering and Consultation Services; Financial Services Industry; Home Maintenance Services; Legal Services and Law Firms

Annual Domestic Revenues: $1.3 billion USD (U.S. Census Bureau, 2009)

Annual International Revenues: $35 billion USD (Urban Land Institute, 2009)

Annual Global Revenues: $90.2 billion USD (Urban Land Institute, 2009)

NAICS Number: 531

INDUSTRY DEFINITION

Summary

The real estate industry affects many aspects of the United States' financial stability. This industry comprises both residential and commercial real estate. It includes anything from the disposition of raw land to development and the value of goodwill in the sale of a commercial establishment. The industry provides real estate services for others and does not include private investors dealing on their own without the use of licensees. Industry employees facilitate the sale, exchange, rental, and leasing of tangible and intangible assets. They also manage, market, and procure those assets, whether with private individuals, with investment corporations, through the banking industry, or through government entities. Real estate licensees provide their services and expertise to assist clients in procuring real estate for the clients' benefit and to ensure that all laws and regulations regarding those transactions are followed.

History of the Industry

What could be termed the first real estate law in England was enacted in 1066, when King William decreed that he owned all of England by right of conquest. He thus had the right to deed the land to other English nobility, who subleased it to commoners in exchange for goods or services. This decree later led to a compilation of English common law and the beginnings of a mortgage system. That law included a provision that a creditor would be given an "interest," or protection in getting his debt paid, by the new owner of a sold property. According to this law, a mortgage was not a final but only a conditional sale until payment was made in full.

After the Industrial Revolution, the banking industry began to provide mortgages. Early mortage recipients were often required to make 50 percent down payments on five-year mortgages. At the end of that term, the unpaid balance would have to be either paid or, if possible, refinanced.

The earliest real estate agents were termed "estate agents," as they were responsible for managing an estate. That role evolved into the role of real estate salesperson. Salespeople worked exclusively for property owners and were given the task of finding buyers. Buyers, for their part, could work only with the agents attached to the properties they wished to purchase. There were no formal standards for conducting this business. By 1913, a group of American real estate agents created bylaws to govern the industry and a code of ethics. In 1916, the term "Realtor" began to be used to identify real estate professionals who were members of the new national association, the National Association of Real Estate Boards (later the National Association of Realtors), and who adhered to its bylaws and code of ethics.

With the Great Depression and the collapse of the banking industry, the Federal Housing Administration (FHA) was created to insure mortgage lenders against losses from default. The FHA developed a thirty-year, fixed-rate loan program. Payments under this program were lower than they had been, so purchasing a house became more feasible for lower-income Americans. Loan terms and interest rates were usually set according to local economies that varied from state to state. In 1938, the government established the Federal National Mortgage Association (FNMA), known as Fannie Mae. It bought those FHA-insured loans and sold them as securities on the financial markets.

The financing arm of real estate evolved to include mortgage bankers and mortgage brokers. Mortgage bankers fund their own loans as direct lenders and have warehouse lines (lines of credit through different banks) to close loans. Just as insurance brokers attempt to find the best policies for their clients' needs from among their selected panels of insurers, loan brokers act as financial intermediaries between borrowers and lenders. Loan brokers originate loans and then broker them to banks or financial institutions. These institutions provide loans to brokers at wholesale rates and pay commissions or fees to brokers for bringing them loan applications. All these financial entities are governed by the department of financial institutions or the department of real estate.

From that small group of people that banded together to form one unified organization, the National Association of Realtors (NAR) has grown to cover all aspects of real estate. Over the years, additional divisions of the industry have occurred to address new specialties and the needs of the public. In the wake of the financial crisis of 2007-2009, the industry continues to evolve, creating training and business practices for handling foreclosures and short sales.

The Industry Today

Today, the NAR has over 1.2 million members. In addition to the specialty divisions of the associa-

Whether representing a client as a buyer or seller, a broker has a duty to negotiate a purchase offer at a price and terms acceptable to that client. (©Dreamstime.com)

tion, affiliates include the National Association of Home Builders Urban Land Institute and Appraisal Institute. Government agencies oversee the licensing guidelines and practices of real estate agents, as well as employing county and city assessors to evaluate private and institutional properties. The U.S. Bureau of Labor Statistics (BLS) projects that real estate broker and sales agent jobs will increase by 14 percent between 2008 and 2018, faster than the average of 11 percent for all occupations. The NAR is one of the largest trade organizations in the country, and it is active in protecting the rights of real estate ownership.

While any individual has the right to contract with another individual to purchase or sell real estate, the complexities and legal ramifications of these transactions motivate most people to use the services of licensed real estate agents. In every U.S. state and the District of Columbia, real estate brokers and sales agents must be licensed. They must pass written examinations according to the guidelines of their states and complete a specific number of hours of classroom instruction.

When a real estate broker is hired to provide a service, an agency relationship is created between the broker and another person, called the principal. All states have laws governing the relationship between real estate agents and clients, whether agents represent buyers, sellers, or both parties. In dual agency, one agent represents both the buyer and the seller in the same transaction. Dual agency is not allowed in some states. Where it is permitted, it must be disclosed to all parties. The buyer and seller must both consent to the dual-agency relationship.

Inputs Consumed by the Real Estate Industry

Input	Value
Energy	$22.9 billion
Materials	$63.0 billion
Purchased services	$641.0 billion
Total	$726.9 billion

Source: U.S. Bureau of Economic Analysis. Data are for 2008.

Brokers have fiduciary duties to their clients or principals. They must act in their clients' best interests and put those interests above all others, including their own. They must also exercise diligent use of their real estate skills and knowledge to represent their clients and carry out all responsibilities of the agency relationship. Brokers are required to safeguard their principals' confidentiality and not disclose any details that could adversely affect a principal unless given permission. However, they are also required to disclose any details of a negotiated property's condition, even if doing so would violate disclosure requirements. If they are involved in property management or in any way handling funds for principals, they must account for all of those funds.

Whether representing a client as a buyer or seller, a broker has a duty to negotiate a purchase offer at a price and terms acceptable to that client. The broker must deliver the offer to the listing agent in a timely manner, and the listing agent is to present any offers to purchase to the seller as soon as is reasonably possible. Brokers are required to provide clients with copies of any agency disclosure forms before writing offers or presenting sellers with offers, so there will be no misunderstanding as to where their loyalties lie.

A real estate agent must be supervised by a real estate broker. Even though the agent may be the only one meeting a given client and drawing up relevant documents, the agent is acting under the au-

The Real Estate Industry's Contribution to the U.S. Economy

Value Added	Amount
Gross domestic product	$1.647 trillion
Gross domestic product	11.4%
Persons employed	1.534 million
Total employee compensation	$80.3 billion

Source: U.S. Bureau of Economic Analysis. Data are for 2008.

		Style	Beds	Baths	Garage	Basmt
SOLD	Main St	Colonial	4	2	2 car	
SOLD	152 Chestnut Ave	Ranch	2	1 1/2	2 car	yes
SOLD	133 Park St East	Ranch	3	2	1 car	no
SOLD	16-B River Ct	Townhouse	2	2 1/2	1 car	no
SOLD	1 Hillside Pl	Victorian	6	3	no	no
SOLD	24 Chestnut Ave	Colonial	3	3	2 car	crawl
SOLD	103 Market St	Row	3	1	no	yes
SOLD	12 Manor Ct	Colonial	4	1	2 car	no
SOLD	11-A River Ct	Townhouse	2	1	1 car	yes
SOLD	214 Oak Ridge Ave	Colonial	3	2 1/2	2 car	no
SOLD	25 Grove St	Ranch	3	2	2 car	no
SOLD	89 Main St	Row	3	1	no	yes
SOLD	184 Sycamore Ave	Split Level	4	2	2 car	no
SOLD***	29 Park St	Colonial	5			
SOLD***	245 Market St					

A listing is an agreement between a property owner and a real estate agent, whereby the agent agrees to find a buyer for the property at a stated price and terms in return for a commission. (©Olivier Le Queinec/Dreamstime.com)

thority of the broker. If an agent leaves a broker's office, the broker's listings—including the ones on which the agent has worked—remain with the broker. Some real estate designations require apprenticeships or specific training programs. These include appraising and commercial sales and leasing. However, all offices train their employees in their specific office procedures. In the field of residential real estate, individual offices also provide some hands-on assistance to new agents to help them through their first few transactions.

Real estate brokers can open their own offices to sell real estate, operate escrow companies, make loans, perform appraisals, provide property management, and run real estate auctions. All these actions entail specific government regulations that attempt to prevent conflicts of interest. Any business associations that have affiliated interests, whether by corporate charter or familial relationship, must be disclosed. Any financial interest gained by completing a real estate transaction must be disclosed,

whether it is an actual part ownership, commission, or potential for profit sharing. As an example, if a real estate brokerage used its own financing company to finance a transaction, it would need to disclose the actual commission on the sale and whether the finance company provides profit sharing to those who work for the brokerage.

Both agents and brokers are required to undergo continuing education as a condition of license renewal. Specific courses required differ from state to state. Failure to complete a state's continuing education requirements within the mandated time frame can result in tempoary suspension of one's license.

Some real estate offices are one-person operations, handling only specific types of real estate transactions, such as property management, appraisals, loans, or sales of specific property types, from residential to commercial. Some offices employ many agents at only one location. Others are parts of national franchises. Many such franchises

During the 2007-2009 economic downturn, many agents and brokerages began specializing in foreclosures. (©Dreamstime.com)

offer full concierge services for their clients. They stage properties for sale, negotiate loans, provide home inspection services, initiate relocation services, and provide referrals for moving companies.

During the financial crisis, many businesses shut down or consolidated offices. However, there is always a need for more agents, as some retire from the industry and others leave to find new careers. During the downturn, many agents and brokerages began specializing in foreclosures, hoping to capture a share of this lucrative field. As many properties began selling at as little as half their previous values, home and commercial ownership became much more affordable than they were at the market's height. These low prices have drawn more buyers into the marketplace.

There is a greater need for licensees to work in the foreclosure segment. Those who have good networking skills and who are willing to research asset management companies can land large contracts with banks and other financial services. This

potential has also increased the need for property management, as financial institutions need assistance in handling their newly foreclosed assets. An agent who can adapt and change will always find a niche in real estate.

INDUSTRY MARKET SEGMENTS

The real estate industry comprises myriad different specialized segments that can be run as individual entities or part of a larger organization including some or all of its aspects. Residential clients can be first-time home buyers, those buying large dream homes, or those downsizing. Agents also work for developers in the tract sale of homes.

The investment side of real estate breaks down into more segments, including transactions for single-family residences, small multiunit dwellings, or large apartment complexes. In commercial real estate, agents deal with sales, exchanges, and leases of commercial buildings, retail centers, or development projects that start from raw land and progress to full construction and development. Property managers handle all types of real estate, from homes to apartments to commercial and business structures. A small subset of the market deals with the exchange of real estate, which can comprise anything from raw land to homes to multiunits to commercial or industrial projects, as well as the exchange of real estate securities.

There are nearly 2 million active real estate licensees across the country. Of these licensees, 1.2 million are Realtors, who account for approximately 60 percent of the licensees nationwide. Although approximately 82 percent of all Realtors specialize in residential real estate, most also have secondary focuses.

Small Businesses

The majority of real estate offices are small businesses. The median staff size is fewer than twenty-five licensees and five or fewer nonlicensed employees. Just over 51 percent of real estate offices are independently owned and run as nonfranchised firms. Firms that are part of larger franchise organizations vary in size from location to location. Some may just be satellite branches of larger offices. While most agents work at offices, more than seven out of ten Realtors have home offices as well. Computer access is the lifeblood of the business, and agents make that access a priority.

Potential Annual Earnings Scale. According to NAR statistics, the median income among Realtors was $36,700 in 2008, down from $42,600 in 2007. Licensed brokers earned a median of $49,300, while sales agents earned a median of $28,400. The gap in income between brokers and agents is accounted for by the fact that they brokers have others working for them and also have more experience in the business. Realtors in the business for two years or less earned a median of $8,600, while those with three to five years of experience earned $27,100. For those with six to fifteen years of expe-

In commercial real estate, agents deal with sales, exchanges, and leases of commercial buildings and retail centers. (AP/Wide World Photos)

rience, the median was $42,400, while members in the business for sixteen years or more earned a median of $53,900. A real estate broker who is a strong producer and who manages a team of agents working exclusively for that broker may be able to earn in excess of $100,000 or even $250,000. As real estate is predominantly a commission-based business, individual earnings can vary greatly depending on the effort put into the business.

Clientele Interaction. Most agents, even those working as members of an office, are responsible for their own business. New agents may be given leads or direct clients to get started. However, to increase their income, they must bring in new clients by promoting their business to family, friends, and other business affiliates.

For a business to continue to grow, it requires a base of repeat clients. Real estate is a person-to-person business in which client relationships are central. Agents must communicate weekly if not daily with active clients to keep them informed of the progress of their transactions. Most real estate business is lost not because an agent is not likable or proficient but rather because a client feels forgotten in the process.

Agents should continue to keep in touch with clients after their transactions are complete. Even if one's clients are not seeking help with any further transactions, they are an important promotional resource. Past and current clients should account for a minimum of 20 percent of an agent's referrals. For new agents, that figure decreases to just 1 percent, as such agents may not have realized the value of referrals to their business—or may not have enough clients to produce sufficient referrals.

Most agents do not work nine-to-five daily schedules. They must be available when their clients are available. Since most clients work themselves, agents must be available during off hours, when the clients themselves are not working. Only 12 percent of Realtors work fewer than twenty hours per week. Some 31 percent work twenty to thirty-nine hours per week, 43 percent work forty to fifty-nine hours per week, and 14 percent work at least sixty hours per week.

Amenities, Atmosphere, and Physical Grounds. Most real estate offices that are run in commercial settings have visible access for new and current clients to find. They include reception areas designed to promote a professional yet relaxed atmosphere for clients. In many instances, front-desk personnel are licensees who are the first contacts for clients. The back office consists in most cases of attached cubicles for individual agents. Those agents who bring in a larger portion of the business may have their own private offices, as well as subordinate staff working for them. Managers also often have private offices. Office personnel that are nonlicensed may have cubicles or sections of private offices. All offices have conference rooms where agents can meet with clients in private. Separate areas are usually set aside for shared office equipment, and most offices have break rooms for coffee. Depending on the size of the office, there may be shared computers or agents may be responsible for providing their own computers.

Typical Number of Employees. According to the BLS, about 61 percent of all business establishments employ fewer than five workers. The median staff size of real estate firms is less than thirty employees. The number of employees at a given firm or in a given area may ebb and flow with the real estate cycle. Only during the boom cycles will a large number of offices employ more thanone hundred people each in a set location.

Traditional Geographic Locations. Most real estate offices are centrally located in business parks or cities for high visibility and easy client access. Some occupy separate buildings, while others are attached to other businesses in strip malls or office complexes. Offices that promote resort properties may be located in tourist-friendly areas, the better to capture potential clients' interest. However, those who specialize in appraisals or residential property management may not have traditional storefronts at all but rather work solely out of their homes. With the growing importance of the Internet and smart phones, physical business storefront locations are no longer necessary for all professionals.

Pros of Working for a Small Business. New agents are likely to receive one-on-one training in small offices. They have greater access to colleagues and superiors to observe the workings of the industry than do agents at larger firms. Seasoned professionals who have opened their own small firms gain control over their business environments, costs, and major decisions. Small businesses are sometimes able to avoid the office politics that are often part of larger offices.

Cons of Working for a Small Business. Small offices are generally limited in scope and must specialize in particular types of real estate or particular services. Employees may find that the particular areas of specialization of their employers do not fit their needs or skills. Moreover, those starting out will be unable to try a full range of transactions and real estate segments to determine which best suit their skills and temperament.

Costs

Payroll and Benefits: Many of the employees in the real estate industry are independent contractors working entirely or partly on commission. Managers are usually the only employees given vacation or sick leave. Agents control their own time, planning work schedules, vacation, and sick leave as appropriate. If business is steady, they may need to work many days in a row without taking any days off. Paid health care benefits are usually reserved for management, but other employees may have the option of participating in company health care plans at their own cost. Depending on the size of the office and its affiliation with a franchise, there may be options for profit sharing, though that is unusual.

Supplies: Small real estate offices require paper and postage, as well as filing cabinets, copiers, scanning equipment, desks, and reception-area furnishings. They also need information technology equipment, such as digital cameras, computers, faxes, and telephones. Those that handle their own cleaning require cleaning supplies.

External Services: Depending on the expertise of management, small real estate offices may contract accounting services or computer maintenance services. Those in freestanding buildings often contract landscapers or groundskeepers. They may also contract security, cleaning, advertising, legal, maintenance, and paper-shredding

Some real estate agents specialize in residential properties, such as these Victorians in San Francisco. (©Dreamstime.com)

services as necessary. Though not a requirement in most states, many real estate companies also purchase a type of malpractice insurance called errors and omissions insurance.

Utilities: Standard utilities for a small office include electricity, telephone, and Internet access. If the office is a freestanding building or in a fully self-contained office space, it may also pay for water and sewage services.

Taxes: Small businesses are required to pay corporate taxes at the local, state, and federal levels. They are also responsible for any applicable business taxes, local and state licensing fees, and property taxes. Self-employed agents may report their business income on personal returns, in which case they must pay self-employment taxes. Otherwise, employers must pay payroll taxes for their employees.

Other Expenses: Other costs include affiliation membership fees and dues.

Midsize Businesses

Midsize firms generally employ between twenty-five people and one hundred people. They may occupy a single office location or multiple locations.

They often include ancillary services that are housed on site or in adjacent locations.

Potential Annual Earnings Scale. Earnings of agents are based on individual productivity, rather than business size. Managers in midsize businesses have greater opportunities to increase their own incomes by motivating their staffs to increase their productivity. According to the BLS, the middle 50 percent of wage earners earned between $27,370 and $63,510 in 2009. During the same period, the middle 50 percent of brokers earned between $35,090 and $93,300. Depending on specialization, there could be as much as a 35 percent difference in income.

Clientele Interaction. In a midsize business, front-office personnel are usually office workers and not licensees. Client interaction is still handled on a one-to-one basis. All licensees are responsible for their own business. However, there is a greater possibility that they will work as teams. Within each team, some members work on paperwork and analysis, while others handle all client interaction. Managers are generally more involved in promoting their companies through their business and social affiliations, increasing the name recognition and prestige of their firms. They also need to maintain close interactions with their employees to make sure that policies are followed and any issues are promptly addressed that could otherwise cause problems for the firm.

Amenities, Atmosphere, and Physical Grounds. To accommodate a larger staff and to generate more revenues to cover their related costs, midsize offices are usually located either in separate buildings or in large sections of office buildings. They tend to have larger front reception areas to accommodate more waiting clients. They are designed to promote a professional atmosphere and to showcase some of their awards and related business affiliations. Midsize offices have several conference rooms and private offices, as well as large areas for office cubicles or freestanding desks. Break rooms may include some vending machines, and technology rooms are larger and contain more shared equipment on average than those of small firms. Midsize businesses may also manage affiliated businesses located within close proximity to facilitate better working relationships. If an office's location is freestanding, it may feature an outdoor patio area with tables and benches.

Typical Number of Employees. Midsize businesses generally employ twenty-five to one hundred people. Staff size often rises and falls as business volume changes.

Traditional Geographic Locations. Midsize offices are predominantly located in suburban or metropolitan areas that are centrally located in business sectors. Real estate offices often seek locations with heavy foot traffic, at busy intersections, or in close proximity to freeways to increase visibility and accessibility.

Pros of Working for a Midsize Business. Employees of midsize businesses have greater opportunities to see how different segments of the real estate business work. They enjoy greater interaction with agents at all different stages of the business. Midsize firms may offer apprenticeship programs, and they generally provide more office promotions and advertising to enhance their corporate image, as well as that of individual agents. Office production is motivated by contests and sales drives for prizes and awards of merit, which are publicized in local media. New agents receive personalized training, and managers are generally available to counsel and guide them. Those ready for management positions will find more options available in midsize companies, as their greater diversity entails a greater variety of managerial roles.

Cons of Working for a Midsize Business. New employees of midsize firms are expected to get up to speed quickly after their initial training and orientation. They must quickly learn to work independently and produce results. They are expected by their supervisors to engage in significant self-promotion and to bear the costs of doing so themselves. Employees of midsize firms must generally attend weekly marketing or regional meetings. They are more likely to be in competition with fellow staffers for awarded clients based on merit.

Costs

Payroll and Benefits: The greatest portion of the staff at midsize firms work entirely or partly on commission. However, these firms have more hourly and salaried employees than do small firms to free up agents to have more time to bring in new business. Paid health care benefits are reserved for management, but highly productive agents may also be given paid health care benefits as retention incentives. Offices with franchise affiliations often have options for profit sharing or provide other cash incentives.

Supplies: Real estate offices require marketing materials, paper, and postage, as well as filing cabinets, copiers, scanning equipment, desks, and conference room and reception-area furnishings. Additional needs are pinpoint presentation materials and equipment for office or client meetings, as well as other information technology equipment such as digital cameras, computers, faxes, and phones.

External Services: Real estate companies may contract accounting services and computer maintenance services. They usually contract interior maintenance service and secure disposal of old files by paper shredders. They may also contract Web design services or other public relations, groundskeeping, landscaping, legal, security, and cleaning services as appropriate. Although not a requirement in most states, midsize offices usually purchase errors and omissions insurance.

Utilities: Standard utilities for midsize offices include electricity, telephone, and Internet access. If the office is freestanding or in a fully self-contained office space, it might also be responsible for water and sewage services

Taxes: Midsize businesses are required to pay corporate taxes at the local, state, and federal levels. They are also responsible for any applicable business taxes, local and state licensing fees, and property taxes.

Other Expenses: Other costs include advertising and affiliation membership fees and dues. There will be additional corporate fees if the business is part of a franchise operation.

Large Businesses

Large real estate businesses may be located in single structures or in multiple locations as part of corporate or franchise operations. They often include ancillary services that are housed on-site or in adjacent locations to offer complete concierge services for their clients. Large businesses employ more than one hundred people.

Potential Annual Earnings Scale. According to the BLS, in 2009, the top 10 percent of real estate sales agents earned more than $96,410 in 2009, while the top 10 percent of brokers earned well in excess of $166,400. It is not usual for top producers to earn in the $250,000 to $500,000 range, and superstars earn in excess of $1 million per year. However, as business cycles change and large contracts move from one office to another, these high income levels may not be consistent from year to year, office to office, or agent to agent.

Clientele Interaction. In large businesses, client interaction is usually more compartmentalized than at smaller firms. Front-office personnel are office workers assigned strictly to meet and greet clients, direct them to the correct associates, and answer incoming telephone calls. Client interaction remains one-to-one, but there are more layers of staff involved that at smaller offices. This staff takes on much of the day-to-day client interaction, freeing agents to bring in more clients. Individuals still need a base of repeat clients, but they also have staff or automated systems to help them keep in touch with past clients for continued business and referrals. Managers are involved in promoting their companies through business and social affiliations, as well as charitable fund-raisers, to increase the name recognition and prestige of their firms.

Amenities, Atmosphere, and Physical Grounds. Large businesses promote themselves by choosing prestigious locations. The layout and design of front offices and client access areas are intended to enhance their images as leaders in the industry. They have separate reception areas for the different concierge services they offer. Each reception or conference area has promotional materials at hand to familiarize clients with all the services the firms provide and to showcase the awards won by offices and individuals.

Large firms are located in their own buildings or occupy multiple floors of office buildings. Back offices, not accessible to clients, include areas for office cubicles or freestanding desks. Large break rooms or multipurpose rooms accommodate the large staffs of these firms and may include vending machines and small kitchen areas. Large technology rooms include shared equipment, and conference rooms are set up to accommodate video meetings or special presentations.

Although large businesses may be in just one location, they usually consist of several satellite or branch offices located throughout a region, state, or country. They may even have international locations. In most cases, they are held by private individuals or investment groups. Branch or satellite offices have amenities similar to those of small or midsize companies.

Typical Number of Employees. Large real estate businesses employ at least one hundred people, and some employ several hundred in differing locations. These numbers increase or decrease in tandem with corporate market share.

Traditional Geographic Locations. Large businesses usually have flagship locations in major metropolitan business districts. Branch locations may be located in suburban, rural, or resort areas or in retail mall settings.

Pros of Working for a Large Business. In a large organization, there are more opportunities to move up the corporate ladder than there are in smaller businesses. Large firms offer concierge services to promote and enhance their business. Employees can see and interact with more fellow agents who work in different aspects of the real estate industry, providing a better idea of what segment of the industry one may wish to specialize in.

Large companies expend greater resources on promotional materials and advertising, enhancing both their corporate images and the images of individual agents. Office production is motivated by contests and sales drives for prizes and awards of merit, which are publicized in the media. New employees receive personalized training, and apprentice programs compensate those who assist new hires. Management staff are available to counsel and guide them as necessary. A greater variety of management positions exists than in smaller firms, providing more opportunities and options for career growth.

Cons of Working for a Large Business. The greatest drawback to working in a large company is its compartmentalization. While large firms are diverse, individual employees may be forced to specialize. They may be assigned to segregated divisions and expected to refer clients who prefer other services to other divisions or branches of their companies, rather than providing those services themselves. Agents may lack one-on-one relationships with clients, as most client needs are handled by support staff and others. In addition, larger offices have greater potential for backbiting and politics, which may not only affect morale but may also draw away clients. Managers at large firms must attend to more and greater complexities and details, which can easily spin out of control and

lead their businesses into downward spirals or total shutdowns if specific licensing requirements are not adhered to properly.

Costs

Payroll and Benefits: Large companies' payrolls are complicated by the several layers of staff the companies employ, as well as the graduated payments involved in commission structures. They employ a greater number of hourly or salaried employees than smaller firms, as well as those temporarily hired to cover large projects. Paid health care benefits are still reserved for management, but other high-revenue-producing employees may also be given such benefits as retention incentives. Many large firms offer profit sharing, stock options, or other cash incentives.

Supplies: Real estate offices require marketing materials, paper, and postage, as well as filing cabinets, copiers, scanning equipment, desks, and conference room and reception-area furnishings. Additional needs are pinpoint presentation materials and equipment for office or client meetings, as well as other information technology equipment such as digital cameras, computers, faxes, and phones.

External Services: Real estate companies may contract accounting services and computer maintenance services. They usually contract interior maintenance service and secure disposal of old files by paper shredders. They may also contract Web design services or other public relations, groundskeeping, landscaping, security, and cleaning services as appropriate. Large companies purchase errors and omissions insurance or have affiliates that provide it. They usually employ their own in-house legal staffs.

Utilities: Standard utilities for large offices include electricity, telephone, Internet access, water, and sewage.

Taxes: Large businesses are required to pay corporate taxes at the local, state, and federal levels. They are also responsible for any applicable business taxes, local and state licensing fees, and property taxes.

Other Expenses: Other costs include advertising and affiliation membership fees and dues. There will be additional corporate fees if the business is part of a franchise operation.

ORGANIZATIONAL STRUCTURE AND JOB ROLES

The organizational structure within the real estate industry and the tasks related to specific job categories are typically based on the size of the company. In small offices, managers deal with most of the major tasks and delegate duties to employees as necessary. In midsize and large offices, managers oversee defined departments, and each employee generally has specific tasks related to his or her position. The duties and responsibilities of those in the real estate industry remain similar, however.

The following umbrella categories apply to the organizational structure of businesses in the real estate industry:

- Executive Management
- Support and Educational Training
- Sales and Marketing
- Real Estate Licensees
- Information Technology
- Human Resources
- Administrative Support
- Maintenance and Security

Executive Management

Executive management handles the general operations of the business. These individuals oversee major operations, set corporate objectives, handle brand development, and chart the financial courses of their organizations. They may manage regional areas or departments within the corporate structure. Executive managers may have advanced degrees in business administration, finance, accounting, or marketing. As real estate is a growing and evolving industry, in many cases experience has served as a substitute for advanced college education; however, industry-related courses and designations are generally necessary for upward mobility in the business. Executive managers usually earn higher salaries than anyone else in their specific sectors of the industry. They are responsible for franchise sales, brand development, corporate communication, implementation of corporate systems, recruiting, training, marketing, and regional development.

Executive management occupations may include the following:

- General Manager
- Chief Executive Officer (CEO)
- Chief Financial Officer (CFO)
- Executive Officer for Affiliated Companies
- Executive Officer for Member Services
- Marketing Director
- Sales Director
- Business Development Director
- Senior Information Technology Officer
- Senior Customer Relations Officer
- General Counsel

Support and Educational Training

Training personnel handle the development of educational materials and training in regards to specific areas of expertise. All segments of real estate entail continuing-education requirements to maintain licensure. Courses to meet these requirements need to be developed within the industry and then approved by relevant state or federal licensing boards as fulfilling their educatioanal criteria. Training materials may be designed for online access only, or they may be intended for use in classrooms. These materials, including curricula, workbooks, quizzes, and other instruction guides, may be developed by a franchise for system-wide use, as general designs applying to a broad range of real estate fields, or as specific to a particular designation.

Support and educational training occupations may include the following:

- Institutional Accrediting Development Specialist
- Instructional Research and Development Specialist
- Compliance Officer
- Graphic Designer
- Customer Service Representative
- Course Instructor

Sales and Marketing

Sales and marketing personnel handle both the expansion and the development of franchises and individual corporations. Their duties may include the design of corporate logos or trademarks, de-

OCCUPATION SPECIALTIES

Property and Real Estate Managers

Specialty	Responsibilities
Apartment house managers	Collect fees for rent, direct maintenance, inspect apartments, and perform other duties.
Land development managers	Negotiate with various organizations to acquire and develop land.
Land leases and rental managers	Direct and manage land leases relative to rights for drilling oil or gas wells.
Leasing managers	Secure leases and other agreements for land, as well as rights for gas and oil companies.
Public events facilities rental managers	Negotiate contracts for arenas, stadiums, or other facilities.
Real estate land agents	Negotiate the purchase and sale of properties and coordinate real estate departments.
Right-of-way agents	Negotiate with property owners and public officials for utilities and other projects.

sign of advertising materials, and placement in the media and implementation of campaigns to enhance revenues within offices. Upper-end sales and marketing personnel usually have at least undergraduate degrees in business management, marketing, or finance-related disciplines, although that may not be the case in more localized operations. Their salaries are competitive and often include performance incentives.

The primary tasks of sales and marketing personnel on a larger corporate level are to track and analyze the production levels of offices and design materials or programs to enhance their revenues. They also promote their companies at trade shows, conferences, and sales conventions. On a more individual-office level, these personnel are responsible for corporate branding, public relations, sponsorship, advertising design and placement, and sales campaigns and incentives.

Sales and marketing occupations may include the following:

- Corporate Sales Manager
- Sales Director
- Marketing Director
- Advertising Manager
- Office Manager

Real Estate Licensees

The bulk of real estate industry employees are licensees. These include independent agents, as well as those working within offices. All real estate offices are required to have licensed brokers in charge of their overall operations. A broker may be in charge of one office or several. Most upper-level managers either are or once were licensed real estate brokers. All personnel who perform the duties of a real estate broker or agent must be licensed according to state and federal regulations. Agents may handle only their own sales or work in teams with other agents or brokers. All licensees are required to complete continuing-education courses to retain their licenses. Their duties include promoting their individual business to the general public, performing specific analyses related to their specialties, meeting with the public, and preparing marketing plans. They also need to adhere to all rules and regulations pertaining to their associational and affiliate designations.

Real estate licensee occupations may include the following:

- Real Estate Broker
- Mortgage Loan Broker
- Real Estate Securities Broker
- Title Officer
- Escrow Officer
- Office Manager
- Property Manager
- Leasing Agent
- Real Estate Counselor
- Real Estate Developer
- Auctioneer
- Asset Manager
- Appraiser
- Exchanger
- Real Estate Trainer

Information Technology

Depending on the size of a business, it may employ on-site personnel to manage its computer and video systems. Smaller firms may contract these services from independent providers. Information technology (IT) personnel are responsible for setting up all devices and hardware typically used during meetings and presentations. They maintain an office's computer networks and systems, and they may also create video presentations or support others in the use of multimedia technology. They must have training in computer and information technology and need to keep abreast of changes in the field and upgrades to existing technology.

IT occupations may include the following:

- Information Technology Director
- Network Administrator
- Multimedia Technician
- Video Assistant

OCCUPATION PROFILE

Real Estate Sales Agent

Considerations	Qualifications
Description	Rents, buys, or sells property for owner; prepares documents.
Career clusters	Business, Management, and Administration; Marketing, Sales, and Service
Interests	Data; people
Working conditions	Work inside
Minimum education level	On-the-job training; high school diploma or GED; junior/technical/community college
Physical exertion	Light work
Physical abilities	Unexceptional/basic fitness
Opportunities for experience	Part-time work
Licensure and certification	Required
Employment outlook	Faster-than-average growth expected
Holland interest score	ESR

Note: See volume 1, "Publisher's Note," for an explanation of the Holland interest score.

Human Resources

Human resources personnel are responsible for salaried, commissioned, and contract employees. They will usually handle employee hiring and dismissal, employee relations, and benefits (such as employee incentives, insurance, and profit sharing). They also assist employees seeking relocation services. Human resources managers are well trained in management, through experience and industry-related, as well as college-level education.

Human resources occupations may include the following:

- Human Resources Director
- Human Resources Coordinator
- Human Resources Manager
- Administrative Assistant

Administrative Support

Administrative personnel are located throughout all levels of the industry, assisting each department in its operations. Administrative staff may be part of the front office or any other office. They may prepare client packages, communicate with clients, input data, assign or perform pickup and delivery of promotional materials, maintain records, or provide support to managers or other employees as the need arises. In some cases, they are— or begin employment as—temporary personnel, but in most instances they are in-house staff. They will usually earn salaries but in some cases earn base pay plus bonuses based on the productivity of the personnel they directly assist.

In larger offices, these personnel are overseen by administrative managers who maintain the smooth operation of their offices. Managers are responsible for the front office, budgeting for equipment and its maintenance, reconciling accounting services or financial departments, and maintaining proper licensing.

Occupations in this area include the following:

- Operations Director
- Office Manager
- Accounting Manager
- Administrative Assistant
- Secretary
- Front-Desk Staff/Receptionist
- Transaction Coordinator
- Intern

Maintenance and Security

Usually only the larger real estate firms employ in-house maintenance or security personnel. In most instances, they contracted such services. Maintenance staff repair malfunctioning building systems. While not an integral part of operations, without their assistance businesses could come to a halt or be financially damaged. Security personnel ensure that any emergency situations are addressed and monitor surveillance cameras, conduct periodic rounds, and respond to relevant calls.

Maintenance and security occupations may include the following:

- Chief Engineer
- Heating, Ventilation, and Air-Conditioning (HVAC) Specialist
- Plumber
- Security Operations Manager
- Security Officer

INDUSTRY OUTLOOK

Overview

The outlook for this industry tentatively shows it to be on the rise. Real estate was at the center of the financial crisis of 2007-2009. In the wake of that crisis, real estate will continue to be a prime indicator of recovery and national economic strength or weakness. When recovery does take place, it will encompass the residential sector first, as the commercial real estate sector traditionally lags behind the former sector. Over the long term, there will always be a demand for real estate, as it is a good long-term investment, and thus there will be increasing demand for agents and brokers as the economy improves.

According to U.S. Census Bureau statistics, housing starts hit a record high of 2.07 million in 2005 and then began to decline. Unemployment in the United States is expected to remain higher than average through at least 2015 or 2020. Mortgage rates are extremely likely to rise in the next decade from the lows they reached during the first decade of the twenty-first century. In addition, the credit crunch instituted during and in the wake of the global financial crisis will continue to affect underwriting guidelines, so home financing will become more difficult to secure for the average borrower.

Real estate offices are becoming leaner and more productive as brokers trim staff and reduce their marketing and advertising expenses to survive the downturn. However, the same offices are increasing their spending on technology and agent recruitment. To stay competitive, they are focusing on technology and online marketing.

Of considerable concern is what has been termed "shadow inventory." These are properties that have been foreclosed, or with loans delinquent ninety days or more, that are not officially on the market. The number of shadow properties has been on the rise, while traditional inventory has only moderately decreased. Depending on how and when these shadow properties come onto the market, they could pose a significant risk to future home-price stability. Many experts believe price stability is what many buyers and sellers are looking for before they make the decision buy or sell a property.

The sought-after price stability is emerging in some markets, while in other markets a pent-up demand for homes is being released as a result of their relative affordability. The latter markets are seeing multiple offers per property and bidding wars.

Economic growth throughout Europe is expected to be subdued, as unemployment is expected to remain high. Capital values of real estate are bottoming out in some cases and then rising quickly in anticipation of recovery. However, the fundamentals of the real estate market in all sectors are still deteriorating and will remain under pressure. Those institutions and corporations that plan to expand in the real estate sector are focusing on prime income-producing properties. In the Asian markets, there has been a small rebound in the real estate markets and a projected prospect of renewed profits. However, transaction levels have remained depressed by historical standards, with many large investors staying on the sidelines for the time being. In Latin America, most economies have been damaged or are unstable—with the exception of Brazil, which is flourishing. In Mexico, the real estate markets are still dropping substantially, mostly as a result of the U.S. recession.

PROJECTED EMPLOYMENT FOR SELECTED OCCUPATIONS

Real Estate Industry

Employment		
2009	Projected 2018	Occupation
50,860	58,800	Bookkeeping, accounting, and auditing clerks
25,950	25,300	General and operations managers
33,220	41,100	Landscaping and groundskeeping workers
234,980	273,600	Maintenance and repair workers, general
90,460	115,500	Office clerks, general
112,610	134,800	Property, real estate, and community association managers
43,270	52,200	Real estate brokers
117,440	156,300	Real estate sales agents

Source: U.S. Bureau of Labor Statistics, Industries at a Glance, Occupational Employment Statistics and Employment Projections Program.

Employment Advantages

Ambitious, people-oriented, persevering, and self-motivated people may find that careers in real estate can help them achieve their goals. In most cases, income is reflective of effort, and significant skill and hard work can result in very high earnings. Working in real estate allows for independence, but it requires flexibility in making time for one's clients.

The real estate industry provides a broad range

PROJECTED EMPLOYMENT FOR SELECTED OCCUPATIONS

Real Estate Rental and Leasing

Employment		
2009	Projected 2018	Occupation
202,870	221,100	Counter and rental clerks
245,700	285,700	Maintenance and repair workers, general
112,760	134,900	Property, real estate, and community association managers
43,310	52,300	Real estate brokers
117,630	156,900	Real estate sales agents

Source: U.S. Bureau of Labor Statistics, Industries at a Glance, Occupational Employment Statistics and Employment Projections Program.

minimal increases in median home prices, whereas Fannie Mae economists expect a slight decline. Fannie Mae does expect sales of new and existing homes to rebound, however.

The commercial real estate market is in a much greater state of decline because of uncertainties relating to changing governmental regulations, financing guidelines, and unemployment. Commercial real estate and rental and leasing job openings fell by 40 percent in 2009. In a slowing economy, well-developed analytical skills and marketing capabilities can often make the difference when downsizing occurs. Graduates of specialized master's degree programs in real estate enjoyed a 1 percent increase in salaries from 2003 through 2007; however, starting salaries for the 2008 graduates of such programs decreased by 4.3 percent. The real estate market overall remains on shaky ground.

of career options, from residential sales to industrial property sales and leasing, land development, property management, mortgage banking, urban planning, real estate counseling, appraisal, real estate investment trusts, and marketing and sales. One may work with a large or small firm or as an independent brokerage.

Most individuals begin their real estate careers as sales trainees or in apprenticeship programs in brokerage firms. Through industry-taught continuing education courses or through college courses and work experience, trainees move up the corporate ladder. Employees have the option of developing specialty skills that make the best use of their personal abilities. Real estate is a rewarding career, offering the opportunity to build a secure future for oneself and also to help shape the future of one's community.

Annual Earnings

The real estate sector has been greatly affected by the global financial crisis of 2007-2009. As property values have decreased, so has the income related to their sales and leasing. The Mortgage Bankers Association and the NAR both project

RELATED RESOURCES FOR FURTHER RESEARCH

APPRAISAL INSTITUTE
550 W Van Buren St., Suite 1000
Chicago, IL 60607
Tel: (888) 756-4624
Fax: (312) 335-4400
http://www.appraisalinstitute.org

CCIM INSTITUTE
430 N Michigan Ave., Suite 800
Chicago, IL 60611
Tel: (800) 621-7027
Fax: (312) 321-4530
http://www.ccim.com

COUNCIL OF RESIDENTIAL SPECIALISTS
430 N Michigan Ave., Suite 300
Chicago, IL 60611-4092
Tel: (800) 462-8841
Fax: (312) 329-8882
http://www.crs.com

INSTITUTE OF REAL ESTATE MANAGEMENT
430 N Michigan Ave.
Chicago, IL 60611
Tel: (800) 837-0706
Fax: (800) 338-4736
http://www.irem.org

NATIONAL ASSOCIATION OF REALTORS
430 N Michigan Ave.
Chicago, IL 60611-4087
Tel: (800) 874-6500
Fax: (312) 329-5962
http://www.realtor.org

U.S. DEPARTMENT OF HOUSING AND URBAN
DEVELOPMENT
451 7th St. SW
Washington, DC 20410
Tel: (202) 708-1112
http://portal.hud.gov

ABOUT THE AUTHOR

Christine Henderson has been working in the real estate industry since the mid-1980's, through the characteristic upturns and downturns experienced by the market. She has continually updated her education and has educated both her clients and other Realtors. She has been the editor of a regional real estate newspaper and has worked on both the Grievance and Professional Standards Committees of the Inland Valley Association of Realtors in Calfiornia to review cases and make decisions on the validity of charges brought against members of the regional board of Realtors.

FURTHER READING

CB Richard Ellis Group. "CB Richard Ellis's 2009 Review and 2010 Outlook for Commercial Real Estate in Europe." December, 2009/January, 2010. http://www.cbre.com/EN/AboutUs/MediaCentre/2010/Pages/011110.aspx.

Harkins, Phil. *Everybody Wins: The Story and Lessons Behind RE/MAX.* Hoboken, N.J.: John Wiley & Sons, 2004.

Keller, Gary, with Dave Jenks and Jay Papasan. *The Millionaire Real Estate Agent: It's Not About the Money . . . It's About Being the Best You Can Be!* New York: McGraw Hill, 2004.

Lindahl, David. *Emerging Real Estate Markets: How to Find and Profit from Up-and-Coming Areas.* Hoboken, N.J.: John Wiley & Sons, 2008.

Malpass, Peter, and Robert Rowlands. *Housing, Markets, and Policy.* New York: Routledge, 2010.

National Association of REALTORS. *Field Guide to the History of the National Association of REALTORS.* July, 2008. http://www.realtor.org/library/library/fg002.

Plunkett, Jack W. *Plunkett's Real Estate and Construction Industry Almanac, 2010.* Houston, Tex.: Plunkett Research, 2010.

Riley, Rowan. *Real Estate: An All-in-One Guide to Navigating Toward a New Career.* New York: Ferguson, 2010.

Urban Land Institute and PricewaterhouseCoopers. *Emerging Trends in Real Estate, 2009-2010.* Washington, D.C.: Author, 2009.

U.S. Bureau of Labor Statistics. *Career Guide to Industries,* 2010-2011 ed. http://www.bls.gov/oco/cg.

U.S. Census Bureau. North American Industry Classification System (NAICS), 2007. http://www.census.gov/cgi-bin/sssd/naics/naicsrch?chart=2007.

U.S. Department of Commerce. International Trade Administration. Office of Trade and Industry Information. Industry Trade Data and Analysis. http://ita.doc.gov/td/industry/otea/OTII/OTII-index.html.

Rental and Leasing Services

©Dreamstime.com

INDUSTRY SNAPSHOT

General Industry: Personal Services

Career Clusters: Architecture and Construction; Manufacturing; Marketing, Sales, and Service; Transportation, Distribution, and Logistics

Subcategory Industries: Automotive Equipment Rental and Leasing; Consumer Goods Rental; General Rental Centers; Commercial and Industrial Machinery; Equipment Rental and Leasing

Related Industries: Automobiles and Personal Vehicles Industry; Construction Equipment Industry; Freight Transport Industry

Annual Domestic Revenues: $90.6 billion USD (U.S. Census Bureau, 2010)

Annual International Revenues: $560 billion USD (*Leasing News* and *World Leasing Yearbook*, 2009 and 2010)

Annual Global Revenues: $650 billion USD (*Leasing News* and *World Leasing Yearbook*, 2009 and 2010)

NAICS Numbers: 532, 5321, 5322, 5323, 5324

INDUSTRY DEFINITION

Summary

The rental and leasing services industry involves businesses that allow consumers to use diverse products distributed from various commercial settings, such as stores, car lots, and warehouses, for a specified period of time without buying the products. This industry provides people an affordable alternative to purchasing equipment that may be expensive or needed only for a short period of time. It also allows them to avoid being financially responsible for upkeep, insurance, and legal costs associated with ownership of those goods. Internationally, this industry thrives by meeting customer needs for common products frequently used by businesses and individuals. Contracts specify the cost and duration of the lease. Some leases incorporate provisions for lessees to purchase rental items.

History of the Industry

The rental and leasing industry has existed for several thousand years. The earliest known lease, in Mesopotamia around 2010 B.C.E., was of agricultural equipment. Ancient Romans, Greeks, Phoenicians, and Egyptians benefited financially from rental agreements, including leasing ships and vehicles for traders to transport goods to markets and providing military troops with weapons and supplies. During the following centuries, the rental and leasing industry expanded to other continents, where people leased modes of transportation, tools, and equipment for diverse purposes.

In the nineteenth century, expenses associated with railroad technology resulted in an early form of equipment leasing. Investors bought costly locomotives and railcars directly from manufacturers and lent them to railroads. Lessees also rented cargo space on ships. Henry Ford's Model T automobile was the catalyst for the rental car industry. In 1916, Nebraskan Joe Saunders began renting out his Model T Ford to traveling salespeople. In 1918, Chicagoan Walter L. Jacobs began leasing a fleet of Model T Fords to customers, and five years later, he was earning $1 million per year. John Hertz, the president of the Yellow Cab Company and the Yellow Truck and Coach Manufacturing Company, acquired Jacobs's business, which he renamed the Hertz Drive-Ur-Self System. He sold it to General Motors Corporation in 1926, but when the Hertz Corporation was formed in 1954, Hertz became its president.

The leasing industry slowed because of the economic crisis during the Great Depression. By the early 1940's, World War II manufacturing demands had reinvigorated the rental industry. The U.S. federal government leased equipment to companies that produced goods necessary for the war effort. After World War II, more people began

The Rental and Leasing Industry's Contribution to the U.S. Economy

Value Added	Amount
Gross domestic product	$195.5 billion
Gross domestic product	1.4%
Persons employed	649,000
Total employee compensation	$30.0 billion

Source: U.S. Bureau of Economic Analysis. Data are for 2008.

flying, creating a need for rental cars to provide transportation from the airport to their final destinations. In 1932, Hertz created a rental car facility at Chicago's Midway Airport; it later would establish franchises at most major airport hubs. In 1946, former pilot Warren Avis started Avis Rent A Car at a Detroit airport.

Consumers, ranging from individuals to corporations, demanded more rental opportunities during the 1950's, seeking leases for items as diverse as medical devices and furniture used in homes and hospitals and machinery and construction equipment needed for postwar building and interstate highway projects. Leasing appealed to businesses that manufactured products incorporating new technologies, such as televisions, and that needed modern machinery for production. Automobile, railroad, and aviation manufacturers relied on leased equipment to manufacture large quantities of vehicles efficiently and profitably.

The Internal Revenue Service (IRS) approved generous deductions for equipment lessors in the Internal Revenue Code of 1954. Lessors were permitted to declare deductions on their taxes for recently acquired equipment for several years, motivating leasing businesses to acquire more rental goods from manufacturers for these tax perks, thus aiding economic growth. As the equipment leasing industry expanded, the IRS adjusted its provisions, clarifying taxable aspects of rental equipment.

In 1963, the U.S. Comptroller of the Currency stated that banks could be lessors, buying equipment and other rental properties and seeking lessees, in addition to lending money for leasing pur-

Inputs Consumed by the Rental and Leasing Industry

Input	Value
Energy	$4.6 billion
Materials	$8.8 billion
Purchased services	$93.8 billion
Total	$107.2 billion

Source: U.S. Bureau of Economic Analysis. Data are for 2008.

poses. During the 1960's, rent-to-own businesses increased to meet customer demand. Companies such as International Business Machines (IBM) and the Xerox Corporation recognized the value of leases in expanding the use of their products, offering businesses rental contracts for access to the most recent computer and electronic equipment.

During the 1980's, some automobile manufacturers invested in car rental businesses that bought the manufacturers' vehicles, providing a way to expose the cars to potential buyers. By the 1990's, about 10 percent of the automobiles sold in the United States were purchased by rental businesses. Consumers also benefited from leasing franchises such as Rent-A-Center, which offered items such as furniture, appliances, and electronics. The Internet made it possible for people to enter into leases electronically, giving birth to the term "e-lease."

The Industry Today

The rental and leasing industry retains its core characteristics, relying on its highly developed reservation systems and offering the same types of products, including vehicles and medical, office, and construction equipment. However, advances in telecommunications technology energized the early twenty-first century rental and leasing services industry, increasing options for consumers, employees, and investors. As more people are able to access the Internet with smartphones and other electronic devices, rental businesses have begun appropriating that technology to market products and services and interact with customers, using social networking sites such as Twitter and Facebook.

Although the rental and leasing industry was negatively affected by the terrorist attacks of September 11, 2001, it resumed growth in the following years. The economic recession of 2007-2009 both negatively and positively affected the rental industry. Consumer demand for the vehicle rental industry decreased, so car rental companies decreased their purchases of vehicles by 63 percent from 2008 to 2009. However, because many consumers were unable to purchase expensive items, such as stereos, appliances, and computers, they leased those items. Rent-to-own options became popular, allowing customers to attain products such as plasma, high-definition, and flat-screen televisions.

Many consumers recognized that renting equip-

ment for parties, meetings, and weddings enabled them to stretch budgets. The furniture rental industry experienced growth as some real estate agents leased attractive furnishings to enhance vacant properties to increase their chances of selling in a slow market. Industry magazines emphasized how rental businesses could use their down time to identify the leasing deals that would appeal to customers with reduced finances.

Online booking of rental cars enables customers to explore the companies' Web sites and discover the available services, including the vehicles offered, rental terms, and prices. Many car rental companies post incentives online, in e-mails, or in collaboration with travel sites to convince customers to choose them. Car rental businesses appeal to customers by offering lower prices, fuel-efficient vehicles, and perks such as Global Positioning System navigation. Businesses stress the convenience

Many car rental companies allow customers to reserve cars online. (©Dreamstime.com)

of their rental procedures, offering services such as transporting customers to their rental vehicles. Some rental businesses focus on providing specialty vehicles such as limousines.

The automobile rental industry faces new rivals. Car-sharing businesses, such as Zipcar.com, present an alternative option. Members pay fees to have access to vehicles in their communities for brief rentals at hourly rates. Established in 2000, Zipcar uses wireless technology to process member reservations on the company's Web site and, through an iPhone application, enables renters to use their smartphones to unlock the vehicles' doors. In 2009, Zipcar counted about 325,000 people, 8,500 companies, and 120 universities as members and generated revenues of $130 million. A year later, U.S. membership reached 400,000. Annually, Zipcar has achieved 30 percent growth. Enterprise Rent-A-Car, Hertz, U-Haul, Avis Rent A Car, and other major rental businesses have developed similar services.

The early twenty-first century rental and leasing industry has become more environmentally friendly. Some rental car companies include hybrid and electric cars in their fleets. Ryder System offers RydeGreen hybrid vehicles to customers. Many rental services emphasize their use of recyclable materials, energy-efficient equipment, and maintenance products that do not harm the environment.

Worldwide, increasing numbers of construction projects ensure a constant demand for equipment leasing for excavation and earth-moving machinery, scaffolds, hoists, cranes, generators, and other essential resources needed to prepare sites and build structures. Many corporations lease multi-million-dollar equipment such as oil rigs, power plants, satellites, and jumbo jets to conduct their businesses.

In the worldwide rental industry, chemical leasing emerged as a thriving sector in the early twenty-first century. Many manufacturers recognize the financial benefits of leasing expensive chemicals used in industrial processes as catalysts, cleaning solvents, and for other roles.

College textbooks can be rented through college bookstores and online. (AP/Wide World Photos)

Textbook rentals are a quickly expanding sector in the leasing services industry. The rising cost of college textbooks motivated entrepreneurs to develop rental alternatives. Inspired by Netflix (the video rental company), businessman Aayush Phumbhra started the textbook rental industry by establishing Chegg.com in 2007. Students can rent textbooks through the company's Web site. Some campus bookstores have begun offering rental textbooks. Textbook rentals are also provided by corporations, such as Barnes & Noble, which provides them online and through its bookstores at schools, and the Follett Higher Education Group, which created Rent-A-Text in 2009. Most services attain profits from a textbook after renting it to three customers.

About three hundred bookstores rented textbooks in 2009. That number increased to fifteen hundred the following year. By fall semester, 2010, almost 50 percent of campus bookstores rented textbooks, according to the National Association of College Stores. Recognizing the importance of this industry, the U.S. Department of Education funded costs associated with textbook rentals at twelve universities. Expenses incurred by universities include investing in textbooks to rent, fees for warehouses to store textbook inventories, training staff to perform tasks involved in these rentals, and electronic equipment and software to process and track rentals.

Although most brides buy their gowns, grooms often rent a tuxedo. (©Dreamstime.com)

Rent the Runway also designed its rental services based on Netflix. Customers examine leading designer fashions, many of which are valued at thousands of dollars, on the Rent the Runway Web site and reserve outfits, which the company ships to them. After wearing the rented garments, lessees return them to Rent the Runway, which arranges for the clothing to be dry-cleaned before it is rented to another customer.

The Web sites of rental and leasing industry associations report industry news and legislation affecting the industry. The American Rental Association (ARA) sponsors one of the leasing industry's most significant conventions, the Rental Show. It also offers training courses on topics such as event rentals and an online driver education course for employees of rental services. Service technicians can be certified through the association's program with the Equipment and Engine Training Council.

Some groups, such as the Canadian Rental Association, present scholarships to students aspiring to rental and leasing services careers. Starting in 2009, the association established the Rental Market Monitor to provide information and research from market analyst IHS Global Insight regarding the leasing industry's future. This service includes access to a current report on the outlook of the industry.

INDUSTRY MARKET SEGMENTS

The rental and leasing services industry is represented by businesses ranging from small to large that lease equipment or other products to individuals as well as companies securing furnishings and devices for hundreds to thousands of employees.

Small Businesses

Drugstores, hardware and farm supply stores, groceries, jewelers, boutiques, and other local businesses often offer rental services aimed at supplying individuals with medical equipment, tools, carpet cleaners, and items for health care, home improvement, or social events. Small leasing businesses sometimes are dealers for manufacturers and specialize in the manufacturer's brands. Patrons often purchase consumer products from these local businesses and choose to rent from them because it is convenient.

Potential Annual Earnings Scale. Most employees receive salaries that cover both their leasing-associated activities and their other tasks such as sales. Some employees are hired specifically for rental work and are compensated depending on their qualifications and experience, starting with minimum wage entry-level positions and increasing to larger amounts for skilled technicians and managers. Commissions and bonuses for performance associated with rentals occasionally supplement incomes.

Clientele Interaction. Small renting and leasing businesses usually rely on a steady customer base that they strive to retain by offering quality rental supplies and responding to customers' concerns. Employees usually know local renters and are familiar with their interests and needs regarding projects, events, or health issues that require rental equipment. Such knowledge helps these businesses appeal to customers by personalizing services and anticipating demands for specific products, enhancing client satisfaction. Party and event planners emphasize the uniqueness of their rental services, often incorporating local themes and imagery associated with schools. Some rental businesses offer customers workshops to teach them how to use the tools and equipment they lease. Leasing services deliver rental medical products to homebound lessees and transport large farming and construction equipment to the sites where renters will use them. Some contracts include demonstrations by experts to help lessees learn how to operate machinery.

Small leasing businesses participate in community chamber of commerce programs and join in holiday celebrations or other civic promotions that highlight local merchants. These businesses sometimes create Web sites advertising items available for renting and including information regarding prices and leasing terms. These online resources often are designed to process reservations electronically. Some small rental businesses send potential and existing customers e-mail messages describing products for lease and rental specials, including previously leased items being offered for sale.

Amenities, Atmosphere, and Physical Grounds. Buildings and sites associated with small rental and leasing businesses vary according to the products they stock and any other commerce and activities they offer. These services are usually located in stores, with rental items displayed on shelves. Larger equipment is stocked in sheds or yards. Many small rental businesses are utilitarian and functional, displaying products for lease by categories so that customers can easily locate items. Lots containing agricultural and construction machinery are designed for safety, with hazardous mechanical parts covered to protect customers.

Displays in small party and event rental businesses tend to be attractive to appeal to customers and indicate how those stores' products can be used to enhance clients' venues. These businesses are sometimes associated with caterers, restaurants, home-design studios, and similar services, so that their offerings can be combined into convenient packages. Some small party service companies have rooms, tents, arbors, gazebos, or landscaped sites on their grounds, where customers who lease products can hold their events.

Rental services include parking lots and storage and maintenance areas to keep and repair inventory until it is displayed. These businesses typically provide offices for customers and employees to discuss leasing terms or plan how they will use rented items at their events. They may also provide refreshments and hand out promotional materials and samples to welcome customers.

Typical Number of Employees. Small rental and leasing businesses hire from one to twenty employees, depending on financial resources, location, and demand. Some owners of small rental services perform the majority of their business's leasing work. Small leasing services occasionally employ part-time or temporary workers to supplement their staff for peak rental times.

Traditional Geographic Locations. Small rental and leasing services are distributed in both rural and urban areas of the United States. They often meet consumers' needs for specific items that those businesses specialize in providing or are convenient to customers' homes or farms.

Kayaks and paddle boats for rent. Recreational equipment is often available for rent. (©Dave Wetzel/Dreamstime.com)

These businesses can be found in downtown locations or on the edge of communities near farms. Some community airports, marinas, train and bus depots, and car dealers maintain small fleets of rental vehicles. Many small rental and leasing services, particularly party and event businesses, located in rural areas are the only source of rental items in the area.

Pros of Working for a Small Rental and Leasing Service. Owners or managers of small rental and leasing businesses often enhance workplace conditions and camaraderie by hiring people from their communities, including friends and relatives. Those positions sometimes are teenagers' first jobs and provide them with the credentials to secure later positions. Most of these positions do not require college degrees, and employees can quickly learn how to perform their assignments from supervisors and colleagues. They sometimes are able to receive training and licenses to operate heavy equipment and commercial vehicles. Employees at small rental and leasing services occasionally contribute their ideas and affect decisions. Recognition for exceptional rental services sometimes includes tips, commissions, or other forms of compensation. Employees often receive discounts for products they lease. Peak rental seasons can provide employees with supplementary income.

Cons of Working for a Small Rental and Leasing Service. Working conditions at small rental and leasing services can be stressful to employees who are responsible for multiple tasks associated with securing, maintaining, and leasing products. Workers may prefer to conduct sales rather than deal with rental contracts. They may feel pressured to acquire training and certification to use heavy equipment or operate commercial vehicles. Recurring contacts with some customers might become unpleasant if those clients frequently complain, expect to receive special discounts, or make other unreasonable demands. Some employees might dislike handling machinery and coming into contact with the grease, oil, or other residues associated with their maintenance. Some rental equipment can be hazardous to employees. Small rental and leasing businesses might expect employees to work extra hours during peak rental times, holidays, weekends, and evenings.

Costs

Payroll and Benefits: Many small rental or leasing employees earn hourly wages. People who provide customers with instruction or other special services associated with using rental equipment often are compensated extra for those assignments. Many small leasing businesses do not hire enough employees for the government to require them to provide benefits. Small rental businesses arrange for vacation and sick leave with their employees based on scheduling needs, in particular coverage during peak periods.

Supplies: Small rental and leasing services use shelving and displays commonly found in most stores to organize their rental products. Larger equipment is often stored outside in warehouses or on fenced lots covered with gravel for drainage. Furniture, such as chairs, couches, and desks, and appliances, such as coffeemakers and water coolers, are placed in areas where customers and employees discuss rental agreements and arrange for credit terms associated with some leases. Most small rental businesses use computers to inventory rental products and process financial transactions. They also use office supplies and cleaners.

External Services: Although employees might perform some routine maintenance tasks, small rental and leasing businesses generally contract with other businesses, such as custodial, pest control, security, and landscaping services, to keep their facilities and grounds clean and safe for both employees and customers. External services sometimes are hired to deliver diesel fuel and repair equipment. These small businesses occasionally use accountants. Legal consultants assist with devising contracts, securing business licenses, and meeting municipal codes. Insurance agents help small leasing businesses secure sufficient coverage in case of theft or damages and to cover liabilities.

Utilities: Small rental and leasing services typically pay for electricity, gas, oil, telephone, and water and sewer. These expenses might be incorporated in real estate leases if businesses rent the buildings and sites where they operate their services.

Taxes: Small rental and leasing services pay local, state, and federal income taxes. Businesses that own buildings and land pay property taxes.

Rental and leasing services pay taxes for registration and licenses to operate vehicles. These businesses collect sales taxes associated with rental transactions.

Midsize Businesses

Midsize rental and leasing services are primarily regional businesses and rental franchises. These businesses often represent manufacturers of equipment and tools and lease customers those manufacturers' brands. Leasing services operating in transportation hubs and car dealerships in midsize cities provide vehicle rentals for travelers, government fleets, and motorists who prefer leasing cars.

Potential Annual Earnings Scale. Incomes for midsize rental and leasing services employees vary according to their position, credentials, experience, and length of employment with a rental franchise or business. Managers' salaries in midsize rental and leasing businesses differ depending on the companies that employ them, their responsibilities, and performance record, but usually range from $45,000 to $100,000 yearly.

Clientele Interaction. Employees working for midsize rental and leasing businesses often have direct contact with customers. Workers guide clients who seek products to rent, providing information and explaining terms for leases and of rent-to-own payment plans. Veterans and college students who work for rental and leasing establishments recognize the needs of their peers for furnishings and equipment for short-term lodgings; they can recommend products they have used and describe available choices. Rental and leasing workers demonstrate how to use rental items when requested. They process rental contracts and advise customers regarding any extra fees they may have to pay for fuel, cable, or Internet service while operating leased items. Workers alert renters to any insurance or maintenance costs associated with renting, provide information on whom to contact if technical problems occur, and inform renters of penalties for damaging leased items.

Employees may deal with customers dissatisfied with products they rented. Workers who remain at midsize renting and leasing businesses for several years may become familiar with returning customers and tell them about products that might meet their professional or personal interests. Employees at midsize rental businesses providing party ser-

vices sometimes assist with civic and sporting events involving celebrities or other prominent people visiting their communities and their discretion regarding arrangements is demanded.

Amenities, Atmosphere, and Physical Grounds. Midsize rental and leasing services facilities, often located by cities' main roads or near shopping or industrial areas, differ in external structure and appearance although they incorporate many similar elements, such as shelving to store and display products, loading docks to receive and ship products, and chairs, couches, and desks for customers and employees to use for business discussions. They may have sound systems to broadcast music or announcements to customer and employee areas.

Stores leasing furnishings, electronics, and other household-related products or party and event rentals usually have an attractive exterior that welcomes customers. Interiors are often designed with neutral paint, lighting, and decorative items appealing to most customers. Party rental businesses may have an area decorated for a sample event to show customers the quality of their merchandise and services. Exterior areas include parking and displays of items too large for showrooms or associated with outdoor use on patios or other sites. Landscaping typically includes shrubbery, trees, and flowers.

Midsize equipment leasing businesses tend to be utilitarian, providing a building where customers can examine tools, offices, and employee areas. Machinery is stored and displayed in adjacent warehouses, sheds, or lots. Function is emphasized over appearance.

Typical Number of Employees. Medium rental and leasing services typically hire twenty to fifty employees, depending on the quantity of merchandise stocked. Specific roles, such as maintenance, might require more workers to keep rental products ready for leasing. Peak rental periods might necessitate hiring more temporary and part-time employees to handle demand.

Traditional Geographic Locations. Midsize rental and leasing services are usually located in cities with a minimum population of fifty thousand people. Many of these businesses are established in college towns or in urban communities adjacent to military bases, industrial parks, airports, depots, or marinas, where rental and leasing services can expect consistent demand for their products and equipment from local businesses, governments, school systems, and residents. They are also located in areas where construction is occurring.

Pros of Working for a Midsize Rental and Leasing Service. Workers employed by midsize services are assured job stability because their communities usually are large enough to produce a sufficient supply of customers. Their work schedule is usually consistent, and overtime, weekend, or holiday hours are typically voluntary and not demanded. Employees may enjoy the quality, diversity, and modern technology available in the products their businesses offer and welcome opportunities to lease those items at reduced rates or purchase discontinued products at reduced prices. Midsize rental and leasing businesses sometimes provide employees with training on the use of rental equipment or computers, which can heighten their professional qualifications and often results in promotions or raises.

Cons of Working for a Midsize Rental and Leasing Service. Employees at midsize rental and leasing services might feel overwhelmed if they are expected to perform numerous roles at their business. Some might feel uncomfortable assisting customers with unfamiliar products, such as heavy equipment, if no specialists are available to handle those requests. Employees might not be interested in learning about new technologies and gaining computer skills associated with their assignments. Some products, especially machinery, might have dangerous components, leak fluids, or present safety concerns. Customer complaints can frustrate employees who lack the authority to resolve issues or adjust contracts and pricing to appease clients.

Costs

Payroll and Benefits: Midsize rental and leasing businesses pay employees based on hourly, monthly, or yearly rates. Temporary and part-time workers receive wages compensating them for the number of hours they work or specific services they perform. Consultants receive fees according to contracts outlining their contributions to businesses. Full-time employees typically receive benefits, including vacation and sick time. They are often provided health care insurance and sometimes company stock and pension plans. Some employees may be given commissions, bonuses, or reduced rental costs, extended lease periods, and upgrades for products they lease.

Supplies: Shelves and display cases are essential to midsize rental and leasing services. These businesses are equipped with office supplies and computers and printers to process transactions. Most midsize rental and leasing services provide basic furnishings in areas where customers and sales representatives can sit to discuss leasing and credit options. These businesses display large rental products in sheds and yards usually adjacent to the stores. Outdoor rental areas are often bordered with fences and sometimes paved or graveled to make it easier for customers to walk around and examine rental equipment. Stereo systems often broadcast music inside and outside rental businesses and occasionally deliver messages about specials. Stores usually stock basic cleaning supplies to keep aisles and rental goods free of grime.

External Services: Midsize rental and leasing businesses use attorneys to prepare leasing agreements. These rental companies frequently contract with external services to clean internal and external areas of stores and warehouses and to maintain yards where large equipment, vehicles, and trailers are stored, thereby ensuring that their sites are clear of hazards that might injure customers and employees. They often contract for fuel deliveries. Some midsize rental businesses purchase employees' clothing from uniform companies and arrange for laundering services. They often hire pest control, security, and landscaping businesses.

Utilities: Midsize rental and leasing businesses typically pay for common utilities, including electricity, gas, oil, water and sewer, and telephone. Utility fees for businesses that lease properties or are located in airports or other large buildings such as malls are often included in property rental costs.

Taxes: Midsize rental and leasing services pay local, state, and federal income taxes in addition to collecting sales taxes from customers. Business owners also pay property tax for any buildings and land belonging to them and used for leasing activities, as well as vehicle registration and license fees.

Large Businesses

Large rental and leasing services are often national and international corporations that typically concentrate on securing contracts with other corporations that require sizable quantities of heavy machinery, office furnishings, and electronic equipment, or services and products leased in bulk amounts. They also provide expensive shipping equipment for manufacturers and luxury goods for individual and corporate clients.

Potential Annual Earnings Scale. Employees working for large rental and leasing services earn varying wages depending on their position, qualifications, responsibilities, and contributions. Compensation ranges from minimum-wage hourly pay for entry-level positions such as rental clerks to salaries in excess of six figures for executives. Workers holding educational credentials for specialized positions can earn salaries from $50,000 to more than $100,000 and often receive bonuses for professional achievements that increase their rental services' profits.

Clientele Interaction. Employees in large rental and leasing services have varied experiences with customers. Some personnel, such as clerks renting transportation, communicate directly with clients, but many executives and managers have limited contact with lessees, interacting primarily by telephone, e-mail, and Internet conferencing with colleagues holding similar positions in companies that are seeking leasing services and products. Workers performing maintenance and other support tasks usually do not meet with customers. Some employees in large rental and leasing businesses are responsible for handling customer complaints, although they may work in a satellite office removed from headquarters or under contract.

Amenities, Atmosphere, and Physical Grounds. Facilities housing large rental and leasing services represent diverse structures. Many of these businesses are located in office buildings. Many companies maintain attractive lobby areas, with furnishings, decorative items, and plants, to accommodate their corporate clients. Executives and employees work in various office spaces, including cubicles, which contain furnishings, computers, telephones, and other supplies. Conference rooms contain electronic and audiovisual equipment for presentations. Large rental and leasing services may provide background music and offer coffee and other drinks or foods to clients. Parking garages or small lots are available for employees and customers. Skyscrapers may have landing pads for helicopters.

Many employees at large rental and leasing businesses are assigned cards with bar codes that enable them to access restricted areas. Some large rental and leasing companies maintain offices and counters within airports or other business facilities. These sites are usually functional to encourage quick transactions and are often painted in the businesses' colors and designed with their names and logos. Parking access is usually provided by the airports or malls in which these rental and leasing services are located.

Large rental and leasing companies might also have warehouses containing the businesses' products or be adjacent to yards, sheds, and garages where vehicles and heavy equipment are stored. Many buildings have docks for delivery or loading equipment. These facilities are often surrounded by security fences and tend to be unattractive because they focus on maintaining large inventories. The areas occupied by these businesses, sometimes vast acreages, are designed for safety, not aesthetics. Parking lots are provided for employees and clients who wish to examine rental equipment before signing contracts. Security and safety equipment includes surveillance cameras, alarms, and intercoms. Some large rental and leasing services require employees and visitors to move through metal detectors at various entrances and exits to prevent theft and sabotage.

Typical Number of Employees. The number of employees working for large rental and leasing services is in the hundreds to thousands depending on the business's staffing requirements. Some rental business employees may be in a central location that includes the company's headquarters, while other workers may be spread throughout a region, a country, or the world, staffing the company's numerous facilities.

Traditional Geographic Locations. Large rental and leasing businesses are often in metropolitan areas with populations exceeding 100,000 people; these areas may include college campuses, military bases, industrial parks, and other institutions with significant populations. Large leasing corporations frequently are established in state capitals. Large rental services maintain sizable fleets of vehicles at major airports, ports, depots, and rail yards. Although offices are usually located in urban areas, large rental services often store rental equipment and products at warehouses and yards at rural sites near transportation routes.

Pros of Working for a Large Rental and Leasing Service. Large rental and leasing businesses often provide entry-level positions to people who are seeking their first job, lack educational credentials, or are unskilled. These workers often appreciate being part of a corporation and the identity and benefits that affiliation offers them. Travel is occasionally involved in some employees' leasing assignments. Large rental and leasing businesses employees sometimes receive perks such as stock dividends, performance awards, commissions, and gifts for employment anniversaries. These services often treat their employees as valued members of the overall corporate community by acknowledging their contributions in company newsletters and offering other forms of recognition. Large rental and leasing businesses sometimes provide employees with training and access to educational, safety, and professional workshops that help them advance professionally.

Cons of Working for a Large Rental and Leasing Service. The size and complexity of large rental and leasing services can make workers feel insignificant and unappreciated. Workers may feel pressure to convince customers to agree to unnecessary extras or add-ons. Personnel who staff rental counters in airports and other large transportation hubs might become tired of people requesting information, complaining, or demanding revised rental agreements and upgraded equipment. Other employees sometimes miss the opportunity to interact with customers, particularly when lessees reserve rental equipment by using company's Web sites or kiosks. Leasing representatives who have to travel for their jobs may dislike being away from home. Employees who work with heavy equipment and chemicals associated with large rental and leasing services risk being injured or exposed to toxins.

Costs

Payroll and Benefits: Salaries paid by large rental and leasing services vary depending on the employee's role, credentials, and contributions to the company's financial status. Entry-level positions, such as rental clerks, often are paid hourly wages. Consultants, part-time, and temporary laborers receive compensation according to the time they work and the type of service performed. Most large rental and leasing businesses offer workers paid vacation and sick leaves. Health insurance, stock options, and pension plans are frequently provided. Employees sometimes receive commissions and bonuses. Large rental services occasionally reward employees with reduced prices for luxury rental goods.

Supplies: Large rental and leasing services need state-of-the-art telecommunications and computer technology to maintain their inventory and reservation databases, to contact rental goods suppliers, and to coordinate with franchises and other facilities functioning within their overall business network. Computers and printers are essential to process credit verifications, rental agreements, and payments, and to print contracts and receipts. These services use large quantities of furnishings, equipment, and office and cleaning supplies to maintain interior and exterior areas where customers interact with rental staff and lease products.

External Services: Most large rental and leasing businesses rely on various professionals to provide essential services. They consult with lawyers to develop contracts. Security is crucial for rental and leasing services, particularly those that own millions of dollars in merchandise, such as thousands of vehicles or high-priced aircraft and yachts. Large rental and leasing businesses usually hire professional cleaners to sanitize their facilities. Specialists are often used to clean upholstery on rental furniture and in rental vehicles. Some large rental and leasing businesses contract for mechanics to repair damaged rental vehicles and equipment. Companies deliver diesel and other necessary fuels. Uniform businesses frequently provide standardized clothing featuring company logos for rental clerks and sales personnel as well as laundry services. Large rental businesses often hire pest control services and landscapers.

Utilities: Large rental and leasing services typically use electricity, gas, oil, water and sewer, and telephone services, which are paid by those businesses or incorporated in leases if the services operate on rented properties.

Taxes: Large rental and leasing businesses usually pay local, state, and federal income taxes. These businesses also collect sales taxes associated with customers' rental contracts and purchases. Companies that own the buildings, land, and vehicles they use for rental business pay property taxes and license and registration fees.

ORGANIZATIONAL STRUCTURE AND JOB ROLES

The organizational structure of the rental and leasing services industry and the roles of its employees are similar in small, midsize, and large companies. The roles of employees vary based on their education, training, and experience, but they tend to fall into employment categories that are standard throughout the industry.

The following general job categories apply to the organizational structure of small, midsize, and large rental and leasing services:

- Business Management
- Customer Services
- Purchasing
- Sales and Marketing
- Reservations
- Facilities and Maintenance
- Security
- Research and Development
- Mechanical and Technical Services
- Operations
- Distribution
- Groundskeeping
- Human Resources
- Information Technology
- Administrative Support

Business Management

The rental and leasing services industry depends on managers to oversee various facets of its business. Owners who also are managers direct many of the business decisions associated with small and midsize rental and leasing services. In larger businesses, a chief executive officer and chief financial officer provide leadership, determining financial goals, dealing with payroll, and delegating assignments to managers. Some department and warehouse managers focus on specific rental products offered by their companies. Larger rental and leasing services often retain finance specialists who oversee securing credit to purchase equipment.

Most rental and leasing services require their managers to have a bachelor's degree in business or an affiliated field and previous employment and leadership experience in the industry. Managers often have obtained a master of business administration (M.B.A.). Managers usually receive the highest salaries at their businesses. The average annual salary for rental and leasing services managers was $95,420 in 2009, ranging from $62,950 to more than $164,120.

Business management occupations may include the following:

- Chief Executive Officer (CEO)
- Chief Financial Officer (CFO)
- Rental and Leasing Services General Manager
- Warehouse Manager
- Rental and Leasing Services Department Manager

Customer Services

Customer services employees in rental and leasing companies assess how existing clientele and the public perceive their companies and determine ways to improve their image. Some employees develop surveys asking rental customers to comment about their experiences and to offer suggestions for products they would like the company to offer. Customer services employees also deal with customers' complaints.

Many customer services personnel have completed programs in public relations or business at universities, community colleges, or vocational schools. Communication skills are necessary for these positions. Some rental and leasing businesses contract customer services through outsourcing.

Customer services occupations may include the following:

- Customer Services Director
- Customer Services Representative
- Public Relations Specialist

Purchasing

Rental and leasing services employ people whose job is to identify sources of rental products and equipment. Purchasing personnel choose specific products and suppliers and place and handle the orders. These employees often attend conferences that showcase products that rental and leasing services might want to procure for their businesses. They acquire information about new products that can supplement or replace existing inventories.

Most rental and leasing services purchasing personnel have a bachelor's degree in a business-related field. Upper-level personnel often have a master of business administration. Businesses value purchasing personnel with knowledge of construction and other industries that frequently rent equipment. Annual salaries for purchasing employees depend on their responsibilities and qualifications.

Purchasing occupations may include the following:

- Purchasing Director
- Senior Purchasing Manager
- Purchasing Agent

Sales and Marketing

Rental and leasing services employ personnel to market their businesses by promoting their rental equipment and products. These businesses also hire people who specialize in convincing customers to rent their merchandise. Marketing personnel often develop appealing perks to persuade customers to choose their businesses. Sales coordinators talk with customers regarding leasing services. Some sales representatives concentrate on leasing accounts with contractors. Sales personnel examine renters' identification, take deposits, and process rental transactions. Some sales employees are responsible for selling vehicles and equipment removed from leasing stock because of their mileage or age.

Marketing and sales personnel working for the rental and leasing services industry usually have bachelor's degrees in marketing or business. Some may have advanced degrees such as an M.B.A. and specialize in a particular area, such as the leasing of luxury items. Employers often seek Web site designers, photographers, and graphic artists for promotional work. Most people working in these de-partments receive annual incomes based on their qualifications and experience. Sales personnel sometimes earn commissions.

Sales and marketing occupations may include the following:

- Sales Director
- Senior Sales Manager
- Marketing Director
- Senior Marketing Manager
- Salesperson
- Marketing Personnel

Reservations

The rental and leasing services industry relies on reservations. Customers can reserve rental vehicles, products, and equipment in various ways, all of which require reservations personnel to record and process these requests. Some rental and leasing reservations personnel answer telephone calls, during which they discuss rental options and terms with clients. Other reservations clerks interact directly with clients who visit their businesses to arrange for leases. Reservations employees also monitor reservations placed through Internet sites.

Most rental and leasing services do not require reservations employees to have education beyond a high school diploma. Reservations work is often entry level. Sometimes rental and leasing companies outsource reservations, using remotely located clerks who may serve more than one business. People with college degrees or experience are usually considered for managerial positions. Counter and rental clerks average $11.38 hourly and $23,670 yearly wages.

Reservation occupations may include the following:

- Reservations Manager
- Reservations Personnel

Facilities and Maintenance

Facilities and maintenance personnel ensure that rental and leasing companies can operate with few disruptions caused by problems associated with electrical, heating, air-conditioning, and plumbing systems. They routinely examine, maintain, and repair machinery. Maintenance personnel are often hired for their specialized skills, including air-conditioning or plumbing expertise. Facilities

OCCUPATION PROFILE

Counter and Rental Clerk

Considerations	Qualifications
Description	Helps customers find appropriate rental equipment and products, prepares rental applications, and processes transactions.
Career clusters	Business, Management, and Administration; Marketing, Sales, and Service; Transportation, Distribution, and Logistics
Interests	Data; people
Working conditions	Work inside
Minimum education level	On-the-job training; high school diploma or GED; high school diploma/technical training
Physical exertion	Light work
Physical abilities	Unexceptional/basic fitness
Opportunities for experience	Military service; part-time work
Licensure and certification	Usually not required
Employment outlook	Slower-than-average growth expected
Holland interest score	CRE; CSE

Note: See volume 1, "Publisher's Note," for an explanation of the Holland interest score.

and maintenance employees for rental and leasing companies also include custodians.

Facilities and maintenance personnel in this industry typically have studied machinery and systems at vocational schools or other institutions. Some have completed engineering or technology degrees at universities. Others are high school graduates hired for entry-level maintenance positions. Facilities and maintenance personnel often have licenses for their specialties. Qualifications and experience determine these employees' incomes, which range from hourly wages to yearly salaries.

Facilities and maintenance occupations may include the following:

- Chief Engineer
- Facility Manager
- Heating, Ventilation, and Air-Conditioning (HVAC) Engineer
- Electrician
- Plumber
- Custodian/Janitor

Security

Rental and leasing companies hire people to secure their facilities from potential threats. Security personnel protect employees and customers and guard rental equipment, patrolling facilities and monitoring surveillance camera images to apprehend people stealing merchandise or carrying weapons. Security personnel guard against attempts to sabotage rental equipment and are on the lookout for signs that a customer intends to use rental equipment to commit an illegal act or engage in terrorism. Guards observe people and vehicles accessing restricted parts of rental facilities. They also monitor sensors that detect smoke, hazardous chemicals, and carbon monoxide.

Security personnel hired by rental and leasing services usually have completed training in public safety and have prior professional experience in that field. Many have worked as firefighters or police officers. Some have performed similar roles while serving in the military. Security personnel typically have completed criminal justice programs and are certified to use firearms. They have usually completed instruction regarding industrial security technologies. Individuals' qualifications and responsibilities determine their wages.

Security occupations may include the following:

- Security Guard
- Security Specialist
- Firefighter

Research and Development

Rental and leasing services often hire consultants to evaluate renting and leasing services and suggest how those businesses will be affected in the future by economic and market changes, consumer demand, and other factors. Market analysts and researchers monitor the development of new technologies and methods that can be applied to leasing services. They inform executives regarding technological changes that will affect their businesses and identify new markets for their services.

People seeking research and development roles within the rental and leasing services industry usually have bachelor's degrees in business subjects or fields such as engineering, and some have masters of business administration. Income varies based on the individual's credentials and contributions, ranging from payments for specific assignments to annual salaries.

Research and development occupations may include the following:

- Market Analyst
- Researcher
- Consultant

Mechanical and Technical Services

Rental and leasing services rely on mechanics and technicians to ensure the proper functioning of equipment used in the course of business, such as delivery trucks, as well as equipment rented to customers. Technicians inspect and maintain vehicles, machinery, and equipment. Mechanics repair vehi-

cles returned with damage, often arranging for external services to perform paint and body work as needed. These personnel sometimes go to the rental customer's location to repair leased equipment.

Mechanics and technicians hired by rental and leasing services usually have completed training at technical schools, in the military, or in special certification programs that teach people how to service vehicles and equipment. Even after being certified, many mechanics seek additional training to learn about new computerized devices used to assess systems in rental equipment. Mechanics and technicians working for rental and leasing services earn annual salaries averaging $38,990 to $57,010, depending on their credentials.

Mechanical and technical services occupations may include the following:

- Head Mechanic
- Mechanic
- Technician

Operations

Rental and leasing services employ entry-level personnel to perform necessary tasks in day-to-day operations and supervisors to oversee those workers. These employees are often assigned to specific duties such as unpacking deliveries of rental equipment. Others may be asked to focus their efforts on a specific type of rental goods, such as being responsible for all power tools offered for leasing. Supervisors might be designated to monitor workers in one or more departments within a rental business.

Rental and leasing services industry supervisors earn yearly salaries averaging $50,270, according to their qualifications. Entry-level workers typically earn hourly wages, with employees often starting at the minimum wage and receiving raises as they gain experience and complete any training associated with their jobs.

Operations occupations may include the following:

- Head Supervisor
- Department Supervisor
- Operations Personnel

Distribution

Some rental and leasing personnel deliver rental equipment and products to customers' homes or to construction sites. Those workers are often expected to set up equipment and demonstrate how it works to lessees. They also are responsible for moving those goods within rental and leasing services facilities, unloading items on delivery docks, placing products in warehouses, and parking equipment in lots. Managers schedule distribution, keeping records noting delivery dates and the distances personnel travel transporting leased equipment. They secure any documents, such as permits, required for moving rental equipment across state or country borders.

Distribution employees for rental and leasing services usually are entry-level workers. They typically have received training, such as driver education programs sponsored by the ARA, and have earned licenses qualifying them to operate a variety of motor vehicles. These personnel might also receive training and be certified to use forklifts and operate large equipment that their businesses rent.

Distribution personnel's wages range from minimum wage to yearly salaries of $24,660 to $38,350, with managers receiving annual incomes averaging $50,000. Some distribution workers are paid by the mileage for each delivery.

Distribution occupations may include the following:

- Distribution Manager
- Distribution Worker

Groundskeeping

Groundskeeping employees are essential to maintain the safety and appearance of the rental and leasing services industry. These personnel clear exterior areas of rental businesses, including parking lots and equipment yards, of hazards that might injure visitors or employees. Rental and leasing businesses focusing on event and party products use landscaping personnel to create appealing areas with shrubbery and flowers where events can be held.

Groundskeeping employees usually have professional gardening experience. Some groundskeeping personnel have educational credentials or certification in horticulture or related fields. Workers performing groundskeeping tasks receive hourly or annual wages according to their qualifications and assignments.

Groundskeeping occupations may include the following:

- Head Groundskeeper
- Groundskeeper

Human Resources

Human resources personnel evaluate and interview applicants for available positions in rental and leasing service businesses. Employees in human resources departments occasionally identify successful rental and leasing services employees at other businesses and offer them incentives to transfer. After employees have been hired, human resources personnel advise them regarding any training necessary to begin work and about benefits, including retirement plans.

Human resources personnel working in the rental and leasing services industry usually have bachelor's degrees in business or human resources management. Many of these employees have previously held similar human resources positions at rental and leasing businesses or at other businesses.

Human resources occupations may include the following:

- Human Resources Director
- Human Resources Manager
- Human Resources Assistant

Information Technology

Rental and leasing businesses rely on employees who can develop and maintain computer systems and other electronic devices essential to process digital information. These employees ensure that equipment is upgraded to enable their companies to be competitive. Specialists in information technology are responsible for maintaining computer systems by installing antivirus programs. Some information technology employees write computer programs for their businesses to inventory and track rental equipment and leasing transactions.

Most rental and leasing services employers require information technology employees to have studied and completed degrees or certification in computer science or information technology at vocational schools or universities. Employees sometimes pursue advanced training and degrees to study new computer and electronics technologies.

Information technology occupations may include the following:

- Information Technology Director
- Computer Programmer
- Information Technology Technician

Administrative Support

Administrative employees in small rental businesses are often responsible for numerous clerical roles. Personnel at midsize and large leasing services may be assigned specific responsibilities according to their qualifications. Bookkeepers maintain records of business transactions. Many administrative workers are assigned clerical tasks such as answering telephones, scheduling appointments, typing correspondence, and filing purchasing orders and invoices.

Administrative employees sometimes begin working for the rental and leasing services industry as temporary or part-time workers. Bookkeepers might have accounting degrees. Some services provide training for administrative support personnel so that they can learn how to use new technologies for office procedures.

Administrative support occupations may include the following:

- Bookkeeper
- Administrative Assistant

INDUSTRY OUTLOOK

Overview

The outlook for the rental and leasing services industry shows it to be stable. According to the Equipment Leasing and Finance Foundation, the global economic recession that began in late 2007 made it difficult for businesses to obtain the financing necessary to lease equipment. The industry suffered economic losses because of the tight credit situation and a drop in consumer demand. During 2008, the volume of leasing in the top fifty countries fell 15.3 percent.

Recovery from the recession has been gradual, with revenues increasing in some rental and leasing services sectors and decreasing in others. Market analysts project this industry will eventually regain its prerecession growth rate because rental and leasing businesses must acquire sufficient rental equipment and products to meet the rental needs of individuals and corporations as they recover economically and can invest in leases.

North American leasing led the industry internationally through 2005 but was surpassed in 2006 by European leasing services. Toward the end of the first decade in the twenty-first century, some countries significantly increased their leasing productivity. The Chinese leasing industry reported an 87.5 percent increase from 2007 to 2008, and Peru expanded leasing activity 60 percent. European leasing represented 48.6 percent of leasing volume in the global industry during 2008, with North America accounting for 20.9 percent, Asia 19.3 percent, and South America 8.7 percent.

An estimated 80 percent of businesses worldwide, ranging in size from small stores to large international corporations, have recognized the benefits, including tax incentives, of leasing equipment to operate their businesses. The *World Leasing Yearbook 2010* evaluated the rental and leasing services industry in one hundred countries, noting that the top fifty markets for leasing were located in the United States, Europe, Asia, and the Pacific region. That yearbook reported that the rental and leasing services industry was expanding in previously undeveloped leasing markets such as Russia and African countries, particularly Nigeria. According to the *China Financial Leasing Industry Report, 2009-2010*, financial leasing in that country grew 138.7 percent from 2008 to 2009.

Before the 2007-2009 recession, Datamonitor had stated the global car rental market was worth $37.7 billion in 2005 and projected that it would increase by 27.5 percent to reach $48 billion by 2010. This report indicated that the Americas, including the United States, Mexico, Canada, and Brazil, represented 60.3 percent of the global car rental market. Within the global car rental market, the United States represented 50.2 percent, the most of any country.

In the late twentieth century and beyond, the car rental industry underwent some consolidation. Major corporations such as Avis Budget Group (Avis, Budget, and Ryder), Enterprise Holdings (Enterprise, Alamo, and National), and Hertz Global Holdings (Hertz and Advantage) purchased midsize car leasing businesses but continued to use these companies' names in order to retain customers loyal to those businesses. As the economy began to rebound after the recession, consumer demand for rental vehicles for business and leisure purposes increased. In 2010, U-Haul International, owned by Amerco International, reported doubling its 2009 profits, with a total of $637 million in revenues. According to the November, 2010, Research and Markets' report on automobile rental and leasing, about five thousand companies in the United States generated an estimated $40 billion in revenues in 2010. Market researchers Frost & Sullivan projected car-sharing rentals could reach $6 billion annually and be used by 10 million people worldwide as of 2016.

Employment Advantages

The U.S. Bureau of Labor Statistics (BLS) predicts that the number of employees in the rental and leasing services industry will increase during the early twenty-first century. It estimates that rental clerk employment will grow by 3 percent from 2008 to 2018, expanding from 448,200 positions to 461,900. About 40.5 percent of leasing executives at the Equipment Leasing and Finance As-

sociation's 2010 convention stated that their businesses would hire new employees in the following year.

People with minimal work experience can find entry-level, temporary, and part-time positions in various categories in this industry, which often provides people with their first jobs. Many employers provide training for their employees, which allows them to advance within their job category or transfer to another specialty. As the industry uses more digital information, leasing companies will train their workers in the appropriate computer skills or seek people with computer competency. Skills gained in this industry can often be applied to other industries and enhance people's employability. Because many rental and leasing services promote diversity, these companies provide women and members of ethnic groups with opportunities to advance professionally.

Annual Earnings

According to *World Leasing Yearbook* and *Leasing News* statistics in 2009 and 2010, yearly revenues generated by the rental and leasing services industry globally totaled at least $650 billion. By 2010, yearly international revenues for the industry were at least $560 billion. According to the U.S. Census Bureau, annual revenues of the U.S. rental and leasing services industry reached about $90.6 billion in 2010, a 0.9 percent growth from $89.793 billion in 2009.

The U.S. industry segments generating the most revenue were commercial and industrial machinery and equipment rental and leasing at $41.1 billion, a 3 percent increase since 2009, and automotive equipment rental and leasing, at $32.3 billion, which was 0.2 percent less than 2009 because of a 1.7 percent decline in automobile rentals, offset by a gain of 3.6 percent in the truck, trailer, and recreational vehicle category. Consumer goods rental, estimated at $14.0 billion, de-

PROJECTED EMPLOYMENT FOR SELECTED OCCUPATIONS

Rental and Leasing Services

Employment		
2009	Projected 2018	Occupation
20,410	26,400	Cleaners of vehicles and equipment
136,540	159,200	Counter and rental clerks
30,160	32,700	First-line supervisors/managers of retail sales workers
15,650	20,700	Retail salespersons
24,770	25,700	Truck drivers, light or delivery services

Source: U.S. Bureau of Labor Statistics, Industries at a Glance, Occupational Employment Statistics and Employment Projections Program.

clined 1.7 percent, and general rental centers, at $3.9 billion, dropped 2.9 percent.

In August, 2010, the Equipment Leasing and Finance Association noted that new commercial equipment financing had expanded 16 percent since the previous year. Corporate profits rose 37 percent since mid-2009, suggesting corporations' investment in leasing equipment was likely to increase.

RELATED RESOURCES FOR FURTHER RESEARCH

AMERICAN RENTAL ASSOCIATION
1900 19th St.
Moline, IL 61265
Tel: (800) 334-2177
Fax: (309) 764-1533
http://www.ARArental.org

ASSOCIATION OF PROGRESSIVE RENTAL ORGANIZATIONS
1504 Robin Hood Trail
Austin, TX 78703
Tel: (800) 204-2776
Fax: (512) 794-0097
http://www.rtohq.org

CANADIAN RENTAL ASSOCIATION
112B Scurfield Blvd.
Winnipeg, MB R3Y 1G4
Canada
Tel: (800) 486-9899
Fax: (888) 270-4440
http://www.CRArental.org

EQUIPMENT LEASING AND FINANCE ASSOCIATION
1825 K St. NW, Suite 900
Washington, DC 20006
Tel: (202) 238-3400
Fax: (202) 238-3401
http://www.elfaonline.org

TRUCK RENTAL AND LEASING ASSOCIATION
675 N Washington St., Suite 410
Alexandria, VA 22314
Tel: (703) 299-9120
Fax: (703) 299-9115
http://www.trala.org

ABOUT THE AUTHOR

Elizabeth D. Schafer earned a Ph.D. from Auburn University in 1993, focusing on the history of technology and science. She specializes in agricultural history, especially the contributions of engineering fields in the designing and improvement of tools, equipment, and machines. Her research and publications have included studies of manufacturers whose equipment and products are frequently leased by agriculturists. She has experience as both a lessee and lessor, primarily concerning the use of goods and services related to livestock, crops, and property.

FURTHER READING

Auto Rental News. "U.S. Car Rental Revenues Rise in 2010." December 1, 2010. http://www.autorentalnews.com/News/Story/2010/12/Revenues-Rise-in-2010.aspx.

Barton, Robert. "American Car Rental Association Chief: I'm 'Adamantly Opposed' to á la Carte Pricing." Interview by Christopher Elliott. Elliott Blog, April 24, 2009. http://www.elliot.org/first-person/6333.

The Economist. "Wheels When You Need Them: Car-Sharing." 396, no. 8698 (September 4, 2010): 70.

Jahn, Tim. "Creating the Textbook Rental Industry—With Aayush Phumbhra, Founder of Chegg.com." *Beyond the Pedway*, November 9, 2010. http://www.beyondthepedway.com/chegg-interview-aayush-phumbhra.

Jakl, Thomas, and Petra Schwager, eds. *Chemical Leasing Goes Global: Selling Services Instead of Barrels: A Win-Win Business Model for Environment and Industry.* New York: SpringerWien, 2008.

Kazanjian, Kirk. *Exceeding Customer Expectations: What Enterprise, America's Number-One Car Rental Company, Can Teach You About Creating Lifetime Customers.* Foreword by Andrew C. Taylor. New York: Currency Doubleday/Random House, 2007.

Keegan, Paul. "Zipcar: The Best New Idea in Business." *Fortune* 160, no. 5 (September 14, 2009): 42-52.

Lacko, James M., Signe-Mary McKernan, and Manoj Hastak. *Survey of Rent-to-Own Customers.* Washington, D.C.: Federal Trade Commission, Bureau of Economics, 2000.

Menkin, Christopher. "The $650 Billion Leasing Industry Has Dramatically Changed." *Seeking Alpha: Financial Stocks*, March 27, 2009. http://seekingalpha.com/article/128189-the-650-billion-leasing-industry-has-dramatically-changed.

Monitor Daily. "Equipment Finance Industry Confidence Shows More Improvement." November 19, 2010. http://www.monitordaily.com/story_page.asp?news_id=26889.

Paul, Lisa, ed. *World Leasing Yearbook 2010.* Colchester, Essex, England: Euromoney Institutional Investor, 2009.

Phelan, Kim. "Soaring Inflatables Industry Gets a Second Look from Insurance." *Rental Pulse.* http://www.rentalpulse.com/Article/tabid/95/smid/426/ArticleID/234/reftab/113/Default.aspx.

Roseman, Brett T. "Rental Car Industry Starts to Emerge from the 'Perfect Storm.'" *USA Today*, April 5, 2010. http://www.usatoday.com/travel/news/2010-04-06-rentalcars06_CV_N.htm.

Saunders, Harris, Sr. *Top Up or Down? The Origin and Development of the Automobile and Truck Renting and Leasing Industry—Since 1916.* Birmingham, Ala.: Harris Saunders, 1985.

Smith, Brandey. "Dreamgirls: Women Succeeding in the Rental Industry." *Rental Equipment Register*, April 1, 2007. http://rermag.com/features/equipment_dream_girls.

Stoller, Gary. "Hertz to Acquire Dollar Thrifty; Cash, Stock Rental Car Deal Valued at $1.2B." *USA Today*, April 27, 2010, 3B.

Transportation Security Administration. *Safeguarding America's Transportation System: Security Guide for Truck Rental Company Employees.* Washington, D.C.: U.S. Department of Homeland Security, 2005.

U.S. Bureau of Labor Statistics. *Career Guide to Industries*, 2010-2011 ed. http://www.bls.gov/oco/cg.

_____. "Counter and Rental Clerks." In *Occupational Outlook Handbook*, 2010-2011 ed. http://www.bls.gov/oco/ocos117.htm.

U.S. Census Bureau. North American Industry Classification System (NAICS), 2007. http://www.census.gov/cgi-bin/sssd/naics/naicsrch?chart=2007.

Wortham, Jenna. "Haute Couture, Available Through the Netflix Model." *The New York Times*, November 9, 2009, B-1.

Residential Medical Care Industry

©Dreamstime.com

INDUSTRY SNAPSHOT

General Industry: Health Science

Career Clusters: Health Science; Human Services

Subcategory Industries: Community Care Facilities for the Elderly; Group Homes for the Disabled; Nursing Care Facilities; Residential Mental Retardation, Mental Health, and Substance Abuse Facilities

Related Industries: Counseling Services; Hospital Care and Services; Hotels and Motels Industry; Insurance Industry; Medicine and Health Care Industry; Scientific, Medical, and Health Equipment and Supplies Industry

Annual Domestic Revenues: $165 billion (Nursing homes and assisted living; Hoovers, 2010)

Annual Global Revenues: $4.5 trillion (Total health care expenditures; The Medica, 2006)

NAICS Number: 623

INDUSTRY DEFINITION

Summary

The residential medical care industry serves patients who require skilled medical or rehabilitative care but who do not carry an illness or injury burden serious enough to qualify for acute hospital care. Residential care facilities are also known as skilled nursing facilities (SNFs). Their primary mission is to provide professional nursing care in an inpatient setting, with a goal of discharging patients to their homes or other appropriate residential environments.

SNFs offer a full spectrum of rehabilitative and recovery services, including occupational therapy, physical therapy, and speech therapy. Registered nurses (RNs) and physicians oversee the care plan of each patient. Twenty-four-hour care is a feature of this care delivery system. Sometimes diagnostics, such as phlebotomy and radiology, may be available on-site; if not, they may be brought via mobile unit, or patients may have to be transported to external testing facilities. Treatments and care are delivered by a number of professionals, from licensed care technicians to RNs and pharmacists.

Limited access to hospitals, cost issues, and advances leading to better survival rates for the chronically ill have led to the development of the specialized services of SNFs. These facilities deliver skilled care much more economically than do acute care facilities, and most insurance companies now mandate transfer to such facilities when patients no longer meet hospital criteria. SNFs pay rigorous attention to the appropriateness of the care they provide, and patients must meet a minimum level of illness severity to qualify for insurance coverage of SNF care. This is especially true of those covered by Medicare.

There are over sixteen thousand SNFs in the United States. This number is projected to grow as a result of the aging of the U.S. population and the longer life spans made possible by medical technology. Health care reform and escalating costs have resulted in a push to deliver more services in SNF settings when appropriate. Medicare and Medicaid, both governmental insurance programs, are the primary payers in the residential care industry, modifying their reimbursement schemata to save their programs from financial crisis. As one example, patients on assisted ventilation used to remain hospitalized until they were weaned from their ventilators. Now, these same patients go to SNFs, whose care and technological expertise has been shown to be successful in achieving more rapid patient recoveries and discharges. In short, hospitals have become places where only the sickest and most resource-intense patients are admitted, and acute inpatient recovery care is being redirected to SNFs. Jobs opportunities in this sector are many and growing.

History of the Industry

In the early twentieth century, senior citizens and others who needed continual care were either housed in private institutions that had been established by ethnic or religious communities or left to their fates in state-supported almshouses. Private institutions had strict criteria for entrance, usually based on moral character, financial means, or social standing, and they housed only a small portion of the people who needed their services. For the rest of the population, who relied on almshouses for care, no regulations or criteria for wellness or illness were established. To call them nursing facili-

The residential medical care industry serves patients who require skilled medical or rehabilitative care but not acute hospital care. (©Alexander Raths/Dreamstime.com)

ties would be to employ a misnomer; often, people went to almshouses to live out their lives in meager and substandard conditions. Workers staffing these facilities were unskilled and often were not even qualified to offer custodial care. Medical care was not available, and mortality rates were high.

In 1935, the federal government instituted Old Age Assistance (OAA), a program for retired workers. As residents in almshouses could not qualify for OAA funds, private institutions began to spring up whose residents would be eligible for OAA payments, which they used to pay for their care. By the end of World War II, governmental oversight structures for elderly care facilities began to mandate that such facilities receive licenses and meet codified standards of care in order to qualify for OAA payments.

In the mid-1950's, federal monies started to be-

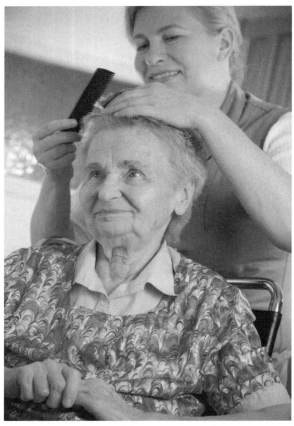

This resident's hair is being fixed by a nurse's aide, but some residents get their hair done by visiting beauticians. (©Alexander Raths/Dreamstime.com)

come available to construct more standardized nursing care facilities. The residents of such facilities had greater needs for regular medical treatment and attention than they had had in the past, so the facilities evolved to embrace more medical missions. They became recognizable as health care institutions and were no longer treated just as elderly homes for the impoverished. Nurses, physicians, and other skilled personnel composed the labor force in these more advanced facilities.

Both the law and federal funding provisions continued to evolve over time; reforms to payment mechanisms occurred, and some monies were withdrawn in response to funding crises. These spending cuts caused difficulties for people who had previously qualified for support and found themselves newly uninsured. Many frail and elderly persons faced barriers to obtaining medical care outside of acute care hospitals. Federal regulatory mandates grew unpopular, and the large number of uninsured citizens was widely publicized. As a result, a new category of "intermediate" care facilities was created to serve elderly and disabled patients and provided federal funding support. Intermediate care facilities had to meet rigorous standards to be paid, and care standards suffered when funding decreased. As a result, more administrative positions were created to monitor and report on facilities' adherence to federal standards.

In 1965, Medicare was enacted to provide health care to senior citizens. SNFs were eligible to receive Medicare reimbursements for their services. More strict eligibility requirements for patient coverage emerged, along with even more strict regulatory oversight of facilities. Nurses, physicians, and administrators ran their facilities and cared for patients, but they found themselves spending increasing amounts of time on compliance and reporting to the government.

The SNF designation was not established until the early 1990's. Originally, these entities were referred to as extended care facilities. SNFs are not custodial care facilities. The federal Medicare regulations spell out the difference between reimbursed medical care and unreimbursed custodial care.

The projected growth of the medical industry will make employment in an SNF a secure career choice for the foreseeable future. The industry, however, is not immune to economic pressures, and difficult financial times can result in unexpected hiring freezes or reductions in noncritical positions. Direct patient care positions are mission-critical and are some of the most secure in the industry. The average age of nurses in the United States is in the mid- to late forties; with an aging workforce and smaller numbers of younger people, jobs will continue to open up as baby boomers retire.

The Industry Today

SNFs are sometimes referred to as nursing homes, a broad term for facilities that offer skilled residential care in combination with restorative or custodial care. Of the sixteen thousand SNFs registered in the United States, about two-thirds are owned by for-profit companies, with the remaining portion owned by not-for-profit organizations. Fewer than 10 percent are owned by the federal government.

Some patients are admitted to SNFs for short-term medical recuperation or rehabilitation; costs of this recuperation are generally borne by a patient's private health insurance carrier. Elderly persons who are unable to care for themselves at home pay for assisted living facilities privately, often through pensions, retirement savings, or the proceeds of selling personal assets such as homes. Those needing more extensive medical care may find that paying for care in skilled nursing facilities becomes more complex, based on medical conditions, functionality, and financial means. In spite of the complex nature of SNF revenue sources, Medicaid is the primary payer for the SNF population in the United States. However, many people qualify for Medicaid only after they have expended their private assets.

People working in residential care facilities currently face stringent expectations for efficiency and economy. Most facilities operate with just enough staff to deliver quality care in a timely manner, and are accountable to the economic bottom line. Because life expectancies are increasing, medical and long-term care costs are rising significantly toward the end of life. Compounding the issue is the fact that aging slows one's recovery processes in general and can make going home immediately posthospitalization challenging.

For these reasons—and because extended families are no longer the norm in the United States—

Some nursing homes have gardens in which patients can walk with visitors. (©Lisa F. Young/Dreamstime.com)

SNF care represents a burgeoning business. RNs with associate's degrees can find supervisory and direct medical positions within SNFs. Licensed patient care technicians or licensed nursing assistants, under the supervision of RNs, provide custodial care and medical treatments within the scope of their licensure. Phlebotomists, radiology technicians, ultrasonographers, and respiratory therapists are just a few of the numerous professionals who may be employed or contracted to care for patients in the residential medical care industry.

SNF employment opportunities are growing faster than are opportunities in acute hospital care facilities. Gone are the days when patients were admitted to hospitals for weeks or months. Exceptional costs preclude long hospital stays, increasing the demand for skilled recuperative care in appropriate and fiscally responsible settings.

Common partnership industries to residential

medical care include long-term residential care facilities. Long-term care facilities and residential care facilities may be owned and operated alongside parent hospitals, or they may be privately owned. Transitioning patients too sick to go home but too well to stay in the hospital is of key importance to hospitals. Keeping patients in the bed too long increases costs and can prevent admissions of sicker patients by limiting bed capacity. Allowing patients who recover well to return home is certainly desirable, but when doing so proves impossible, residential care facilities allow hospitals to shift as much nonnecessary inpatient care as possible to an outpatient setting as soon as it can be done safely.

INDUSTRY MARKET SEGMENTS

Individual skilled nursing facilities range in size from small establishments with only a few beds to large facilities with more than one hundred beds. These facilities may be individual private entities, or they may be owned and managed by larger corporations. For example, Genesis HealthCare Corporation operates more than two hundred SNFs in thirteen states. Some corporations specialize in managing SNFs, whereas others may also own and operate hospitals and private medical office buildings, among other properties.

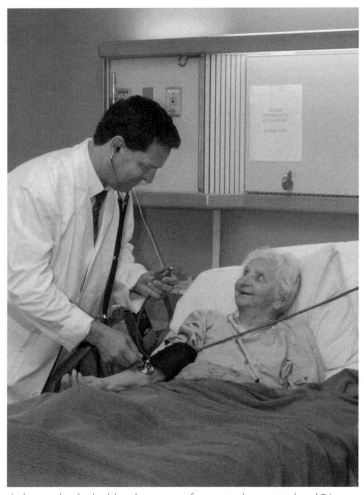

A doctor checks the blood pressure of a nursing home resident. (©James Steidl/Dreamstime.com)

Small Skilled Nursing Facilities

Small SNFs have fewer than fifty beds and employ as few as twenty-five people full time. They are often rural facilities, since most urban areas support significantly larger establishments.

Potential Annual Earnings Scale. According to the U.S. Bureau of Labor Statistics (BLS), an RN in a nursing care facility in 2008 earned a median annual income of $57,060; a licensed practical nurse earned an annual salary of $40,580; and a home health aide earned a median hourly wage of $10.20. Employees of small SNFs are likely to earn wages at or below the median.

Clientele Interaction. Patients, their families, government payers, federal facility surveyors, colleagues, referring hospitals, and vendors are the primary clients for SNFs. Patients in SNFs, as inpatients, are often in a highly vulnerable state, frightened and suffering maladies of various sorts. Many arrive at SNFs from independent homes and find themselves in unfamiliar surroundings, feeling a loss of autonomy and self. Patients rarely arrive alone, and employees of SNFs must be cognizant of extended families' pressures and fears.

Financial worries, child care, lost wages, and social concerns for the patient and the family require care providers to have compassion, understanding, a good sense of timing, and empathy. SNF nursing staff face particular challenges posed by competing demands for their time. High levels of bureaucracy and regulated oversight of staff make it all the more important for them to make the effort to connect directly with their patients. Everyone, from physicians to housekeepers, must maintain professional and respectful decorum; they should promote the quality of their SNFs to help allay fears and aid recovery, and they must be ever aware of the need to protect patients' privacy and confidentiality. In short, taking on the responsibility of working in health care requires employees to provide the medical, social, and psychological support necessary for recovery.

Amenities, Atmosphere, and Physical Grounds. Cleanliness and a calm atmosphere are critical in the SNF setting. Surgical-patient recovery requires sterility and designated treatment areas. Increasingly, SNFs are developing a patient-centered approach, with innovative designs that strive to be more "homelike," as comfort and peace of mind speed the recovery and discharge processes. Facilities seek to make access for family members relatively simple, providing sufficient parking and clear signage. Within an SNF, an attended receiving area assists in quickly routing visitors. However, the most important consideration within the care delivery areas is the comfort of the patients. Controlled humidity and temperature, rigorous attention to maintaining modest noise levels, and utmost attention to privacy and confidentiality are important to recovery.

Typical Number of Employees. Small SNFs of less than fifty beds generally employ a total of around twenty-five persons. They are often situated in sparsely populated areas, so they may find it difficult to find sufficient staffing for even those few positions. However, these smaller SNFs are likely to be fairly near acute-care facilities, and they provide strong economic stability in their locales, employing staff of all grades, from entry-level personnel to professional physicians and chief operating officers.

Traditional Geographic Locations. Small facilities are likely to be located in rural communities, with populations of under twenty thousand within their service areas. It is not uncommon to find such SNFs colocated with hospitals. While staff are drawn primarily from the immediate locale, higher-level administrative positions are attractive for their growth potential, and SNFs cast wide nets when recruiting for such positions. Finding physicians to staff SNFs can be challenging, because such a high proportion of the facilities' payments are made through Medicare and Medicaid, which have relatively low reimbursement rates. Contracts are required to reimburse physician travel time to small rural facilities.

Pros of Working for a Small Residential Care Facility. Providing local care at a small SNF allows employees to work in a more intimate community atmosphere. Direct health care providers at such facilities see many types of diagnoses and are exposed to stimulating technical and cognitive challenges in their work. Small SNFs are therefore attractive to many who value the unique learning opportunities they provide.

Smaller facilities often involve less bureaucracy and greater personal relations for employees with patients and their families. The U.S. Centers for Disease Control and Prevention Nursing Home Statistics Database suggests that smaller facilities have higher staff-to-patient ratios than do larger facilities. This higher ratio is likely to decrease stress levels and facilitate better distribution of workloads among caregivers. Small SNFs are likely to provide more intimate settings for staff and patients than do large SNFs, and those seeking close relationships with their patients should seek facilities housing no more than fifty to seventy-five beds.

Cons of Working for a Small Residential Care Facility. One challenge that professional staff face in an SNF is the lack of continuous and personal relationships with patients, given the technical resource requirements of their jobs. Nurses, therapists, and others delivering skilled services spend much time attending to medications, technologically administered treatments, and oversight of less skilled staff. Time spent in a nurturing role can be limited, which can be a dissatisfying situation.

Small SNFs may not have the financial resources of their larger counterparts, depending on whether they are run for profit. For-profit facilities tend to seek lower staff-to-patient ratios, raising concerns over patient safety and staff burnout due to stress and overwork. Capital dollars to improve equipment or enhance facilities may be more limited than at larger facilities. Additionally, small SNFs may have trouble recruiting and retaining trained staff, including physicians. Their lack of resources and inability to match the salaries of larger organizations are two primary drivers behind staffing challenges.

At small SNFs that lack sufficient depth in their work pools, employees are at risk of being required to work extra shifts or, at times, to work on shifts that are short-handed. The purchasing power that comes with a large workforce can also be compromised at small facilities, and employee benefits may not be as robust at smaller SNFs as they are at larger SNFs. Larger organizations have better risk ratings and can likely offer employees more and better benefit options. However, small SNFs that are part of larger chains may be able to offer the benefits common at larger organizations. Small SNFs provide high-level medical and procedural services, but health care providers who value the opportunity to work with the latest technology, with critically ill patients, or with younger populations may not feel fully challenged in these facilities.

Costs

Payroll and Benefits: SNFs employ both hourly and salaried employees, and benefits include health and dental insurance, long- and short-term disability, and Family Medical Leave Act coverage. Continuing professional education time and dollars are usually provided, as are malpractice insurance and sick and earned time. According to the U.S. Census Bureau, the vast majority of health care employees work part time, probably owing to the high proportion of them who are women either starting or raising families. Benefits, if available to part-time staff, are prorated to their total work commitments.

Supplies: SNFs require general medical supplies, disposables, pharmaceuticals, radiological products, and surgical and wound-care supplies and equipment; capital costs include such equipment investments as physical therapy equipment and whirlpools. Administrative and general operating supplies, such as cleaning and sterilization products, as well as office supplies, are also required.

External Services: SNFs experiencing a shortage of doctors or nurses may contract temporary physicians or travel nurses. They may also contract outside legal counsel, accountants and tax preparation professionals, medical record-keeping services, information technology experts, or billing consultants.

Utilities: Utilities for any medical facility are critical and include electricity, heat, backup energy sources, telephone, and Internet access.

Taxes: Governmental and publicly owned SNFs may enjoy tax breaks; not-for-profits are exempt from many taxes. Privately owned facilities, the majority of those in operation, must pay corporate income and property taxes. All facilities must pay employer payroll taxes and withhold payroll and income taxes from employees.

Midsize Skilled Nursing Facilities

Midsize SNFs have bed capacities of from fifty to one hundred. Net income after expenses varies widely, depending on the amount of bad debt burden, insurance payments (including Medicare and Medicaid, which pay poorly compared with private pay or other insurers), direct and indirect expenses, and overhead. SNFs' margins can be very small as the result of external factors; the broader economy plays a role, especially in driving competition to obtain privately paying patients who can afford skilled care.

Potential Annual Earnings Scale. According to the BLS, an RN in a nursing care facility in 2008 earned a median annual income of $57,060; a licensed practical nurse earned an annual salary of $40,580; and a home health aide earned a median hourly wage of $10.20. Employees of midsize SNFs are likely to earn wages that approximate the median salaries for their occupations.

Clientele Interaction. For the most part, the core mission of an SNF is to deliver medical and rehabilitative services. Working purely in a service industry, staff must be customer-focused, possess excellent communication skills, and have a desire to work in a hands-on, interactive, and caring industry. Midsize SNFs are likely to have lower staff-to-patient ratios than do small facilities, putting more pressure on care staff to maintain a safe and personal environment for their patients. The reputation of a facility is public knowledge because Medicare survey results on safety and quality are publicly accessible. Similarly and importantly to businesses, word-of-mouth referrals are more likely when personal service and good client interaction are delivered. Facilities have far too many overhead expenses to be able to leave beds unfilled, so reputation and interaction are priorities.

Amenities, Atmosphere, and Physical Grounds. Cleanliness and a calm atmosphere are critical in the SNF setting. Surgical-patient recovery requires sterility and designated treatment areas. Increasingly, SNFs are developing a patient-centered approach, with innovative designs that strive to be more "homelike," as comfort and peace of mind speed the recovery and discharge processes. Facilities seek to make access for family members relatively simple, providing sufficient parking and clear signage. Within an SNF, an attended receiving area assists in quickly routing visitors. However, the most important consideration within the care delivery areas is the comfort of the patients. Controlled humidity and temperature, rigorous attention to maintaining modest noise levels, and utmost attention to privacy and confidentiality are important to recovery.

Typical Numbers of Employees. A midsize SNF of up to one hundred beds will likely employ fifty to sixty staff members. Patient-to-staff ratios need to be explicitly understood, so employees are ensured of a responsible and manageable workload. A major factor in total staffing numbers is the centralization of functions or external contracting of services such as billing, collections, and communications systems.

Traditional Geographic Locations. Midsize facilities are typically located near populated areas. Two-thirds of SNFs are located in metropolitan areas. This makes sense, given that a sufficient population density is needed to support such a facility. Most U.S. SNFs are located in the Midwest and the South. (Retirement to warmer climes and older populations in these areas probably explain this distribution.) Many SNF admissions come from discharges following surgery or medical service; the closer it is to referring physicians and hospitals with technology and ancillary services, the more attractive an SNF will be to investors (if privately run) and to patients. Close links to physician staff and private-practice physicians should be paramount to maximize referral sources. While socioeconomics in the SNF's local area can play a role, the demand for easily accessible SNFs can bring midsize facilities to more populated locales despite sour economic conditions. Reputation and quality reports play a much larger role than location in an organization's sustainability, however.

Pros of Working for a Midsize Residential Care Facility. Well-established organizations provide employment security, and their purchasing power allows them to offer better benefits at more favorable rates for their employees, especially if they are part of larger chains of privately owned nursing facilities. Employees of midsize SNFs have access to health insurance for themselves and their families at group rates, which are more favorable than those a smaller employer might be able to offer. Pay incentives may be available as well, usually based on productivity and expense controls. Every employee of an SNF is responsible for contributing to the financial bottom line of the organization.

Physicians, nursing leaders, and administrators generally share responsibility for being on call at night and during weekends. Midsize and larger facilities are able to spread this responsibility out over larger staffs, making the burden less onerous on each individual. Any facility providing service twenty-four hours a day, seven days a week faces unique staffing challenges, but skilled employees are in high demand, creating a favorable scenario for job seekers.

Cons of Working for a Midsize Residential Care Facility. Midsize SNFs are more complex organizations than their smaller counterparts. Their higher patient-to-staff ratios can contribute to staff dissatisfaction. With complexity comes increased communication challenges and, potentially, less autonomy; this situation is sometimes challenging for medical service professionals. When ratios are low, staff can become antagonistic to coworkers who call in sick or are not seen as pulling their weight. The danger of overwork, including mandatory overtime, is one of many factors affecting employee retention and satisfaction.

Multiple equally worthy individuals and units may have to compete for limited resources. Thus, medical staff—in addition to already demanding jobs—may need to be strong advocates for themselves and their clients when confronting their own institutions' bureaucracies. Pressures to be more efficient and work with fewer staff while providing excellent care will be felt.

Costs

Payroll and Benefits: Midsize SNFs hire professional staff and pay on salary. Benefits often include health insurance, dental coverage, short- and long-term disability, malpractice premium reimbursement, continuing education funds (including money and time), and retirement plans such as 401(k)s.

Supplies: SNFs need paper or electronic medical records, basic office supplies, computers, telephones, décor conducive to a health care setting, disposable medical supplies, uniforms, and other noncapital supplies, among many other necessities. Capital expenses relative to medical equipment vary, depending on the tests and services available on-site, but equipment investments and maintenance costs can be considerable.

External Services: SNFs may contract external vendors to clean their facilities or linens and to provide uniform services, accounting, legal advice, public relations and marketing services, cell phones and pagers, medical records storage and destruction, and hazardous waste removal. Nonfederal consultants may be contracted to assure continued licensure.

Utilities: SNFs must pay for electricity, water, backup systems, telephone service, and Internet access.

Taxes: Governmental and publicly owned SNFs may enjoy tax breaks; not-for-profits are exempt from many taxes. Privately owned facilities, the majority of those in operation, must pay corporate income and property taxes. All facilities must pay employer payroll taxes and withhold payroll and income taxes from employees.

Large Skilled Nursing Facilities

Large SNFs have more than one hundred inpatient beds. Their patient demographics and staffing qualifications are identical to those of small and midsize SNFs. Patient-to-staff ratios tend to be higher in large SNFs, likely as a result of economies of scale, though larger SNFs that are privately owned are known to cut staffing and costs to improve their financial bottom lines. Higher patient-to-staff ratios can raise safety and quality concerns. Large facilities can draw business from up to 100 miles away or even further, depending on competition and patient willingness to travel. Competition exists in the health care industry, and grappling for market share while maintaining sufficient staffing is a constant challenge for a large SNF.

Revenue from patient care services is in the millions of dollars for large chain SNFs. Earnings in these settings are targeted at maintaining favorable operating margins. A favorable margin, depending on the legal structure of the organization, can result in profits for stakeholders or reinvestment into not-for-profit entities. Not-for-profits struggle for revenues and a sustainable bottom line because of their charity-care and uncompensated-care requirements (as well as their expensive medical education missions if they are associated with training programs). Facilities seeking to remain current, viable, and competitive in the industry must reinvest in their capital funds and infrastructure. Continuing to pass federal site reviews is even more important, as negative findings can result in loss of Medicare funding or even threaten facilities with closure.

Potential Annual Earnings Scale. According to the BLS, an RN in a nursing care facility in 2008 earned a median annual income of $57,060; a licensed practical nurse earned an annual salary of $40,580; and a home health aide earned a median hourly wage of $10.20. Employees of large SNFs are likely to earn wages at or above the average for their occupations.

Clientele Interaction. Larger organizations offer more diversity and opportunity for professionals. SNF care, which can be long term (months), can force patients to spend months away from their homes and familiar environments. Removing patients from familiar settings and family can delay recovery, however. Physicians, nurses, and other staff can become surrogates for family, and they must have excellent interpersonal caring skills. Staff should advocate for patients and encourage their families to assign guardians or family advocates to closely monitor patient care and progress.

Physicians and nurses employed by large SNFs work as part of a large group of similar professionals, sharing on-call duties. Collaboration and patience are required, and staff may face challenges scheduling their obligations around holidays and school vacations. Professionals represent their organizations and their colleagues when they interact with clients, and they are expected to be available and responsive when they are on call.

Amenities, Atmosphere, and Physical Grounds. Large SNFs are typically freestanding, with sizable grounds. Investments in aesthetics are important to develop client security and trust in an organization, which in turn is important for maintaining the organization's client base. Open space and a trend toward less clinical environments are common, as the focus of those designing amenities and interiors lies more on patient comfort than on optimal medical-care-delivery design or the convenience of deliverers.

Typical Number of Employees. Large health care facilities employ thousands of staff members, including medical, administrative, financial, operations, and support staff. From the first phone call, to patient admission, to patient discharge and follow-up, numerous staff members representing a given SNF come in direct or indirect contact with patients. This size and structure requires a synergistic, well-coordinated effort to meet the needs of patients and to fulfill the mission of the SNF.

Traditional Geographic Locations. Large SNFs are generally located in densely populated areas, mostly in the Midwest and the South. A sufficient population base, with actuarial promise of growth, is critical to the livelihood of a medical facility. Unlike a business that relies on product sales through the Internet, for example, a health care facility provides a face-to-face service to its clients.

Pros of Working for a Large Residential Care Facility. Large health care facilities offer many people the opportunity for advancement. Throughout their careers, people working in SNFs can develop leadership skills and move into growth positions, such as administrative or management roles. Large SNFs provide significant areas for growth, especially if employees are motivated and committed to learning. Larger organizations tend to have the financial capacity and structure to promote such advancement, particularly if their missions include academic opportunities alongside clinical care. The SNF industry, embedded in an overarching and mammoth health care industry that contributes nearly 20 percent of the U.S. gross domestic product (GDP), offers job security and strong opportunities for advancement.

Cons of Working for a Large Residential Care Facility. Internal politics become more evident in larger service organizations. The employees of large SNFs can expect more bureaucracy and delays inherent in decision making; sometimes, it can take what seems a very long time to move initiatives forward. The higher ratio of patients to each nurse creates employee tension, as well as higher risks for patients. While minimum staffing ratios are set by oversight bodies such as Medicare, the higher the ratio of patients to staff members, the longer recovery will take for patients.

No area of SNFs is exempt from financial challenges: Leadership and managers must advocate regularly for resources and be mindful of staff burnout and overwork. Working in any large organization can cause employees to feel unnoticed or underappreciated. Large SNFs with robust postsurgical and medical services must remain competitive. Investment in facilities for growth is a priority. Information technology, for example, is exploding in SNFs, as diminishing revenues force greater efficiency and rapid management to discharge. Surgical and diagnostic advances represent major capital investments, but without them SNFs can lose their competitive edge.

Costs

Payroll and Benefits: Large organizations hire professional staff under a salary structure. Common benefits include health and dental insurance, disability coverage, Family Medical Leave Act protection, retirement accounts, malpractice insurance, continuing medical education (including reimbursement for travel, time, and registration for courses), and even tuition reimbursement for additional degree work. Benefits are generally prorated to the standard number of hours worked, with a minimum set for eligibility.

Supplies: SNFs need paper or electronic medical records, basic office supplies, computers, telephones, décor conducive to a health care setting, disposable medical supplies, uniforms, and other noncapital supplies, among many other necessities. Capital expenses relative to medical equipment vary, depending on the tests and services available on-site, but equipment investments and maintenance costs can be considerable.

External Services: SNFs may contract external answering services, cleaning services, sterile supply companies, uniform services, cell phone and pager providers, waste disposal companies, medical records storage and destruction services, and risk management and legal counsel, among other medical, support, and business services.

Utilities: SNFs must pay for electricity, water, backup systems, telephone service, and Internet access.

Taxes: Governmental and publicly owned SNFs may enjoy tax breaks; not-for-profits are exempt from many taxes. Privately owned facilities, the majority of those in operation, must pay corporate income and property taxes. All facilities must pay employer payroll taxes and withhold payroll and income taxes from employees.

ORGANIZATIONAL STRUCTURE AND JOB ROLES

Any size entity providing medical services has to function as a business. An SNF represents a complex, integrated system that requires many key critical functions to interrelate daily. At small facilities, multiple functions and roles may be filled by the same individual. Large facilities are more likely to employ specialists in each role.

The following umbrella categories apply to the organizational structure of businesses in the residential medical care industry:

- Business and Operations Management
- Medical Staff
- Contracting, Reimbursement, and Billing
- Human Resources
- Customer Services/Risk Management
- Public Affairs and Marketing
- Facilities and Security
- Housekeeping
- Nutrition
- Information Technology and Communication Systems

Business and Operations Management
Business and operations managers guide the business decisions of their organizations. They set

OCCUPATION SPECIALTIES

Activities Therapists

Specialty	Responsibilities
Art therapists	Plan and direct activities that help mentally ill and physically disabled patients use art for nonverbal expression and communication.
Dance therapists	Plan, organize, and lead dance and body movement activities to improve patients' mental outlook and physical well-being.
Horticultural therapists	Plan, coordinate, and conduct therapeutic gardening programs to facilitate the rehabilitation of physically and mentally handicapped patients. They conduct gardening sessions and revise the programs to conform and grow with the progress of the patients.
Manual-arts therapists	Plan and organize woodworking, photography, metalworking, agriculture, electricity, and graphic arts activities in collaboration with a rehabilitation team and prepare reports that show development of patient work tolerance, emotional and social maturity, and ability to meet physical and mental demands of employment.
Music therapists	Plan, organize, and direct instrumental and vocal music activities and experiences to help patients with their communication, social, daily living, or problem-solving skills.

OCCUPATION PROFILE

Medical Records Administrator

Considerations	Qualifications
Description	Helps plan, design, develop, evaluate, and manage health care record systems.
Career clusters	Business, Management, and Administration; Health Science
Interests	Data
Working conditions	Work inside
Minimum education level	Bachelor's degree
Physical exertion	Light work
Physical abilities	Unexceptional/basic fitness
Opportunities for experience	Internship
Licensure and certification	Usually not required
Employment outlook	Faster-than-average growth expected
Holland interest score	SIE

Note: See volume 1, "Publisher's Note," for an explanation of the Holland interest score.

goals and measure success. They drive any moves toward expansion or consolidation of services or facilities. Underlying these decisions is the company's financial success. The business and operations group is also responsible for financial management—budgeting for revenues, expenses, and capital investments. The chief executive officer (CEO) and chief financial officer (CFO) work together to manage financial performance and oversight.

A business and operations group protects the jobs of everyone working in their organization by ensuring fiscal stewardship and maximizing financial performance. Typical employees in this area have undergraduate or graduate degrees in finance or business. Many management positions are salaried, and they are often the highest-paid positions within an organization.

Managers' relationships with stakeholders both within and outside the SNF are important. Good relations with referring hospitals are needed for consistent business. In particularly large organizations, chief officers direct from the highest levels,

leading vision, strategy, and investment goals for their organizations, and their compensation reflects the risk involved in decision making when more is at stake. According to the BLS, the median annual income in 2008 for a medical and health services manager in a nursing care facility was $71,190.

Business and operations management occupations may include the following:

- Chief Executive Officer (CEO)
- Chief Financial Officer (CFO)
- Chief Operating Officer (COO)
- Nursing Director

Medical Staff

SNFs depend heavily on their reputations, which can make or break them. The quality and professionalism of those providing medical care, from doctors to health aides who work directly with patients, determine the greatest share of their facilities' reputations. They have the most direct contact

OCCUPATION PROFILE

Nurse Practitioner

Considerations	Qualifications
Description	Performs both nursing and other medical duties that may include treating uncomplicated illnesses in infants, children, and adults; conducting a physical exam; developing a plan of patient care; providing emergency treatment; and teaching and counseling patients on matters such as prevention of illness, family planning, and care of the terminally ill.
Career cluster	Health Science
Interests	Data; people; things
Working conditions	Work inside
Minimum education level	Bachelor's degree; master's degree
Physical exertion	Light work
Physical abilities	Unexceptional/basic fitness
Opportunities for experience	Volunteer work
Licensure and certification	Required
Employment outlook	Faster-than-average growth expected
Holland interest score	ISA

Note: See volume 1, "Publisher's Note," for an explanation of the Holland interest score.

with patients and guide their care. Successful organizations thrive on high standards of patient care, excellent communication, and a shared understanding of best practices in providing care.

Compensation is tied to training and expertise; according to the Medical Group Management Association's Physician Compensation and Production Survey, the 2008 median annual salary for a primary care physician was $186,044. According to the BLS, the average salary for an RN was $57,060; a licensed practical nurse earned an average of $40,580; and a home health aide earned a median hourly wage of $10.20 during the same period.

Medical staff occupations may include the following:

- Physician
- Registered Nurse
- Licensed Practical Nurse
- Home Health Aide

Contracting, Reimbursement, and Billing

Contracting, reimbursement, and billing personnel ensure that their SNFs are reimbursed as expected by Medicare and other payers. They submit all charges and documentation and manage accounts receivable, as well as accounts payable. For nongovernmental contracts, rate negotiation and oversight are the responsibility of contracting departments. Personnel also work with in-house legal counsel and inside and outside stakeholders to develop fair and reasonable contracts, and they work with business and operations managers to ensure that contractual conditions are met. They also contract with private physicians to provide medical care and directorship. Contracting personnel generally have bachelor's or advanced degrees, and some may require legal expertise as well.

Contracting, reimbursement, and billing occupations may include the following:

- Chief Financial Officer (CFO)
- Chief/Vice President/Manager of Contracting
- Revenue and Reimbursement Manager
- Financial Analyst
- Charge Master Manager
- Denials Manager
- Data Entry Clerk
- Accounts Receivable Clerk
- Accounts Payable Clerk

Human Resources

Human resources (HR) personnel recruit, hire, train, and fire staff. They administer payrolls and benefits, evaluate employee performance, and provide performance management expertise. A growing area of responsibility within the domain of human resources is employee wellness and function. In larger organizations, human resources staff members hold undergraduate or graduate degrees, sometimes with training in social work or counseling. Human resources professionals are responsible to managers and supervisors, providing them guidance in all functions of human resources and ensuring fair and equitable treatment of employees.

Human resources occupations may include the following:

- Nurse Recruiter
- Development and Education Specialist
- Benefits Manager
- Human Resources Manager
- Payroll Clerk
- Employee Health Adviser

Customer Services/Risk Management

Customer services and risk management staff are responsible for responding to patient complaints and protecting their SNFs from legal actions. They receive and resolve customer concerns, direct front-line managers and employees in how to interface with customers, and handle malpractice claims, injuries, and other legal liability issues in collaboration with legal and senior medical counsel. Pertinent to SNFs are the routine quality surveys conducted by external auditors. Negative findings are publicly reported and must be managed appropriately to mitigate damage to a facility's reputation and market share. According to Salary.com, the median annual salary for a risk management specialist in 2010 was $94,606.

Customer services and risk management occupations may include the following:

- Relations Manager
- Risk Management Specialist
- Legal Counsel
- Service Recovery Specialist

Public Affairs and Marketing

Marketing and public affairs personnel maintain and grow their organizations' market share. Despite an aging population driving more need for SNF care, competition for their business is real. Public affairs personnel advertise their facilities, interact with customers inside and outside the organization, and develop marketing strategies alongside operations strategy. They cooperate closely with operations, overseeing and directing local departmental initiatives to retain and grow their customer base. They also work closely with the customer services and risk management department.

Public affairs and marketing occupations may include the following:

- Referring Physician Liaison
- Administrator of Public Affairs and Marketing
- External Relations Manager
- Advertising Executive

Facilities and Security

Facilities and security are responsible for maintaining the buildings, equipment, and grounds of SNFs, as well as controlling access to the facilities. Keeping buildings in good repair is both a safety requirement and a marketing and public relations requirement. Included in this area of responsibility are snow removal, ice management, signage, parking, and some transportation.

Security professionals provide twenty-four-hour service and usually bring with them law enforcement or similar backgrounds. Nurses and others finishing shifts after dark should have escorts available, vehicle assistance if needed, and the ability to request assistance if necessary. Depending on the level of security responsibility, a high school diploma or a bachelor's degree is required.

Facilities and security occupations may include the following:

- Security Director
- Facility Management Director
- Security Guard
- Parking Attendant
- Building Engineer
- Maintenance Contractor

Housekeeping

Housekeepers maintain a clean, safe environment for patients, visitors, and employees. They interact with people during much of their workdays. Because SNFs provide hospital-level services, housekeepers must have specialized training and expertise in maintaining a hygienic environment, knowing standards, and protecting employees and patients alike from biological, chemical, and physical hazards. Housekeepers typically have high school diplomas or college degrees, depending on the level of their positions. Wages are generally hourly, with shift differentials for evening and night work. These positions are staffed twenty-four hours a day, seven days a week.

Housekeeping occupations may include the following:

- Housekeeping Director
- Housekeeper

Nutrition

Nutrition and dietary personnel prepare patients' meals. Dieticians must provide for those patients with food restrictions related to pathologies such as diabetes, kidney disease, or hypertension and must coordinate with food managers to ensure safety and compliance. Nutrition staff also work in employee dining areas, and they can provide healthful eating education to patients and employees alike.

Nutrition occupations may include the following:

- Nutritionist
- Chef

- Cook
- Dietician
- Food Preparer/Kitchen Staff
- Meal Delivery Staff
- Cashier

Information Technology and Communication Systems

Networking systems, computer workstations, electronic medical records, and related software are the responsibility of the information technology (IT) department. Communications, interconnectivity for programs supporting clinical care, and diagnostic technologies such as radiology, laboratory, and medication management systems are examples of the high-end technological needs in this setting. IT professionals generally have bachelor's or advanced degrees in computer science or related fields and often have practical experience in IT support as well.

IT and communication systems occupations may include the following:

- Systems Analyst
- Hardware Specialist
- Help Desk Staff
- Computer Security Specialist

INDUSTRY OUTLOOK

Overview

The outlook for the residential medical care industry shows growth to be an ongoing trend. Demand for workers and career opportunities are very favorable. Growth in this industry is steady, with health care contributing 17 percent to the U.S. GDP. Contributing to this growth is the largest aging population in U.S. history. Americans expect to live longer and are treating illnesses aggressively, creating a market for skilled nursing facilities that will extend for a significant portion of the early twenty-first century. Threats to the industry come from diminishing Medicare and Medicaid funds. State-run Medicaid funding is also under threat, as the recession of 2007-2009 threatens the financial health and stability of state governments across the country.

Employment and job security in this sector are strong. Challenges for those entering the industry include greater competition for college-educated professionals in direct care positions and some administrative roles. Physicians, psychologists, pharmacists, and other direct care providers with advanced degrees should see greater opportunities in this highly competitive job market. SNFs seek those who are self-directed and have an affinity for the elderly and disabled.

SNFs have the potential to earn significant profits if managed closely and efficiently. Troublesome trends are emerging, however, in which investors purchase facilities and then cut corners in terms of cost and quality. Whether privately or publicly owned, regulatory complexity and declining Medicare funds suggest challenging times for SNFs. Overall, nursing homes collected more than $75 billion in revenues from federal (Medicare) and state (Medicaid) funding, money that presents an attractive opportunity for investors. The aging U.S. population will keep SNFs in business, but astute management will be of utmost importance for them to remain financially viable.

Employment Advantages

Positions in medicine, nursing, and pharmacology are in demand. Whether part-time or full-time, these positions are often salaried and very secure relative to the general economic environment. Those interested in medical technical work will find much opportunity, as complex treatments require increasing use of medical technology in the industry. Shortages in key professional positions help keep salary and benefits competitive.

Additionally, SNFs hire skilled, white-collar workers in such fields as administration, finance, and management. Professionals in such careers may find SNFs to be rewarding settings in which to work. Caring for the elderly or debilitated provides the personal reward of seeing patients through to recovery and back home. The challenges in this area lie in the balance of providing excellent care while managing operating expenses.

SNFs offer work experiences that were once found only in hospitals. Nursing and medical students will likely find themselves doing clinical rotations in these settings, but they may find that working in acute-care hospitals initially after graduation will hone their skills and confidence prior to working in SNFs. Clinical academic rotations can only give a flavor of the independence that professionals may enjoy in SNFs. Today, one of the greatest advantages of SNF work is job security, as millions of baby boomers are aging and demand in this area is growing.

Annual Earnings

Reports of annual earnings and revenues in SNFs are usually combined with the revenues from assisted living facilities, which usually work closely with skilled nursing organizations. In fact, many of those in the aging population, as they become less able to care for themselves or develop debilitating illnesses such as Alzheimer's or heart disease, are moved from assisted living to skilled nursing care because SNFs are better equipped to administer the full range of medical procedures such patients may require.

While assisted living costs are

PROJECTED EMPLOYMENT FOR SELECTED OCCUPATIONS

Nursing and Residential Care Facilities

Employment		
2009	Projected 2018	Occupation
399,600	546,100	Home health aides
263,520	315,900	Licensed practical and licensed vocational nurses
34,100	38,900	Medical and health services managers
797,110	956,700	Nursing aides, orderlies, and attendants

Source: U.S. Bureau of Labor Statistics, Industries at a Glance, Occupational Employment Statistics and Employment Projections Program.

calculated at a monthly rate, skilled nursing care rates are significantly higher and, because of specific Medicaid requirements, are calculated on a per diem basis. More complex patients and conditions require costly procedures that only licensed facilities can provide. Some insurers pay flat day-or-stay rates, while other insurers negotiate discounted fees. Revenues vary by facility, the number of beds, the severity of the illnesses being treated, and billing conventions. Gross fees never translate to net fees in the medical industry; allowances (discounts) that vary by payer and by contract prohibit reliable projections of annual revenues.

That said, Hoovers estimates the 2010 revenues of all U.S. nursing homes and assisted living facilities at $165 billion. According to the U.S. Census Bureau, 2007 revenues in the areas of continuing care retirement communities grew by 10.1 percent, while the growth rate for hospital revenues in the same year was 6.5 percent. SNFs have a proven track record of growth and are also proving to be sound investments and to constitute a solid industry for career development.

RELATED RESOURCES FOR FURTHER RESEARCH

AARP
    601 E St. NW
    Washington, DC 20049
    Tel: (888) 687-2277
    http://www.aarp.org

AMERICAN COLLEGE OF HEALTHCARE EXECUTIVES
    1 N Franklin, Suite 1700
    Chicago, IL 60606-3529
    Tel: (312) 424-2800
    Fax: (312) 424-0023
    http://www.ache.org

AMERICAN HOSPITAL ASSOCIATION
    155 N Wacker Dr.
    Chicago, IL 60606
    Tel: (312) 422-3000
    http://www.aha.org

HEALTHCARE FINANCIAL MANAGEMENT ASSOCIATION
    2 Westbrook Corporate Center, Suite 700
    Westchester, IL 60154
    Tel: (708) 531-9600
    Fax: (708) 531-0032
    http://www.hfma.org

MEDICAL GROUP MANAGEMENT ASSOCIATION
    104 Inverness Terrace East
    Englewood, CO 80112-5306
    Tel: (303) 799-1111
    http://www.mgma.com

ABOUT THE AUTHOR

Nancy Sprague holds a bachelor of science degree from Granite State College and a master of science in health policy from the Dartmouth Institute, Dartmouth College. She is a member of the National Medical Group Managers' Association, the Healthcare Financial Management Association, and the American College of Healthcare Executives. She is a fellow in the American College of Healthcare Executives, a registered nurse, and a health care operations consultant. Sprague has spent her career in medical practice and hospital operations, both in private practice and in a large academic tertiary hospital. She has extensive experience in physician and staff relations, and she is an expert in human resources, compliance, risk, billing, health care business management, hospital administration, and patient-centered care.

FURTHER READING

Giacolone, Joseph A. *The U.S. Nursing Home Industry.* Armonk, N.Y.: M. E. Sharpe, 2001.
New Strategist Publications. *American Health: Demographics and Spending of Health Care Consumers.* Ithaca, N.Y.: Author, 2005.
Parker, Philip M. *The 2007-2012 Outlook for Nursing Homes in the United States.* San Diego, Calif.: ICON Group, 2006.
Santerre, Rexford E., John A. Vernon, and the National Bureau of Economic Research. *Testing for Ownership Mix Efficiency: The Case of*

the Nursing Home Industry. Cambridge, Mass.: National Bureau of Economic Research, 2005.

U.S. Bureau of Labor Statistics. *Career Guide to Industries,* 2010-2011 ed. http://www.bls.gov/oco/cg.

U.S. Census Bureau. North American Industry Classification System (NAICS), 2007. http://www.census.gov/cgi-bin/sssd/naics/naicsrch?chart=2007.

U.S. Congressional Budget Office. *The Impact of Medicare's Payment Rates on the Volume of Services Provided by Skilled Nursing Facilities.* Washington, D.C.: Author, 2007.

U.S. Department of Commerce. International Trade Administration. Office of Trade and Industry Information. Industry Trade Data and Analysis. http://ita.doc.gov/td/industry/otea/OTII/OTII-index.html.

Verity, Jane, and Daniel Kuhn. *The Art of Dementia Care.* Clifton Park, N.Y.: Thomson Delmar Learning, 2008.

Restaurant Industry

©Danie Nel/Dreamstime.com

INDUSTRY SNAPSHOT

General Industry: Agriculture and Food
Career Clusters: Agriculture, Food, and Natural Resources; Hospitality and Tourism
Subcategory Industries: Drinking Places; Full-Service Restaurants; Limited-Service Eating Places
Related Industries: Farming Industry; Fishing and Fisheries Industry; Food Manufacturing and Wholesaling Industry; Food Retail Industry; Food Services; Livestock and Animal Products Industry; Themed Entertainment Industry; Travel and Tourism Industry
Annual Domestic Revenues: $566 billion USD (National Restaurant Association, 2009)
Annual Global Revenues: $1.367 trillion USD (Research and Markets, 2007)
NAICS Number: 722

INDUSTRY DEFINITION

Summary

The restaurant industry is a segment of the food service industry, which includes all businesses that prepare and sell food that is ready for consumption. Restaurants differ from other types of food vendors in that they provide an area for patrons to dine after purchasing a meal. The restaurant industry is one of the largest service industries in the United States and is closely related to the tourism and leisure industry. Restaurants can be divided into numerous subcategories, including quick service or fast food, casual dining, and fine dining. As of 2009, there were an estimated more than 945,000 restaurants employing more than 13 million full- or part-time workers in the United States.

History of the Industry

Restaurants were an essential part of the economies of ancient societies, including those of preindustrial China, Japan, Europe, and the Middle East. In thirteenth century China, the affluent city of Hangzhou, the most populous city of that time, was the site of many cultural and technological innovations. It was there that restaurants began to develop into something resembling their modern incarnation. Food was cooked to order, and guests chose their meals from a menu. Before this, most early restaurants were inns or boarding houses that offered food to guests for an additional fee. Food at these establishments was usually served "family style," with guests gathering at tables to serve themselves from communal dishes.

Though food vendors were common in medieval Europe, the first public cafés, or restaurants, serving gourmet food to customers appeared in the mid-seventeenth century in Paris, France. (The term "restaurant," in fact, first appeared in the sixteenth century and is derived from the French word *restaurer*, which means "to restore" and which originally referred to a medicinal soup. Early purveyors often marketed their restaurants as providing a medicinal service and concentrated on the healthy aspects of their cuisines.) Seventeenth century Paris was one of Europe's largest cities and the center of the French economy. As in thirteenth century China, the proliferation of the economy and a large population with sufficient disposable income created a niche within the food market.

By the mid-eighteenth century, Paris had a variety of restaurants that concentrated not only on

Restaurants can be divided into numerous subcategories, including quick service or fast food, casual dining, and fine dining. (©Dreamstime.com)

preparing food but also on providing an atmosphere for socializing. Dining in Parisian restaurants soon became a symbol of status and a fixture of the metropolitan entertainment market. It was not long before technological innovations followed and the modern restaurant spread throughout Europe—by 1770, restaurants were using printed menus and the burgeoning industry had diversified into a number of specialized establishments selling different types of cuisine.

The evolution of the dining industry in the United States resembled the development of the European industry. The early inns and boarding houses serving food gave way to simple food vendors operating on the streets and eventually to small cafés and taverns selling food from menus. The first "official" restaurant on record in the United States was Jullien's Restarator, which opened in Boston, Massachusetts, in 1794. The restaurant was operated by Jean-Baptiste Gilbert Payplat, who came to be known as the Prince of Soups, reflecting the French origins of the word "restaurant." (Boston is also home to the oldest continuously operating American restaurant, the Union Oyster House, which opened its doors in 1826.) Early eating establishments in the United States were characterized by heavy and mostly mediocre—if not outright poor—food. Few were successful.

The development of the restaurant industry during the nineteenth century was soon driven by competition among eating establishments. Some restaurants specialized in extravagant cuisine or presentation, while others capitalized on unique cuisine. As the twentieth century unfolded, the restaurant industry began to develop in the opposite direction. A number of restaurants began offering simple, affordable cuisine that contrasted with the elaborate, gourmet fare of earlier restaurants. These new establishments became widespread since they catered to the general population and not just the upper classes.

The simplification of restaurant food eventually led to the establishment of the fast-food industry, which concentrates on providing simple, quick, low-cost food. The origins of fast-food restaurants are usually traced to New York City, where vendors working at fairgrounds began to sell precooked items such as hot dogs to passing customers. At the 1904 World's Fair in St. Louis, Missouri, vendors sold a variety of fast, affordable food items, providing a model for what would become one of the largest facets of the food industry. By the 1920's, small establishments such as White Castle (which eventually became a national chain of restaurants) cropped up, offering "to-go" food items such as hamburgers and soft drinks.

By the 1930's, the first fast-food chains began to appear all over the United States. This growth was spurred by the development of the automobile industry in the 1930's and 1940's, which helped usher in the next wave of the quick-service industry: drive-in restaurants. The prototypical fast-food model was established by McDonald's restaurant, which emerged in 1940 in San Bernardino, California. McDonald's became the first restaurant chain to employ an assembly line in the food preparation area, increasing efficiency and speed. This trend was soon employed by hundreds of similar establishments.

By the twenty-first century, American cities boasted a variety of eating establishments, drive-in and fast-food eateries, banquet centers, full-service casual or fine dining, and specialty restaurants. Restaurant offerings range from healthy or organic food options to any type of international cuisine. The restaurant industry has continued to grow, as entrepreneurs attempt to compete in a crowded marketplace by introducing innovations across the board, whether in cuisine, presentation, or price.

The Industry Today

In the first decade of the twenty-first century, the U.S. restaurant industry was one of the most di-

Inputs Consumed by Food Services and Drinking Places

Input	Value
Energy	$14.5 billion
Materials	$123.3 billion
Purchased services	$106.6 billion
Total	$244.4 billion

Source: U.S. Bureau of Economic Analysis. Data are for 2008.

verse service industries in the nation. Restaurant sales accounted for more than $500 billion in 2008, nearly 4 percent of the U.S. gross domestic product (GDP), and the industry employed some 13 million full- and part-time workers, 9 percent of the workforce. In fact, more than 40 percent of U.S. adults will work in the restaurant industry at some point in their lives. More than 90 percent of restaurants are considered small or midsize and employ fewer than fifty people.

Even as the industry continues to diversify, most restaurants can still be placed into one of three categories: quick service, casual dining, or fine dining. The latter two categories encompass full-service establishments, which provide table service to patrons. Quick-service restaurants, which include fast-food purveyors, specialize in fast preparation time and affordable menu options, while casual restaurants occupy a middle ground between quick service (in which turnover is more intimately tied to revenue) and fine dining. (Restaurants termed "fast casual" represent another, emerging category.) The vast majority of restaurants fall under the casual-dining umbrella, which includes pubs, cafés, and most national chains. Fine-dining establishments are typically characterized by quality and reputation, rather than value and volume. There are many varieties of fine-dining establishments, ranging from small neighborhood eateries to large, banquet-style restaurants.

The Contribution of Food Services and Drinking Places to the U.S. Economy

Value Added	Amount
Gross domestic product	$288.3 billion
Gross domestic product	2.0%
Persons employed	9.691 million
Total employee compensation	$188.2 billion

Source: U.S. Bureau of Economic Analysis. Data are for 2008.

Within each category, restaurants may specialize in one or more ways. They may, for instance, limit their hours and menus to cater to specific clienteles or meals. For example, restaurants in areas with heavy foot traffic at midday often specialize in serving lunch to business customers, and they may remain open for only five or six hours each day. Other restaurants specialize in evening dining and may therefore remain closed throughout the morning and afternoon. Regardless, factors such as atmosphere and type of cuisine vary across all three categories; for example, international cuisine is represented across the service spectrum, and atmosphere may be as important to the success of a pub or national chain as it is to a fine restaurant.

The industry continues to evolve, incorporating such trends as organic, vegan, and vegetarian dining; restaurants that serve only locally produced ingredients; and fusion cuisine, in which chefs blend favors from different geographic areas. There are hundreds of fusion varieties, including French-Asian and Afro-European. Combining the basic restaurant concept with the many categories of international and fusion cuisine creates a multitude of possibilities, from quick-service Indian food to fine Afro-Asian cuisine.

The vast majority of restaurants fall under the casual-dining umbrella, which includes pubs, cafés, and most national chains. (©Diego Vito Cervo/ Dreamstime.com)

The 2007-2009 global economic crisis proved a challenge to the national restaurant industry. Since restaurants tend to depend on the disposable income of consumers to survive, and many Americans consider dining out to be a luxury rather than a necessity, the restaurant industry is particularly susceptible to economic downturns. From January to May of 2009, for example, approximately 60 percent of restaurants experienced sales lower than their average. During such periods, restaurants often seek to make their food more affordable and advertise their products in terms of value to gain a competitive edge.

While economic factors and consumer trends present challenges to restaurant operators, the U.S. restaurant industry remains robust, as patronizing restaurants has become an ingrained and central part of American recreation and entertainment. On an average day, more than 130 million Americans eat out, whether purchasing a hamburger from a fast-food vendor or enjoying a gourmet meal at a fine-dining establishment.

Small-restaurant chefs may earn anywhere from $15,000 to more than $100,000. (©Monkey Business Images/ Dreamstime.com)

INDUSTRY MARKET SEGMENTS

Each of the three basic restaurant categories can be further divided into small businesses, midsize businesses, and large businesses. Each type of restaurant, from large quick-service provider to small fine-dining establishment, offers specific advantages and challenges. An analysis of each business category, organized by size, is provided below.

Small Businesses

Small restaurants are those with twenty or fewer employees and a capacity to serve fifty or fewer clients at a time. Small restaurants may provide quick-service, casual, or fine dining and are often closely linked to their immediate communities. The vast majority of independent restaurants in the United States fall into this category.

Potential Annual Earnings Scale. Earnings for restaurant owners and managers depend less on the size of the restaurant than on location, type of food served, and the average turnover rate—that is, the average time needed to service a single group of customers and turn the tables for the next seating. The salary range for restaurant managers ranges from $20,000 to over $100,000 per year, with the majority earning an annual average salary of about $50,000 in 2005, according to Star Chefs. Owners of small restaurants can be expected to earn salaries in the lower half of that scale.

According to Star Chefs, executive and head chefs in the United States earned an average of $75,000 per year in 2005, but individual salaries vary widely depending on the type of restaurant and location. Small-restaurant chefs may earn anywhere from $15,000 to more than $100,000. In 2008, the average annual salary for chefs and head cooks was $42,410 according to the U.S. Department of Labor. Some restaurant owners calculate employee earnings based on the percentage of sales to which they contribute.

Kitchen staff, including dishwashers, line or prep cooks, and other "back of the house" workers, make a modest wage—often the federal minimum wage, which was $7.25 in 2009. The U.S. Bureau of Labor Statistics (BLS) reports that the 2008 estimated median hourly wage for dishwashers was $8.19. For food prep workers, it was $9.39. Wait staff and "front of the house" staff generally rely on an hourly base wage plus tips. Because a small restaurant can be an exclusive bistro with a high-priced menu or a small café serving coffee and baked goods, earnings vary widely. Assuming an average of between 15 and 20 percent for tips at all establishments, wait staff at expensive restaurants can earn dramatically more than wait staff at inexpensive cafés that serve the same number of customers each day. The BLS estimates that the median hourly wage of waiters and waitresses in 2008 was $8.01 per hour. Bartenders, like waitresses, rely heavily on tips. The BLS estimates the 2008 median hourly wage of a bartender at $8.54.

Clientele Interaction. The level of client-staff interaction at a restaurant depends on the size of the restaurant and the type of service offered. The nature of the quick-service industry, which focuses on affordable fare and efficient turnover time, generally prevents customers and staff from developing a high level of familiarity, regardless of restaurant size. By contrast, employees of small fine and casual restaurants have the opportunity to cultivate relationships with frequent customers. In fact, small fine and casual restaurants often rely on repeat customers and may be heavily tied to a certain neighborhood or area. It is more common in small restaurants for members of the staff to know customers by name and to develop working friendships with members of their clientele.

Amenities, Atmosphere, and Physical Grounds. The décor of a small restaurant depends largely on the type of food being served. Whether quick-service, casual, or fine, small restaurants have to find a balance between making the most of their limited space and creating a friendly, inviting environment. Smaller quick-service restaurants are usually organized so as to maximize efficiency, including the placement of the service counters, the arrangement of seating, and the location of restrooms and other facilities. Small casual and fine restaurants are more concerned with environment and ambience. For example, small casual restaurants may choose eclectic decorations, opting to make the space appear unique rather than elegant. By contrast, small fine restaurants may choose minimalist decorations in an effort to create an environment of elegance.

The choice of decoration also generally reflects the type of cuisine being served. A small French restaurant might, for instance, attempt to replicate the environment of a Parisian café with its table linens and other decorations. National or regional music and arts also play a large part in setting the ambience of small international restaurants. Amenities in smaller restaurants are often basic. In larger cities, where space is often limited, many restaurants lack environmental controls such as air-conditioning. Even fine restaurants, which focus on creating a luxurious atmosphere, are often forced to make do with fewer amenities in urban areas.

Smaller quick-service restaurants are usually organized so as to maximize efficiency. (©Monkey Business Images/ Dreamstime.com)

Typical Number of Employees. Small businesses are typically not as insulated against changes in patronage as are larger restaurants because they often operate on lower levels of income. The number of employees working at a small restaurant may range from four or five to more than twenty employees, depending on the size of the space, the volume of customers, the number of shifts available per day, and the type of cuisine served.

It is not uncommon for small restaurants to have only a single server working during any given shift, though some restaurants require several staff members to accommodate heavy customer traffic. A small breakfast restaurant might, for instance, have to employ several servers during Saturday and Sunday service because of increased patronage, while a single server might suffice during a Tuesday or Wednesday morning.

The number of employees in a restaurant kitchen also varies widely. The smallest establishments may have only one or two kitchen workers for any shift. They will prepare food, prep ingredients for service, and clean the kitchen area. Other restaurants may hire additional support staff, including dishwashers, prep cooks, line cooks, and other kitchen employees.

Traditional Geographic Locations. Small restaurants may appear in a variety of locations, from residential neighborhoods to busy commercial areas. They are especially common in large cities, where they are ideally situated to make use of the limited commercial space available. Many small towns and rural communities have one or more small restaurants in the center of town, and these establishments often serve as gathering places for their communities.

The only areas in which small restaurants do not often appear are those that are very sparsely populated, such as the long stretches along interstate highways that are more often populated with midsize casual and quick-service restaurants situated in strip malls and similar commercial areas. The lack of foot traffic and repeat clientele make these areas unattractive to the typical freestanding small restaurant.

Pros of Working for a Small Restaurant. Small restaurant environments are often extremely closely knit and may be informal by comparison to larger restaurants. Often, the intimate, community environment lends itself to personal interaction.

Even in the more formal environment typical of the fine-dining industry, smaller restaurants tend to have a more unique and personal feel.

During periods of economic turmoil, as many larger businesses are unable to afford their overhead, small restaurants may have an advantage in that they require fewer customers to generate sufficient revenue to afford ingredients and staffing costs. In addition, small restaurants are better able to adjust to changing market trends by altering their approach or presentation to suit their changing clientele.

Because small restaurants are often tied closely to the surrounding community, owners may benefit from a more loyal base of customers, who feel personally invested in the success or failure of the restaurant. This customer loyalty can benefit restaurant owners in times of financial turmoil, as regular customers will often continue to patronize their favorite establishments even while cutting back on other spending.

Cons of Working for a Small Restaurant. Because of limited space and staff, small restaurants are limited in the total revenues that they can generate during an average business day. Lower revenues ultimately render small restaurants vulnerable to economic changes. When consumer spending falls, small restaurants must adjust quickly to avoid financial collapse. About 30 percent of new restaurants fail within the first year and the number climbs to 60 percent within three years of opening, according to the *Cornell Hotel and Restaurant Administration Quarterly*. Restaurants fail for a variety reasons but mostly because of poor financials, bad marketing decisions, and inadequate management.

Another limitation of the small restaurant business is that the cost of ingredients and other supplies is higher when they are purchased in small quantities, preventing small restaurants from maximizing their profits. Limited resources for supplies also force small restaurants to avoid wasting material as much as possible, because their costs per unit for raw ingredients are higher.

In addition, some owners and employees of small restaurants may find that the familiarity and informal interactions between staff and clients create a unique set of interpersonal problems. For instance, if a staff member develops a personal issue with a certain customer, that customer may decide not to return to the restaurant. Losing a single repeat customer may not significantly affect a midsize or large restaurant, but it might affect the daily income of a smaller establishment.

Costs

Payroll and Benefits: While payroll costs vary widely depending on the average daily income of each restaurant, payroll expenses generally constitute about 30 percent of every revenue dollar according to Restaurant Resource Group. Many small restaurants do not offer insurance and other benefits to most employees. However, small quick-service restaurants may offer such benefits, especially if they are part of a larger chain.

Supplies: In addition to ingredients for cooking, small restaurants require cookware and utensils for preparation and food service. The most costly expenditure for many restaurants is purchasing stovetops, ovens, and ventilation equipment for their kitchens, as well as cold-storage units to keep perishable supplies. Numerous other necessary supplies include linens, sanitary supplies, and cleaning products.

External Services: Many small restaurants hire a credit card service to process credit and debit transactions. They may also contract accounting and payroll services to handle monetary transactions and bookkeeping, as well as uniform companies to bring clean napkins, linens, rugs, and other supplies.

Utilities: Restaurants may need to pay for water and sewage, electricity, heating (gas or electric), and telecommunications and Internet services. Utilities may vary depending on whether the restaurant owner also owns the property in which the restaurant is housed.

Taxes: Small restaurants pay federal, state, and sometimes city taxes. Many restaurants also pay additional annual licensing costs, including liquor license fees, food preparation permits, and inspection permits. Property owners also need to pay property taxes annually.

Midsize Businesses

Midsize restaurants seat between fifty and one hundred customers. There are many different types of midsize restaurants, from quick-service restaurants and diners to fine-dining establishments. Most midsize restaurants fall into the casual-dining category, which includes a number of national and statewide chain restaurants that offer affordable, basic meals and welcome groups.

Potential Annual Earnings Scale. The earnings of midsize restaurants often exceed those of small restaurants, but they vary widely depending on the type of restaurant, location, and average number of clients served per dining period. Typically, the investment in staff and materials for midsize restaurants is only slightly more than for small restaurants. However, midsize restaurants often provide higher profit margins because they can serve more clients.

Owners and managers of midsize restaurants generally earn more than $60,000 annually. Similar to small restaurants, the individual salaries of executive or head chefs range widely depending on the type of restaurant and location, though a high percentage draws annual salaries between $70,000 and $90,000. As of 2008, the average annual salary for chefs and head cooks was $42,410.

Clientele Interaction. The environment of a midsize restaurant is often more formal than that of a smaller restaurant, with less personal interaction among members of the staff and between staff and customers. Midsize restaurants must be prepared to serve large groups and therefore require a more rigid system for determining roles and functions among the staff.

While midsize restaurants may attract repeat customers, their larger volume requires them to draw customers from outside the immediate community. These customers are less likely to become regulars and therefore less likely to form personal attachments to the restaurant. In addition, because midsize restaurants may serve one hundred or more customers during a lunch or dinner rush, members of the staff have less time to engage in casual, friendly interactions with their customers. Staff at midsize restaurants must therefore find a balance between presenting a friendly, inviting atmosphere and maximizing efficiency.

Amenities, Atmosphere, and Physical Grounds. Unlike smaller restaurants, which can still attract clientele while maintaining an informal atmosphere, midsize restaurants must provide certain basic amenities for their customers. Air-conditioning is essential in midsize restaurants, where the volume of customers can have a significant effect on the ambient temperature. In addition, midsize restaurants may, for example, provide changing tables in restrooms for the convenience of customers with infants and young children. Midsize restaurants also typically have high chairs and booster seats available for young children. Other amenities in "family style" midsize restaurants may include toys such as crayons and coloring books for children.

Many midsize restaurants are part of restaurant chains, and their choices in décor and atmosphere may reflect decisions made by the owners of the chain, rather than the local management and staff. A popular decorative scheme in midsize casual dining is the "knick-knack" approach, where the restaurant is decorated using a variety of eclectic items intended to give customers something to look at while they enjoy their meal. For example, sports-themed establishments are often decorated with a variety of athletic equipment, sports team memorabilia, and similar items.

Midsize fine-dining establishments often use sparse decoration and strategically contrasting colors to create a dignified, luxurious look. Black and white is a common color scheme in fine-dining establishments, along with candles for the tables, fine art pieces on the walls, and soft, ambient lighting.

Typical Number of Employees. Midsize restaurants typically handle large volumes of customers and must therefore hire sufficient employees to facilitate efficient service. While small restaurants sometimes expect servers to clean and reset tables between customers, midsize restaurants usually hire support staff to assist the servers and kitchen staff. Midsize restaurants might have as many as thirty employees working during a busy shift, including servers, support staff, kitchen workers, and a floor or shift manager.

Traditional Geographic Locations. Midsize restaurants may appear in a variety of geographic areas but are usually concentrated in areas with significant automobile or foot traffic. The vast majority of midsize restaurants are quick-service and casual-dining establishments that attempt to attract customers who are already in the area for other reasons.

Midsize restaurants are especially common in commercial zones, along portions of an expressway or highway, where they can benefit from proximity to other retail stores and shopping malls.

Many midsize restaurants establish themselves near a major recreational venue, such as a concert hall or sports stadium. A small number of midsize fine-dining establishments may also choose a strategic location next to upscale recreational venues, such as opera houses or symphony orchestra venues. Some midsize fine restaurants appear in busy downtown areas, where they can capitalize on a variety of foot traffic.

Pros of Working for a Midsize Restaurant. Midsize restaurants offer several advantages over small restaurants. With increased capacity and customer volume, restaurant owners stand to make more profit and have a better chance of insulating their business to withstand slow periods. In addition, because a midsize restaurant often employs a larger staff, the business is protected in case a staff member must leave unexpectedly, a situation that can be disastrous for smaller restaurants.

For the staff in midsize restaurants, the division of labor that comes with having a larger staff provides the opportunity to do less work than in a small restaurant for similar pay. Unlike the situation in small restaurants, servers, chefs, and other workers at midsize restaurants have well-defined roles and are usually only responsible for one part of the service.

Cons of Working for a Midsize Restaurant. While midsize restaurants have greater earning potential than do small restaurants, they are also dependent on attracting a larger number of customers to make ends meet. On a slow business day at a midsize restaurant, the restaurant may waste a significant amount of the material that was prepared to cook the day's meals.

Similarly, the cost of maintaining a large staff can become financially draining when business lulls. Utility and rent payments are also significantly higher for a typical midsize space.

Costs

Payroll and Benefits: Kitchen staff and other support staff are usually paid hourly wages and are more likely to be given benefits at midsize restaurants and chain restaurants. Servers and other support staff (bussers, bartenders, hosts/hostesses, and so forth) are often paid a small hourly wage and expected to supplement this base wage with tips.

Supplies: Midsize restaurants require a variety of supplies for daily operation. In addition to ingredients, they must have cleaning supplies, cookware, dishes, utensils, linens, and sometimes uniforms for the staff. Most midsize restaurants also have computer systems to handle orders and payment and may require various other electronics, such as telephones, televisions, and stereo systems.

External Services: Many midsize restaurants hire external companies to handle credit and debit transactions and to aid with bookkeeping and other financial data. They may also hire supply companies to deliver sanitary supplies, dishware, linens, and other items that must be renewed or replaced on a regular basis. Restaurants may also contract outside services to provide royalty-free music and gaming entertainment, while some establishments maintain an entertainment budget that includes payments for live music.

Utilities: Midsize restaurants must typically pay for gas/oil, telephone, Internet access, sewage, water, and electricity.

Taxes: Midsize restaurants must pay local, state, and federal income taxes, as well as property taxes. They may also need to pay annual licensing fees to maintain their liquor licenses, vending licenses, and other permits that must be renewed.

Large Businesses

Large restaurants are the most specialized of the three size categories. With the capacity to serve between one hundred and one thousand diners at a time, large restaurants specialize in attracting large groups and catering to special events. Banquet halls and country clubs are the standard models for large restaurants, but there are some large fine and casual restaurants in metropolitan areas. These include very large themed restaurants that market themselves as tourist destinations, as well as niche restaurants that cater to many customers at once, such as dim sum palaces.

Potential Annual Earnings Scale. While management in large restaurants may earn salaries exceeding those offered in midsize and small restaurants, the standard wage for staff members differs little between large and midsize restaurants. Large restaurants also incur the highest costs for materials and staffing, which offset their earnings from increased volume.

Within a general salary range of $20,000 to $100,000 for owners and managers in the United States, those operating large restaurants tend to earn salaries in the upper half of the scale. However, a manager of a large chain restaurant may not earn more than a similar manager in a smaller chain restaurant. Executive chefs in large restaurants, such as those serving country clubs or banquet halls, also tend to earn salaries at the upper end of the scale, ranging from $70,000 to $100,000 per year.

Clientele Interaction. Because large restaurants more often serve large groups, the environment of such establishments is less intimate and less personal than those of midsize and small restaurants. To handle a large volume, larger restaurants require a well-defined division of labor and usually require that all members of their staffs concentrate on efficiency, without sacrificing friendliness and basic customer relations. Large restaurants often employ a staff of greeters, whose role is to welcome customers as they enter and show them to their seats, among other small tasks.

Amenities, Atmosphere, and Physical Grounds. Depending on the type of cuisine being served, the atmosphere of a large restaurant can range from basic to elegant. Banquet centers are often established in historic buildings, with attractive interiors adding to the elegance of the atmosphere. Employees of large restaurants commonly wear formal uniforms.

Large restaurants may choose from many different potential organizational styles, depending on the space. Some large restaurants have single, large dining rooms with many tables organized in such a way as to facilitate efficient service. Others have several dining rooms in order to accommodate multiple parties or to better partition service.

Because they serve many customers, large restaurants must be equipped with basic amenities, including bathrooms capable of accommodating multiple occupants. Large restaurants often also have public telephones and may provide wireless Internet for business customers. They usually require attached parking facilities or at least paid parking areas that are within a convenient distance. Often, they have amenities designed to accommodate large parties, such as weddings and other celebrations. For example, a restaurant might have a lawn with a tent in summer or a large function hall with or without a separate kitchen, restroom facilities, a bar, dance floor, and small rooms for bridal parties.

Typical Number of Employees. A large restaurant may have anywhere from thirty or forty full-time employees to more than one hundred, depending on the size of the company and the number of customers served on an average business day. The division of labor for service personnel usually requires one server and at least one server's assistant for every three to five tables. More may be required if tables have more than five to ten seats.

Large restaurants also typically have sizable staffs to support the chefs in the kitchen. Dishwashers, expediters (food runners), and cleaning staff may be required, in addition to persons responsible for preparing raw ingredients and handling inventory. Some restaurants also hire staff specifically to deal with their liquor inventory, including purchasing and organizing stock. This may include a bar manager, who is also responsible for tending bar.

Traditional Geographic Locations. Large restaurants are usually found only in cities, either in busy downtown areas or on the outskirts of the city. Some large country clubs, resorts, and hotels also have large restaurants on the premises. Business for large restaurants typically comes from pre-planned events rather than from customers who walk into the restaurant in passing (called "walk-ins" in the industry). Though a large restaurant is perhaps best situated in a location that is convenient for potential customers, these restaurants rarely rely on their locations as the primary means of attracting customers.

Pros of Working for a Large Restaurant. Owners and managers of large restaurants have a high earning potential and are often provided with competitive benefits. Employees of large restaurants typically earn wages commensurate with those of the staff at smaller restaurants, but they are more likely to be offered benefits such as health insurance and retirement plans in addition to their wages. Because large restaurants typically have a sufficient number of supporting staff members, workers in any one position may not be required to handle as many competing tasks as are employees of small restaurants.

Because large restaurants often focus on catering large events, parties, and other social events, they are not as reliant as are small and midsize restaurants on impulse customers. Large restaurants may therefore enjoy continued revenues during times when consumers' impulse spending is in decline.

Cons of Working for a Large Restaurant. Working at a large restaurant is an entirely different type of experience than working at a small or midsize establishment. Employees at large restaurants must function as a team, so personality conflicts among staff members can harm the business, and the need for teamwork can complicate the tasks associated with serving, cleaning, or working in the kitchen. In addition, the cost of purchasing huge quantities of ingredients and paying for a large number of staff members hampers large restaurants' ability to endure extended periods without significant business.

Costs

Payroll and Benefits: Most employees at large restaurants are paid hourly wages, and many are offered benefits packages. Having a large number of employees working in different positions complicates the salary and wage structure within a large restaurant. Managers and chefs generally receive a salary and are usually given some form of benefit package.

Supplies: The most significant expenditure for a large restaurant is food, alcohol, and ingredients. In addition, large restaurants require dishes, cookware, utensils, cleaning supplies, and linens, as well as computer systems to facilitate ordering and payment and other electronic items to facilitate high-volume business.

External Services: Large restaurants typically hire outside companies to deliver basic restaurant supplies, including laundered goods, paper goods, and other dry goods. They may also use payroll services and accounting services, and many restaurants use outside laundry services to clean uniforms, rugs, and other items. Other services include pest control and maintenance for utility units, including heating and air-conditioning.

Utilities: Most large restaurants pay for gas/oil, electricity, telephone, Internet access, and water. Many pay additional fees for use of public parking areas and other services that are shared with other businesses.

Taxes: Large restaurants pay local, state, and federal income taxes, as well as property taxes where applicable. Large restaurants also need to pay annual fees to keep their licenses in order, including liquor licensing and food permits.

ORGANIZATIONAL STRUCTURE AND JOB ROLES

The division of labor within a restaurant depends on a number of factors, including the size of the restaurant and the type of food being served. Larger restaurants tend to have more employees and usually use a more defined and sometimes hierarchical division of labor. Similarly, fine-dining establishments typically have a pronounced division of labor, especially in the kitchen, where there may be multiple personnel, each specializing in one facet of food service.

In the smallest restaurants, job roles tend to blend together, as a single individual may need to handle tasks from a variety of categories. Small cafés, coffee shops, and family-run restaurants often have fewer employees, each of whom is responsible for duties ranging from sanitation and cleaning to customer service and accounting.

The following umbrella categories apply to the organizational structure of restaurants:

- Management
- Advertising and Marketing
- Kitchen Staff
- Kitchen Support
- Liquor and Beverage Staff
- Dining Staff
- Dining Assistants

Management

A manager at a typical restaurant is responsible for a wide variety of tasks. Few restaurants have separate human resources departments, so managers are responsible for hiring and firing employees, mediating conflicts between staff members, and overseeing the daily operations of the restaurant. Some restaurant owners function as managers, while other owners hire managers.

Depending on the size of a restaurant, management may be divided into several levels. Many restaurants, for instance, have one manager who is responsible for overseeing business in the dining and service areas while another manager oversees the kitchen. Each is responsible for overseeing operations, hiring and firing staff, and handling inventory in his or her respective area. Restaurants that handle large volumes of customers may hire multiple dining and kitchen managers, each responsible for a specific shift. Other restaurants hire special managers to oversee certain functions of the restaurant, including accounting, human resources, and inventory management.

Managers are typically salaried, and many restaurants choose to promote former servers or other dining staff to management positions to ensure that their managers are familiar with all procedures in the kitchen and dining areas. Similarly, kitchen managers are usually former chefs or at least individuals with significant prior cooking experience.

Management occupations may include the following:

- General Manager
- Kitchen Manager
- Dining Manager
- Shift Manager
- Executive Chef
- Financial Manager
- Inventory Manager

Advertising and Marketing

The amount of money spent on advertising varies widely among restaurants. Small, independent restaurants typically spend little on advertising, other than placing occasional ads in local publications, while many quick-service restaurants and casual-dining chains spend a significant amount on ads, including radio, television, and print campaigns.

While few small restaurants hire full-time staff for advertising and marketing, larger restaurants and chain restaurants often have at least one employee who is responsible for facilitating and updating their advertising. Advertising specialists may also be responsible for finding alternative ways to market their restaurants, such as by participating in local and national charities or catering prominent public events. Advertising and marketing specialists are typically salaried and usually earn pay commensurate with that of restaurant managers.

Advertising and marketing occupations may include the following:

- Advertising Director
- Marketing Director
- Special Events Coordinator
- Advertising and Marketing Manager

Kitchen Staff

The chef or head cook of a restaurant is typically the head of the kitchen, except in cases where the owner or general manager hires a kitchen manager to take executive control of food preparation. The role of a chef or head cook differs depending on the type of restaurant and the type of cuisine being served. In addition, a restaurant may hire a number of employees to assist the head cook in the kitchen. The difference between a cook and a chef is imprecise and often based on qualitative charac-

teristics, such as the prestige of the restaurant, the individual's level of training, and the quality of the cuisine being served.

Executive chefs oversee all aspects of the business related to the kitchen, including cost control for staff and ingredients, menu design and creation, and the hiring and firing of kitchen staff. Many fine restaurants also have sous chefs (under chefs), who serve as the second in command of the kitchen and principal assistant of the executive or head chefs. Executive and sous chefs function as members of both the kitchen staff and the management staff.

Beneath head chefs and sous chefs, many restaurants employ a variety of line cooks, also called *chefs de partie*, who are responsible for various food preparation activities. Each line cook may be responsible for a variety of preparation tasks or may be highly specialized. In some fine restaurants, individual chefs are assigned such tasks as grilling, baking bread and pastries, preparing fish, preparing

---

OCCUPATION PROFILE

Cook/Chef

Considerations	*Qualifications*
Description	Plans and prepares food for consumption in restaurants and other eating facilities.
Career cluster	Hospitality and Tourism
Interests	Data; people; things
Working conditions	Work inside
Minimum education level	On-the-job training; high school diploma or GED; high school diploma/technical training; apprenticeship
Physical exertion	Medium work
Physical abilities	Unexceptional/basic fitness
Opportunities for experience	Apprenticeship; military service; volunteer work; part-time work
Licensure and certification	Usually not required
Employment outlook	Slower-than-average growth expected
Holland interest score	ESR; RES; RSE

Note: See volume 1, "Publisher's Note," for an explanation of the Holland interest score.

OCCUPATION SPECIALTIES

Cooks/Chefs

Specialty	Responsibilities
Bakers	Prepare bread, rolls, muffins, and biscuits and supervise other bakers in various institutions.
Chefs de froid	Design and prepare decorated foods and artistic food arrangements for buffets in formal restaurants.
Institutional cooks	Prepare soups, meats, vegetables, salads, dressings, and desserts in large quantities for schools, cafeterias, hospitals, and other institutions.
Pie makers	Prepare and bake pies, tarts, and cobblers.
Short-order cooks	Prepare and cook to order foods requiring short preparation time.
Specialty fast-food cooks	Prepare such foods as fish and chips, tacos, and pastries for window or counter service.

sauces and condiments, cooking vegetables, making soups, and staffing other specialized stations.

While most executive chefs and other managing members of a kitchen staff are usually on salary, many line cooks and subordinate cooks are paid hourly wages. The leading chefs in a fine restaurant usually occupy the highest-paying positions in the restaurant.

Kitchen staff occupations may include the following:

- Executive Chef
- Head Chef
- Line Cook
- Junior Cook
- Sous Chef
- Saucier (Sauce Chef)
- Pastry Chef
- Grill Chef
- Fish Chef

Kitchen Support

In addition to a head chef and a supporting chef, many kitchens also hire a number of supporting personnel who do not cook or prepare ingredients. Instead, they support cooks and other kitchen workers and may be responsible for tasks such as dishwashing, waste disposal, cleaning and sanitization, and other general services. In large restaurants and ones that handle large numbers of customers during a typical shift, supporting kitchen staff members and cooking personnel are equally essential to the functioning of the kitchen. Most supporting kitchen staff members are paid hourly wages and generally earn less than cooking staff. In large restaurants and restaurant chains, supporting kitchen staff may be offered benefits in addition to their regular wages.

Kitchen support occupations may include the following:

- Dishwasher
- Cook's Assistant
- Cleaning Assistant
- Kitchen Maintenance Worker

Liquor and Beverage Staff

Some restaurants, especially fine-dining establishments, hire liquor and beverage specialists to maintain their liquor stocks, assist chefs and cooks in pairing liquor with certain dishes, and aid customers in choosing and purchasing beverages and liquor. Restaurants with full-service bars usually hire bartenders with knowledge of cocktails, wine, and other types of spirits and liquor.

The sommelier is the pinnacle of restaurant liquor specialists. Sommeliers are specialists in wine and aid restaurants by handling all aspects of wine service, including purchasing wine from distributors, organizing storage and inventory, and recommending and serving wine to customers. Sommeliers are usually salaried employees, while bartenders and liquor-service assistants may be paid hourly wages.

Liquor and beverage staff occupations may include the following:

The quality of any restaurant, whether quick service, casual dining, or fine dining, depends on the customer-relations skills of the restaurant's service personnel. (©Dreamstime.com)

- Sommelier
- Assistant Sommelier
- Liquor Manager
- Bartender
- Bartender's Assistant (or Barback)

Dining Staff

The quality of any restaurant, whether quick service, casual dining, or fine dining, depends on the customer-relations skills of the restaurant's service personnel. The service personnel are responsible for taking customer orders and delivering orders to the kitchen. The exact duties of servers and other service personnel differ depending on the structure of the restaurant and the type of food being served.

Some restaurants, especially fine-dining establishments, hire a headwaiter, or maître d', who acts as head of the dining department. This individual functions as both a manager and a member of the service staff and is usually responsible for handling server assignments, greeting customers, handling problems with dining service, and overseeing servers and server assistants. Alternatively, some restaurants hire hosts and hostesses to perform some of the duties typically assigned to a maître d'. These employees are generally given similar authority to that of servers rather than functioning as managing servers.

While a maître d' may work on salary, most other positions in the service department are paid hourly wages. Salaries for many service personnel are low, because it is expected that servers and other dining workers will earn some or most of their income from customer gratuities (tips).

Dining staff occupations may include the following:

- Server
- Host/Hostess
- Maître d'
- Head Server
- Greeter

Dining Assistants

To ensure the efficient operation of the dining area, a variety of support personnel is often hired to assist servers and customer-service personnel. Servers' assistants are responsible for cleaning tables and refilling beverages, and they often help servers keep track of customer needs. Dining assistants are also usually responsible for turning over tables—that is, cleaning them after one service and setting them up for new customers.

An expediter (or aboyeur) is part of both the kitchen and the dining staff. Expediters retrieve food from the kitchen and deliver it to either the tables or the servers. Expediters are also typically responsible for ensuring that orders brought to the kitchen are completed in the correct order. An expediter therefore serves as an important line of communication between the kitchen and the dining area.

Most dining assistants earn hourly wages, and they are not usually offered benefits, except in larger restaurants. Server assistant positions typically have high turnover rates in many restaurants, as employees in assistant positions often transition to become servers. In addition, assistant positions often attract individuals who want temporary or seasonal work, such as students who want to work during the summer before returning to classes.

Dining assistant occupations may include the following:

- Server's Assistant
- Expediter
- Maintenance Staff

INDUSTRY OUTLOOK

Overview

Growth and decline in the restaurant industry are closely tied to recreational consumer spending. During an economic surge, the industry thrives, as customer volume increases and the average customer spends more on a typical meal. During a recession, customer numbers fall, as does average spending per customer.

While the restaurant industry is closely linked to economic performance, restaurants are often better able to withstand economic fluctuations than are other types of recreational businesses. Food and drink are essentials of everyday life, rather than pure indulgences. While individuals can choose to prepare their own meals in order to save money, they must continue to eat, and the vast majority will frequently turn to restaurants, whether out of necessity, convenience, or pleasure. Restaurants, moreover, are a basic and ingrained part of social culture around the world. From business lunches, to romantic dinners, to family meals, individuals often justify recreational spending in favor of the social benefits of eating out with friends, colleagues, and family.

The 2007-2009 global economic crisis provides a recent example of how the restaurant industry can fare in times of economic decline. According to the National Restaurant Association (NRA), restaurants across the board—from independent establishments to local and national chains—reported declines in sales for more than twelve consecutive months between summer, 2008, and summer, 2009. Though the NRA predicted that nationwide sales would rise by as much as 2.5 percent in 2009, when the statistics are corrected to account for inflation, the result was a net decline of more than 1.3 percent. Full-service restaurants, which have greater expenditures compared to income, were expected to suffer declines of as much as 2.5 percent in 2009.

While the NRA report painted a poor picture for the industry, Technomic, a consulting firm specializing in food-industry analysis, believed that losses would be even more significant in 2009, with as much as a 6 percent decline in sales for U.S. restaurants. Technomic also predicted that the casual dining industry would bear the brunt of the economic collapse because there are simply too many casual restaurants to compete in a flooded market. Technomic predicted in early 2009 that more than one thousand casual restaurants would close in the United States by the middle of the year. (In contrast, fast-food outlets stand to gain from economic downturns, as some spending-cautious consumers opt for waiter-free and more affordable dining options.)

Fine-dining establishments are also vulnerable during an economic downfall, because the price of an average meal at a fine dining restaurant may be too high for consumers wary of spending and concerned about job losses. Fine restaurants, however, have one major advantage—their marketing is based on offering high-quality or unique cuisine, whereas the quality of fare offered at casual restaurants differs little from restaurant to restaurant. Diners seeking a meal that cannot be duplicated at home or looking for a place to celebrate a major event often turn to fine and unique independent restaurants before they choose to spend their money at casual restaurants or chains. Some fine restaurants modify their menus during economic downturns to offer high-quality but lighter and less expensive meals. French restaurants convert to bistros (or open bistros next door to their flagship restaurants). Italian osterias similarly convert to or open supplementary trattorias.

Another factor that plays a major role in the fortunes of the industry is the price of ingredients. Rising food costs in 2007 and 2008 severely cut into the profits of many restaurants. Food cost fluctuations stem from a variety of factors, including production levels in the agricultural industry, plant and animal illnesses, fossil fuel prices (industrial agriculture is heavily dependent upon fossil fuel), and seed monopolies, as well as the ongoing evolution of foreign trade agreements. Even as profits decreased in the United States in 2008 and 2009, food prices began to fall, owing to bumper crops (unusually large or productive harvests) of some ingredients and discounts from vendors designed to offset loss of business during the recession. Between January and May of 2009, average food costs declined by almost 12 percent, providing much-needed relief for many restaurants struggling to stay in business during the fiscal crisis.

While many organizations, including the NRA and Technomic, report that the recession-related declines in sales were the worst recorded in as many as forty years, economic booms and declines have always played an important role in the evolution of the restaurant industry. As many casual chains and fine-dining establishments are forced to close, space opens for new restaurants and concepts. Restaurants that fail to survive in times of recession are often those whose services and cuisine fail to meet the needs of a changing consumer climate, and their decline paves the way for restaurateurs nimble enough to respond to and address consumer needs.

Food trends, like fashion, also have a significant impact on the industry. One of the most significant dining trends in the early twenty-first century has been restaurants' promotion and support of locally procured and organic ingredients. In its annual survey of member chefs, conducted in 2009, the NRA found that local produce was the top choice for the hottest food industry trend, especially at fine dining establishments. More than 80 percent of chefs surveyed reported using locally grown or locally sourced ingredients on their menus. In addition, more than 70 percent of adults interviewed reported that they would be more likely to visit a restaurant that offered local produce, meat, and other items. The same trend has been responsible for an increase in the number of small, independent businesses in cities across the country, as consumers are more likely to favor spending to support their own communities rather than opting for the convenience of nationwide chains and brands.

The local food trend is also linked to an overall increase in health consciousness among U.S. consumers. This increasing focus on healthy eating has affected every facet of the food industry, from snack-food purveyors to fine restaurants. According to Chicago-based analysis firm Mintel International Group, more than 50 percent of food products launched in 2007 used the terms "organic" or "natural" in their advertisements. The trend has also begun to see expression in governance and legislation. New York City, for instance, passed an ordinance in May, 2008, requiring that quick-service and chain restaurants post calorie counts on their menus to help consumers make more informed decisions in the effort to re-

PROJECTED EMPLOYMENT FOR SELECTED OCCUPATIONS

Restaurants

Employment		
2009	Projected 2018	Occupation
31,780	38,400	Bartenders
2,229,440	2,536,300	Combined food preparation and serving workers, including fast food
514,660	570,800	Cooks, fast food
849,920	910,900	Cooks, restaurant
2,128,120	2,319,100	Waiters and waitresses

Source: U.S. Bureau of Labor Statistics, Industries at a Glance, Occupational Employment Statistics and Employment Projections Program.

duce obesity. Many restaurants are also offering smaller portions, healthier dining options for children, and dishes low in salt and fat.

Another related trend affecting the restaurant industry is the demand for restaurants to become more ecologically conscious, both in terms of their menu options and in terms of community involvement, which includes proper waste disposal and charitable and community-building activities. Restaurants around the country are advertising their use of recycled materials, their contributions to local and national environmental organizations, and their choice to purchase produce and meat products from sources using only sustainable agricultural practices.

The combination of economic changes and trends in consumer spending may give an advantage to smaller, independent restaurants. It is easier for a small restaurant to alter its menu, advertising strategies and overall approach to the market than for larger restaurants and chains, which may require a considerable expenditure to alter their basic approach. Moreover, any individual restaurant will have an easier time finding local ingredients than will a nationwide chain, which would likely need to change its entire distribution structure if it wished to adopt a local food or sustainable model.

Conversely, while smaller restaurants are more adaptable, larger restaurants and chains have greater investment capital and can therefore afford to invest in new menu items and décor as consumer preferences evolve or change. As the healthy, organic food trend progresses, the cost of organic ingredients will likely increase, which may in turn prove an advantage for restaurants with the financial capability to buy in bulk.

Employment Advantages

The BLS predicts that restaurant-industry jobs will increase by 11 percent between 2006 and 2016, which is about the same rate as the overall rate of job increases during the same period. Employment opportunities at the bottom level of the food service industry, which will include maintenance, cleaning, and serving positions, are expected to remain steady in coming years. Opportunities for management in restaurants is expected to grow more slowly, at only 3 to 6 percent.

While economic stagnation has caused full-service casual and fine restaurants to decline in the short term, demographic trends suggest that, overall, these restaurants will increase as a proportion of the total restaurant market during the 2006-2016 period, as the number of families with children and the number of affluent older consumers increases to represent a larger proportion of the total population.

One of the primary economic benefits of the restaurant industry is the number of employment opportunities it provides for unskilled, semiskilled, and young workers. More than 20 percent of those employed in restaurants in 2009 were between the ages of sixteen and nineteen. That proportion is more than five times the proportion for similarly aged workers in other industries. Restaurants also provide a variety of temporary, part-time, and supplementary employment opportunities, which are in higher demand as economic conditions increasingly require individuals to seek additional sources of income.

The restaurant industry is one of the largest private sector employers in the United States, and employment opportunities within the industry are expected to continue increasing. The NRA predicts that the industry will add more than 10 million jobs between 2010 and 2020. In addition, the industry will continue to be an important source of employment and career opportunities for women and minority workers in the United States, making the industry an important factor in maintaining the diversity of the national workforce.

Annual Earnings

The fallout from the 2007-2009 global economic crisis may continue to have a negative effect on the restaurant industry for several years. Estimates of annual revenues vary widely among sources, but the U.S. restaurant industry earned $566 billion in 2009, and it should continue to constitute roughly 4 percent of the national GDP. Measurements of the global restaurant industry are less precise, as many countries produce no internal estimates regarding earnings from their restaurant industries. However, the global industry is worth roughly $1.367 trillion in revenues. A 2009 study by Global Industry Analysts indicates that the global food service industry, which also includes catering and grocery services, will reach $2.2 trillion in revenues by 2015.

According to the U.S. Department of Labor, average weekly earnings for nonmanagement food service employees were $215 in 2006, which is well below the national average of $533 for the private sector as a whole. However, this low figure does not include tips, which typically constitute a large percentage of a service person's annual income. In addition, many restaurants provide bonuses to employees, including discounted or staff meals and other perks that do not figure into measurements of income.

RELATED RESOURCES FOR FURTHER RESEARCH

AMERICAN CULINARY FEDERATION
180 Center Place Way
St. Augustine, FL 32095
Tel: (800) 624-9458
Fax: (904) 825-4758
http://www.acfchefs.org

AMERICAN INSTITUTE OF WINE AND FOOD
26364 Carmel Rancho Ln., Suite 201
Carmel, CA 93923
Tel: (800) 274-2493
Fax: (831) 622-7783
http://www.aiwf.org

INTERNATIONAL ASSOCIATION OF CULINARY PROFESSIONALS
1100 Johnson Ferry Rd., Suite 300
Atlanta, GA 30342
Tel: (404) 252-3663
Fax: (404) 252-0774
http://www.iacp.com

INTERNATIONAL HOTEL AND RESTAURANT ASSOCIATION
41 Ave. General Guisan (Lausanne)
1009 Pully
Switzerland
Tel: 41-21-711-4283
http://www.ih-ra.com

NATIONAL RESTAURANT ASSOCIATION
1200 17th St. NW
Washington, DC 20036
Tel: (202) 331-5900

Fax: (202) 331-2429
http://www.restaurant.org

TECHNOMIC
300 S Riverside Plaza, Suite 1200
Chicago, IL 60606
Tel: (312) 876-0004
Fax: (312) 876-1158
http://www.technomic.com

ABOUT THE AUTHOR

Micah L. Issitt is a freelance writer and researcher working in Philadelphia, Pennsylvania. He has been involved in the restaurant industry since 1994, working in various capacities from clerk to manager. Issitt has written industry profiles for the International Directory of Company Histories and Standard Business, published in the United Kingdom.

FURTHER READING

Beriss, David, and David Evan Sutton. *The Restaurants Book: Ethnographies of Where We Eat.* Oxford, England: Berg, 2007.

"Economics and the Origin of the Restaurant." *Cornell Hotel and Restaurant Administration Quarterly,* August, 2002. http://www.arts .cornell.edu/econ/kiefer/Restaurant.PDF.

Fine, Gary Alan. *Kitchens: The Culture of Restaurant Work.* Berkeley: University of California Press, 2008.

Fullen, Sharon L. *Restaurant Design: Designing, Constructing, and Renovating a Food Service Establishment.* Ocala, Fla.: Atlantic, 2002.

Gabriel, Vincent A. *Success in the Food Business.* Singapore: Rank Books, 2008.

Lee, Ronald. *The Everything Guide to Starting and Running a Restaurant.* New York: Everything Books, 2005.

Miller, Richard K. *The 2009 Retail Business Market Research Handbook.* 11th ed. Loganville, Ga.: Richard K. Miller and Associates, 2009.

National Restaurant Association. "Restaurant Industry: Facts at a Glance." http://www .restaurant.org/research/ind_glance.cfm.

Pilzer, Paul Zane. *The New Wellness Revolution:*

How to Make a Fortune in the Next Trillion Dollar Industry. New York: John Wiley & Sons, 2007.

Research and Markets. "Leisure: Global Industry Guide." http://www.researchandmarkets.com/reports/838291/leisure_global_industry_guide.

Simon, Michèle. *Appetite for Profit: How the Food Industry Undermines Our Health and How to Fight Back.* New York: Nation Books, 2006.

StarChefs.com. "Salary Survey." http://www.starchefs.com/features/editors_dish/salary_survey/2008/html/index.shtml.

U.S. Bureau of Labor Statistics. *Career Guide to Industries,* 2010-2011 ed. http://www.bls.gov/oco/cg.

U.S. Census Bureau. North American Industry Classification System (NAICS), 2007. http://www.census.gov/cgi-bin/sssd/naics/naicsrch?chart=2007.

U.S. Department of Commerce. International Trade Administration. Office of Trade and Industry Information. Industry Trade Data and Analysis. http://ita.doc.gov/td/industry/otea/OTII/OTII-index.html.

U.S. Internal Revenue Service. "Food Industry Overview." http://www.irs.gov/businesses/article/0,,id=175715,00.html.

Walker, John R. *The Restaurant: From Concept to Operation.* New York: John Wiley & Sons, 2007.

Watson, James L., and Melissa L. Caldwell. *The Cultural Politics of Food and Eating: A Reader.* New York: Wiley-Blackwell, 2005.

Retail Trade and Service Industry

©Outline205/Dreamstime.com

INDUSTRY SNAPSHOT

General Industry: Manufacturing

Career Clusters: Manufacturing; Marketing, Sales, and Service

Subcategory Industries: Automobile Dealers; Automotive Parts, Accessories, and Tire Stores; Building Material and Garden Equipment and Supplies Dealers; Clothing and Clothing Accessories Stores; Electronics and Appliance Stores; Food and Beverage Stores; Furniture and Home Furnishings Stores; Gasoline Stations; General Merchandise Stores; Health and Personal Care Stores; Miscellaneous Store Retailers; Motor Vehicle and Parts Dealers; Nonstore Retailers; Other Motor Vehicle Dealers; Sporting Goods, Hobby, and Music Stores

Related Industries: Household and Personal Products Industry; Motion Picture and Television Industry; Textile and Fabrics Industry; Travel and Tourism Industry

Annual Domestic Revenues: $4.1 trillion USD (U.S. Census Bureau, 2009)

Annual International Revenues: $9.8 trillion USD (U.S. Census Bureau, 2009)

Annual Global Revenues: $13.9 trillion USD (Economist Intelligence Unit, 2010)

NAICS Numbers: 44-45

INDUSTRY DEFINITION

Summary

The retail industry is one of the most significant components of the economies of most developed and a growing number of less-developed countries. The industry focuses on the sale of finished products to consumers. Retailers are found in a wide range of industry areas, such as automobiles and other vehicles, clothing and accessories, furniture, electronics, grocery stores, and gasoline stations. The industry is represented in virtually every country around the world, employing countless individuals who work in a broad array of professional fields.

History of the Industry

The practice of selling finished products finds its roots in ancient civilizations. The ancient Egyptians were known to engage in commercial trade with their Mediterranean neighbors, purchasing and selling cloth, utensils, pottery, and foodstuffs. Over time, trade and commerce would become the most prominent driving force for the expansion of the human populace around the world. During the eighth century B.C.E., the Greeks developed the use of gold and silver as currency for the purchase of goods and honed their commercial skills, thanks in large part to their conquering and assimilation of the Phoenicians (a civilization that excelled in trade and commerce). During the second century B.C.E., the rising Roman Empire developed a type of commerce that lasted for five hundred years, establishing trade guilds and manufacturing networks. The retail industry thrived during this period, with a broad array of goods and products for purchase and sale throughout the Empire's vast reach.

For several centuries after the fall of Rome, the early retail industry (like other trades) remained irrelevant to the tribal and nomadic cultures of Europe. In the eighth century, however, Charlemagne, king of the Franks and emperor of the Romans, breathed new life into commerce and retail, and over the next several centuries, trade began to evolve in Europe, representing the foundation of such commercial cities as Genoa, Sicily, and Venice (now in Italy). Commerce also played a major role in the age of exploration, particularly in trade with India, China, Africa, and the Americas.

It was in North America that the first retail stores began to appear. These general stores, established in the eighteenth century, offered consumers a wide range of products and goods. Not long after these smaller stores emerged, larger, "department" stores evolved, offering larger inventories of goods. Simon Lazarus, an immigrant from Poland, established such a store in Columbus, Ohio, in 1851. In 1858, Rowland Hussey Macy founded a store that would become Macy's. Many historians argue that the first true department store, Zions Cooperative Mercantile Institution, was founded in 1868 in Salt Lake City by Mormon leader Brigham Young, although many others point to The Wanamaker's Grand Depot, opened by John Wanamaker in 1876 in Philadelphia, as the first incarnation of the modern department store. Wanamaker would also be credited with creating the first modern price tag, in-store restaurants, and white sales (sales of linens and towels). Wanamaker and other department store entrepreneurs soon realized the value of buying goods wholesale (purchasing products in large quantity for resale), which cut costs and reduced retail prices.

During the twentieth century, shopping centers and malls, reminiscent of historical marketplaces, were introduced. They combined independent stores, parking, and other services in a single location. The first enclosed mall, the Southdale Mall, opened in 1956 in Minnesota. In the 1980's, enormous malls, some of which included hundreds of stores, hotels, amusement park rides, and other amenities, opened. Malls continue to operate, although economic and market conditions (including changes in consumer behavior that favor less-hectic shopping environments) have caused a decline in the long-term health of malls since the mid-1990's.

In the latter decades of the twentieth century, the rapid growth of the Internet enabled retailers to generate business with customers around the globe. The Internet has also helped retailers reduce costs by, in many cases, eliminating the need for storefronts and large staffs to manage them. Today, retail is a thriving industry, fueled by the development of the Internet and the continued viability of retail stores around the world.

The Industry Today

The retail industry is expansive and diverse. Of the ten largest retailers in the world, five are from the United States and five are from Europe. However, there are a number of growing retailers in

One way to attract customers is with sales. (©Infomages/Dreamstime.com)

The Retail Trade Industry's Contribution to the U.S. Economy

Value Added	Amount
Gross domestic product	$866.0 billion
Gross domestic product	6.0%
Persons employed	15.563 million
Total employee compensation	$503.9 billion

Source: U.S. Bureau of Economic Analysis. Data are for 2008.

China, India, and Dubai, United Arab Emirates, all of which have the potential to become major global retailers. The global retail industry employs countless individuals. In the United States alone, about 15 million people work in this industry. Although this industry (like most other industries) has been affected by the 2007-2009 global economic crisis, the industry remains strong. Because retailing is such a tremendous contributor to the gross domestic product of the United States, any upward or downward trend in retail sales is considered a major economic indicator.

The two general areas in which this industry operates are in the store and online. There are countless storefront retailers of varying size and focus. Stores are alike in that they are designed to provide direct, personalized service to customers, but they vary considerably in size, type, and clientele. Stores may be traditional, owner-managed establishments, or they may offer more specialized products and have a less typical appearance. For example, kiosks are small stores that do not have an entrance at all and are situated in high-traffic areas such as street corners, shopping centers, and public transportation stations, where they offer inexpensive, disposable goods such as periodicals, snacks, and souvenirs. Some other stores—such as used automobile dealers and consignment shops—do not offer new products but rather pre-owned goods at lower prices. Warehouse stores and shopping clubs, such as BJ's and Sam's Club, provide items in bulk, rather than in individual packaging, to provide customers with items at prices that resemble wholesale prices.

Smaller stores include convenience stores, boutiques, and kiosks. These stores are usually independently owned or franchised (the operators purchase the rights to use the trademarks and business practices of a larger, parent company) and employ only a few employees. Such stores are sometimes located in a separate building, although many owners of small stores rent space in a larger building, such as a mall or shopping center.

Like small stores, many larger retail stores occupy rent space in larger shopping centers and malls, although some are located in their own individual buildings. Larger retail stores hire more employees to perform tasks such as sales, delivery, or shelf stocking and organization. Larger stores are usually independently owned or part of a larger corporation, although some retailers are franchised.

Retail stores, depending on their size, must be staffed with competent employees. In smaller stores, employees tend to do more—restocking shelves and storerooms, handling purchases, performing accounting, addressing customer complaints, and ordering new inventory. In larger stores that employ greater numbers of employees, those employees' respective tasks may be more compartmentalized.

With the development of the Internet, the retail industry began to surge. The Internet has created the second major vehicle for retail sales. The World Wide Web has proven invaluable for attract-

Inputs Consumed by the Retail Trade Industry

Input	Value
Energy	$16.6 billion
Materials	$93.7 billion
Purchased services	$309.2 billion
Total	$419.5 billion

Source: U.S. Bureau of Economic Analysis. Data are for 2008.

ing customers to stores and providing pricing and information about goods available at a store to make the shopping process easier. Increasingly, however, retailers are becoming online stores, enabling retail customers to shop for and purchase products from their home computers and mobile devices.

The prevalence of online retailing has presented the retail industry with a number of challenges. Among these issues are matters of customer privacy and protection. Just as a thief would rob a retail store at gunpoint, identity thieves are constantly attempting to illegally access online stores' payment systems in order to gain credit card numbers and other personal financial information. Retailers continue to seek ways to secure their payment processing systems, as would-be thieves continue their efforts.

Another issue facing online retailers is that there are literally thousands of sales tax codes in the United States alone. If an individual in one state purchases a new computer from a retailer based in another state (which has lower tax rates), the individual's resident state stands to lose tax revenues from that sale. Without uniformity in the sales tax code, retailers, their customers, and the states involved in that purchase are often caught in confusion, lawsuits, and even reciprocity issues (a state seeking to compensate for lost tax revenues by imposing heavier taxes on other transactions with another state). As online stores evolve within the retail industry, these issues are likely to continue and new issues to develop.

Because of its sheer breadth and tremendous diversity, the retail industry remains a powerful contributor to any economy. Although the more-developed countries of Western Europe, East Asia, and North America continue to dominate the industry in terms of sales and profits, retailers in less-developed countries, powered by local and regional consumer demand, are also showing continued growth in this area.

Some stores try to offer a little of everything, while others specialize in one product. (©Matty Symons/Dreamstime.com)

INDUSTRY MARKET SEGMENTS

The retail industry ranges in size from smaller to larger stores and also encompasses online stores. These segments have varying characteristics and issues.

Small Stores

Small stores typically have ten or fewer employees and occupy a limited amount of real estate. Work at such a store is diverse, primarily because such establishments employ so few workers. Small stores succeed largely because they are able to offer products that attract consumers over the long term and to generate enough sales to enable them to afford rent, utilities, and other monthly expenses.

Potential Annual Earnings Scale. The average earnings for a storekeeper vary from region to region. However, the range in the United States for such positions is between about $26,000 and $35,000 per year.

Clientele Interaction. Small retail store owners and storekeepers work directly with customers. They must be prepared to help customers find the products that best fit their needs, to answer any questions about use, and to know enough about the product to provide the best service. Because small stores succeed largely on the basis of the service they provide, small storekeepers must have strong communication and interpersonal skills (including diplomatic skills when customers have a complaint). Furthermore, as some small stores (such as antique shops and used goods establishments) may be flexible in their asking price for certain goods, a small store owner or storekeeper must develop good business skills. Willingness to lower a price must take into account the store's needs as well as those of the customer.

Amenities, Atmosphere, and Physical Grounds. In many cases, small stores (such as boutiques, kiosks, and shops that cater to tourists) must be attractive to those who are passing by. Furthermore, most small stores must have their items in plain view for customers to see, with prices well marked. Small stores are often at their busiest during high-traffic periods, such as during morning and evening rush hours, at lunch, and during holiday shopping periods.

Consumers expect small stores to foster a personable, relaxed atmosphere, particularly in comparison with larger businesses. Those who work in such establishments must therefore be personable, friendly, helpful, and knowledgeable. Furthermore, to compete with larger stores, many stores seek to offer products that cannot be found elsewhere.

With the exception of kiosks, small stores typically occupy only one or two main rooms, either in a stand-alone building or as part of a larger shopping center or mall. These establishments often have a store room and office adjacent to the main store (and, in the case of clothing retailers, changing rooms).

Typical Number of Employees. Small store-owners must work to ensure that their profits are not lost to major expenses. Therefore, most small stores have only a handful of staff, many of whom are part time and hourly. In peak seasons and during holiday periods, many small retail establishments temporarily hire additional personnel on an hourly basis to handle the larger number of customers.

Traditional Geographic Locations. Small stores are found in most areas in which consumers live and visit. They may rent space in malls or shopping centers, but many are located in stand-alone buildings that the owner may or may not own. Small stores do not require a great deal of geographic space, but they do need to be located in areas where there is consumer need. These areas include downtown areas, tourist attractions, along major roadways, and near major businesses.

Pros of Working in a Small Retail Store. Employees of small retail stores, by virtue of not being subject to a corporate mentality, tend to experience a less formal and more relaxed working atmosphere. Such an environment fosters a spirit of camaraderie among the relatively small number of employees. Additionally, the work performed at a small retail establishment is highly diverse. Employees rarely fall into a rut, as they may need to meet with customers, take inventory, order new products, restock shelves, and perform many other tasks. Because the jobs performed by employees at small stores are myriad, workers rarely are idle.

Cons of Working in a Small Retail Store. Individuals who work in a small retail store are often called on to manage multiple tasks simultaneously. During peak customer times, juggling these responsibilities can be challenging. Furthermore, because these establishments have only a handful of employees, they often do not provide health care and other benefits that larger stores typically offer full-time employees.

Additionally, salaries for employees of small retail establishments are not highly competitive. Significant pay increases are not easily obtained, especially during down times. Small stores, especially those that cater to tourists and passers-by, are subject to peaks and valleys in terms of their business. When business becomes stagnant, employees can lose benefits or suffer layoffs.

Costs

Payroll and Benefits: With the exception of the store proprietor, most workers at a small retail establishment earn hourly wages. The cost of living and the store's fiscal health play a major role in the determination of employee wages. Because small retail stores employ so few individuals, these establishments are generally not required to offer health care or other benefits, although many employers do in order to retain employees.

Supplies: Small stores require a wide range of supplies to ensure effective operation. Among these items are office supplies (including computers, file cabinets, and telephone systems), price tags, cash registers, credit card machines, and cleaning supplies. Additionally, small stores will need bags, boxes, and wrapping paper for customers.

External Services: Many owners of small retail stores use an external accountant to manage tax filings and the employee payroll. Those with a Web site and online purchasing services must also hire a Web designer and Web site administrator. Furthermore, stores that provide deliveries, towing, and other customer services often use external contractors, such as moving companies, parcel companies, and tow truck providers. Finally, these establishments look to external wholesalers for products that they may sell to the consumer.

Utilities: Typical utilities for a small retail store include water and sewer, electricity, gas or oil service, telephone, cable, and Internet access.

Taxes: Small retail stores are required to pay local, state, and federal income taxes as well as applicable property taxes. They must also withhold and pay state and federal income taxes for hourly employees and collect and repay sales taxes collected from consumers.

Midsize and Large Retail Stores

Potential Annual Earnings Scale. Wages for employees working at midsize and large retail stores vary based on the position and the particular industry segment in which the work is performed. In 2008, for example, U.S. retail salespeople working in clothing stores earned $8.94 per hour, while automobile dealer salespeople earned $18.94 per hour. Store managers and supervisors earned between $30,480 and $37,710 in 2008, depending on the industry.

Clientele Interaction. Employees working in midsize and large retail stores have varying degrees of customer interaction. Those working in stockrooms and warehouses, for example, interact less with customers than floor salespeople and cashiers do. However, during times of peak activity in such stores, most employees are expected to assist in checkout areas, near shelves, and in other parts of the store where customers need assistance. Most individuals employed at midsize and large retail stores must therefore demonstrate a degree of customer relations skills.

Amenities, Atmosphere, and Physical Grounds. Midsize and large retail establishments will typically be found in stand-alone facilities or as part of a larger shopping center or mall. Some warehouse and shopping club establishments may even have other stores—such as fast food restaurants and coffee shops—operating independently within them.

Midsize and large retail stores will typically be compartmentalized, with aisles and departments separated for easy customer access. Because of the occasional complexity of such store layouts, these establishments may be hectic during peak shopping periods. Employees are expected to quickly become familiar with the various departments and sections of these establishments to better serve customers.

Many larger stores will have lounge areas, cafeterias, locker rooms, and other employee-oriented facilities and services. Midsize and large retail stores usually have ample parking for their customers and for their employees as well.

Typical Number of Employees. Midsize and large retail stores can have dozens, if not hundreds, of employees working in shifts throughout the day. The number of employees on staff at a given establishment depends on the size of the store and whether the store is operating during peak shopping hours.

Traditional Geographic Locations. Midsize and large retail establishments are typically located in stand-alone buildings or as part of larger shopping centers and malls. Such stores are ideally established in or near high-traffic areas, such as a city's downtown or outskirts, or along major roadways. Midsize and large retail stores are limited by their need for a large parcel of land for the store itself and off-street parking, as well as to provide access for large delivery trucks.

Pros of Working in a Midsize or Large Retail Store. Working in a midsize or large retail store offers a sense of job security that smaller retailers cannot often promise. Additionally, these establishments often offer health care and other benefits (including discounts on store merchandise) to employees as a way to ensure that they are happy and loyal to the store. Furthermore, midsize and large retailers are often linked to much larger corporations (either through franchising or directly), giving employees the opportunity to rise up the corporate ladder or transfer to different locales.

Presentation of the merchandise and service are important for a retailer's survival. (©Marco Scisetti/Dreamstime.com)

Cons of Working in a Midsize or Large Retail Store. Although there is stability in working for a midsize or large store, the corporate mentality that typically exists in such establishments leaves very little room for individual creativity. Additionally, midsize and large retail establishments may be too complex and high-pressure for some people, especially because they must work with a diverse group of fellow workers. From a management point of view, midsize and large retail stores are extremely challenging to operate, particularly because of the number of employees who require compensation and the significant number of other expenses that must be covered regularly.

Costs

Payroll and Benefits: Payroll and benefits are some of the most significant portions of a midsize or large retail store's budget. This figure varies based on job description, the industry, and the fiscal health of the business itself. As for many other businesses, health care coverage is one of the largest expenditures paid by a midsize or large retailer.

Supplies: Midsize and large retail stores require items such as office supplies, computer and telephone equipment, intercom systems, storage room hardware (such as ladders and dollies), cash registers, and credit card payment systems.

External Services: Although larger than small stores, midsize and large stores must call on external vendors to help with operations. For example, accounting professionals, external security personnel, information systems technology professionals, and even marketing consultants are often called into service. External consultants are also used to manage Web sites and online purchasing centers, marketing campaigns, and legal affairs.

Utilities: Typical utilities for midsize and large retail stores include water and sewer, waste disposal, electricity, gas and oil service, telephone, cable, and Internet access.

Taxes: Midsize and large retail stores are required to pay local, state, and federal income taxes as well as applicable property taxes. They must also withhold state and federal income taxes from employees and collect and report all sales taxes collected from consumers.

Online Retail Stores

Potential Annual Earnings Scale. Salaries for professionals working at online retail stores vary based on the position, the individual's experience, the cost of living, and the financial strength of the company itself. In one region, for example, average salaries for online retail sales people are approximately $72,000 per year.

Clientele Interaction. Online retail sales require a somewhat different form of customer service. Although direct client interaction is rare, online stores still require communication with customers, typically through e-mail or by telephone. Such in-teraction usually occurs when the customer has a problem using the system, seeks a refund, or seeks information on the status of an order.

Amenities, Atmosphere, and Physical Grounds. Online retail stores are not typical brick-and-mortar storefronts. Rather, these facilities usually take the form of offices, with no inventory visible. Online store facilities are usually staffed by younger individuals. As such, they may feature flexible schedules and a relaxed atmosphere. Some online stores even include some on-site perks for employees, such as lounges, video games, and other amenities. Still, employees are expected to meet their sales goals. Online retailers must take the initiative to seek out the best venues for generating business.

Typical Number of Employees. The number of employees working at an online retailer varies based on the size and financial strength of the company as well as the service area in which the online

---

OCCUPATION PROFILE

Merchandise Displayer

Considerations	Qualifications
Description	Designs, builds, and arranges displays of merchandise to attract the attention of prospective buyers through eye-catching displays in windows, in showcases, and on sales floors.
Career clusters	Marketing, Sales, and Service
Interests	Data; things
Working conditions	Work inside
Minimum education level	On-the-job training; high school diploma/technical training; junior/technical/community college
Physical exertion	Light work; medium work
Physical abilities	Unexceptional/basic fitness
Opportunities for experience	Internship; volunteer work; part-time work
Licensure and certification	Usually not required
Employment outlook	Average growth expected
Holland interest score	AES

Note: See volume 1, "Publisher's Note," for an explanation of the Holland interest score.

store operates. One of the world's largest online retail stores, Amazon, has more than twenty-four thousand employees, although some retailers are one-person operations.

Traditional Geographic Locations. Online retailers may be found in any geographic location. As business is conducted on the Internet, an online retailer needs only a computer, Internet access, and space to store inventory for shipping. Many online retailers work out of their own homes. Even developing nations are starting to see an increase in the number of online retailers because of the ease of launching such businesses.

Pros of Working in an Online Retail Store. For many online retailers, the greatest benefit is the ability to work from home. Also, because most independent online retailers use an established Internet commerce system to process transactions, the work is often easy. The offices of larger online retailers are typically casual workplaces, and if the enterprise is profitable, salaries and benefits are highly competitive.

Cons of Working in an Online Retail Store. Individuals who enjoy a high level of customer interaction or a highly professional environment are likely to be a good fit for the online retail industry. Additionally, the burst of the dot-com bubble that occurred at the beginning of the twenty-first century demonstrates the unpredictability that characterizes the online industry. Companies in this industry may be quickly bought, sold, or put out of business. Furthermore, if the business fails to generate strong profits over the long term, online retailers who are sole operators and proprietors may suffer a loss.

Costs

Payroll and Benefits: For online retailers with staff, employee pay and benefits are some of the most critical elements of the budget. To attract the best and brightest employees, online retailers must offer competitive salaries and excellent benefits. For online retailers who are sole proprietors, this area of the business is not an issue, except in terms of the owner's income.

Supplies: Central to an online retailer is the necessary computer hardware to conduct business, including a high-quality computer system, server, and relevant equipment. For online stores with office space, office supplies, including computers and printers, are important. Because shipping plays a central role in online sales, mailing supplies (such as overnight forms and packing materials) are essential.

External Services: Online retail stores rely on a Web site administrator to oversee the effective operation of the site. For understaffed retailers, these services are acquired from external consultants. Additionally, shipping is conducted by such companies as FedEx, UPS, DHL, and the U.S. Postal Service. Furthermore, many retailers may turn to accountants and financial advisers to ensure that the company's money is well managed.

Utilities: Online retailers use a number of utilities, such as electricity, telephone, cable, and Internet access. Those companies with office space must also pay for water, sewer, and garbage disposal.

Taxes: Online retailers must pay corporate income taxes based on profits earned as well as property taxes (for office space). If the company has full-time employees, it must withhold federal and state income taxes. Online retailers must collect sales taxes, where applicable, although the rates of those taxes vary based on where the purchase was made.

ORGANIZATIONAL STRUCTURE AND JOB ROLES

The organizational structure and distribution of tasks within a retail establishment are typically based on its size. The owner and sole operator of a small retail store or online business usually handles most of the major tasks because he or she is the only major employee, and an executive or senior manager of a larger retail establishment organizes and distributes tasks among a team of employees. Nevertheless, the tasks themselves, in a general sense, remain similar throughout the retail industry.

The following general job categories apply to the organizational structure of small, midsize, and large retailers and online retail businesses:

- Executive Management
- Sales
- Cashiers

- Delivery Personnel
- Accounting
- Purchasing
- Managers
- Stockroom Clerks
- Maintenance Personnel
- Security
- Human Resources
- Web Designers/Administrators
- Marketing
- Customer Service
- Administrative Personnel
- Front-Line Personnel

Executive Management

Executive management handles the general operations of the retail business. Employees in this area help oversee major operations, goal setting, and the implementation of business plans. They also manage individual teams and departments (or in the case of the chief executive officer, oversee all departments). Many executive managers have advanced degrees, particularly in business management, accounting, and similar fields. As with many industries, experience can sometimes serve as a substitute for advanced education.

Executive managers generally earn higher salaries than people in other positions within the company. Their job is to manage the overall functions of the retail company, address systemic issues, and ensure that all departments are functioning in a fluid fashion.

Executive management occupations may include the following:

- Chief Executive Officer (CEO)
- President
- Vice President of Sales
- Vice President of Operations
- Chief Financial Officer (CFO)
- Controller
- Director of Marketing
- Vice President of Human Resources

Sales

Retail sales personnel are in many ways the business's front line of customer relations. They will approach customers, answer any questions the consumer may have about products, and based on customer needs, work to present them with the best possible product to meet those needs. In this regard, sales personnel are essential business generators for retail establishments. Additionally, many store sales personnel will be asked to work in other areas of the store, including at the cash register and other locations, as needed.

Retail sales personnel are expected to have strong interpersonal and customer service skills. Although advanced schooling is not typically a requirement for sales associates, they usually will undergo some form of training upon joining a company to familiarize them with the inventory and, where relevant, the corporate philosophy, systems, and expectations. Retail sales personnel salaries vary based on the position involved. Some work on an annual salary with bonuses, while others work on commission in addition to a modest base salary.

Sales occupations may include the following:

- Retail Sales Associate
- Senior Sales Manager
- Director of Sales
- Business Development Associate

Cashiers

Cashiers are individuals whose primary task is to process customer payments within the store. This responsibility entails operating cash registers and processing checks, credit cards, and coupons. At times, cashiers are called on to handle customer service activities, issuing refunds and replacing defective products. Cashiers are expected to keep a careful accounting of all monies they manage during their shifts.

Cashiers are paid hourly and are often offered benefits packages based on union negotiations. Pay varies based on the industry and experience, although the median salary for cashiers in all industries for 2008 was about $8.50 per hour. Such positions do not require any formal education, although some in-house training does occur.

Delivery Personnel

Many retail stores hire personnel whose primary responsibility is to deliver purchased items to customers. These individuals load the items onto a delivery truck, organize the truck inventory to match customer invoices, and retain any relevant paperwork.

Delivery personnel do not necessarily require any formal education, although they are expected to have a valid driver's license and may be required to obtain a truck driver's license as well. Furthermore, drivers must have strong interpersonal skills to maintain a professional attitude when working with customers in their own homes. In addition, they may require some training on how to assemble the items being delivered, as they may be asked to do so by the customer for an additional fee.

Accounting

Accounting personnel are responsible for maintaining a careful record of the retail store's finances. They must collect, record, and file receipts; review expenses; and file tax returns. Store accountants do not have much direct interaction with customers, as their jobs focus more on the store's internal operations. As the fiscal watchdog of the business enterprise, these accountants must have a careful eye for details, a strong grasp of numbers, knowledge of state and federal corporate tax laws and requirements, and an understanding of the company's activities and departments. Additionally, they will need computer skills, as many stores use software to categorize various products to better record sales.

Full-time accountants are usually paid on an annual basis, although some receive an hourly wage, with competitive benefits. Most have some postsecondary education and ideally have received certification as a Certified Public Accountant (CPA).

Accounting occupations may include the following:

- Store Accountant
- Steward
- Accounts Payable/Receivable Manager
- Administrative Assistant

Purchasing

Retail stores rely on a team of personnel who purchase goods and products wholesale from merchants for resale at their respective stores. Purchasing requires strong business and negotiating skills and an appreciation of product quality. As many merchants offer their wares at convention-style marketplace events in large exhibit halls, purchasing agents may be required to travel as part of their jobs.

Merchandise purchasers must also be careful analysts of market trends, competitors' prices, and consumer behavior. Such skills are useful in their pursuit of top-quality goods that consumers will purchase. Additionally, because of their central role in delivering products for resale at the store, purchasing professionals may also be called on to offer their insights to marketing and advertising departments on how best to promote the items in question. Furthermore, purchasers must be proficient in understanding the merchants themselves, assessing their manufacturing and delivery schedules and taking into account any issues these companies may be experiencing.

Because purchasing requires a great deal of business savvy, technical skills (such as computer software and even engineering,) and careful analytical skills, many larger retailers require a bachelor's, master's, or professional degree, and many are professionally certified as accredited purchasing practitioners or certified purchasing managers. Smaller retailers may not have such requirements, however.

Purchasing occupations may include the following:

- Retail Planner
- Retail Buyer
- Associate Buyer
- Online Buyer-Merchandiser
- Purchasing Manager
- Merchandise Manager
- Purchasing Clerk
- Junior Buyer

Managers

Managers are the individuals responsible for ensuring that the retail business operates smoothly and according to the business plan. Managers set employee schedules, lead individual departments and teams, address employee concerns and disciplinary actions, and ensure that corporate goals are met. Every facet of the store requires the oversight of a manager, including a store manager, who oversees the entire establishment.

Managers come from a variety of backgrounds and areas of expertise. They must be knowledgeable of the department in which they work as well as the enterprise as a whole. They must be capable of leading others and working with customers.

OCCUPATION PROFILE

Retail Store Sales Manager

Considerations	Qualifications
Description	Plans and controls some or all of the sales activities of retail organizations, stores, and departments, generally supervising stock clerks, sales clerks, and assistants.
Career clusters	Agriculture, Food, and Natural Resources; Business, Management, and Administration; Marketing, Sales, and Service
Interests	Data; people
Working conditions	Work inside
Minimum education level	On-the-job training; high school diploma or GED; high school diploma/technical training; apprenticeship
Physical exertion	Light work
Physical abilities	Unexceptional/basic fitness
Opportunities for experience	Internship; apprenticeship; military service; part-time work
Licensure and certification	Usually not required
Employment outlook	Slower-than-average growth expected
Holland interest score	ESR

Note: See volume 1, "Publisher's Note," for an explanation of the Holland interest score.

They are responsible for submitting staff and sales reports and, in the case of store managers, opening and closing the establishment.

Many senior managers have an undergraduate degree or other advanced educational credentials. Other managers are promoted from lower-level hourly wage jobs and have no advanced degree, although they are highly experienced and knowledgeable about the company. Salaries vary based on the level of management, the industry, and the individual's experience. For example, a store manager may earn nearly $42,000 per year, while a district manager may earn about $65,000 per year.

Manager occupations may include the following:

- Store Manager
- Senior Sales Manager
- Director of Sales

- Human Resources Manager
- Department Manager

Stockroom Clerks

Stock clerks control the flow of merchandise and supplies into and out of the stockroom, warehouse, or other storage facility. They track inventories, and reorder products when supplies are low. Stockroom clerks receive incoming deliveries and open and examine the products to ensure there are no defects and no damage has occurred. If the products are acceptable, they place them in an easily cataloged and retrievable location in the facility. Clerks keep track of products using a variety of methods, including electronic scanners, coding systems, and other approaches.

There is no general educational requirement for stockroom clerks, although individuals who assume such responsibilities must have strong reading, mathematical, and writing skills to perform their tasks. Entry-level stock clerks usually begin their jobs at the minimum wage, but may receive pay increases as they become experienced.

Stockroom clerk occupations may include the following:

- Shipping/Receiving Clerk
- Inventory Clerk
- Warehouse Manager
- Traffic Clerk
- Order Filler

Maintenance Personnel

Maintenance personnel are responsible for ensuring that the many systems of the retail establishment are operating properly. They monitor and, where necessary, repair heating, ventilation, and air-conditioning systems (HVAC), bathrooms, lighting, and other elements of the business's infrastructure. Maintenance employees must be generally proficient in a wide variety of fields, including electrical, plumbing, carpentry, and heavy equipment systems.

Maintenance professionals generally have vocational educational training in several fields, and some have degrees in engineering. Salaries for these employees vary based on the industry, the position involved, and the individual's experience. Building maintenance professionals earn an average of $46,000 per year. Custodians are at the low end of the pay spectrum, earning $19,000 per year, and heavy equipment repair personnel and licensed electricians earn about $36,000 annually.

Maintenance personnel occupations may include the following:

- Custodian
- Electrician
- Heavy Equipment Repairer
- Mechanic
- Plumber

Security

The security of the customers and staff of a retail establishment is charged to a security team. Store security personnel ensure that unruly customers are disciplined or removed from the premises, that no illegal activity takes place in or around the property, and that emergency situations are addressed.

Security personnel conduct periodic rounds on foot and in parking lots, monitor surveillance cameras, write reports on daily activities, and respond to relevant calls for assistance.

Store security personnel are expected to have training in public safety that varies based on the job level. They may obtain this training through vocational education or a number of security certification programs. Additionally, they may be required to obtain certification in cardiopulmonary resuscitation (CPR) and other first-aid techniques. Salaries vary based on experience and job responsibilities.

Security occupations may include the following:

- Store Detective
- Entry-Level Personnel
- Technical Support

Human Resources

The human resources department oversees employee relations. Human resources professionals hire and dismiss employees, interview candidates, and evaluate employees. They also help employees obtain on-the-job and off-site training to enhance their skills and professional qualifications. Furthermore, human resources professionals administer employee benefits, such as insurance, retirement funds, and other employee incentives.

Human resources professionals must demonstrate a number of important professional skills and attributes. They have a strong understanding of the business itself, its goals and expectations— an attribute that is useful for recruiting strong candidates for vacant posts that facilitate the pursuit of those goals. Additionally, these professionals must be knowledgeable about insurance, retirement funds, stock options, and other employee benefits to offer the best possible employment packages to staff. Human resources departments may be responsible for designing in-house training courses, and therefore human resources professionals must have effective communication and presentation skills. They often have the responsibility of hearing and resolving employee complaints and must use conflict resolution skills to address these issues in such a way that the company is best served.

Human resources managers are well trained in human resources management, which is learned both through experience and college-level training. On average, human resources managers in the retail industry earn about $57,000 per year, although salaries vary from business to business.

Human resources occupations may include the following:

- Director of Human Resources
- Human Resources Coordinator
- Human Resources Manager
- Administrative Personnel

Web Designers/Administrators

Retail stores and online retailers alike use Web designers and administrators to develop and maintain their Web sites. These individuals will work with company executives, managers, and other personnel to create a Web site that is attractive and easy to navigate and that generates profits for the business. As such, they must be able to work with others, have an understanding of the store and its clients, and be competent in the latest in Web site software and technology.

Web designers and administrators generally have bachelor's degrees in computer science, engineering, or similar fields. Salaries in this area vary based on the business, industry, and individual experience. Some Web site administrators earn more than $52,000 per year, including bonuses and other benefits such as profit sharing.

Web site design and administration occupations may include the following:

- Web Developer
- Web Content Administrator
- Webmaster
- Information Technology Manager

Marketing

The job of promoting the retail business and enticing customers to patronize the establishment falls to the store's marketing department. Marketing professionals are very well trained in understanding customer behavior and develop and implement campaigns that are designed to meet consumer demand. Marketing professionals work at the heart of the retail business, as they carefully research market and consumer preferences and coordinate with executives, managers, and other professionals throughout the retail organization to create and set forth marketing strategies, such as sales, coupons, and customer satisfaction programs.

Marketing professionals have exceptional business, analytical, and communications skills. These professional attributes are important because these individuals must understand the type of customer the store seeks to attract, create and work within marketing budgets, and effectively present marketing campaigns to the rest of the employees of the retail establishment. Additionally, they should have strong computer skills so that they can use software for research and presentations.

Marketing personnel usually have undergraduate degrees in marketing, business, or similar professional areas. Senior personnel in the marketing field may have advanced degrees, such as an M.B.A. Salaries for marketing professionals vary based on the position level, the industry, and the amount of experience the individual has. Entry-level marketing positions in the retail field generally earn just more than $43,000 per year, according to the U.S. Bureau of Labor Statistics (BLS), while marketing managers can earn nearly $109,000 per year.

Marketing occupations may include the following:

- Marketing Coordinator
- Marketing Manager
- Director of Marketing
- Account Manager
- Intern

Customer Service

Customer service personnel are charged with addressing the needs and concerns of consumers who have purchased or seek to purchase goods from a retail store. They field customer complaints, handle refunds and exchanges, and special order items that are not in stock. Online retailers use customer service personnel in a similar vein, through telephone, e-mail, or Internet chat room features. Customer service employees should have a strong understanding of the store's policies, demonstrate knowledge of its products, and above all, have strong interpersonal and problem-solving skills, particularly when customers are unhappy with their shopping experience.

Customer service personnel are generally paid by the hour, at salaries that vary based on the industry, employee experience, and the financial strength of the store. They do not necessarily require a formal education but will need some training on store policies as well as the computer systems they will use during the course of their jobs.

Customer service occupations may include the following:

- Help Desk Consultant
- Customer Services Representative
- Technical Support Specialist

Administrative Personnel

Administrative personnel are located in the retail establishment's office, assisting with the overall operations of the business. Administrative staff may be needed to answer telephones during high-traffic periods, run errands for managers, make photocopies, send faxes, and perform other tasks. In many cases, they are the nucleus of the store, providing support to managers through scheduling, data entry, filing, and other activities as warranted by the organization.

Administrative personnel have a wide range of backgrounds and professional experience. Many are temporary employees, and others are brought in as entry-level staff to assist managers and other personnel.

Administrative occupations may include the following:

- Administrative Assistant
- Secretary
- Intern
- Cooperative Employee

Front-Line Personnel

Many major retailers have employees who are responsible for enhancing the customer experience. Some stores, for example, have greeters to welcome customers and answer any questions they may have. Other front-line personnel include baggers, shopping cart attendants, and other individuals. Front-line staff are usually paid minimum wage and do not necessarily require a formal education to perform their tasks.

Front-line personnel occupations may include the following:

- Greeter
- Bagger

- Shopping Cart Attendant
- Sample Provider
- Valet

INDUSTRY OUTLOOK

Overview

The two periods of economic decline and stagnation that constituted much of the first decade of the twenty-first century have taken their toll on the retail industry. The impact was particularly significant during the 2007-2009 economic crisis, when a collapsing mortgage system, a subsequent consumer credit crunch, and a combination of high food and energy prices spurred a severe recession. Consumer spending spiraled downward while the costs of managing a business continued to increase. Many retailers of all sizes and industries severely cut budgets and staffs, closed stores, reorganized, or simply went out of business during this period. Recovery has been slow, primarily because of tightening credit market conditions, which means that sales and mergers and acquisitions are severely hampered.

The end of the recession has not sent consumers flocking back to retail stores. Rather, the recession left consumers far more wary of spending their money. Retailers had to find ways to entice customers back to stores and to their Web sites, and many have significantly shifted their strategies.

The first change in strategies is from large stores to smaller, more specialized storefronts. This approach is motivated by two factors. The first is that retailers save significantly on rent, utilities, and other expenses, including large staffs. The second is the notion that smaller stores will cause customers to make short, frequent shopping trips. Retailers hope that customers will take note of the personalized approach offered in the smaller stores. They also believe that this approach will generate more profits. As larger retailers focus on ways to lower prices to better compete with rivals, the so-called niche approach may improve profit margins.

The second major change is taking advantage of consumer sentiment regarding the environment. Going green is an extremely popular theme in many industries, including the retail field. The green approach has become an effective marketing strategy, one that is increasingly popular among retailers and their customers. Merchants are offering more eco-friendly products, including offering reusable bags instead of plastic bags. They are also promoting their use of clean energy, such as solar and wind power, to power stores and servers. A retailer's efforts to highlight recycling programs, waste reduction, and energy efficiency can drive customers to shop at the store. Additionally, such endeavors can render the retailer eligible for government benefits, such as tax credits and lower fees, which can further lower costs.

In addition to the smaller, greener store approach to retailing, companies are investing more heavily in their online stores. The prevalence of the BlackBerry, iPhone, and other smart phones means that more and more shopping will be done using mobile technology. Retailers are taking note of this evolution and directing more resources toward accommodating this demand. Some are even offering multichannel retailing, moving from simple Web sales to using social networking and other multimedia vehicles to build relationships with entire communities of customers.

Retailers are embracing an important element of the business—business development. Many companies are launching marketing campaigns designed to reach out to existing and past customers. By using social networking systems and other approaches, retailers seek to drive repeat business. By opening up communication with customers, retailers are also able to gauge consumer behaviors, identify trends and attitudes, and as a result, provide customers with the type of service and products they seek.

The retail industry has long been one of the largest employers of and contributors to the U.S. and global economy. The industry has a vast number of subindustries, and demand for retail goods remains strong. A recent study by the National Retail Federation showed that consumer spending began to rebound in 2010, led by a double-digit increase in online sales. The study also showed that members of Generation X, who are in a position to shop more for themselves and their families, are more careful and savvy about spending but are still willing to do so. Higher-income consumers are also showing an increased willingness to go shopping.

In the light of these trends, the retail industry is expected to continue its evolution to meet the needs of customers. The outlook for the industry around the globe, at least in the short term, is one marked by cautious optimism. Worldwide national leaders in this industry continue to be found in the United States and Europe, but recovery from the recession has been modest at best. Meanwhile, the industries of India, China, and northern Africa are growing in size and global influence, although it remains to be seen if these rising retail powers will continue their upward trend after the global economy fully recovers from the recession.

Employment Advantages

According to the BLS, the retail industry will continue to grow at a modest pace over the next decade. The BLS estimates that by 2018, the number of wage and salary jobs in all fields within the retail industry will increase

PROJECTED EMPLOYMENT FOR SELECTED OCCUPATIONS

Retail Trade Industry

Employment 2009	Projected 2018	Occupation
2,828,730	3,012,400	Cashiers
243,080	281,800	Customer services representatives
1,037,570	1,091,100	First-line supervisors/managers of retail sales workers
3,891,310	4,299,600	Retail salespersons
1,303,730	1,345,200	Stock clerks and order fillers

Source: U.S. Bureau of Labor Statistics, Industries at a Glance, Occupational Employment Statistics and Employment Projections Program.

by 11 percent. Although there are changes occurring in how the industry is shaped, there will be a continued growth.

The diversity of the industry in terms of the broad range of career paths continues to be a great benefit to those seeking advancement. Most employees begin in an entry-level position, such as cashier or customer services representative, moving upward within the store or at another store. Most major retailers offer management training, certification, and other programs designed to give employees the opportunity to thrive in their current positions and move upward in the future.

The new directions in which the retail industry is moving are exciting, particularly for younger employees who have grown accustomed to the technological advances that are helping reshape the industry. Potential employees of the retail industry have an opportunity to be a part of building a new shopping experience that their parents never knew.

Annual Earnings

Because of the lingering effects of the economic recession of 2007-2009 and its effects on consumer behavior, it is believed that the retail industry will grow at a modest rate. According to Moody's, the U.S. retail industry will most likely see earnings increase by about 3.5 percent in 2011. Most industry analysts estimate that this increase will depend highly on the overall condition of the economy as it slowly rebuilds.

During the recession, most major retailers saw declines in their sales. At the end of 2010, however, these stores saw significant increases over the previous year. Abercrombie and Fitch, for example, saw a 32 percent increase in sales in September, 2010, over the same period a year earlier. Most retailers saw improvement during the holiday season of 2010 when compared with the same period in the previous two years.

RELATED RESOURCES FOR FURTHER RESEARCH

GLOBAL ENTERTAINMENT RETAIL ASSOCIATION-
    EUROPE
    Colonnade House, 1st Floor
    2 Westover Road

Bournemouth, Dorset BH1 2HY
    United Kingdom
    Tel: 44-1202-292063
    Fax: 44-1202-292067
    http://www.gera-europe.org

INTERNATIONAL COUNCIL OF SHOPPING CENTERS
    1221 Avenue of the Americas, 41st Floor
    New York, NY 10020-1099
    Tel: (646) 728-3800
    Fax: (732) 694-1755
    http://www.icsc.org

NATIONAL GROCERS ASSOCIATION
    1005 N Glebe Rd., Suite 250
    Arlington, VA 22201-5758
    Tel: (703) 516-0700
    Fax: (703) 812-1821
    http://www.nationalgrocers.org

NATIONAL RETAIL FEDERATION
    325 7th St. NW, Suite 1100
    Washington, DC 20004
    Tel: (800) 673-4692
    Fax: (202) 737-2849
    http://www.nrf.com

RETAIL INDUSTRY LEADERS ASSOCIATION
    1700 N Moore St., Suite 2250
    Arlington, VA 22209
    Tel: (703) 841-2300
    Fax: (703) 841-1184
    http://www.rila.org/pages/default.aspx

ABOUT THE AUTHOR

Michael P. Auerbach has over sixteen years of professional experience in public policy and administration, economic development, and the hospitality industry. He is a 1993 graduate of Wittenberg University and a 1999 graduate of the Boston College Graduate School of Arts and Sciences. He is a veteran of state and federal government, having worked for seven years in the Massachusetts legislature and four years as a federal government contractor.

FURTHER READING

Fisher, Marshall L., and Ananth Raman. *The New Science of Retailing: How Analytics Are Transforming the Supply Chain and Improving Performance.* Boston: Harvard Business Press, 2010.

JobBank USA. "Training, Certifications, Skills and Advancement: Purchasing Managers, Buyers, and Purchasing Agents." http://www.jobbankusa.com/career_employment/purchasing_managers_buyers_purchasing_agents/training_certifications_skills_advancement.html.

Krafft, Manfred, and Murali K. Mantrala. *Retailing in the Twenty-first Century: Current and Future Trends.* New York: Springer, 2010.

Lichtenstein, Nelson. *The Retail Revolution: How Wal-Mart Created a Brave New World of Business.* New York: Metropolitan Books, 2009.

Miller, Michael. *Selling Online 2.0: Migrating from eBay to Amazon, Craigslist, and Your Own E-commerce Website.* Indianapolis, Ind.: Que, 2009.

Moody's Investor Services. "Annual Outlook: U.S. Retail Industry." Alacra Store. http://www.alacrastore.com/research/moodys-global-credit-research-Annual_Outlook_U_S_Retail_Industry_Sluggish_Economy_Will_Limit_Earnings_Growth_in_2011-PBC_128312.

PayScale.com. "Salary for Industry: Retail." January 11, 2011. http://www.payscale.com/research/US/Industry=Retail/Salary.

_____. "Salary Snapshot for Web Administrator Jobs." January 7, 2011. http://www.payscale.com/research/US/Job=Web_Administrator/Salary.

Salary.com. "Salary Wizard: Storekeeper." http://www1.salary.com/Storekeeper-salary.html.

Simply Hired. "Average Building Maintenance Salaries." http://www.simplyhired.com/a/salary/search/q-building+maintenance.

_____. "Average Online Retail Sales Salaries." http://www.simplyhired.com/a/salary/search/q-online+retail+sales/l-logan,+ut.

StateUniversity.com. "Stock Clerk Job Description, Career as a Stock Clerk, Salary, Employment." http://careers.stateuniversity.com/pages/633/Stock-Clerk.html.

U.S. Bureau of Labor Statistics. "Clothing, Accessory, and General Merchandise Stores." In *Occupational Outlook Handbook,* 2010-2011 ed. http://www.bls.gov/oco/cg/cgs022.htm.

_____. "Retail Salespersons." In *Occupational Outlook Handbook,* 2010-2011 ed. http://www.bls.gov/oco/ocos121.htm.

_____. "Sales Worker Supervisors." In *Occupational Outlook Handbook,* 2010-2011 ed. http://www.bls.gov/oco/ocos025.htm#earnings.

U.S. Census Bureau. North American Industry Classification System (NAICS), 2007. http://www.census.gov/cgi-bin/sssd/naics/naicsrch?chart=2007.

Scientific and Technical Services

©James Steidl/Dreamstime.com

INDUSTRY SNAPSHOT

General Industry: Science, Technology, Engineering, and Math

Career Cluster: Science, Technology, Engineering, and Math

Subcategory Industries: Engineering Services; Research and Development in Biotechnology; Research and Development in the Physical, Engineering, and Life Sciences

Related Industries: Environmental Engineering and Consultation Services; Pharmaceuticals and Medications Industry; Scientific, Medical, and Health Equipment and Supplies Industry

Annual Domestic Revenues: $279.1 billion USD (U.S. Census Bureau, 2007)

Annual International Revenues: $10.2 billion USD (U.S. Census Bureau, 2007)

Annual Global Revenues: $289.3 billion USD (U.S. Census Bureau, 2007)

NAICS Numbers: 54133, 54169, 54171

INDUSTRY DEFINITION

Summary

The scientific and technical services industry includes organizations that provide research and development services in the life sciences and engineering, as well as those that supply scientific and technical consulting services to others. People working in this industry usually have education and training in the sciences or engineering; many have advanced degrees.

One of the major services provided by this industry is research and development, in which workers with scientific and technical expertise apply their skills to make scientific discoveries or develop new products. Biotechnology and pharmaceutical companies, for example, conduct biomedical research and development, including biochemistry, molecular biology (such as recombinant deoxyribonucleic acid [DNA] and genetic engineering), protein engineering, nanotechnology, and materials science research. Practically all of the research activities at for-profit biotechnology and pharmaceutical companies are focused on or relate to the discovery of new tools and therapies to prevent and treat diseases. These companies are funded by profits from product sales and by money from investors and venture capitalists.

Publicly traded companies also receive funding from selling shares on the stock exchanges. Nonprofit organizations, including government laboratories, universities, and research institutes, perform a broader range of scientific and engineering research services to advance scientific knowledge and deliver clinical and technological benefits. This research addresses a wide range of questions and knowledge gaps in science, engineering, and medicine. Some of the research at nonprofit establishments is geared toward understanding the mechanism of diseases and how to treat them, while other research advances scientific knowledge in a particular area but may not have a large impact on disease treatment. Much of the research at nonprofit organizations is funded by competitive grants from federal entities such as the National Institutes of Health and the National Science Foundation, or by grants from private and/or charitable foundations. Fed-

The Contribution to the U.S. Economy of Scientific, Technical, and Miscellaneous Professional Services

Value Added	Amount
Gross domestic product	$691.3 billion
Gross domestic product	4.8%
Persons employed	5.313 million
Total employee compensation	$426.7 billion

Source: U.S. Bureau of Economic Analysis. Data are for 2008.

eral, state, and city laboratories and private companies provide forensic laboratory services to uncover causes of death and help to solve homicides and other crimes.

Forensic laboratory services are provided by fed-

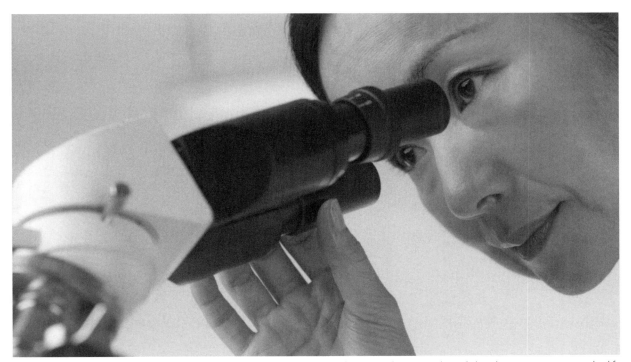

The scientific and technical services industry includes organizations that provide research and development services in the life sciences and engineering, as well as those that supply scientific and technical consulting services to others. (©Imagez/Dreamstime.com)

Inputs Consumed by Scientific, Technical, and Miscellaneous Professional Services

Input	Value
Energy	$6.1 billion
Materials	$47.9 billion
Purchased services	$314.1 billion
Total	$368.1 billion

Source: U.S. Bureau of Economic Analysis. Data are for 2008.

eral and state laboratories as well as by private companies. Forensic specialists use their expertise in molecular biology, microbiology, chemistry, ballistics, and materials to help solve crimes; they may also act as expert witnesses in criminal trials.

Academic and research institutes, as well as for-profit companies, provide a variety of engineering services, including services in the fields of chemical engineering, mechanical engineering, materials engineering, environmental engineering, and waste management and decontamination. Individuals working in these organizations apply engineering principles to designing and building structures, machines, instruments, materials, and systems. Engineers also use their scientific and mathematical training to improve production processes, making them more efficient and economical, and to solve technical problems affecting machines and electronics. They use their knowledge to turn raw materials into useful and/or consumable products such as paper products, plastics, metals, detergents, gasoline, and pharmaceuticals. Other engineering services include overseeing production of electronic parts and industrial machines in factories and testing or quality control of the products.

Meteorologists apply knowledge of weather patterns, climate, and principles of physics to predict weather patterns. Meteorologists work in a variety of industries including television or radio broadcasting, air pollution, and hydrology. Some meteorologists perform research at academic institutes or government organizations in areas such as climate change, oceanography, polar meteorology, and desert meteorology.

History of the Industry

The history of the scientific and technical services industry can be broken down by the type of service provided. The biotechnology industry has its origins in the field of zymotechnology, which is the production of beer using fermentation. Life science research and development received an enormous boost in 1953, when the discovery of the structure of DNA ushered in the field of molecular biology. Recombinant DNA techniques and the polymerase chain reaction (PCR), a method for amplifying specific genes or sections of DNA, made it possible to produce large amounts of human proteins in the laboratory using such humble vehicles as bacteria and yeast. Genentech, arguably the first biotechnology company, opened in 1978 with a single product—human insulin. More drugs were subsequently produced and marketed, including human growth hormone, hepatitis B vac-

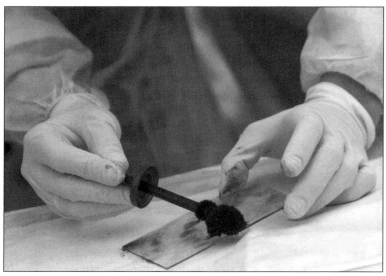

Forensic specialists use their expertise in molecular biology, microbiology, chemistry, ballistics, and materials to help solve crimes. (©Dreamstime.com)

Engineers use their scientific and mathematical training to solve technical problems affecting machines and electronics. (©Dreamstime.com)

cine, alpha-interferon, and tissue plasminogen activator, a protein that breaks down blood clots. Advances in synthetic organic chemistry also facilitated the chemical synthesis of many medically important compounds in the laboratory, including drugs active against different types of cancer.

The origins of chemical engineering can be traced back to the ancient Greeks and Chinese, who invented methods of distilling alcohol. Aristotle described a strategy for purifying fresh water from the sea by evaporation and condensation. Modern chemical engineering began during the Industrial Revolution in eighteenth century England, when a growing need for chemicals such as sulfuric acid, alkali (used in soap, glass, and textiles) and potash spurred the development of industrial methods of producing chemicals. Chemical methods and instruments for large-scale production were developed and fine-tuned to produce these chemicals on a large enough scale to meet huge demands.

In 1887, George Davis, an alkali inspector in England, delivered a series of lectures at the Manchester Technical School about operations in the chemical industry. This was probably the first chemical engineering course; formal education programs in chemical engineering were still lacking. The first bachelor's degree course in chemical engineering started in 1888 at the Massachusetts Institute of Technology, and it was followed by similar courses at the University of Pennsylvania and Tulane University within the next decade. In Germany in the nineteenth century, batch reactors started to be used for large-scale production of chemicals. Following a decline in the industry during the stock market crash of 1929, production ramped up again during World War II and expanded even more rapidly after the war.

Mechanical engineering started with the invention of the steam engine in the eighteenth century, which provided an impetus for the invention of other machines that were put to use in the Industrial Revolution. The Institution of Mechanical Engineers was founded in 1847 in Birmingham, England, providing credibility and momentum to the burgeoning field. Electrical engineering originated in the 1600's, when William Gilbert discovered magnetism and static electricity. Later, Alessandro Volta discovered the electric current. This was followed by the invention of the telegraph, the telephone, the lightbulb, and the electric motor in the 1800's. The American Institute of Electrical Engineers was formed in 1884.

The Industry Today

The scientific and technical services industry is one of the fastest-growing industries today, spurred by the revolutionary scientific and technical advances of the previous century and by discoveries that are continuing to occur on a daily basis in the twenty-first century. The workforce has also grown in number and qualifications, supplied by the increasing ranks of newly minted Ph.D.s and engineering graduates. Today's Ph.D. scientists and specialized engineers usually undergo extensive education and training before they embark on their first jobs. Many hold internships at laboratories or companies while undergraduates, earn advanced degrees, and undergo further training and mentorship years after receiving those degrees.

Scientific and engineering research in the twenty-first century is a collaborative and interdisciplinary enterprise. To be successful, scientists and engineers must be cognizant of scientific and technical areas outside their chosen specialties. In academic institutions and companies, researchers with different expertise frequently collaborate on a project. The National Institutes of Health, which provide funding for the majority of academic research projects, favor projects that propose a multidisciplinary approach to scientific questions. Present-day science has many tools that can be used to discover new therapies and decipher the mechanisms of diseases. These biotechnology tools include recombinant DNA technology, stem cells, cancer cell lines (cells cultured from cancer patients that are propagated for research use), and X-ray crystallog-raphy to determine how drugs interact with proteins and DNA in the body at the atomic level.

Engineering research is also progressing rapidly, with exciting advances in the fields of nanotechnology and robotics. For example, nanotechnology research has been explored for drug delivery in medicine. "Smart" particles are attached to substances that are made to function as "homing missiles," directing them to specific cells or tissues in the body. The idea is for these smart particles to deliver drugs or gene sequences only to affected cells or tissues (such as cancer cells), selectively killing these cells without damaging surrounding healthy tissue. Nanotechnology is also being applied to the production of novel materials and devices for medical and industrial purposes. Chemical engineering today is a sophisticated profession that uses engineering principles to solve complex problems in many different fields, ranging from medicine to the petroleum industry. Chemical engineers also turn raw materials into an ever growing array of useful products.

INDUSTRY MARKET SEGMENTS

Scientific and technical service providers range in size from individual self-employed consultants to major research and development corporations with budgets in the billions of dollars.

Small Businesses

Small biotechnology (biotech) and pharmaceutical companies, academic and research institutes, and small companies providing engineering services, meteorological services, and forensic laboratory services fall under this category. Small biotech and pharmaceutical companies include start-up businesses that have a modest amount of funding capital and one to several potential drugs or therapies in development. The goal for most of these companies is to produce their therapies (sometimes only one therapy), test them in clinical trials, and obtain approval for treating specific diseases from the Food and Drug Administration (FDA). After FDA approval, the company can sell its therapies on the market. Small companies providing engineering services, meteorological services, or forensic laboratory services are usually private and provide services for large companies or other industries that occasionally require these services. They may also offer consulting services.

Potential Annual Earnings Scale. According to the U.S. Bureau of Labor Statistics (BLS), the average annual salary for an engineer in the engineering services industry in 2009 ranged from $74,900 for a marine engineer to $129,890 for a nuclear engineer. The most common type of engineer in the industry was a civil engineer, with a mean salary of $82,300. Engineering managers earned an average of $123,510. In the scientific research and development services industry, scientists' average salaries ranged from $60,510 for zoologists and wildlife biologists to $107,660 for physicists. The most common type of research scientist in the industry was a medical scientist, with a mean average salary of $925,350. Natural sciences managers earned an average of $152,200.

Average annual salaries at small companies or academic centers are $33,200 for research technicians (almost all of whom have at least a bachelor's degree) and $83,000 for "Scientist I" workers (about 60 percent of whom have Ph.D.s). Many Ph.D. scientists undergo further training as postdoctoral fellows in academia or in companies before starting their own laboratories in universities or research centers or taking jobs as research scientists at private companies. The National Institutes of Health publishes pay recommendations for postdoctoral fellow stipends. As of fall, 2009, the institute-recommended pay scale ranged from $37,368 for a fellow with no experience to $51,552 for a fellow with seven or more years of postdoctoral experience. Postdoctoral fellows' salaries generally follow this pay scale across company size.

Clientele Interaction. Because of the relatively small number of employees at small firms, engineers in small engineering companies may have a considerable amount of interaction with customers, typically project managers working for government organizations or private companies. Business skills are essential for engineering managers; many engineers take business courses to help them move up the management ladder. Research and development scientists in small biotechnology companies have little contact with customers unless they are providing a contract research service and need to clarify experimental details with their clients. Scientists in academia do not have customers as

such, although they have certain obligations to the government bodies that fund their research.

Amenities, Atmosphere, and Physical Grounds. Employees at small companies may work a forty-hour week, but most work longer hours because the workload of an individual employee is often greater at smaller establishments than at larger ones. Also, because of smaller amounts of capital or tighter profit margins, small companies may offer fewer amenities such as free meals and free gym memberships. Because engineering, biotech, and pharmaceutical companies depend on productive scientific and technical ideas, these companies usually cultivate an open atmosphere to facilitate discussion and communication among technical workers (scientists or engineers) and between technical workers and administrators. Small companies may resemble small universities or colleges. The physical grounds vary from converted office buildings or warehouses to small but landscaped compounds; some companies may even have small cafeterias and gyms.

Typical Number of Employees. According to the Small Business Administration's Small Business Size Standards, a small company conducting research and development in the physical, engineering, and life sciences is defined as one having five hundred or fewer employees. However, other sources define a small business as one that has one hundred or fewer employees.

Traditional Geographic Locations. Small businesses in this industry can be found in a variety of locations, including in small towns, suburban areas, and metropolitan downtown areas. Although many small businesses have limited capital, owners may decide that the convenience and easy access to clients provided by a metropolitan location justifies the higher costs.

Pros of Working for a Small Scientific Service Provider. It may be easier for an individual with less work experience to secure a position at a small business than at a larger establishment. Working in a small business also allows employees to gain broader professional experience; for example, a scientist at a small biotechnology company could have the opportunity to conduct research as well as manage projects and laboratory operations. It may also take less time to get promoted or become a manager with reporting employees at a small business than at a bigger company. Some small companies provide more paid vacation time and the options of flexible work hours and part-time or full-time telecommuting to compensate for lower average salaries and less attractive benefit packages.

Cons of Working for a Small Scientific Service Provider. On average, workers in small businesses earn less than those in midsize and large businesses. Employee benefits, such as medical, dental, and vision plans, as well as performance-based bonuses, stock options, and reimbursements for gym memberships and utilities, may be more limited than at larger businesses. Although some small companies offer better nonmonetary benefits than their larger counterparts, other small companies provide less paid vacation time and pressure employees to work longer hours in order to match the output of larger competitors.

Although the opportunities for promotion may be better at a small company, titles may mean less. For example, a director at a small company may manage one or two (or even no) employees, whereas directors at midsize or large companies could have entire departments with hundreds of employees reporting to them. Holding a position of seniority or authority at a small business does not necessarily equip an individual to transition smoothly to a management position in a larger business. Employees at small companies also gain experience working with the particular company's management style and may be unfamiliar with processes common in larger companies, such as Six Sigma streamlining procedures, legal and compliance review, and coordination between many different departments or branches within the company. If an employee's ultimate career goal is to work at a large company, he or she may gain valuable and more diverse work experience at a small company but will need to learn these "larger company" skills to be successful at a bigger establishment.

Costs

Payroll and Benefits: Small scientific service providers may be staffed entirely by salaried employees, or they may have salaried employees in managerial and professional positions (scientist or engineer level) and hourly employees in technician positions. Many businesses offer benefits, including medical, dental, and sometimes vision insurance; paid vacation time; retirement programs with company matching contributions; and year-end bonuses. However, the company contribution may not be as generous as that of larger businesses. Almost all small businesses are privately owned, so they do not offer stock options to their employees.

Supplies: Most small scientific service providers require specialized equipment. Some pieces of equipment are extremely expensive, costing hundreds of thousands of dollars, and purchasing such equipment could mean that small companies have to forgo other purchases. Small biotechnology and chemical engineering companies also require a continuous supply of chemicals, reagents, kits, and biological materials, such as cell lines, bacteria, and yeast. Businesses that conduct animal research also need laboratory animals, as well as food, cages, and bedding for the animals.

External Services: Small businesses may contract some projects or parts of projects to other companies if they do not have the necessary expertise or resources to complete them in-house. Although many small businesses have several employees in charge of marketing and sales, they often contract outside vendors to fulfill their marketing and medical education needs. Small businesses also hire housekeeping, security, and landscaping staff from companies specializing in these services.

Utilities: Utilities include water, sewage, gas, electricity, telephone, and Internet access.

Taxes: Small businesses, the majority of which are for-profit, pay federal, state, and local taxes on revenue, as well as property taxes.

Midsize Businesses

Midsize companies providing scientific and technical services are more likely to be public than smaller companies. That is, they raise funding by selling shares to the public. Midsize academic and research institutes may be funded through a combination of federal grants (for example, from the National Institutes of Health) and grants from pharmaceutical companies and private foundations. Midsize biotechnology companies usually have several products either on the market or in the developmental pipeline. These companies may perform their own clinical trial research but often partner with a larger company to market and sell their products, with profits shared between the partners. Midsize companies providing engineering services typically specialize in one or a few areas of engineering and also hire engineers as managers and in upper management positions. Midsize establishments providing meteorological services include state-run organizations and local television and radio stations. Midsize forensic laboratories offer consulting services for law enforcement and for legal cases.

Potential Annual Earnings Scale. According to the BLS, the average annual salary for an engineer in the engineering services industry in 2009 ranged from $74,900 for a marine engineer to $129,890 for a nuclear engineer. The most common type of engineer in the industry was a civil engineer, with a mean salary of $82,300. Engineering managers earned an average of $123,510. In the scientific research and development services industry, scientists' average salaries ranged from $60,510 for zoologists and wildlife biologists to $107,660 for physicists. The most common type of research scientist in the industry was a medical scientist, with a mean average salary of $925,350. Natural sciences managers earned an average of $152,200.

Average annual salaries at midsize companies or academic centers are $50,000 for research technicians (almost all of whom have at least a bachelor's degree). Scientists at midsize biotechnology and pharmaceutical companies, more than 60 percent of whom have doctoral degrees, earn an average annual starting salary of $85,000. An engineer at a midsize company, who typically has a bachelor's or master's degree, earns an average annual starting salary of $60,000 to $90,000. After five years, salaries increase to an average of $75,000, and engineers with twenty years of experience frequently earn more than $100,000. Engineering technicians such as biomedical engineering technicians, who maintain and operate medical equipment, earn an average starting salary of $53,000 per year.

OCCUPATION SPECIALTIES

Engineering Technicians

Specialty	Responsibilities
Civil engineering technicians	Help civil engineers plan and build highways, buildings, bridges, dams, wastewater treatment systems, and other structures; they also conduct related surveys and studies. Some inspect water and wastewater treatment systems to ensure that pollution control requirements are met. Others estimate construction costs and specify materials to be used.
Electrical technicians	Apply electrical theory and related knowledge to test and modify developmental or operational electrical machinery and electrical control equipment and circuitry in industrial or commercial plants and laboratories.
Industrial engineering technicians	Study and record time, motion, methods, and speed of maintenance, production, clerical, and other work operations to establish standard production rates and improve efficiency.
Mechanical engineering technicians	Help engineers design, develop, test, and manufacture industrial machinery, consumer products, and other equipment.

Clientele Interaction. Employees in midsize engineering companies may have a fair amount of interaction with customers, typically project managers working for government organizations or private companies. Business skills are essential for engineering managers; many engineers take business courses to help them move up the management ladder. Research and development scientists in midsize biotechnology companies have minimal to no contact with customers. Scientists in midsize academic centers do not have customers as such, although they have certain obligations to the government bodies that fund their research.

Amenities, Atmosphere, and Physical Grounds. Midsize companies frequently offer on-site full-service cafeterias, cafes, gyms, and communal spaces where scientists and managers can meet and discuss ideas. These companies may also provide free or heavily discounted meals or vending machine food items for employees who need to work longer hours. Although a forty-hour workweek is fairly common, many employees work longer hours and on weekends when necessary. The physical grounds of midsize engineering services companies include office buildings and industrial plants. Midsize scientific research establishments, both academic and for-profit biotech companies, are often self-contained, landscaped campuses.

Typical Number of Employees. Midsize businesses have 500 to 999 employees.

Traditional Geographic Locations. Midsize scientific or technical service companies may be located in suburban or urban areas. Biotechnology companies are often located in research hubs, where there is a high concentration of academic institutions and biotechnology and pharmaceutical companies.

Pros of Working for a Midsize Scientific Service Provider. Working in a midsize business offers a degree of interaction and camaraderie that may be similar to that of a small company, while providing some of the advantages of a large company (better benefits, more perks, and more delegation of responsibility).

Cons of Working for a Midsize Scientific Service Provider. Midsize businesses may have more business-oriented managers than smaller establishments, which may emphasize profits over innovation and creativity. Scientists and engineers who want to rise up the corporate ladder in a midsize

business will need to have strong business and interpersonal skills besides their technical expertise.

Costs

Payroll and Benefits: Midsize businesses have a majority of salaried staff with full benefits, including medical, dental, and sometimes vision insurance; paid vacation time; retirement program with company match; and year-end bonuses. Publicly traded businesses also frequently offer stock options or a discounted stock-purchase plan to their employees.

Supplies: Most midsize businesses in this industry require specialized equipment. Some pieces of equipment cost hundreds of thousands of dollars. Research centers and biotechnology and chemical engineering companies also require a continuous supply of chemicals, reagents, kits, and biological material such as cell lines, bacteria, and yeast. Businesses that conduct animal research also need laboratory animals as well as food, cages, and bedding for the animals.

External Services: Midsize businesses may contract some projects or parts of projects to other companies if they do not have the expertise or resources. Midsize biotechnology companies frequently partner with larger biotechnology or pharmaceutical companies; after the midsize company develops the drug, the larger company produces the drug on a large scale and markets it. Although midsize companies have marketing and sales personnel as well as medical writers on staff, they often contract specific marketing projects to advertising and medical education companies. Midsize companies often hire housekeeping, security, and landscaping staff from companies specializing in these services, although some companies have their own staff on payroll.

Utilities: Utilities include water, sewage, gas, electricity, telephone, and Internet access.

Taxes: For-profit businesses pay federal, state, and local taxes on revenue, as well as property taxes. Some midsize establishments are nonprofit research centers, which are either tax exempt or considered government organizations (for example, state universities). These organizations do not need to pay federal taxes on surplus money that is used solely for the organization's purposes and not to benefit individuals. Property and state tax exemption varies depending on the organization and the state.

Large Businesses

Large companies providing scientific and technical services are often publicly traded because the technology-intensive work they do requires a large amount of capital and overhead costs. Large academic and research institutes tend to receive a disproportionately large share of federal grants and grants from pharmaceutical companies and private foundations, compared to smaller institutes. One of the reasons for this is their ability to attract researchers with top-notch reputations who perform the type of cutting-edge, interdisciplinary research that is most attractive to grantors. Large biotechnology and pharmaceutical companies always have several to many products on the market and in the developmental pipeline. They typically have their own clinical trial divisions and have marketing and sales budgets and infrastructure. Large companies providing engineering services are either industries that manufacture products or design systems, or they are engineering consulting companies that provide engineering expertise on a project-by-project basis to industries. Government organizations such as the National Weather Service and the National Oceanic and Atmospheric Administration are large establishments that provide meteorological services that are useful for a wide variety of industries, including transportation, construction, and environmental engineering. National television and syndicated radio services are additional large employers offering meteorological services. Similarly, the largest forensic laboratories are operated by federal government agencies, such as the Federal Bureau of Investigation.

Potential Annual Earnings Scale. According to the BLS, the average annual salary for an engineer in the engineering services industry in 2009 ranged from $74,900 for a marine engineer to $129,890 for a nuclear engineer. The most common type of engineer in the industry was a civil engineer, with a mean salary of $82,300. Engineering managers earned an average of $123,510. In the scientific research and development services industry, scientists' average salaries ranged from $60,510 for zoologists and wildlife biologists to $107,660 for physicists. The most common type of research scientist in the industry was a medical sci-

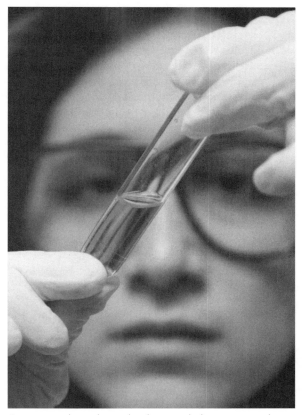

Scientists at large biotechnology and pharmaceutical companies, more than 60 percent of whom have doctoral degrees, earn an average annual starting salary of $85,000. (©Paul Hakimata/Dreamstime.com)

entist, with a mean average salary of $925,350. Natural sciences managers earned an average of $152,200.

Average annual salaries at large companies or academic centers are approximately $55,000 for research technicians (almost all of whom have bachelor's degrees and some of whom have master's degrees). Large biotechnology or pharmaceutical companies sometimes employ postdoctoral fellows. These fellows often earn higher salaries than their counterparts in academia and often transition to scientist positions at the same company after completing their postdoctoral training. Scientists at large biotechnology and pharmaceutical companies, more than 60 percent of whom have doctoral degrees, earn an average annual starting salary of $85,000. An engineer at a large engineering services company, who typically has a bachelor's or master's degree, earns an average annual starting salary of $60,000 to $100,000, depending on experience. Large companies are more likely to hire a larger number of engineering technicians, earning an average of $58,000 per year, than smaller companies.

Clientele Interaction. Employees in large engineering companies may have a fair amount of interaction with customers, typically project managers working for government organizations or private companies. Business skills are even more important for engineering managers in large companies because these companies place more emphasis on streamlining costs and driving profits. Research and development scientists in large biotechnology companies have minimal to no contact with customers. Scientists in large academic centers do not have customers as such, although they have certain obligations to the government bodies that fund their research.

Amenities, Atmosphere, and Physical Grounds. In a larger company supplying scientific and technical services, the importance of cultivating and nurturing effective communication between scientific and technical workers and management is even greater. Management needs to understand the realities of developing products, the challenges to development and production time lines, and the complexity of research data. The physical grounds of a large scientific and engineering services company is usually a self-contained campus with several large buildings, multiple cafeterias and break rooms, a gym, and several conference rooms of different sizes to accommodate smaller group meetings as well as meetings for the entire company.

Typical Number of Employees. Employees number from one thousand up to tens of thousands.

Traditional Geographic Locations. Large scientific companies are located in suburban areas close to major metropolitan areas or in and around technology hubs. Large businesses in this industry rely heavily on finding the most talented and experienced workers. Being situated in these locations increases the chances of businesses finding such employees from surrounding academic centers and companies.

Pros of Working for a Large Scientific Service Provider. Workers in large businesses earn more on average than workers doing similar jobs in small and midsize businesses. They may also enjoy better benefits such as a more comprehensive health plan, reimbursement for further education, and an expense account. In addition, employees at larger research and engineering companies have the experience of working at a well-known, established company, which will help them find jobs at similar or even larger companies in the future. If a researcher or engineer at a large business makes a discovery or invents a new device, the company has the legal resources and experience to carry out the patent process in an efficient way.

Cons of Working for a Large Scientific Service Provider. Getting a job at a large business can be difficult, especially for workers with little experience in their particular fields. Once an employee is hired, it may be more challenging to distinguish himself or herself from the crowd. There is often a steep learning curve at the beginning while the new employee becomes familiar with the many processes that the company has in place. Some large businesses are also very hierarchical, and it can take several years to be promoted to the next level.

Costs

Payroll and Benefits: Large businesses have key staff, including management, professional, technical, and administrative employees, in salaried positions with full benefits, including medical, dental, and sometimes vision insurance; paid vacation time; retirement program with company match; and year-end bonuses. Some large businesses have a large number of hourly laboratory technicians, usually with full benefits. Many large businesses are publicly traded and offer stock options or a discounted stock purchase plan to their employees.

Supplies: Large businesses in this industry have a wide range of specialized equipment, some of which is very costly. Research centers and biotechnology and chemical engineering companies also require a continuous supply of chemicals, reagents, kits, and biological material such as cell lines, bacteria, and yeast. Businesses that conduct animal research periodically purchase laboratory animals as well as food, cages, and bedding for the animals.

External Services: Large businesses usually conduct all of their research in-house, but they may contract parts of their production process or testing to other companies. Likewise, many large companies have their own marketing, sales, and medical writer employees, but they may contract specific marketing projects to advertising and medical education companies. Large companies commonly have their own housekeeping, security, and landscaping staff, although some companies hire external companies to provide these services.

Utilities: Utilities include water, sewage, gas, electricity, telephone, and Internet access.

Taxes: For-profit businesses pay federal, state, and local taxes on revenue, as well as property taxes. Some large establishments are nonprofit research centers, which are either tax exempt or considered government organizations (for example, state universities). These organizations do not need to pay federal taxes on surplus money that is used solely for the organization's purposes and not to benefit individuals. Property and state tax exemption varies depending on the organization and the state.

ORGANIZATIONAL STRUCTURE AND JOB ROLES

Research and development in the physical sciences, life sciences, and engineering is conducted in laboratories in government organizations, academic institutions, and companies. For meteorological research and services, organizational structures and job roles vary according to the type of organization. One-third of meteorologists are employed at National Weather Service weather stations, which are operated by the federal government. Other meteorologists work for television and radio stations, for academic institutions, and for environmental consulting companies. Meteorologists at small weather stations or television and radio stations may work alone, while those at companies and in academia often work in collaboration with other meteorologists or scientists from other disciplines.

Biotechnology and pharmaceutical companies typically have a scientific advisory board to oversee the scientific direction of the company. The scientific advisory board is closely linked to the corporate board of directors, which provides business direction for the company. The chief executive officer (CEO) is responsible for putting the scientific and business advice of the boards into action to generate profits for the company. A chief operating officer (COO) oversees the daily operations of the company. Most companies have vice presidents or directors of research and development, marketing, finance, business development, and investor relations, who are in charge of their respective divisions.

Engineers working in-house for manufacturing, petroleum, energy, and water treatment companies design processes and equipment to improve production and delivery of services. Some engineers are responsible for maintenance of processes, machines, and equipment. Engineers working in engineering consulting companies usually work as part of a team, with a supervising engineer in charge of a project. These supervising engineers may meet with clients to pitch projects when vying for a contract and to present updates throughout the project. Supervising engineers require considerable business and management skills in addition to engineering knowledge and experience. Generally, engineers need to acquire such business and management skills in order to advance their careers to the next level.

The following umbrella categories apply to the organizational structure of businesses in the scientific and technical services industry:

- Research and Development
- Business Management
- Technology and Design
- Production and Operations
- Sales and Marketing
- Administrative Services
- Intellectual Property/Legal Services
- Regulatory Affairs
- Human Resources
- Facilities and Security

Research and Development

One of the most important departments of a technical services company is research and development. Because many of these companies sell products or services that are based on intellectual property, their success depends on the quality and innovativeness of their research. For example,

OCCUPATION SPECIALTIES

Science Technicians

Specialty	Responsibilities
Artificial breeding laboratory technicians	Measure the quality of animal semen to improve artificial breeding.
Assayers	Test ores and minerals for values and components, and separate and weigh components.
Biological aides	Assist researchers with experiments in agricultural sciences by setting up, testing, record keeping, and cleaning.
Chemical laboratory technicians	Assist chemical engineers and chemists in laboratory work.
Food testers	Test and report on food for flavor, color, purity, odor, and content quantities.
Laboratory animal care veterinarians	Examine, diagnose, and treat diseases of laboratory animals to ensure health of animals used in scientific research and to comply with regulations governing their humane and ethical treatment.
Laboratory testers	Examine, measure, test, and photograph synthetic fiber samples to assist quality control.
Scouts	Collect information about oil and gas drilling, geological prospecting, and land or lease contracts.
Spectroscopists	Examine metals and minerals for density and intensity, and record procedures and results.
Weather observers	Observe weather and visibility using various equipment for pilot briefings or forecasts.

choosing the right treatment to develop and bring to market is crucial to the success of biotechnology or pharmaceutical companies. Developing a treatment (for example, a drug for atherosclerosis) is a lengthy process. Out of multiple promising drug candidates, for example, only a small fraction will be selected for clinical trial testing. Out of these, only the candidates that show efficacy in clinical trials and do not have detrimental side effects will be earmarked for further development. Drug characteristics and clinical trial data are then submitted to the FDA and, following approval for a specified disease state and sometimes in specific patient types, the drug can be marketed and promoted.

Biomedical engineers also engage in research and development activities that are related to health care and diseases. They are more concerned with applying engineering principles to the design and development of prosthetic limbs, medical instruments, and medical devices, including heart valves, catheters, and imaging systems (such as magnetic resonance imaging and ultrasound). Led by a vice president or director, this department may be divided into several divisions based on broad research areas (for example, biochemistry,

chemistry, immunology, and molecular biology) or by target disease classifications (for example, oncology, autoimmune diseases, and endocrinology). Scientists and technicians work in teams under the supervision of a principal scientist or director, performing scientific research in laboratories that is focused on a particular purpose.

Although companies and government organizations providing forensic services focus more on processing specimens and generating data, some establishments perform research to develop better techniques, reagents, and equipment to help determine the cause of death and solve crimes. Forensics research and development occurs across a broad range of forensics specialties, including ballistics, chemistry, molecular biology, microbiology, and biometrics (fingerprints).

Larger engineering services companies may also have research and development departments that develop new processes, machines, and instruments for specific purposes. Burgeoning new fields such as nanotechnology provide the opportunity for innovative engineering research, producing new tools that can be used for a wide range of applications in fields such as materials science, electronics, and medicine.

Research meteorologists, who usually work for the government or in industries requiring weather prediction, are involved in researching air pressure, temperature, and impact of weather on the environment. Meteorologists may also develop new devices and methods for detecting weather changes and predicting weather patterns.

Research and development occupations may include the following:

- Vice President of Research and Development
- Research Director in Chemistry
- Research Director in Immunology
- Principal Investigator/Scientist/Engineer
- Scientist
- Research Engineer
- Scientific Associate
- Research Technician

Business Management

Although businesses in this industry are mostly driven by intellectual knowledge, with the scientifically and technically trained employees making up the core, a significant proportion of upper management consists of people with business rather than technical experience. These business managers, including the CEO, the director of business development, and the director of investor relations, use their business knowledge and experience to identify business opportunities, products to develop, and the business direction of the company. The business managers are in charge of ensuring strong returns on investment (ROI) for investors and for increasing profits for the company as a whole. In a publicly traded company, the business managers are also responsible for driving profits for stockholders.

Business management occupations may include the following:

- Chief Executive Officer (CEO)
- Vice President/Director of Communications and Investor Relations
- Vice President/Director of Business Development
- Vice President/Director of Product Development
- Business Development Analyst
- Account Manager

Technology and Design

Chemical engineers participate in design and development processes for chemical manufacturing, as well as energy, paper, clothing, and food production. Some chemical engineers specialize in nanotechnology, which uses nanoparticles (microscopic particles in the nanometer size range) for a wide range of applications. Electrical engineers design and develop production of electrical components and machines, including electric motors, wiring in buildings, radar and navigation instruments, telecommunications components, and instruments involved in the generation and distribution of electricity to homes and businesses. Electrical engineers are also involved in developing and fine-tuning processes for more efficient transmission of electricity. Mechanical engineers design and develop machines, tools, and devices for a variety of purposes, ranging from manufacturing and agriculture to energy production and utilization.

Technology and design occupations may include the following:

- Chief Information Officer (CIO)
- Technology Director
- Design Engineer
- Applications Engineer
- Testing Engineer

Production and Operations

Although some research and development activities produce intangible results (for example, a weather forecast or increased scientific knowledge of a disease), biotechnology research often produces a drug, therapy, or medical device that has to be produced on a large scale and distributed to customers. Because large-scale production is extremely expensive, small companies often license the intellectual property of their product to larger companies that are responsible for large-scale production, distribution, and, in some cases, marketing.

Midsize and large companies may have production facilities in different locations from their administrative or research facilities. For example, a company's research and administrative offices may be located in an expensive town in New Jersey, while its production facilities may be situated in a more rural location where leasing and employment costs are lower. Quality control and assurance are an essential function during the production process. Quality control specialists are trained in different characteristics of the product and are responsible for performing testing and verification procedures to ensure that national and international standards are met.

In engineering services companies, many engineers are involved in some aspect of production, and some engineering jobs are focused on one or more steps in the production process—streamlining, troubleshooting, or testing and quality control. For example, production engineers are involved in day-to-day operations and responsible for production efficiency, scheduling of workers, and worker safety. Project engineers are responsible for managing all aspects of a specific project, including time line, resources, workers, and meeting client needs. Testing and systems engineers are involved in testing and improving equipment and processes in industrial manufacturing and in the delivery of utilities to consumers. These engineers may work collaboratively with design engineers to refine the design of machinery and processes throughout a project.

Production and operations occupations may include the following:

- Chief Operating Officer (COO)
- Operations Director
- Production/Manufacturing Director
- Production/Manufacturing Manager
- Technician, Production/Manufacturing Manager
- Plant Manager/Supervisor
- Plant Maintenance Manager
- Production Engineer
- Systems Engineer
- Maintenance and Repair Technician

Sales and Marketing

Marketing managers and the sales force are integral to the success of a scientific and technical services company. Depending on the type of services provided and the size of the company, the number of marketing managers and the size of the sales force can range from a few people to thousands.

In a pharmaceutical or biotechnology company, marketing managers are often involved in marketing a specific brand, usually a drug or type of treatment. The brand managers are in charge of shaping and controlling the marketing message for the drug, through advertising as well as promotional and continuing medical education (CME) programs tailored for the target group (clinicians who treat patients with diseases targeted by the drug). Often, these marketing personnel may work with research directors in research and development to pinpoint the drug characteristics that make the drug stand out among its competitors. Marketing managers then incorporate these characteristics into the marketing message; this message will be a thread running through the advertising and educational programs, which include presentations at national conferences by key opinion leaders (usually clinicians or researchers who are well known and highly respected in their field), scientific articles, printed materials, and online content.

Marketing managers are also in charge of conveying the marketing message to the sales force attached to that drug. As a brand evolves, brand managers often streamline the marketing message to focus on emerging aspects of the drug that can be translated into a competitive advantage, such as the efficacy of the drug for a particular patient group or a better side-effect profile compared to competitor drugs. These qualities may be apparent only after the drug has been on the market for a while and used by a sufficient number of patients.

Although marketing personnel decide whom to target and what to say, they do not usually interact directly with the target audience, the clinicians. Instead, the face of the company is its sales force. Salespeople see clinicians regularly and develop relationships with them; these relationships allow salespeople to convey the latest results, advances, and marketing messages directly to clinicians. Pharmaceutical and biotechnology salespeople are often scientifically trained and receive further training about the company, the drug, and the diseases targeted by the drug; they may also receive more in-depth training about drug characteristics and disease states that provides competitive advantages. For drugs that are used by specialists, salespeople with specialized knowledge and experience may be employed to more effectively engage the target group.

Marketing and sales at engineering services companies focus on discovering and addressing specific client needs. Marketing and sales personnel include engineers who have firsthand knowledge of the problems clients face and can propose practical engineering solutions. Engineering sales personnel often interact directly with clients to identify key issues and needs and devise the best strategies to meet these needs. Some of these salespeople have titles such as technical sales engineer, reflecting the fact that they are trained engineers who are experienced in selling specialized products and services.

Sales and marketing occupations may include the following:

- Vice President of Marketing
- Marketing Director
- Marketing Manager
- Market Analyst
- Medical Education Director
- Medical Writer
- Technical Writer
- Medical Science Liaison
- Vice President of Sales
- Regional Sales Director
- District Sales Director

- Sales Representative
- Technical Sales Engineer

Administrative Services

This group of employees provides support functions for the company, ranging from accounting and billing to administrative services. Some departments, including accounting and payroll, support the entire company. Administrative assistants, by contrast, may support an individual manager, several managers, or a team.

Administrative services occupations may include the following:

- Controller
- Accountant
- Payroll Services Director
- Payroll Services Manager
- Payroll Coordinator
- Billing Operations Director
- Billing Operations Manager
- Billing Specialist
- Executive Assistant
- Administrative Assistant
- Receptionist

Intellectual Property/Legal Services

Intellectual property lawyers in the legal departments of scientific and engineering companies are responsible for analyzing the intellectual value of each new drug or technique and whether it can be patented. These employees also monitor similar products or techniques in other companies or in academia to determine if there is a patent infringement. Intellectual property lawyers have degrees from law schools; many also have degrees such as doctorates in science or engineering. They may have worked as intellectual property lawyers in law firms before taking a job in industry. Some companies employ patent agents, many of whom have scientific or engineering education and training. Patent agents work with intellectual property lawyers to determine the patent value of discoveries and inventions.

Intellectual property and legal services occupations may include the following:

- General Counsel
- Intellectual Property Attorney
- Litigator

- Patent Agent
- Paralegal
- Legal Secretary

Regulatory Affairs

Biotechnology companies have regulatory departments that are responsible for putting together new drug applications to the FDA. The FDA requires a comprehensive and rigorous assessment of a drug's efficacy, side-effect profile, safety, and other characteristics. If these are favorable and the drug's efficacy compares well with other drugs in its class, the FDA will approve the drug for sale. Regulatory specialists and regulatory medical writers usually have science degrees and training in regulatory processes and FDA rules.

Regulatory services occupations may include the following:

- Regulatory Affairs Director
- Regulatory Affairs Manager
- Regulatory Affairs Specialist
- Regulatory Writer

Human Resources

The human resources department is in charge of hiring and terminating employees, as well as mediating disagreements between employees and between employees and their managers. Human resources personnel in the scientific and technical services industry encounter unique challenges, including having to hire highly qualified and specialized individuals for research, administrative, marketing, and legal positions. For many of these positions, the management will highlight specific qualities and experience that the successful candidate should possess. Depending on the candidate pool at the specific location and the attractiveness of the package, it can be challenging to find suitable candidates who meet these requirements.

Another unique challenge involves the personalities and working styles of many research scientists and engineers. For example, the field of academic science, where many scientists are trained, encourages creative, unconventional thinking and sometimes emphasizes results over personal interactions. Some scientists thus emerge from graduate school with difficulty interacting with others in a respectful and tolerant way, especially with those whom they perceive as less intelligent. This attitude can create tense, disruptive situations with coworkers or managers that may escalate to the point that human resource specialists or managers need to intervene. The role of the human resource specialist or manager is to help resolve these and other disagreements as quickly and completely as possible to avoid lost productivity, resignation of talented employees, and lawsuits by employees or former employees. All these situations can have negative ramifications for the institute or company as a whole. It is also common for the human resources department in larger companies to perform employee surveys to determine if employees are contented (or not) with the work environment, company management, their managers, salaries, benefits, advancement, and professional development opportunities. Human resource specialists will highlight areas that need improvement and work with managers to implement appropriate action.

Human resources occupations may include the following:

- Vice President/Director of Human Resources
- Human Resources Manager
- Human Resources Specialist
- Administrative Assistant

Facilities and Security

Biomedical research facilities in academic centers and companies are typically state-of-the-art, with equipment that can cost up to millions of dollars. Facility personnel are in charge of maintaining these pieces of equipment and fixing problems that arise, even if they occur after the regular workday. Refrigerators, freezers, incubators, and cold rooms need to be maintained at constant temperatures to preserve the integrity of research materials such as chemicals, cell cultures, bacteria, protein, and DNA. These pieces of equipment are fitted with sensors, and some are wired to call the researcher or facilities worker in charge if a problem occurs. Regardless of the time of day, the facilities worker is expected to go to work, check the equipment, and repair it if possible to prevent the loss of valuable samples.

Most research facilities have security guards who check employee identification cards and patrol the facilities. These guards work in shifts to provide security coverage twenty-four hours per day. Security in research facilities is important to prevent industrial spies, rival research groups, and animal right activists from breaking into laboratories and removing animals or removing and destroying laboratory records, data, and equipment. The laboratories can be a security challenge because they are typically open throughout the day, and also open at night if researchers are working late. Security guards and security managers are even more important in facilities conducting primate research, which are at higher risk of invasion and vandalism by animal rights activists. These places tend to be very low-key and to avoid publicizing the type of research that they do, even to other departments within the same organization (if there is a sign on the outside the building, it usually does not include the words "primate research").

Facilities and security occupations may include the following:

- Security Manager
- Security Guard
- Maintenance Manager
- Maintenance and Repair Worker
- Custodian/Janitor

INDUSTRY OUTLOOK

Overview

The scientific and technical services industry is a growing field, driven by advances in science and technology and increasing awareness of environmental concerns. The employment outlook for engineers and research and development scientists is good. However, competition is expected to be strong in all scientific fields, partly because of the increasing number of science graduates. In 2008, approximately 91,300 biological scientists (who perform medical and genetic research) were employed; this number is projected by the BLS to increase by 21 percent to approximately 110,500 in 2018. Research chemist jobs are projected to grow by 3 percent between 2008 and 2018, which is lower than the 11 percent average rate of increase for all occupations. In 2008, there were an estimated 84,300 employed chemists. This number is expected to grow very modestly to 86,400 in 2018. Most of these chemists will be employed in scientific and technical service companies, especially biotechnology firms, where they are needed for discovery and manufacture of new drugs for diseases that will likely increase in severity and compli-

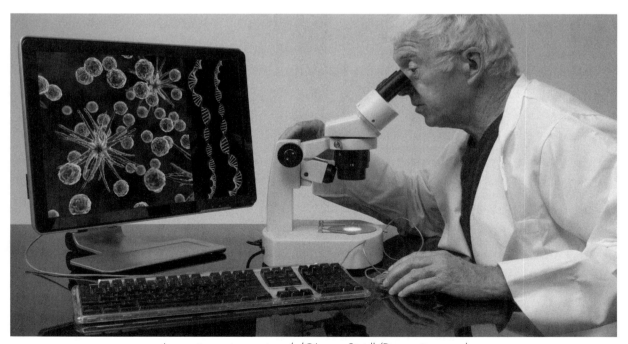

A genetic engineer at work. (©James Steidl/Dreamstime.com)

cations as the population ages. Chemist jobs in the manufacturing industry are expected to decline in the coming years. Materials scientist jobs are projected to increase by 12 percent between 2008 and 2018 (from 9,700 to 10,900), which is similar to the projected growth for all jobs. However, the relatively small total number of materials scientist jobs may skew the percentage increase. Thus, job growth in this field may not be as rosy as it appears.

The outlook for engineering jobs is also somewhat mixed. In 2008, there were 1.6 million engineering jobs. This total number is projected to increase by 11 percent between 2008 and 2018, on par with the projected growth for all occupations. However, not all engineering specialties will experience growth similar to the overall rate, while other specialties are projected to undergo enormous growth, far beyond the overall rate for all jobs. Biomedical engineers, for example, are expected to experience 72 percent job growth between 2008 and 2018, largely because of the increasing medical needs of an aging population. Engineers working in the field of nanotechnology are also expected to have good job prospects.

In 2007, the global medical market for nanotechnology products was $1.7 billion. As the field continues to advance and more products using nanotechnology reach the market, revenues should increase accordingly. The total number of chemical, mechanical, and electrical engineering jobs is expected to remain stable or increase slightly. Most of the increase is predicted to be caused by job growth in engineering consulting companies rather than in traditional industries. This shift is because industries are expected to cut down on the number of in-house engineers employed in favor of contracting engineering consultants when projects require their services. Scientists and engineers with advanced degrees may have better opportunities for obtaining a job in their field and for being promoted to senior and upper management positions. Research jobs in academic research institutions will remain scarce, and competition for these jobs will continue to be very intense. In addition, researchers may have to compete more aggressively for fewer and smaller research grants.

Employment Advantages

Overall, technical and scientific jobs have remained relatively stable in the face of the worldwide recession because of the dependence on federal funding for nonprofit research centers, which has not been as severely affected by the economic downturn as many other sources of funding. Many for-profit companies in this industry also provide essential goods and services, including drugs for chronic diseases, making them relatively recession-proof. Workers in this industry have the advantage of being highly trained and technically proficient, making them attractive candidates for a wide variety of jobs in other industries. Some companies, for example management consulting firms, actively recruit scientific and engineering employees because of their ability to think critically and unconventionally about problems.

Annual Earnings

The 2007 annual earnings for this industry were estimated at $279.1 billion by the U.S. Census Bureau.

PROJECTED EMPLOYMENT FOR SELECTED OCCUPATIONS

Professional, Scientific, and Technical Services

Employment		
2009	Projected 2018	Occupation
371,430	540,200	Accountants and auditors
86,390	105,100	Architectural and civil drafters
372,050	424,800	Lawyers
215,500	359,400	Management analysts
70,200	107,400	Market research analysts

Source: U.S. Bureau of Labor Statistics, Industries at a Glance, Occupational Employment Statistics and Employment Projections Program.

RELATED RESOURCES FOR FURTHER RESEARCH

AMERICAN INSTITUTE OF CHEMICAL ENGINEERS
3 Park Ave.
New York, NY 10016-5991
Tel: (800) 242-4363
Fax: (203) 775-5177
http://www.aiche.org

AMERICAN SOCIETY OF MECHANICAL ENGINEERS
3 Park Ave.
New York, NY 10016
Tel: (800) 843-2763
Fax: (973) 882-1717
http://www.asme.org

BIOTECHNOLOGY INDUSTRY ORGANIZATION
1201 Maryland Ave. SW, Suite 900
Washington, DC 20024
Tel: (202) 962-9200
Fax: (202) 488-6301
http://www.bio.org

NATIONAL INSTITUTES OF HEALTH
9000 Rockville Pike
Bethesda, MD 20892
Tel: (301) 496-4000
http://www.nih.gov

NATIONAL SCIENCE FOUNDATION
4201 Wilson Blvd.
Arlington, VA 22230
Tel: (703) 292-5111
Fax: (703) 292-9055
http://www.nsf.gov

NATIONAL SOCIETY OF PROFESSIONAL ENGINEERS
1420 King St.
Alexandria, VA 22314
Tel: (703) 684-2800
Fax: (703) 836-4875
http://www.nspe.org

ABOUT THE AUTHOR

Ing-Wei Khor holds a bachelor's degree in zoology, a master's degree in marine science, and a Ph.D. in biochemistry. She discovered the exciting world of scientific research during an off-campus semester in college when she interned at a national government laboratory for five months. This experience was followed by more than a decade of scientific research experience in academia, where she delved into the fields of fish immunology, parasitology, virology, cell biology, and cancer biology. During her time in academic research, she published several peer-reviewed articles in scientific journals and presented posters at numerous national and international conferences. In 2006, she became a medical writer, combining her love of both science and communication. Her clients have ranged from pharmaceutical and biotechnology companies to the diagnostics industry to general reference publishers, and she has researched and prepared educational materials from CD-ROMs, Web site content, slide presentations, and video case studies. Her work is geared toward condensing a large amount of scientific literature and research data into clear, simply stated, and easily read educational pieces for busy clinicians. The ultimate goal of these pieces is to drive better and more informed health care decisions for patients.

FURTHER READING

Adeola, Bayo. *Engineering Is Development: Towards a New Role for Consultancy in Nation Building.* Lagos, Nigeria: Comprehensive Project Management Services, 2009.

Camenson, Blythe. *Opportunities in Forensic Science Careers.* New York: McGraw-Hill, 2009.

Careers in Focus: Engineering. 2d ed. New York: Ferguson, 2007.

Erickson, Aaron. *The Nomadic Developer: Surviving and Thriving in the World of Technology Consulting.* Upper Saddle River, N.J.: Addison-Wesley, 2009.

Gartner, John. *Confessions of a Consultant: Survival Business Skills for Scientists and Engineers.* Belleville, Ont.: Epic Press, 2008.

Kenney, Martin. *Biotechnology: The University-Industrial Complex.* New Haven, Conn.: Yale University Press, 1986.

Simon, Françoise, and Philip Kotler. *Building Global Biobrands: Taking Biotechnology to Market.* New York: Free Press, 2003.

Skrzeszewski, Stan. *The Knowledge Entrepreneur.* Lanham, Md.: Scarecrow Press, 2006.

U.S. Bureau of Labor Statistics. "Biological Scientists." In *Occupational Outlook Handbook,* 2010-2011 ed. http://www.bls.gov/oco/ocos047.htm.

_____. *Career Guide to Industries,* 2010-2011 ed. http://www.bls.gov/oco/cg.

_____. "Engineers." In *Occupational Outlook Handbook,* 2010-2011 ed. http://www.bls.gov/oco/ocos027.htm.

U.S. Census Bureau. North American Industry Classification System (NAICS), 2007. http://www.census.gov/cgi-bin/sssd/naics/naicsrch?chart=2007.

_____. Service Annual Survey. 2008. http://www.census.gov/services/sas/historic_data.html.

U.S. Department of Commerce. International Trade Administration. Office of Trade and Industry Information. Industry Trade Data and Analysis. http://ita.doc.gov/td/industry/otea/OTII/OTII-index.html.

Yates, J. K. *Global Engineering and Construction.* Hoboken, N.J.: Wiley, 2007.

Scientific, Medical, and Health Equipment and Supplies Industry

©Søren Sielemann/Dreamstime.com

INDUSTRY SNAPSHOT

General Industry: Health Science

Career Cluster: Health Science

Subcategory Industries: Dental Equipment and Supplies Manufacturing; Medical, Dental, and Hospital Equipment and Supplies Merchant Wholesalers; Medical Diagnostic Apparatus Manufacturing; Ophthalmic Goods Merchant Wholesalers; Ophthalmic Instruments and Apparatus Manufacturing; Orthopaedic Appliances Manufacturing; Prosthetic Appliances Manufacturing; Surgical and Medical Instruments Manufacturing; Surgical Appliance and Supplies Manufacturing

Related Industries: Medicine and Health Care Industry; Scientific and Technical Services

Annual Domestic Revenues: $130 billion USD (Market Research, 2009)

Annual International Revenues: $160 billion USD (Market Research, 2009)

Annual Global Revenues: $290 billion USD (Market Research, 2009)

NAICS Numbers: 42345-42346, 334516-334517, 339112-339114

INDUSTRY DEFINITION

Summary

The scientific, medical, and health equipment and supplies industry engages primarily in the development, manufacturing, and distribution of equipment that is utilized by the health care industry. Products manufactured by this industry span a wide range of technologies. From disposable rubber gloves, to syringes, to high-tech diagnostic imaging systems and linear accelerators, an extensive assortment of supplies, instruments, and devices is produced by this industry. The industry also drives the innovation and development of new health-science technologies that are designed with the ultimate goal of optimizing patient care.

History of the Industry

Up until the nineteenth century, the world of medical technology was very small and specialized. Doctors were dependent on their creativity and whichever instruments they carried in their black bags to provide patient care. Their instruments were often designed and fabricated by themselves or by local blacksmiths. The twentieth century heralded a new age of advances in technology and the sciences. The world of medicine was given a dramatic face-lift with the advent of improved anesthesia, biotechnology, and radiology.

Some of the most important inventions of the

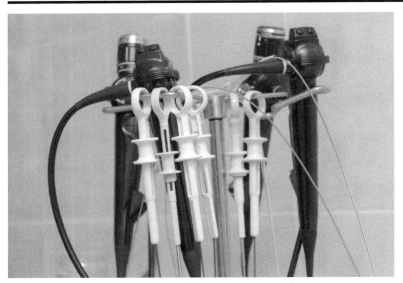

Endoscopy tools. (©Dreamstime.com)

twentieth century were in the field of diagnostic medicine. Near the turn of the century, Wilhelm Röntgen discovered the X ray, one of the eminent discoveries of modern medicine. In 1905, Willem Einthoven developed the electrocardiograph (ECG), a tool that measures the electrical activity of the heart and provides crucial information to diagnosticians. The endoscope, developed in 1956, is able to examine the interior of hollow organs or body cavities and helped replace exploratory surgeries.

The field of radiology uses various noninvasive imaging technologies to diagnose and assess disease. From the plain X ray, to the ultrasound scanner, to more advanced technologies, such as computed tomography (CT), magnetic resonance imaging (MRI), and positron emission tomography (PET) scans, the twentieth century has given physicians an array of tools to aid in the diagnosis of disease. Medical laboratory equipment has become increasingly efficient at analyzing blood, urine, and deoxyribonucleic acid (DNA) samples from patients. The automation of such analysis has resulted in quicker diagnoses and more efficient treatment plans.

Therapeutic medical equipment has seen a similar growth over the last century. Although the skilled hands of a surgeon are irreplaceable, new technologies aid in the management of patients; these include infusion pumps, medical ventilators,

anesthetic machines, medical lasers, and dialysis machines. The treatment of cancers has been revolutionized through the clinical use of linear accelerators to irradiate tumors.

Health care equipment is no longer confined to hospitals or medical clinics, as an increasing amount of such equipment is being produced for use within the home. For example, patients with diabetes possess glucometers to monitor their blood-sugar levels at home, and those with high blood pressure can check their pressures at home with portable blood-pressure cuffs.

Medical technology is forever being researched and improved. The twenty-first century will see continued advances in the field of therapeutic and diagnostic health care equipment. As with all other industries, the scientific, medical, and health equipment and supplies industry is driven by profit. In becoming more profitable, new technologies must strive not only to reduce production costs but also to optimize patient care, for example, by treating more patients per day, reducing recovery times, providing early diagnosis of medical problems, and providing patients with a higher quality of life.

The Industry Today

Establishments within the industry are primarily engaged in manufacturing medical equipment and supplies. Today, the main industry-manufactured products fall into the following categories: surgical appliances and supplies (which account for 28 percent of the U.S. market), surgical and medical instruments (25 percent), dental equipment and supplies (16 percent), ophthalmic equipment (9 percent), electromedical equipment (8 percent), in vitro diagnostic devices (4 percent), and irradiation equipment (3 percent); 7 percent of products fall in other minor categories.

The surgical appliances and supplies sector includes products ranging from sutures to artificial limbs, from cervical collars to infant incubators, and from safety masks to surgical implants. Electromedical equipment includes the various types of endoscopes (such as colonoscopes and broncho-scopes); X-ray, ultrasound, CT, MRI, and PET scanning devices; and pacemakers and dialysis machines. Dentists' tools, instruments, enamels, teeth, and so on are all supplied by the dental equipment and supplies sector. The ophthalmic equipment sector produces equipment for opticians, optometrists, and ophthalmologists. The field of irradiation is a small but high-value sector, as it is responsible for producing machines such as the linear accelerator, which irradiates cancer tumors. Laboratory equipment and furniture also constitute major sources of revenue for this industry, with products such as operating tables, hospital beds, and centrifuges.

As the population ages, the number of diseases and illnesses that require advanced medical equipment rises. Today, the medical equipment and supplies industry is driven by the expectation that new technologies will enhance the quality of patients' lives as they get older. The U.S. medical equipment industry is known for producing high-quality devices using advanced technology resulting from heavy investment in research and development. There are nearly eight thousand medical equipment companies in the United States, employing over 300,000 individuals. Most firms are small start-up companies, but there are a limited number of large firms and relatively few midsize businesses. More than 80 percent of medical technology companies have fewer than fifty employees.

The U.S. medical device market, the world's largest, was worth $130 billion at the end of 2009. The industry is highly concentrated, as the fifty largest companies account for approximately 75 percent of industry revenue. Seven of the world's top ten medical device manufacturers are U.S. companies. The top ten U.S. companies in the medical device sector are Johnson & Johnson, GE Medical Systems, Baxter International, Tyco Healthcare, Medtronic, Abbott Laboratories, Becton Dickinson, 3M Healthcare, Guidant, and Stryker.

During the early 1990's, rising health care costs led many hospitals to form alliances and make group purchasing decisions in order to buy equipment in bulk at lower costs. In order to sell to these large buying groups, sellers needed to provide a wide assortment of products. This development left suppliers facing unprofitable margins, and many smaller companies folded or were acquired by larger companies. Other factors that have driven consolidation among supply firms are shorter product life cycles and the high cost of new technology development. Moreover, the medical community has faced increasing pressure to reduce its impact on the environment, as costs related to the disposal of medical waste have been mounting. These increasing costs have resulted in a demand for medical products that are able not only to serve patients' needs but also to reduce waste—a demand that increases production costs. Many of the larger firms have therefore been investing heavily in research and development in order to develop innovative products, as such products remain the key to market success.

In the United States, imports are beginning to form an increasingly significant part of the medical equipment and supplies market, accounting for approximately 34 percent of the total market. The growth in this sector is explained by the lower man-

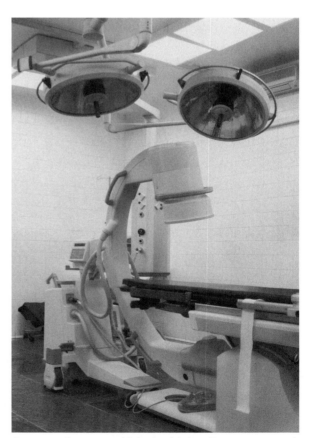

Equipment for surgery. (©Andrei Malov/Dreamstime.com)

ufacturing costs that can be achieved by producing goods in other countries, such as Mexico, and then reimporting the goods back into the United States. The U.S. market is highly regulated and can be an expensive one in which to operate. The process of product regulation can be very extensive and time-consuming. In 1992, the Global Harmonization Task Force (GHTF) was conceived to help achieve uniformity among global regulatory systems. The GHTF is a collaboration among the United States, the European Union, Canada, Japan, and Australia. Medical device companies have also begun applying for regulatory approval in other countries concurrently, or prior, to seeking approval from the U.S. Food and Drug Administration (FDA). These ventures have helped ensure that this transparent and rules-based industry continues to appeal to entrepreneurs and professionals alike.

Reimbursement rates for medical devices are a primary concern not only for American manufac-

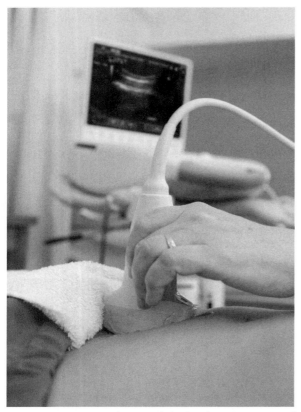

A patient receives ultrasound. (©Stephen Mcsweeny/Dreamstime.com)

turers but also for the global market as a whole. In the United States, there are several key organizations involved in establishing reimbursement rates. The Department of Health and Human Services' Centers for Medicare and Medicaid Services (HHS/CMS) is the central agent of control. The HHS/CMS is very closely involved in determining the rates of reimbursement paid by Medicare and Medicaid. Within the U.S. market, health maintenance organizations (HMOs) and private health insurance companies set or negotiate their own reimbursement rates. A low reimbursement rate for a medical device in the U.S. market can make the device uneconomical to produce elsewhere in the world because the United States represents such a large percentage of the global market.

The complementary industries on which the medical device industry relies include microelectronics, telecommunications, instrumentation, biotechnology, and software development. The growth in recent years of these sectors has positively affected the medical device industry. Announcements of progress in medical technologies that allow for earlier detection of diseases and more effective treatment options are now almost daily occurrences. As an example, the integration of radiology with information systems is the most significant trend affecting diagnostic imaging. The Picture Archiving and Communications Systems (PACS) store medical images digitally, eliminating the need for film or chemical processing. Doctors can access these images remotely, increasing efficiencies within health care. Broad nationwide initiatives, such as the adoption of electronic health records and the use of personal health records, are another way in which technology has the potential to transform the health care system.

Medical device manufacturers are benefiting from a new generation of materials and manufacturing processes. As medical device and biotechnological products converge, one area that is seeing tremendous growth is drug-delivery devices: Many treatments and therapies derived from research will not necessarily be available in pill form. Medical devices will act as delivery systems for new products that result from genetic engineering and biotech research.

Technological advances in areas separate from the medical equipment industry are also having an impact on that industry's trends. One of these ar-

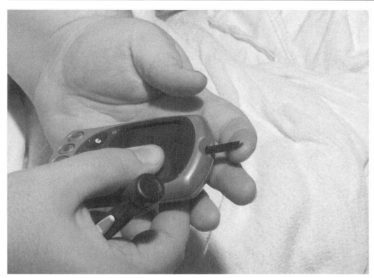

A patient with diabetes monitors his sugar levels with a glucometer. (©Robert Byron/Dreamstime.com)

eas is harnessing the power of the Internet. Online purchasing of medical products has proliferated, saving both time and money for buyers and sellers.

The medical device industry is at the forefront of health care delivery, as it manufactures the tools necessary to provide patient care. The health care industry as a whole remains the largest and fastest-growing industry market worldwide. The intimate relationship shared by the medical device and health care industries ensures that the medical supplies sector remains competitive in today's market.

INDUSTRY MARKET SEGMENTS

The medical equipment and supplies industry encompasses businesses ranging in size from small start-ups to large multinational enterprises. It caters to a wide range of clients, from small medical clinics, to research laboratories, to large tertiary-care hospitals. The following sections provide a comprehensive breakdown of each of these different segments.

Small Businesses

Most of the firms in the health care equipment and supplies industry tend to be small start-up com-

panies. More than 80 percent of medical technology companies have fewer than fifty employees. The customers of these companies are primarily resellers of their equipment. The success of a small firm normally depends on its ability to find a specialized niche in which to market and sell its products.

Potential Annual Earnings Scale. According to the U.S. Bureau of Labor Statistics (BLS), the average annual salary of an electro-mechanical technician working in the medical equipment and supplies manufacturing industry in 2009 was $48,750. The average salary of a mechanical engineer was $74,810, the average salary of a materials engineer was $87,260, and the average salary of a biomedical engineer was $81,590. Medical scientists in the industry earned $91,200, on average, while laboratory technologists earned $54,440 and laboratory technicians earned $39,710. The average salary of all production positions in the industry combined was $34,380, and production supervisors earned an average of $58,110. Medical managers earned $133,980, engineering managers earned $119,320, general and operations managers earned $128,990, and chief executives earned $203,900. Employees of small start-ups are likely to earn salaries below these averages, although they may be offered stock options and other forms of deferred compensation should the venture succeed. In general, small businesses in the medical supplies industry generate yearly revenues of $200,000 to $3,500,000. Revenues are directly related to the number of employees within the business, as well as the number of years the firm has been in business.

Clientele Interaction. Small-business proprietors tend to be more intimate with their customers and clients than are owners and managers of larger firms. The relationships that small businesses cultivate lead to a greater degree of loyalty on the part of customers and accountability on the part of producers. Face-to-face interactions are often necessary when presenting new technologies. Sales personnel have to be well-versed in how a particular medical device operates. For example, when introducing a new surgical device, a salesperson may scrub into the operating room with surgeons to ensure the device is functioning properly.

For small businesses, keeping travel costs to a minimum is a necessity, but clientele interaction can often take place via telecommunication. Gaining the trust of clients is paramount for small businesses. Because they often work in niche markets, small companies have to overcome barriers relating to the abilities of their products. Clients need to feel confident that a company's products are suitable as well as reliable. Because of their size, small companies usually lack brand power and, therefore, need to work harder to convince their clients of their products' capabilities.

Amenities, Atmosphere, and Physical Grounds. The smaller the business, the more intimate the office space. Normally, small medical equipment and supply companies have team office spaces, as well as some private executive offices and at least one meeting room. Amenities for employees are usually minimal, with restrooms and small kitchen facilities being necessities. At a minimum, all business offices need private telephone lines, fax machines, and Internet connectivity. Small businesses' office spaces are usually rented within business centers, and, as a result, some services such as parking and security are often shared with other businesses. Many small businesses employ professional receptionists to greet visitors and answer phones.

The manufacturing areas of small medical equipment firms are often crowded; free space tends to be scarce. As a result, it is vitally important for small businesses efficiently to lay out their manufacturing equipment to make the best use of the area. Many smaller companies have limited storage space for raw materials and finished goods. Their loading docks often become overcrowded, hampering deliveries and shipments.

Typical Number of Employees. Small medical equipment and supply businesses try to minimize costs wherever possible. Each employee usually adopts numerous roles within such businesses. Normally, these firms have fewer than one hundred employees, and most have less than fifty employees.

Traditional Geographic Locations. Medical device manufacturers are dispersed throughout America. The states with the highest concentrations of medical equipment companies are California, New York, Florida, Massachusetts, Illinois,

Minnesota, and Georgia. Medical equipment firms consider several factors when deciding where to locate a new facility. The four main considerations include the following:

- Being in close proximity to a knowledgeable, highly trained, and productive workforce. This consideration normally requires businesses to locate in metropolitan areas.
- Being part of a cluster of other medical device or high-tech companies to share in the infrastructure built to support such industries.
- Locating facilities near education and research institutes.
- Locating near customers in order to minimize transportation and travel costs.

Pros of Working for a Small Medical Equipment Manufacturer. A small business can often be started at low cost and on a part-time basis. There is a level of satisfaction associated with being a small-business owner and making one's own decisions, albeit within the constraints imposed by one's economic environment. Small businesses have greater flexibility in changing their profiles to meet the changing needs of their customers. As a result, they are often able to move quickly to exploit new technologies or methodologies in order to gain a competitive advantage. Another pro of working in a small business is the ability to learn a variety of processes. Because small businesses often require their employees to wear multiple hats, employees gain a better understanding of how their companies' products pass through the many stages of the production cycle.

Cons of Working for a Small Medical Equipment Manufacturer. Small firms often have a difficult time marketing new products. Introducing a new product requires devoting a significant amount of financial resources to research, development, and marketing. Such resources are often not available in the smaller firms.

Another hindrance for small businesses is their limited geographic and commercial range. Larger firms are able to export their products on a global scale, whereas smaller firms are usually limited to local markets. Moreover, it is difficult for smaller businesses to negotiate deals with group purchasing organizations (GPOs), such as HMOs and health care companies.

Costs

Payroll and Benefits: Most workers in this industry have professional designations, and they usually earn annual salaries. Paid vacation and sick leave are normally included in compensation packages. Small companies do not always provide health care benefits, although many professionals require them. In addition, it is unusual for small firms to offer employees other than executives any type of profit-sharing incentives.

Supplies: Depending on the products being produced, medical equipment manufacturers may require raw materials such as glass, steel, or plastics; assembly-automation equipment; packaging equipment; information technology; office furniture; and so on. Because they require commodity raw materials, such firms are susceptible to price changes in these commodities that result from changes in supply and demand. In addition, small firms do not have much bargaining power with their suppliers and are unlikely to receive major discounts.

External Services: In order to focus on the manufacturing process, many small companies employ external accounting, legal, and human resources firms, as well as external janitorial, cleaning, and delivery companies.

Utilities: Small businesses pay for electricity, water, cable television, telephone, Internet access, and gas.

Taxes: Companies are responsible for federal, state, and local income and property taxes.

Midsize Businesses

Midsize companies attempt to sell their products directly to end users, such as hospitals and medical laboratories. With increasing business volume, these companies have to learn to streamline administrative aspects of the business and decentralize decision making. Like small firms, midsize businesses tend to operate in specialized niches. For example, Medrad, a midsize medical equipment company located in Pittsburgh, operates in three product market groups: vascular injection systems, ancillary magnetic resonance products, and imaging products.

Potential Annual Earnings Scale. According to the BLS, the average annual salary of an electromechanical technician working in the medical equipment and supplies manufacturing industry in 2009 was $48,750. The average salary of a mechanical engineer was $74,810, the average salary of a materials engineer was $87,260, and the average salary of a biomedical engineer was $81,590. Medical scientists in the industry earned $91,200, on average, while laboratory technologists earned $54,440 and laboratory technicians earned $39,710. The average salary of all production positions in the industry combined was $34,380, and production supervisors earned an average of $58,110. Medical managers earned $133,980, engineering managers earned $119,320, general and operations managers earned $128,990, and chief executives earned $203,900. Midsize businesses are likely to pay salaries roughly in line with these averages. They generate revenues of between $4 million and $30 million annually.

Clientele Interaction. Midsize businesses are more likely to sell directly to end users of their products than are small businesses, which sell more at wholesale to retailers. While this arrangement still requires midsize businesses to cultivate close relationships with their customers, they are likely to have far more customers than small businesses. As a result, midsize companies cannot deal with each client as intimately as small businesses do. Midsize companies do not generally have sufficient sales forces to assign individuals to specific products. Instead, their salespersons are responsible for one or more lines of products. Selling different products to different customers requires salespersons to be very well rounded, as they must understand the workings of multiple products. For example, when introducing a new surgical device, a salesperson may have to scrub into the operating room with a surgeon to ensure that the device is functioning properly. Many midsize firms are attempting to grow and seek clients in other countries. Their salespersons thus need to be trained to interact with clients whose social and business cultures differ substantially from their own.

Midsize companies may be able to attract larger clients. These clients have higher expectations regarding the quality of their interactions with their medical equipment suppliers. They may expect suppliers to train their staffs to use the equipment they purchase. As a result, midsize businesses have higher costs associated with developing and maintaining their clients than do small businesses.

Amenities, Atmosphere, and Physical Grounds. Midsize firms often have more than one office, and their offices can be regional, national, or international. Each office is usually more expansive than those of smaller firms. They include team office spaces for separate departments and private executive offices. Conference facilities are also generally available. In addition to restrooms and kitchenettes, amenities available to employees may include exercise facilities, free parking, and daycare centers. Employers try to ensure availability of food services, including cafeterias, fast-food courts, and coffee bars. Midsize companies may separate their business offices from their production and design plants, locating their headquarters in downtown office buildings rather than industrial parks.

The atmosphere at midsize businesses is likely to become more segmented than at small firms, as a gap appears between the manufacturing and the business sides of companies. A less family-oriented atmosphere prevails. Manufacturing at this scale requires a larger space, and it may not be possible to combine the two separate aspects of the business in the same building.

Typical Number of Employees. Midsize businesses have a structure, similar to that of many large firms, in which decision making is decentralized. Managers are hired to be responsible for the functioning of each department within the company. A midsize company normally has less than five hundred employees spread out over more departments than at small businesses. Those employees are less likely to have dual roles and are instead more likely to specialize in one specific function.

Traditional Geographic Locations. Medical device manufacturers are dispersed throughout America. The states with the highest concentrations of medical equipment companies are California, New York, Florida, Massachusetts, Illinois, New York, Minnesota, and Georgia. Corporate headquarters are often located in downtown cores, while manufacturing plants are usually located in industrial areas, where costs are less. In addition, some midsize firms conduct manufacturing operations in developing countries, such as Mexico or India, where labor costs are far less than they are in North America.

Medical equipment firms consider several factors when deciding where to locate a new facility. The three main factors include the following:

- Being in close proximity to a knowledgeable, highly trained, and productive workforce.
- Being part of a cluster of other medical device or high-tech companies to share in the infrastructure built to support such industries.
- Locating facilities near education and research institutes.

Pros of Working for a Midsize Medical Equipment Manufacturer. Midsize businesses offer opportunities that small businesses cannot, while at the same time they do not have the inbuilt bureaucracy that is often found in large businesses. This situation provides employees with more opportunities to transfer to a different department or to seek promotion. Employees also get to work with a greater range of products at midsize firms than at small ones, not only because midsize firms produce more products but also because their product teams are less specialized than are those of large companies. Midsize companies are also able to allocate greater funds to research and development than can smaller firms, while at the same time being more flexible than large companies.

Cons of Working for a Midsize Medical Equipment Manufacturer. Midsize businesses face many of the same problems faced by small businesses. Raising funds for expansion can be problematic, as a result of relying on a relatively small number of customers. Successful midsize companies are also seen as threats by larger companies that may target their customers or suppliers in an attempt to impede their success.

Costs

Payroll and Benefits: Most workers in this industry have professional designations, and they tend to be salaried. Paid vacation and sick leave are normally included in compensation packages. Health care benefits are usually provided by midsize companies. Other benefits may include pension plans, flex hours, bonuses, dental insurance, parental leave, and the ability to telecommute from home.

Supplies: Depending on the products being produced, medical equipment manufacturers may require raw materials such as glass, steel, or plastics; assembly-automation equipment; packaging equipment; information technology; office furniture; and so on. Because they require commodity raw materials, such firms are susceptible to price changes in these commodities that result from changes in supply and demand.

External Services: Midsize businesses make less use of external services than do small businesses; however, they are still likely to contract external auditing, consulting, employment, and logistics companies. They must also carry insurance against legal action.

Utilities: Manufacturing firms pay for electricity, water, cable television, telephone, Internet access, and gas.

Taxes: Employers are responsible for federal, state, and local income and property taxes.

Large Businesses

Large medical manufacturing companies are likely to have operations and customers in multiple countries, as well as a wide range of products. In addition, they are more likely to be vertically integrated along their supply chains. Such integration entails a company producing the components needed for its products, as opposed to purchasing them. Large businesses also outsource many aspects of their operations that fall outside their core competencies. These include accounting, finance, and human resources. While small and midsize businesses hire firms to deal with these aspects of their operations, large companies outsource the entire function, giving control of those aspects to other companies. Large companies also have far greater economies of scale in manufacturing and research and development.

Potential Annual Earnings Scale. According to the BLS, the average annual salary of an electromechanical technician working in the medical equipment and supplies manufacturing industry in 2009 was $48,750. The average salary of a mechanical engineer was $74,810, the average salary of a materials engineer was $87,260, and the average salary of a biomedical engineer was $81,590. Medical scientists in the industry earned $91,200, on average, while laboratory technologists earned $54,440 and laboratory technicians earned $39,710. The average salary of all production positions in the industry combined was $34,380, and production supervisors earned an average of $58,110. Medical managers earned $133,980, engineering managers earned $119,320, general and operations managers earned $128,990, and chief executives earned $203,900. Large corporations generally pay salaries equal to or greater than these averages. They often consist of a main company and several other companies that operate within the control of the main company. The annual revenues of such consolidated entities range from $30 million to $2 billion.

Clientele Interaction. Large companies often interact with their clients at the executive level. Very large clients need to be treated more as partners than as customers, and they often dictate the features of the products they purchase. Thus, manufacturers and clients must attain a high level of mutual trust. In addition, large businesses often try to impose high switching costs on their clients to ensure that clients do not replace them with one of their competitors. Large businesses often spend a lot of money to keep their most important clients happy. They send private jets to collect clients for meetings, entertain clients by taking them to sporting events, and hold meetings in exotic locations.

Amenities, Atmosphere, and Physical Grounds. Large businesses can afford to offer their employees in-house amenities that are not often available at smaller firms. In addition to a kitchen, a company may provide its employees with free beverages and a full-service cafeteria. They may also provide gymnasiums, swimming pools, neck and back massages, mailing services during holidays, day-care services, or lactation rooms. The atmosphere at many of the larger businesses is one of "work hard, play hard." Expectations are very high in large companies, and competition among employees is rampant, as there are more employees than there are opportunities for advancement.

Typical Number of Employees. Large firms have workforces of more than five hundred employees, sometimes far more. For example, Toshiba Medical Systems Corporation has 875 employees, while Johnson & Johnson has a total of 117,000 employees worldwide.

Traditional Geographic Locations. Medical device manufacturers are dispersed throughout America. The states with the highest concentrations of medical equipment companies are California, New York, Florida, Massachusetts, Illinois, New York, Minnesota, and Georgia. Large businesses, however, tend to have offices in metropolitan areas throughout the world, as well as production facilities in many different countries. To take advantage of low labor prices and tax rates, many large companies strategically place themselves in areas far away from their suppliers and customers.

Medical equipment firms consider several factors when deciding where to locate a new facility. The three main factors include the following:

- Being in close proximity to a knowledgeable, highly trained, and productive workforce.
- Being part of a cluster of other medical device or high-tech companies to share in the infrastructure built to support such industries.
- Locating facilities near education and research institutes.

Pros of Working for a Large Medical Equipment Manufacturer. Most large companies are publicly traded and are able to issue debt in the form of bonds. This enables them to invest a substantial amount of financial resources in research and development. Large companies are also able to acquire smaller companies that become threats to them or that offer new products that would be of interest to their customers.

Cons of Working for a Large Medical Equipment Manufacturer. Employees of large businesses can often feel insignificant. They may find their working environment to be cutthroat, with each employee trying to stand out from the crowd. Large companies may have more legal battles to deal with, as they tend to attract the attention of government and regulatory agencies. They often have to engage in intellectual-property litigation to protect their innovations from competitors. As many of their sales are to overseas customers, they must also manage foreign currency exposure.

Costs

Payroll and Benefits: Large companies are often able to provide compensation packages that include base salaries and incentive pay, such as cash bonuses or stock-based compensation. They provide comprehensive benefits that vary by country, region, and role. Employers ensure that employees are able to meet their health care, income-protection, financial, retirement, and time-off needs. Paid vacation and sick leave, health care benefits, pension plans, flex hours, dental insurance, parental leave, telecommuting from home, and wellness packages are normally provided by such firms. However, many large firms are now trying to reduce their payrolls by carrying out certain business functions in developing countries, where the price of producing is far lower.

Supplies: Large companies require an extensive amount of supplies. Because of their size, some companies produce the supplies they need themselves, thus reducing their overall costs. In addition, they are able to purchase the supplies they need at heavily discounted prices by buying in bulk.

External Services: Large companies make use of many external services, including accounting, finance, human resources, and logistics. Many of the external vendors they engage are based in foreign countries.

Utilities: Manufacturing firms must purchase electricity, water, cable television, telephone, Internet access, and gas.

Taxes: Large companies, because of their international status, can often avoid paying high taxes through the use of tax-haven countries such as Ireland. Multinational firms are responsible for paying taxes required in each relevant local jurisdiction, as well as those required by the country in which they report their financial statements.

ORGANIZATIONAL STRUCTURE AND JOB ROLES

The organization and structure of the medical equipment supplies industry is largely based on its size. Smaller firms devote fewer financial resources toward research and development; therefore, they have fewer employees in this division. Larger companies have highly specialized personnel involved in the development of specific kinds of new products. The organizational structure of most firms, however, is representative of the majority of business models, with departments involved in management, production, sales and marketing, accounting, and distribution. Additional departments may be needed as a company grows and diversifies its market interests.

The following umbrella categories apply to the organizational structure of businesses in the scientific, medical, and health equipment and supplies industry:

- Business Management
- Clinical and Medical Affairs
- Accounting and Finance
- Communications
- Engineering
- Sales
- Research and Development
- Production
- Quality Assurance
- Marketing
- Legal Counsel
- Information Technology
- Distribution
- Human Resources

Business Management

The primary goal of business managers is to satisfy the stockholders of their companies. At small companies, this may simply mean satisfying themselves. Managers seek to ensure that companies realize profits, satisfy customers, and maintain effective working environments. Often, shareholders appoint boards of directors that hire senior managers. Senior managers then hire middle and lower-level managers, such as supervisors and team leaders.

The salary for an administrative assistant averages $33,000 per year. Administrative managers have mean annual salaries of $40,000. Senior managers earn approximately $90,000 annually, although the range can be quite large. The average salary of a chief executive officer (CEO) varies greatly based on the size of the company, but the national mean in 2009 was $203,900. The CEO of a small business may earn a base salary of approximately $150,000, on average. The CEO of Johnson & Johnson has a base salary of $1.73 million, but with incentive pay and stock options, his annual salary amounts to well over $25 million.

Business management occupations may include the following:

- President/Chief Executive Officer (CEO)
- Chief Financial Officer (CFO)
- Chief Operating Officer (COO)
- Chief Technology Officer (CTO)
- Vice President
- Supervisor

- General and Operations Manager
- Production Manager
- Engineering Manager
- Biomedical Manager
- General Counsel
- Administrative Assistant

Clinical and Medical Affairs

Clinical and medical affairs personnel play an important role in the licensing and marketing of products worldwide. They design, conduct, and report on clinical studies for new and currently licensed products. They also provide clinical guidance for product development and represent their companies before professional regulatory agencies. A strong clinical background is usually required for these positions. A bachelor's degree is a necessity; however, some roles require further clinical expertise, and advanced degrees in nursing or medicine may be necessary.

Clinical and medical affairs occupations may include the following:

- Clinical Analyst
- Clinical Technician
- Clinical Affairs Representative
- Medical Affairs Representative
- Chief Science and Technology Officer

Accounting and Finance

The finance department plays a central role in driving the performance of a business. Accounting and finance personnel use financial tools and techniques to evaluate business opportunities and communicate their findings to decision makers in their organizations. Their skills—combined with their access to data and intelligence about their businesses' performance, risks, and opportunities—are essential to making key business decisions. Larger companies often outsource these positions to established accounting firms.

Financial professionals normally require bachelor's degrees in finance or accounting. In addition, they need experience in financial analysis and decision making, accounting and reporting, risk management, and business management. Accountants hired in-house had average salaries of $67,460 in 2009, while financial analysts earned $74,000 on average. Firms may also utilize financial consultants, who bill at $100 to $500 per hour.

Accounting and finance occupations may include the following:

- Financial/Business Analyst
- Financial Manager
- Accountant/Auditor
- Financial Consultant
- Chief Financial Officer (CFO)

Communications

Communications personnel provide communications support across their companies' operations. They are involved in media relations, internal employee communication, and community relations. Strong written and verbal skills are essential for these jobs. A high school diploma or bachelor's degree may be necessary to secure a job in this field.

Communications occupations may include the following:

- Technical/Medical Writer
- Technical/Medical Editor
- Publications Editor
- Web Designer/Content Provider
- Electronic Communications Specialist
- Community Relations Staff
- Public/Media Relations Staff
- Corporate Identity Manager

Engineering

Engineers play an essential role in the design, development, and manufacturing of new, innovative products. They work in three major areas within the medical supplies industry: research and development, manufacturing, and quality assur-

---

OCCUPATION PROFILE

Biomedical Engineer

Considerations	Qualifications
Description	Conducts research into the biological aspects of humans or other animals to develop new theories and facts or to test, prove, and modify known theories of life systems.
Career clusters	Agriculture, Food, and Natural Resources; Health Science; Manufacturing; Science, Technology, Engineering, and Math
Interests	Data; things
Working conditions	Work inside
Minimum education level	Bachelor's degree; master's degree; doctoral degree
Physical exertion	Light work
Physical abilities	Unexceptional/basic fitness
Opportunities for experience	Internship; military service
Licensure and certification	Required
Employment outlook	Faster-than-average growth expected
Holland interest score	IRE

Note: See volume 1, "Publisher's Note," for an explanation of the Holland interest score.

OCCUPATION PROFILE

Technical Sales Representative

Considerations	Qualifications
Description	Sells goods and services that require technical expertise to describe and explain to potential buyers; their clients include retail, industrial, and commercial firms and institutions.
Career clusters	Agriculture, Food, and Natural Resources; Architecture and Construction; Business, Management, and Administration; Human Services; Marketing, Sales, and Service
Interests	Data; people
Working conditions	Work inside
Minimum education level	On-the-job training; bachelor's degree
Physical exertion	Light work
Physical abilities	Unexceptional/basic fitness
Opportunities for experience	Part-time work
Licensure and certification	Usually not required
Employment outlook	Average growth expected
Holland interest score	ESR

Note: See volume 1, "Publisher's Note," for an explanation of the Holland interest score.

ance. Larger businesses that are heavily involved in research tend to have very large engineering departments with heavy emphasis on research and development. Smaller businesses hire engineers in their manufacturing departments, where they focus on ensuring that manufacturing processes are efficient and effective. Engineers normally possess a bachelor or master of science degree in electrical, mechanical, computer, or biomedical engineering. Average salaries for engineers range from $75,000 to $90,000 annually.

Engineering occupations may include the following:

- Engineering Technician
- Mechanical Engineer
- Electrical Engineer
- Industrial Engineer
- Computer Engineer
- Software Engineer
- Biomedical Engineer
- Director of Engineering

Sales

Sales personnel provide sales support to their firms' buyers. They are often required to travel extensively to meet with potential buyers. When companies hire for sales positions, they normally look for individuals with sales experience in the health care sector who are well versed in medical jargon. Medical sales staff must be able to communicate proficiently with physicians and nursing staff. Their customers include not only medical professionals but also patients, payers, governments, purchasing groups, and others involved in the global delivery of health care.

The base salary for salespeople is normally less than $30,000 per year. However, they have the po-

OCCUPATION PROFILE

Biomedical Equipment Technician

Considerations	Qualifications
Description	Maintains and repairs the sophisticated electronic equipment used in the health care field.
Career clusters	Manufacturing
Interests	Data; things
Working conditions	Work inside
Minimum education level	Junior/technical/community college; apprenticeship
Physical exertion	Light work
Physical abilities	Unexceptional/basic fitness
Opportunities for experience	Apprenticeship; part-time work
Licensure and certification	Recommended
Employment outlook	Faster-than-average growth expected
Holland interest score	RIE

Note: See volume 1, "Publisher's Note," for an explanation of the Holland interest score.

tential for much higher earnings based on commissions. Thus, a career in sales requires strong and consistent motivation. Sales representatives had total mean incomes of $76,480 in 2009, while sales managers had mean salaries of $120,790.

Sales occupations may include the following:

- Sales Manager
- Sales Representative

Research and Development

Research and development is essential to the growth of a large medical manufacturing firm. New and innovative products are continuously being designed to meet the health care needs of a growing population. Most companies specialize in a select number of technical competencies, such as drug delivery, diagnostics, surgical supplies, or software development. Engineers compose a large proportion of research and development employees, although individuals with medical and scientific backgrounds are also required to form

well-rounded research teams.

Research and development occupations may include the following:

- Mechanical Engineer
- Electrical Engineer
- Computer Engineer
- Software Engineer
- Biomedical Engineer
- Research Scientist
- Laboratory Technologist
- Laboratory Technician

Production

The production department is the foundation on which a manufacturing company stands. Most production personnel work within a manufacturing plant, often as assembly line workers. This department has the role of safely, efficiently, and expeditiously producing goods. Production workers on average earn between $25,000 and $35,000 per year.

Production occupations may include the following:

- Team Assembler
- Machine Operator
- Production Supervisor
- Production Planner
- Service Operations Manager
- Laboratory Technician

Quality Assurance

Quality assurance personnel ensure that the medical devices that reach patients and clinicians are both safe and effective. They protect the reputations of their companies, as well as guarding against civil and criminal liabilities for negligence or infringement of safety regulations. They normally have engineering, scientific, or manufacturing backgrounds.

Quality assurance occupations may include the following:

- Mechanical Engineer
- Electrical Engineer
- Computer Engineer
- Software Engineer
- Biomedical Engineer
- Engineering Technician
- Scientist
- Laboratory Technician
- Compliance Officer

Marketing

Marketing personnel determine the needs of the marketplace, communicate them to decision makers, and deliver products and services to meet those needs. Nearly every aspect of the medical manufacturing business involves the functions of marketing—from initial market research; to research and clinical trials; to product launches, pricing, and advertising; to postmarket surveillance. A marketing department's goal is simply to increase the number of interactions between its company and potential customers, with the ultimate aim of generating a larger customer list. This depart-

ment is essential for both small, up-and-coming companies that need to advertise their names and larger, well-established companies that need to market new products.

The salaries of marketing managers vary based on the department in which they work. Annual mean salary for marketing managers is \$121,520; for advertising and promotions managers, it is \$93,700.

Marketing occupations may include the following:

- Market Development Manager
- Advertising and Promotions Manager
- Distribution Manager
- Marketing Representative
- Market Research Analyst
- Product Manager
- Media Relations Specialist

Legal Counsel

The role of a legal department is to ensure that its company's business activities comply with all ap-

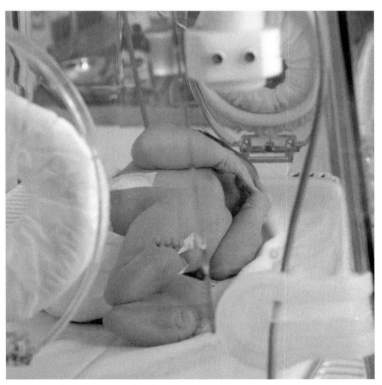

An infant in an incubator. (©Alvera/Dreamstime.com)

plicable laws and regulations and to represent its company's legal interests in court proceedings and before other government entities, such as legislatures and regulatory agencies. Passage of the bar exam is necessary for all practicing attorneys, and all attorneys require either law degrees or formal apprenticeships as prerequisites for taking the exam. Medical attorneys must have knowledge and expertise in litigation, ethics, government affairs, patents, and regulations. The salary for a paralegal ranges between $35,000 and $50,000. Corporate attorneys are paid well over $100,000, salaries being largely dependent on the size of the firm. Lawyers directly employed by medical equipment manufacturers earned an average of $164,100 in 2009.

Legal occupations may include the following:

- General Counsel
- Paralegal
- Patent Counsel
- Legal Secretary
- Lobbyist

Information Technology

Information technology (IT) personnel are responsible for meeting their companies' technology needs. They seek to improve operations while simplifying user experience. They require a thorough understanding of the various IT functions. Computer programmers in the industry earned an average of $70,500 in 2009, while computer support specialists earned $51,890 and system administrators earned $72,060.

IT occupations may include the following:

- Computer Programmer
- Computer Support Specialist
- Software Engineer
- System Administrator
- Help Desk Staff
- Development Specialist
- Business Solutions Specialist
- Project Manager

Distribution

Supply chain and distribution personnel ensure the safe and efficient delivery of products to patients and clinicians. At smaller companies, this involves ground transportation of products locally or regionally. Larger firms transport products world-wide, utilizing the most efficient modes of transport they can find.

Distribution occupations may include the following:

- Customer Service Representative
- Shipping and Receiving Clerk
- Materials Manager
- Supply Chain Analyst
- Delivery Truck Driver
- Heavy Truck Driver

Human Resources

Human resources (HR) personnel recruit, hire, train, and fire employees. They administer payrolls and benefits, enforce company discipline, and respond to employee grievances. They may adopt roles such as employee advocates, strategic business partners, change agents, and process experts.

HR occupations may include the following:

- Recruiter/Hiring Manager
- Talent Manager
- Human Resources Manager
- Human Resources Director
- Human Resources Generalist
- Payroll Clerk
- Benefits Specialist

INDUSTRY OUTLOOK

Overview

The outlook for the medical supplies and equipment industry shows it to be on the rise. There are two competing factors in the outlook for this industry: an aging world population, which spends more on health and medical treatment as it ages, and the global recession of 2007-2009, which is prompting hospitals and consumers to decrease spending. Although the medical device market will continue to grow based on population demographics, its growth will be curbed by the global recession. Growth in the aftermath of the recession is expected to be slow initially, but the pace should increase within four years. The annual growth rate is expected to be around 4-6 percent. Major market reports estimate that the global market for medical devices will generate revenues of $367 billion by 2014.

The global market for medical devices has been

affected by the 2007-2009 worldwide recession. According to the American Hospital Association, hospitals in the United States reduced their capital spending by 77 percent. Of health projects already in progress, 46 percent of hospitals scaled back and 14 percent of hospitals put a halt to such projects. Similar trends in health care spending are being seen worldwide. Cuts to spending by hospitals are expected in the United Kingdom and Japan. The Japanese government is looking at medical tourism as a way of generating revenue to keep up with domestic health care costs. Nonetheless, two of the world's major emerging economies, India and China, are projecting increased spending in health care.

The positive trend for the medical supplies industry is the aging world population. Baby boomers are fast approaching the ages when chronic conditions such as diabetes, arthritis, and heart disease traditionally emerge, and the number of U.S. seniors is expected to grow to 70 million by 2030, according to the U.S. Administration on Aging. As a result, the need for medical supplies and equipment will continue to grow. Specifically, cardiologic, neurologic, and orthopedic device manufacturers are expected to profit. As the population ages, there will be increasing pressure to discourage lengthy hospital stays and deliver health care in more cost-effective settings, such as patients' homes. The home health care products sector is therefore expected to become one of the fastest-growing segments of the medical equipment industry.

Some of the types of medical products and technologies that are expected to grow most rapidly include technologies that allow for less invasive procedures and require less recovery time while improving clinical outcomes. Moreover, procedures performed in low-cost, less specialized settings that utilize fewer specialized professionals are also expected to rise. These trends apply to both the medical and the dental equipment industries. With greater awareness among the general population about dental health, the dental equipment and supplies industry is expected to experience continual expansion.

The Internet is also driving new trends within the medical industry. Online medical equipment auctions are a growing trend, as they allow health care providers to buy and sell used medical devices conveniently. Members of the public are also purchasing medical devices over the Internet, to benefit both from increased convenience and from lower costs. Although the financial crisis has affected most major industry sectors worldwide, the medical devices industry appears to have a brighter future than do other sectors. Profits in this industry will continue to be driven by a demand for innovative products and by favorable demographic trends.

Employment Advantages

The medical equipment industry is continuing to grow and remains a source of high-income jobs within the United States. In 2008, the International Trade Administration reported that employees in the medical device industry earn 49 percent more than private-sector employees generally and 18 percent more than general manufacturing workers. According to the BLS, the average annual salary for all occupations within this industry is $46,270; the national average for all industries is $43,460.

Nearly one-third of all U.S. bioscience jobs are found within the medical devices industry. According to the U.S. Labor Department, the number of jobs in this sector is increasing. The total number of employees in the industry is expected to rise from 308,690 to 312,000 by 2014. The states that are expected to see the greatest increase in industry jobs are California, Minnesota, Florida, Massachusetts, New York, and Pennsylvania. Employees in this sector tend to be highly educated and possess specialized training. Given the high salaries and prestigious positions available, competition for jobs is very robust in this field.

Annual Earnings

The medical device industry is expected to grow and will be fueled by an aging population, increased hospital visits, and product innovation. The global market reached $290 billion in 2009; by 2014, it is projected to be close to $367 billion. Growth between 2010 and 2013 is expected to be slow, but it should pick up immensely after 2013, as a result of emerging markets in India and China. The Chinese government plans to build two thousand new community hospitals and to spend $850 billion by 2011. Although the United Sates is by far the largest market for medical devices, with a market value of $130 billion (representing 44.8 percent of total market share), the markets emerging in Asia will provide significant competition in the future. Overall, the medical device industry is an increasingly competitive field with numerous multinational firms pursuing a global market. Over the next few years, greater attention will be paid to international sales and revenue, joint ventures, and mergers and acquisitions, as companies try to stay abreast of this competitive market.

RELATED RESOURCES FOR FURTHER RESEARCH

ADVANCED MEDICAL TECHNOLOGY ASSOCIATION
701 Pennsylvania Ave. NW, Suite 800
Washington, DC 20004-2654
Tel: (202) 783-8700
Fax: (202) 783-8750
http://advamed.org

ASSOCIATION FOR THE ADVANCEMENT OF
MEDICAL INSTRUMENTATION
1110 N Glebe Rd., Suite 220
Arlington, VA 22201-4795
Tel: (800) 332-2264
Fax: (703) 276-0793
http://www.aami.org

EUCOMED-MEDICAL TECHNOLOGIES INDUSTRY IN
EUROPE
Place des Maieurs 2
1150 Brussels
Belgium
Tel: 32-2-772-2212
Fax: 32-2-771-3909
http://eucomed.be

MEDEC (MEDICAL DEVICES CANADA)
405 The West Mall, Suite 900
Toronto, ON M9C 5J1
Canada
Tel: (416) 620-1915
http://medec.org

MEDICAL EQUIPMENT SUPPLIERS ASSOCIATION
509 S Chickasaw Trail, Suite 178
Orlando, FL 32825
Tel: (800) 722-2310
http://www.mesanet.org

MEDICAL TECHNOLOGY AND PRACTICE PATTERNS
INSTITUTE
4733 Bethesda Ave., Suite 510
Bethesda, MD 20814
Tel: (301) 652-4005
Fax: (301) 652-8335
http://www.mtppi.org

ABOUT THE AUTHOR

Ravinder Pandher is an alumnus of the University of British Columbia, Vancouver. She obtained a bachelor of science in biology in 2004 and a medical doctor degree in 2009. Dr. Pandher is currently a resident physician at the University of Calgary, pursing a specialization in the field of Radiation Oncology through the Tom Baker Cancer Centre. Her interest in and passion for the field of medicine and specifically for oncology are exemplified through her clinical and research pursuits.

FURTHER READING

Babler, Scott D. *Pharmaceutical and Biomedical Project Management in a Changing Global Environment.* Oxford, England: Wiley-Blackwell, 2010.

Baxter, Jenny. *Market Report, 2009: Medical Equipment.* Hampton, England: Key Note, 2009.

Bronzino, Joseph D. *Medical Devices and Systems.* Boca Raton, Fla.: CRC Press, 2006.

Mehta, Shreefal S. *Commercializing Successful Biomedical Technologies: Basic Principles for the Development of Drugs, Diagnostics, and Devices.* New York: Cambridge University Press, 2008.

Parker, Philip M. *The 2009-2014 World Outlook for Health Care Equipment and Supplies.* San Diego, Calif.: ICON Group, 2008.

_____. *The 2009-2014 World Outlook for Surgical and Medical Instruments.* San Diego, Calif.: ICON Group, 2008.

Teixeira, Marie B., and Richard Bradley. *Design Controls for the Medical Device Industry.* New York: Marcel Dekker, 2003.

U.S. Bureau of Labor Statistics. *Career Guide to Industries,* 2010-2011 ed. http://www.bls.gov/oco/cg.

U.S. Census Bureau. North American Industry Classification System (NAICS), 2007. http://www.census.gov/cgi-bin/sssd/naics/naicsrch?chart=2007.

U.S. Department of Commerce. International Trade Administration. Office of Trade and Industry Information. Industry Trade Data and Analysis. http://ita.doc.gov/td/industry/otea/OTII/OTII-index.html.

U.S. International Trade Commission. *Medical Devices and Equipment: Competitive Conditions Affecting U.S. Trade in Japan and Other Principal Foreign Markets.* Washington, D.C.: Author, 2007.

Wiklund, Michael E., Jonathan Kendler, and Allison S. Yale. *Usability Testing of Medical Devices.* Boca Raton, Fla.: Taylor & Francis, 2011.

Zenios, Stefanos, et al. *Biodesign: The Process of Innovating Medical Technologies.* New York: Cambridge University Press, 2009.

Shipbuilding, Submarines, and Naval Transport Industry

©Andrew Dobrzanski/Dreamstime.com

INDUSTRY SNAPSHOT

General Industry: Transportation, Distribution, and Logistics

Career Cluster: Transportation, Distribution, and Logistics

Subcategory Industries: Boat Dealers; Boiler, Tank, and Shipping Container Manufacturing; Coastal and Great Lakes Freight Transportation; Coastal and Great Lakes Passenger Transportation; Deep Sea, Coastal, and Great Lakes Water Transportation; Deep Sea Freight Transportation; Deep Sea Passenger Transportation; Inland Water Freight Transportation; Inland Water Passenger Transportation; Marine Cargo Handling; Motorcycle, Boat, and Other Motor Vehicle Dealers; Navigational, Measuring, Electromedical, and Control Instruments Manufacturing; Other Support Activities for Water Transportation; Port and Harbor Operations; Ship and Boat Building; Ship Building and Repairing; Specialized Freight (except Used Goods) Trucking, Local Support Activities for Water Transportation; Water Transportation

Related Industries: Defense Industry; Freight Transport Industry; Travel and Tourism Industry; Warehousing and Storage Industry

Annual Domestic Revenues: $14.5 billion USD (2007 NAICS Economic Census)

Annual International Revenues: $430 billion USD at contracted values (Clarkson Research, 2010)

Annual Global Revenues: $442 billion USD at contracted values (Clarkson Research, 2010)

NAICS Numbers: 336611-336612, 481-486, 488, 491-493

INDUSTRY DEFINITION

Summary

The water transportation industry supports a vast global network of goods and services that includes provisions for inland and oceanic trade, national defense, and international travel and recreation. Shipping is a capital-intensive mode of transport. It is one of the most expensive sectors of a nation's economy. It is supported by complex, tightly orchestrated sets of statutes established to protect the best interests of international governments, municipal port authorities, manufacturers, financiers, and labor organizations.

Commercial shipping jurisdictions in the United States are monitored by the Maritime Administration (MARAD) agency within the Department of Transportation. The U.S. Coast Guard is a civilian organization within the Department of Homeland Security whose mission is to protect the nation's ports and waterways. Within the U.S. Navy, the Military Sealift Command maintains a fleet of more than one hundred civilian cargo ships used to deliver military supplies to Navy ships worldwide. The Navsea Shipbuilding Support Office works directly with the Naval Sea Systems Command to monitor the Navy's shipbuilding program as required by the Department of Defense.

A shipyard is a fixed facility equipped to build and repair ships of different sizes and structures. There are more than 125 commercial and defense shipyards in the United States employing more than 145,000 people. Commercial vessels include barges, cargo and container ships, dredges, drilling platforms, ferryboats, fishing boats, oil and gas vessels, patrol boats, roll-on/roll-off (RORO) vessels, submersibles, towboats, tugboats, yachts and passenger liners, and recreational watercraft. Military watercraft include aircraft carriers, battleships, cruisers, destroyers, frigates, submarines, cargo ships, minesweepers, auxiliaries, and support craft.

History of the Industry

The design and use of watercraft is considered one of the greatest technological achievements of early human societies. Human waterborne transport and navigation are prehistoric skills whose origins are uncertain. Primitive shoreline communities became adept at binding together bundles of reeds and tree branches to create simple rafts that could be paddled by hand. The invention of the sewing needle and the art of basket weaving made

A U.S. Navy aircraft carrier docked in a New York harbor. (©Richard Goldberg/Dreamstime.com)

it possible to sew together lengths of animal skin over a bone or wicker framework to create waterproof, lightweight floating vessels suitable for inland and coastal fishing, transport, and trade. In communities where greatwoods were plentiful, the axe, knife, and fire were used to fashion heavy wooden dugouts and outriggers, hollow log vessels from which all subsequent construction principles are derived. The progression and innovation of the shipwright's craft is evident in cultures worldwide. Models of prehistoric vessels still remain in use. These include the *madel paruwa* of Sri Lanka, the Indian catamaran, the *butuan* boats of Southeast Asia, the *sambuqs* of Dhofar, the Arabian *dhow*, and the Indonesian *jangollan*.

Archaeological excavations have made it possible to reconstruct or restore early models of sea transport. Advances in framing, planking, ribbing, dowelling, smithing, and joinery; the replacement of paddles with oars; and the use of the mast and sail transformed maritime commerce, greatly enriching those ancient societies that realized the lucrative potential of global maritime trade. The development of maritime transport in Egypt, Africa, China, India, Southeast Asia, the Middle East, the Mediterranean states, and Northern Europe and the Americas transformed the material and intellectual cultures of the known world. To the present day, the maritime arts have had a profound influence on the human mind and spirit, made manifest in countless cultural icons, artifacts, commodities, technologies, watercraft activities, and traditions.

The mastery of ancient mercantile trade routes and sea lanes gave rise to two classes of ships—those of trade and those of war. The enormous capital infrastructure needed to support maritime trade necessitated the concentration of national and private assets to underwrite the costs and risks of lengthy sea voyages. International financial markets and trading partnerships flourished as a consequence of the increasing sophistication and capacity of seaworthy ships capable of delivering and receiving cargo within networks of exchange that are thousands of years old. Piracy and conflict among nations have always been an inevitable part of the contest for markets. It is for this reason that navies are assigned to protect the ports and waterways vital to the commerce of sovereign nations.

Small, locally built sailing vessels were essential to the commercial development of the early American colonies. By the eighteenth century, many ship designs had become standards of maritime trade; these included carracks, caravels, cats, cutters, ketches, galleons, snows, schooners, spritsails, barges, brigs, brigantines, floyts, frigates, and pinnaces. European shipwrights settled along the Atlantic seaboard and the Great Lakes and were quick to capitalize on the value of interior woodlands; by the early 1700's, British shipwrights were calling for the suppression of shipbuilding in the colonies as a means of curtailing the booming American maritime industries. One of the first legislative acts of the newly formed Congress, under the leadership of President George Washington, was the creation of a merchant marine corps. Tonnage dues of fifty cents per ton collected from foreign vessels quickly offset the discriminatory duties and taxes suffered by early American merchants.

The maritime interests of the country flourished up to the time of the Civil War. During that period, massive capital outlays were diverted from shipping to the railroads. The British Empire was at its zenith. It was not until the early twentieth century that American shipwrights would embrace the new power technologies of the Industrial Revolution, creating the impetus for the resurgence of American maritime influence.

Marine insurance was essential to the conduct of business among colonial mari-

The Water Transportation Industry's Contribution to the U.S. Economy

Value Added	Amount
Gross domestic product	$14.1 billion
Gross domestic product	0.1%
Persons employed	66,000
Total employee compensation	$5.9 billion

Source: U.S. Bureau of Economic Analysis. Data are for 2008.

Inputs Consumed by the Water Transportation Industry

Input	Value
Energy	$11.1 billion
Materials	$1.6 billion
Purchased services	$11.4 billion
Total	$24.1 billion

Source: U.S. Bureau of Economic Analysis. Data are for 2008.

time tradespeople. It is the subject of the most successful applications of general common law in American commercial litigation. Northern and southern colonists depended on established English entities such as Edward Lloyds Coffee House in London to leverage the risks of trans-Atlantic shipping. Ship logs, maps, and nautical instruments of increasing precision made it easier to calculate the risks of operable ventures. These risks were underwritten by private and corporate financiers. Over time, the corporate model of investment became dominant because of the higher risks investors were able to assume. As a result of the 1775 Royal Navy blockade of the Atlantic coast and subsequent colonial independence, American maritime interests scrambled to create their own network of underwriters for the nation's fledgling European and Caribbean markets. Nevertheless, English investors continued to secure American maritime trade well into the nineteenth century. Early colonial insurers included principals from the Insurance Company of North America, the Virginia Marine Insurance Company, the Alexandria Marine Insurance Company, John Copson of Philadelphia, Joseph Marion and Benjamin Pollard of Boston, and John Benfield of Charleston.

The Industry Today

Two events occurred in 1890 that set the stage for the modern era of shipbuilding. Robert Gair, a Scottish printer living in Brooklyn, accidentally created a batch of corrugated papers when his ruler shifted position. That mechanical glitch was the foundation of a process for manufacturing folded corrugated boxes. Corrugated shipping materials have become a universal staple of the packing process, allowing merchants around the world to safely transport any number of delicate and perishable commodities. Refinement of container technologies during the twentieth century allowed exporters to crate their shipments into individual segments, reducing the time and labor of dockworkers who loaded and unloaded shipments for delivery. Post-World War II tankers in Europe were retrofitted in 1951 to carry large steel containers suitable for transport via rail and truck. In 1955, Malcolm McLean, a trucking fleet magnate, purchased a tanker and introduced container shipping in the United States. Today, more than 90 percent of the bulk cargo worldwide is delivered in container vessels.

Also in 1890, Alfred Thayer Mahan published his classic work, *The Influence of Sea Power Upon History, 1660-1783*. It was one of several volumes of lectures he wrote in preparation for his career as a founding lecturer and president of the U.S. Naval War College, established at Newport, Rhode Island, in 1884. His published works caught the eye of Theodore Roosevelt, a War College lecturer known for his scholarly narrative *The Naval War of 1812* (1882). Roosevelt later served as the assistant secretary of the Navy under President William McKinley. His clear-sighted understanding of the relevance of a strong naval fleet to national security set the groundwork for America's rise as a sea power in the twentieth century. The settling of the American West, the annexation of Alaska and Hawaii, the completion of the transcontinental railroad, corporate investments in river transport, the opening of the Suez Canal, plans for a future canal in Panama, and a growing commitment to hemispheric autonomy initiated legislation to secure the country's eastern, southern, and western oceanic borders. A strong navy and merchant marine were essential if the nation was to maintain its position in a rapidly changing economic world order.

Labor unions played prominent industrial roles in the years after the Civil War. Massive dislocations of personal wealth and property followed in the upheaval of global industrialization and migration. Trade unions were essential in the early commercial ventures of the founding colonies. The right to organize to protect and to promote a trade or a

A container ship heads toward Vancouver. (©Andrew Dobrzanski/Dreamstime.com)

skilled profession was a time-honored English tradition protected by common law. With the introduction of the factory system and the mass production of commodities, the role of the skilled worker often took a backseat to the mechanical uniformity of factory production. The shift to cheap, unskilled wage labor had a profound effect on shipbuilding, a highly skilled craft, and related manufacturing, warehousing, and transport industries. Early attempts to organize occurred along California's Pacific coastline, where shipping industries worked feverishly to fulfill charters for the lucrative Alaskan trade. Between 1898 and 1900, seventy-four new ships were built along the Pacific coast.

The American Federation of Labor was founded in 1886 by Samuel Gompers; six years later, the International Longshoremen's Association (ILA) was formed to protect dockworkers on the Great Lakes. Today, the ILA represents sixty-five thousand workers from the Great Lakes, Canada, the Atlantic and Gulf coasts, Puerto Rico, and major U.S. inland waterways.

At the turn of the century, America's city streets were crowded with myriad horse-and-carriage businesses. Teamsters and carriage drivers labored long hours for paltry wages. Without insurance, the individual driver was held accountable for the cargo he hauled. The Team Drivers International Union was formed in 1901 with a membership of seventeen hundred. In 1903, Gompers intervened in the union's internal disputes to form the International Brotherhood of Teamsters. This organization expanded its influence to provide legal protection for a variety of transport industries, setting the stage for the organization of the trucking industries of the twentieth century. The Teamsters are proud of their legacy of racial and gender equality, established at a time when these principles were not always practiced in the workplace. Both labor organizations played important roles on dockyards across the nation.

After the Civil War, the United States was far behind European nations in shipbuilding and design. Before the turn of the century, lawmakers made no provision for the construction of new warships. Great Britain capitalized on advances in naval architecture: armor plating, iron and steel hulls, screw propellers, compound and triple expansion engines, forced draught systems, life systems engineering, and efficient weapon carriers. Because of its plentiful natural resources of coal, Great Britain surged ahead in ironworks industries. The *Aaron Manby* and *The Great Britain* were among the world's first iron ships. Wood continued to be the primary building material of all American ships, a material that beautifully supported paddleboats and steamers. Iconic vessels such as the *Zebulon M. Pike*, the *Constitution*, the *Western Engineer*, the *Clermont*, and the *Mississippi* transformed the inland rivers and port cities of the nation but proved inadequate for the rigors of ocean transport. As the nineteenth century came to a close, U.S. congressmen approved legislation drafted to bolster the status of the Navy and its maritime fleet. In 1880, the Report of the Commis-

sioner of Navigation documented 902 new ships built that year; in 1901, the total number of ships built rose to 1,580.

Inequality in the workplace was an inevitable reality of the seaman's contract. The shipowner selected the captain, who wielded direct authority over all ship personnel for the duration of a voyage. Once a seaman agreed to work the voyage, he was legally compelled to complete it, with little leeway for compensation for injury during the contract. In 1920, Section 27 of the Merchant Marine Act (P.L. 66-261), also known as the Jones Act, was passed by Congress; it mandated that all U.S.-flagged ships be built, owned, operated, and documented within the United States. The Jones Act also provided legal redress for seamen injured because of negligence on the part of a shipowner, captain, or crew member. In 1927, the Longshoremen's and Harbor Worker's Compensation Act (LHWCA) was enacted by Congress, providing federal recourse for injuries occurring on navigable waters. This act

A tug assists a cargo ship in the port of Los Angeles. (©Dreamstime.com)

was amended in 1972 to include shipbuilders, longshoremen, ship repairmen, and shoreside workers. On October 6, 2006, the Jones Act was restated and codified as 46 U.S.C. 30104.

In 1893, Congress appropriated $200,000 for an "experimental submarine." Designs and prototypes for submersible vessels had piqued inventive minds since antiquity. The Confederate *H. L. Hunley* was one of the first submarines successfully fitted with a torpedo. J. P. Holland won the 1893 congressional design contest; his *USS Holland* was the first submarine to be adopted by the U.S. Navy in 1900. In 1906, Germany launched the first U-boat (*Unterseeboot*). On the brink of war in 1914, a world fleet of four hundred submarines served sixteen navies. By 1918, German U-boats had destroyed more than four thousand vessels, nearly one-fourth of the world's maritime fleet.

In the postwar period, Japan began its own military buildup in anticipation of an attack on the United States. The Pacific coast became an important front for U.S. naval operations. In 1913, the first U.S. submarine base opened at San Pedro, California. Critical submarine design issues included improvements in torpedo launch systems, radar intercept, and improved underwater fuel systems. In September, 1940, Germany launched its first "wolf pack"—a coordinated attack against merchant convoys in the Atlantic. Attacks against civilian vessels motivated a shift in American public opinion away from neutrality toward full engagement in the war. In December, 1941, Japan attacked the U.S. naval base at Pearl Harbor, Hawaii. This event transformed the nation's naval operations; warships, aircraft carriers, and submarines were instrumental in the war effort. The *USS Gato* (SS-212) and the *USS Baleo* (SS-285) were classic vessels of the time. Nearly 60 percent of Japan's merchant marine was destroyed by American submarines. Submarines continued to play an important role in

Fishing boats at a marina in Northern California. (©Daniel Raustadt/Dreamstime.com)

global military defense during the Cold War era. The introduction of the U-235 isotope as a source of nuclear power transformed submarine technologies in the second half of the twentieth century.

As the twentieth century came to a close, commercial and naval shipbuilders lobbied against legislation that slashed funding for the U.S. Maritime Administration (MARAD). After 1987, the nation's fleet shrank from 600 to 327 ships, forcing shipyards across the nation to close or to consolidate their services. It was estimated that a build rate of 10 ships per year was required to secure a future minimum fleet of 300 ships. The Navy's requirement is 313 vessels. In July, 2000, the American Shipbuilding Association reported that the Department of Defense's thirty-year shipbuilding program did not provide sufficient funding to maintain a minimum fleet of more than 300 ships. The September 11, 2001, terrorist attacks on New York City and Washington, D.C.; military engagements in Iraq, Afghanistan, and Kosovo; and the aggressive military buildup of the People's Republic of China highlighted the need for a coordinated Homeland Security program that included building a stronger naval fleet. In 2006, Admiral Michael C. Mullen, chief of naval operations, proposed a defense budget of $14.1 billion for new ships in 2008, with annual increases to $19.1 billion in 2012. In 2010, the fleet counted 290 vessels, the smallest fleet on record.

On July 15, 2010, the fiscal year (FY) 2011 Homeland Security Appropriations Bill was passed by the Senate Appropriations Committee. This bill provided $966 million for Coast Guard surface ships. It also provided $648 million for the National Security Cutter program, completing funding for the fifth of eight cutters requested by the U.S. Coast Guard. On July 22, 2010, the Senate Appropriations Committee approved $5 million in new loan guarantees for the controversial Title XI Ship Loan Guarantee Program. The FY 2011 Transportation Appropriations Bill provided American shipowners with a federal guarantee of 87.5 percent on commercial bank loans over twenty-five years. This legislation provided essential capital to maintain the nation's energy transport, commercial, and military capacity. These funds are administered by MARAD. On September 16, 2010, the Senate Appropriations Committee approved its version of the FY 2011 Defense Appropriations Bill,

recommending $15.2 billion for the Navy's Shipbuilding and Conversion account and $1.5 billion for the National Defense Sealift Fund.

The shipbuilding and repair industries play important roles in the physical health of global ports and ocean communities. Sustainable development, the protection of marine biodiversity, biosecurity, and climate change are expected to challenge the maritime trades to take leading roles in promoting policies and practices that minimize their effect on marine ecosystems. For instance, Section 3516 of the 2004 National Defense Authorization Act required that MARAD and the U.S. Environmental Protection Agency (EPA) jointly develop an environmentally friendly best-practices program to prepare inoperable vessels for sinking in areas best suited for artificial reef habitat construction.

INDUSTRY MARKET SEGMENTS

Small Shipyards

On February 13, 2009, Congress passed the American Recovery and Reinvestment Act (ARRA). In August, 2009, the Department of Transportation designated $98 million in ARRA funding for seventy grants to be awarded through the Assistance to Small Shipyards program. On April 15, 2010, an additional $14.7 million was awarded to seventeen small shipyards by MARAD, funded through the FY 2010 Department of Transportation Appropriations Bill. Many of the shipyards receiving assistance will invest in new equipment, upgrades to dock areas, computer technology, storage systems, training systems, and environmental compliance programs. Small shipyards are defined as those that reported receipts of up to $500,000 in the 2007 Economic Census.

Potential Annual Earnings Scale. The 2007 Economic Census posted that 621 small shipyards collected a total of $125.7 billion in receipts. This is an average of $203,000 in yearly earnings. A total of $30.557 million was paid in salaries to 1,037 employees for an average salary of $29,000.

Clientele Interaction. Small shipyards play an important role in local communities, providing the resources needed to build and repair vessels for independent fleets and individual owners. They are producers of inland watercraft, such as boats and barges, intended for use on inland and coastal waters. Small shipyards may or may not have drydock capabilities for repairs.

Amenities, Atmosphere, and Physical Grounds. Shipyards encompass a variety of open and closed environments. Working in a marine environment carries risks of exposure to changes in weather. Strenuous activity, heavy workloads, slippery surfaces, and cold and wet conditions are unavoidable in most working seaboard communities. Many shipyards are built within harbors or marine enclaves that provide secure docks and moorings for vessels needing repairs or for new construction. State-of-the-art railways, climate-controlled service bays, carpenters' shops, and machine shops are important features of shipyard design. Three-dimensional computer-aided design (CAD) drawings offer the shipyard builder or renovator precise renderings for the effective staging of future projects. Some smaller shipyards still use vast lofts for the modeling and design of ships.

Typical Number of Employees. Many small shipbuilding and repair businesses are sole proprietorships or family businesses. According to the 2007 Economic Census, small shipbuilding and repair enterprises employed a total of 1,037 people. That averages to about 2 employees per enterprise.

Traditional Geographic Locations. Typically, smaller shipyards are located on inland waterways, suitable for the building and repair of barges, tugboats, and towboats.

Pros of Working for a Small Shipyard. One of the great benefits of working in smaller shipyards is the opportunity to contribute to a unique communal culture and history. Many employees represent families whose involvement in a particular yard or community goes back several generations. Some operational yards have distinguished histories that go back to the colonies. Others have played memorable roles in world affairs and function as historical landmarks. Ships are some of the largest self-sufficient structures built. Regardless of the shipwright's specialty, the building processes are always complex and synthetic, incorporating centuries-old practices with state-of-the-art technologies. Small businesses often contribute to the preservation and restoration of classic shipbuilding techniques and materials, creating new masterpieces of workmanship guaranteed to last several generations. For those who love the challenges of owning a business, the trades and craft of shipbuilding can mean a lifetime of independent satisfaction and achievement.

Cons of Working for a Small Shipyard. Marine environments are vulnerable to storms that can cause catastrophic damage to a facility. That is a particular danger to small shipyard owners and partners with personal investments in a shipbuilding enterprise. Market fluctuations also can play havoc with investments in a particular shipbuilding enterprise. Years of apprenticeship study and guided practice are required of anyone desiring to learn the essentials of building a ship. It is an art that is mastered over a lifetime.

Costs

Payroll and Benefits: A wide variety of payroll and benefits packages exist within the shipbuilding industry. Many tradespeople earn hourly wages; other professionals earn an annual salary. Health and retirement benefits also depend on the size of the operation. Small shipyard industries frequently are privately owned.

Supplies: Shipyards require the materials used in shipbuilding as well as construction tools. Electronic as well as structural components all must be fabricated or purchased. Ships built for human habitation require heating, ventilation, and air-conditioning systems and indoor plumbing. Hotel and restaurant suppliers are essential providers for ships housing staffs or passengers.

External Services: Basic external services include accountants, computation services, office supply vendors, food and beverage services, banking and credit card support, heating and air-conditioning maintenance and repair, and general contractors as needed. Electronic fire and safety systems are essential.

Utilities: Typical utilities for a small shipyard include electricity, water, sewer, telephone, cable, Internet, and fuel service.

Taxes: Fees and taxes are assessed as applicable by local, state, and federal agencies.

Insurance: Property insurance, particularly in hurricane-prone areas, is essential.

Midsize Shipyards

The 2007 Economic Census reported that 650 shipbuilding facilities collected receipts ranging from $500,000 to $5 million. These midsize shipyards have the capacity to produce seaworthy ocean vessels. They offer a full range of facilities with in-house design capabilities. There is some overlap in the size and types of ships built in midsize and large yards.

Potential Annual Earnings Scale. The 2007 Economic Census reported that 650 midsize shipbuilding facilities collected $1.2 billion in revenues. Annual earnings averaged about $1.8 million per yard. A total of $307 million in payroll supported 8,750 employees for an average salary of $35,000.

Clientele Interaction. Midsize shipyards typically offer a world-class program of commercial vessel construction and repair. Clientele interaction may not be as frequent or in-depth as at a smaller company, where more personalized attention is given to each job.

Amenities, Atmosphere, and Physical Grounds. Shipyards encompass a variety of indoor and outdoor environments. Working in a marine environment carries risks of exposure to changes in weather. Strenuous activity, heavy workloads, slippery surfaces, and cold and wet conditions are unavoidable in most working seaboard communities. Marine environments are vulnerable to storms that can cause catastrophic damage to a facility. Many shipyards are built within harbors or marine enclaves that provide secure docks and moorings for vessels needing repairs or for new constructions. State-of-the-art railways, climate-controlled service bays, carpenters' shops, and machine shops are important features of shipyard design. Three-dimensional computer-aided design (CAD) drawings offer the shipyard builder or renovator precise renderings for the effective staging of future projects.

Typical Number of Employees. In the 2007 Economic Census, midsize shipyards reportedly employed a total of 8,750 people for an average shop population of 14 people.

Traditional Geographic Locations. Midsize shipyards are built on a variety of riverine and oceanic waterways, depending on the type of vessels they produce.

Pros of Working for a Midsize Shipyard. Resilience is an important strength of midsize vessel construction and repair operations. Midsize shipyards that keep abreast of changes in shipping technologies and markets are able to serve a broad base of commercial interests. During economic downturns, flexibility is an asset, making it possible to consolidate or relocate key divisions and products. Those companies with diversified portfolios are able to integrate their shipbuilding services with contracts in complementary service sectors. Ships are among the largest self-sufficient structures built. Shipbuilding combines centuries-old practices with state-of-the-art technologies.

Cons of Working for a Midsize Shipyard. One of the dangers of working in a midsize commercial or naval shipyard is the uncertainty of world markets and their effects on the shipbuilder. These vulnerabilities are greatly magnified in geographic areas heavily dependent on maritime commerce for their base economies. For instance, it is estimated that in 2005 hurricanes Katrina and Rita cost shipyards in Louisiana billions of dollars in damages, putting thousands of employees out of work. The recovery of ocean economies was complicated by the dramatic financial losses suffered in world markets beginning in late 2007. Gulf state officials are working hard to retain the viability of their shipbuilding industries. Mergers and buyouts continue to threaten the displacement of ship workers nationwide as large corporate entities struggle to leverage their risks and liabilities in a volatile commercial and defense contract environment. The architecture and systems design of commercial and naval vessels can be very complex, requiring advanced study in electronics, physics, and hydraulics. Years of apprenticeship study and guided practice are required of anyone desiring to learn the essentials of building commercial vessels. It is an art that is mastered over a lifetime.

Costs

Payroll and Benefits: A wide variety of payroll and benefits packages exist within the shipbuilding industry. Many of the tradespeople are paid hourly wages; professionals are paid an annual salary. Health and retirement benefits also depend on the size of the operation. Federal employees enjoy the full range of benefits supported by the U.S. government.

Supplies: Shipyards require the materials used in shipbuilding as well as construction tools. Electronic as well as structural components all must be fabricated or purchased. Ships built for human habitation require heating, ventilation, and air-conditioning systems and indoor plumbing. Hotel and restaurant suppliers are essential providers for ships housing staffs or passengers.

External Services: Basic external services include accountants, computation services, office supply vendors, food and beverage services, banking and credit card support, heating and air-conditioning maintenance and repair, and general and private contractors as needed. Electronic fire and safety systems are essential.

Utilities: Typical utilities for a midsize shipyard include electricity, water, sewer, telephone, cable, Internet, and fuel service.

Taxes: Fees and taxes are assessed as applicable by local, state, and federal agencies.

Insurance: Property insurance, particularly in hurricane-prone areas, is essential.

Large Shipyards

The 2007 Economic Census reported that five hundred shipbuilding facilities collected receipts from $5 million up to and above $100 million. Large shipyards produce world-class commercial and naval oceangoing vessels. They offer a full range of in-house design and construction services, including full dry dock capabilities for repairs. In 2009, the U.S. Coast Guard reported the delivery of seventeen large, deep-draft naval vessels, merchant ships, and drilling rigs. These included one U.S. Navy submarine, six commercial product carriers, one U.S. Coast Guard cutter, two assault ships, two destroyers, one fisheries research vessel, one aircraft carrier, two replacement ships, and one drill rig. These ships were built by companies such as Northrop Grumman, Aker Philadelphia, National Steel and Shipbuilding, and NG Ingalls. The Coast Guard also delivered eleven large oceangoing barges. In September, 2010, Bollinger Shipyards was awarded a $166.1 million U.S. Coast Guard contract for the construction of four Sentinel-class Fast Response Cutters (FRCs).

Potential Annual Earnings Scale. The 2007 Economic Census (NAICS 3366) reported that 500 large shipyards collected some $27 billion in revenues, averaging $14.5 million in individual yard incomes. They paid a total of $6.1 billion in salaries to 138,781 employees for an average salary of $44,000.

Clientele Interaction. Large shipbuilding enterprises provide the technology and expertise to produce vessels for government agency contracts and large corporations. Some also manufacture submersibles for domestic and security purposes. Large shipbuilders tend to serve major corporations and U.S. government and military agencies.

Amenities, Atmosphere, and Physical Grounds. Shipyards encompass a variety of open and closed environments. Working in a marine environment carries risks of exposure to changes in weather. Strenuous activity, heavy workloads, slippery surfaces, and cold and wet conditions are unavoidable in most working seaboard communities. Marine environments are vulnerable to storms that can cause catastrophic damage to a facility. Many shipyards are built within harbors or marine enclaves that provide secure docks and moorings for vessels needing repairs or for new constructions. State-of-the-art railways, climate-controlled service bays, carpenters' shops, and machine shops are important features of shipyard design. Three-dimensional computer-aided design (CAD) drawings offer the shipyard builder or renovator precise renderings for the effective staging of future projects.

Typical Number of Employees. Large shipyards employed a total of 138,781 people as of the 2007 Economic Census, for an average shop population of 278 people. Northrop Grumman is the nation's largest private shipbuilder. Specializing in defense systems, it has a total employee base of 120,000 working in five production sectors: aerodynamics, electronics and information systems, shipbuilding, technical services, and life cycle. On October 7, 2010, it was announced that the U.S. Navy awarded the Northrop Grumman Corporation a $107.2 million contract for the construction of state-of-the art submarines, facilities, and interfaces. The work will be completed at the company shipyard in Newport News, Virginia, one of only two sites in the nation capable of building nuclear-powered submarines. The Norfolk Naval Shipyard in Virginia is owned by the U.S. Navy and is one of the largest in the world. Other prominent shipyards include Bollinger in Lockport, Louisiana; Ingalls Shipbuilding of Pascagoula, Mississippi (now a Northrop Grumman subsidiary), and North American Shipbuilding in Larose, Louisiana.

Traditional Geographic Locations. Large shipyards typically are found on major waterways on the Pacific and Atlantic seaboards and the Gulf Coast.

Pros of Working for a Large Shipyard. Many

of the nation's large shipyards are recognized for superior standards of health and safety. Competitive apprenticeships, excellent health and retirement benefits, opportunities for a lifetime of professional growth, and high levels of professionalism at all levels of organization are essentials of the trade. Many work closely with area unions. Some operational yards have distinguished histories that go back to the founding colonies. Others have played important strategic and commercial roles in world affairs and function as highly acclaimed military landmarks. Ships are some of the largest self-sufficient structures built. Regardless of the shipwright's specialty, large ships are always complex and synthetic, incorporating centuries-old practices and know-how with state-of-the-art technologies using robotics, electronics, and computer design.

Cons of Working for a Large Shipyard. One of the dangers of working in a large commercial or naval shipyard is the uncertainty of world markets and their effects on the shipbuilder. These vulnerabilities are greatly magnified in geographic areas heavily dependent on maritime commerce for their base economies. For instance, it is estimated that in 2005 hurricanes Katrina and Rita cost shipyards in Louisiana billions of dollars in damages, putting thousands of employees out of work. This is only one of many coastal areas that sustained catastrophic damages to their operations. The recovery of ocean economies was complicated by the dramatic financial losses suffered in world markets beginning in late 2007. Gulf state officials are working hard to retain the viability of their shipbuilding industries. Mergers and buyouts continue to threaten the displacement of ship workers nationwide as large corporate entities struggle to leverage their risks and liabilities in a volatile commercial and defense contract environment. The architecture and systems design of large commercial and naval vessels and submersibles can be very complex, requiring advanced study in strategic defense systems. Years of apprenticeship study and guided practice are required of anyone desiring to learn the essentials of building large ships. It is an art that is mastered over a lifetime.

Costs

Payroll and Benefits: A wide variety of payroll and benefits packages exist within the shipbuilding industry. Many tradespeople are paid by the hour; other professionals are paid an annual salary. Health and retirement benefits also depend on the size of the operation. Larger shipbuilding enterprises offer excellent benefits for their employees. Federal employees enjoy the full range of benefits supported by the U.S. government.

Supplies: Shipyards require the materials used in shipbuilding as well as construction tools. Electronic as well as structural components all must be fabricated or purchased. Ships built for human habitation require heating, ventilation, and air conditioning systems and indoor plumbing. Hotel and restaurant suppliers are essential providers for ships housing staffs or passengers.

External Services: Basic external services include accountants, consultants, computation services, office supply vendors, food and beverage services, banking and credit card support, heating and air-conditioning maintenance and repair, and general and private contractors as needed. Electronic fire and security systems are essential. Transportation vehicles are either owned or leased.

Utilities: Typical utilities for a large shipyard include electricity, water, sewer, telephone, cable, Internet, and fuel service.

Taxes: Fees and taxes are assessed as applicable by local, state, and federal law.

Insurance: Property insurance, particularly in hurricane-prone areas, is essential.

ORGANIZATIONAL STRUCTURE AND JOB ROLES

Shipyards, regardless of size, require employees in a number of positions. In small companies, one or a few employees may take on multiple tasks. The following umbrella categories apply to the organizational structure of small, medium, and large shipyards.

- Management
- Ship Design
- Shipfitting
- Customer Services

- Sales and Marketing
- Facilities and Security
- Human Resources

Management

The enormous expense and complexity of the shipbuilding process and the volatile effects of global markets on essential industrial production systems make the shipbuilding profession a tightly coordinated corporate venture. Public, private, and international stakeholders participate in a complex, reiterative process of contract negotiation, management, and review; cost control planning and procedures; project planning and management; procurement; quality control; research and development; human health and safety control; and environmental assessment. In a small business enterprise, these functions may be divided among a group of partners. The scope of production for larger vessels is managed by full corporate and government entities.

Midshipmen may qualify for the Marine Engineering and Shipyard Management program offered by the United States Merchant Marine Academy. This training prepares qualified candidates to serve as licensed officers in the Merchant Marine; to understand the engineering principles required for the construction and maintenance of sophisti-cated ships and their mechanical systems; to succeed in auxiliary business, manufacturing, and transportation professions; and to prepare as graduates for licensure as professional engineers or graduate studies.

Occupations in the management category include the following:

- Member of Board of Directors
- Financial Officer and Accountant
- Contract Supervisor
- Business Manager
- Purchasing Agent
- Travel and Transport Specialist
- Strategic Planning and Product Development Director
- Research and Development Specialist
- General Project Manager
- Health, Safety, and Environment Specialist
- Quality Assurance and Inspections Specialist
- Legal Arbitration and Negotiations Specialist

Ship Design

The shipwright is the master builder of a ship. He or she works directly with the shipowner or cor-

---

OCCUPATION SPECIALTIES

Marine Engineers and Architects

Specialty	Responsibilities
Marine equipment design engineers	Design marine equipment and machinery.
Marine equipment research engineers	Conduct research on marine machinery and equipment.
Marine equipment test engineers	Test marine equipment and machinery.
Marine surveyors	Survey marine vessels and watercraft, such as ships, boats, tankers, and dredges, to check the condition of hull, machinery, equipment, and equipage and to determine the repairs required for vessels to meet insurance requirements.
Port engineers	Coordinate the repair and maintenance functions of operating fleets to minimize loss of revenue and costs of repairs.

OCCUPATION PROFILE

Marine Engineer and Architect

Considerations	Qualifications
Description	Designs, develops, and evaluates marine vessels and equipment.
Career clusters	Architecture and Construction; Manufacturing; Science, Technology, Engineering, and Math
Interests	Data; things
Working conditions	Work both inside and outside
Minimum education level	Bachelor's degree; master's degree; doctoral degree
Physical exertion	Light work
Physical abilities	Unexceptional/basic fitness
Opportunities for experience	Internship; military service; part-time work
Licensure and certification	Required
Employment outlook	Slower-than-average growth expected
Holland interest score	IRE

Note: See volume 1, "Publisher's Note," for an explanation of the Holland interest score.

porate representative to determine the type of vessel needed and how the vessel is to be used, to prepare the ship's specifications, and to clarify what special features need to be included in its design and construction. The shipowner can be an individual, a private or public entity, a government agency, or an international contractor. He or she is usually the owner of a merchant vessel designed to carry cargo or other commodities. The shipowner is legally and financially responsible for the ship's maintenance and is officially registered in the Certificate of Registry for the vessel.

Ship architects, systems (production) engineers, and draftsmen use computer-aided design software and traditional blueprint sketches to ensure that the components and logistics of a ship or submarine are seaworthy and built to code. Computer-aided drafting programs and other interoffice communications software are essential tools for tracking a project and ensuring that the design meets the demands of the ship or submersible's intended use. Foremen and computer draftsmen

earn anywhere from $30,000 to $60,000 in annual salaries. Architects' and engineers' salaries range from $50,000 to $95,000 per annum.

Occupations in the ship design category include the following:

- Shipwright
- Naval Architect
- Marine Engineer
- Structural Designer
- Structural Engineer
- Electrical Designer
- Mechanical Designer
- Piping Designer
- Drafter
- Foreman
- Computer Technician

Shipfitting

The term "shipfitter" refers to the coordinator of all the mechanical trades involved in the shipbuilding process. Ships are generally built from the keel up. Extensive modeling of the design and its components occurs either in traditional lofts or with the use of new computer technologies. Shipfitters are responsible for preparing the large plates, frames, and bulkheads for riveting and welding. Working with a construction supervisor, shipfitters create the major components of the ship, which are then connected and finished by riveters, welders, caulkers, and sanders. The shipfitter is skilled in the use of a variety of power tools and shop machinery necessary for the seamless and detailed construction of the ship. Final detailing is handled by the outfitter. Skilled craftspeople (welders, riggers, machinists, and carpenters) can earn $42,000 to $45,000 per annum.

Occupations in this area include the following:

- Construction Supervisor
- Boilermaker
- Burner
- Carpenter
- Crane Operator
- Electrician
- Engineer
- Inspector
- Machinist
- Painter
- Pipefitter
- Riveter
- Sheet Metal Worker
- Welder
- Rigger
- Robotics Technician

Customer Services

The shipbuilding industries serve a variety of international and domestic entities. Contractors include private individuals, corporations, cruise ships, passenger ferry providers, and fisheries. Other contractors include the U.S. Navy, the U.S. Coast Guard, the Military Sealift Command, the National Oceanic and Atmospheric Administration (NOAA) Marine Operations, and the U.S. Army.

Occupations in the customer services category include the following:

- Purchasing Agent
- Systems and Equipment Inspector
- Warranties Supervisor
- Electronics Maintenance and Repair Worker
- Transportation and Delivery Worker

Sales and Marketing

Sales and marketing is an important part of the corporate mission of professional shipbuilders. Whether large or small, each individual shipyard provides services that are valuable to a particular constituency or locale. The Internet, the proliferation of desktop publishing packages, and maritime trade shows and conventions make it possible to promote the key products that set a firm apart from its competitors. In some communities, bids for lucrative contracts are highly competitive and public approval ratings are essential, demanding a high-profile program of positive press releases and publications intended to keep a yard or program in the public eye.

Occupations in the sales and marketing category include the following:

- Brokerage and Charter Salesperson
- Communications Specialist
- News and Media Coordinator
- Web Designer
- Community Relations Director
- Customized Project Design Specialist

Facilities and Security

Shipyards may vary in size and location, but they are usually very large and open spaces. Some take on the dimensions of a small manufacturing city employing thousands of people. One of the first legislative acts to address vessel security was passed in 1914 after the catastrophic loss of the *Titanic*. The Safety of Life at Sea Convention was revised in 1929, in 1948, and in 1960, when it was adopted by the newly formed International Maritime Organization. It was amended and restated in 1974; subsequent amendments include provisions for tanker security; safety procedures for RORO vessels, bulk carriers, and high-speed craft; emergency towing and reporting procedures; fire safety; helicopter landing safety; and other general safety provisions. In response to the September 11, 2001, terrorist attacks, on July 1, 2004, the International Maritime Organization enforced the International Ship and Port Facility Security Code (ISPS). This protocol was initiated to enhance previous security policies.

The U.S. Coast Guard played a lead role in drafting these protocols. The codes apply to cargo and passenger ships, drilling vessels, and port facilities. Security communications systems, personnel, and emergency planning programs are required. In the United States, maritime administrators also follow the Maritime Transportation Act of 2002. Industry leaders like Northrop Grumman specialize in cybersecurity systems to protect their facilities and their products.

Occupations in this area include the following:

- Custodian/Janitor
- Maintenance and Repair Worker
- Security Supervisor
- Security Guard

Human Resources

Shipyards comply with all federal laws and regulations regarding the health and security of grounds and personnel assigned to vessels and ports. Human resources employees monitor a company's compliance with these regulations in addition to administering benefits, screening candidates for open positions, resolving employee inquiries or grievances, and other administrative duties. Staff members in this department also must be aware of applicable union rules and jurisdictions.

Occupations in human resources include the following:

- Benefits Specialist
- Industrial and Employee Relations Specialist
- Health, Safety, and Environment Compliance Specialist
- Computer Security Specialist
- Training Director

INDUSTRY OUTLOOK

Overview

The outlook for this industry shows it to be on the rise. In September, 2010, the International Union of Marine Insurance reported one of the deepest contractions in global trade output since the 1930's. Seaborne trade dropped 4.5 percent in 2009; exports dropped seven times faster than the global gross domestic product (GDP). Never-theless, economic indicators show a steady comeback, with an expected 3.5 percent growth in 2010.

In 2005, the Gulf Coast economies of Florida, Louisiana, Mississippi, Alabama, and Texas sustained about $85 billion in damages as a result of hurricanes Katrina and Rita. The economies of the coastal zones account for nearly 25 percent of the states' total revenues. Ocean economies are based on key industries including marine construction, the harvesting of seafood resources, shipbuilding and boat building, oil and mineral extraction, and tourism and recreation industries. Nearly one-third of all marine construction, more than 20 percent of all shipbuilding and fisheries, and nearly half of all ocean-related oil and gas exploration and production in the United States takes place on the Gulf Coast.

On June 15, 2006, Congress approved the Emergency Supplemental Appropriations Act for Defense, the Global War on Terror, and Hurricane Recovery. This bill approved emergency appropriations for operating expenses incurred by the U.S. Coast Guard and authorized funding for the Department of Defense to repair Gulf Coast naval shipyard infrastructures damaged during Hurricane Katrina. Emergency appropriations also were made for the Department of the Army and the Department of the Interior for dredging, flood control, inspections, and repairs of coastal facilities.

In August, 2009, the state of Mississippi awarded a $20 million Housing and Urban Development community development grant for the construction of the Jackson County Maritime Trades Academy. The facility will be able to accommodate one thousand apprentices in the art of shipbuilding, securing the future of the Gulf Coast and its prominent role in shipbuilding.

The crash of world financial markets in late 2007 had a sharp and lasting effect on global seaborne trade. The Clarksea Index is a weighted index of the value of earnings based on the number of vessels worldwide. Between the end of May, 2008, and April, 2009, the index fell from $50,000 per day to $7,350 per day. The value of the index as of January 8, 2010 was $16,783 per day.

Employment Advantages

One of the great advantages of a career in ship-building is the wide range of skills and technologies available for career advancement. Excellent benefits, competitive salaries, educational stipends, and an opportunity to contribute to an industry that is vital to the commercial and security interests of nations around the world can open doors for a lifetime of achievement and job satisfaction.

Annual Earnings

GDP world averages are expected to rise by 3.5 percent over the next twenty years, with a doubling in world trade. Major developing countries are expected to increase their trade output by 5.9 percent. Shipweight capacity also increased in 2010. In its 2009 Review of Maritime Transport, the United Nations Conference on Trade and Development (UNCTAD) reported that sharp declines in global demand for goods has had a deleterious effect on orders for new ships. This trend is complicated by the numbers of new ships completed and delivered in compliance with orders placed before the 2008 financial slide. In 2009, the world merchant fleet capacity was estimated at 1.2 billion deadweight tons, with an annual increase of 6.7 percent. The oversupply is juxtaposed against falling freight and charter rates.

RELATED RESOURCES FOR FURTHER RESEARCH

AMERICAN ASSOCIATION OF PORT AUTHORITIES
  HEADQUARTERS
  1010 Duke St.
  Alexandria, VA 22314
  Tel: (703) 684-5700
  Fax: (703) 684-6321
  http://www.aapa-ports.org

AMERICAN SHIPBUILDING ASSOCIATION
  600 Pennsylvania Ave. SE, Suite 305
  Washington, DC 20003
  Tel: (202) 544-8170
  http://www.americanshipbuilding.com

AMERICAN SOCIETY OF NAVAL ENGINEERS
  1452 Duke St.
  Alexandria, VA 22314-3458
  Tel: (703) 836-6727
  http://www.navalengineers.org

INTERNATIONAL BROTHERHOOD OF
  BOILERMAKERS, IRON SHIPBUILDERS,
  BLACKSMITHS, FORGERS, AND HELPERS
  753 State Ave., Suite 570
  Kansas City, KS 66101
  Tel: (913) 371-2640
  http://www.boilermakers.org

INTERNATIONAL MARITIME ORGANIZATION
  4 Albert Embankment
  London SE1 7SR
  United Kingdom
  Tel: 44-020-7735-7611
  Fax: 44-020-7587-3210
  http://www.imo.org

INTERNATIONAL TRADE ADMINISTRATION,
  U.S. DEPARTMENT OF COMMERCE
  1401 Constitution Ave. NW
  Washington, DC 20230
  Tel: (800) 872-8723
  http://www.ita.doc.gov

MARITIME ADMINISTRATION, U.S.
  DEPARTMENT OF TRANSPORTATION
  1200 New Jersey Ave. SE
  Washington, DC 20590
  Tel: (800) 996-2723
  http://www.marad.dot.gov

NAVAL VESSEL REGISTER
  Norfolk Naval Shipyard
  Code 284, Building 705
  Portsmouth, VA 23709-5000
  Tel: (757) 396-0913
  Fax: (757) 967-2953
  http://www.nvr.navy.mil/class.htm

PUBLIC AFFAIRS OFFICE, MILITARY SEALIFT
  COMMAND
  914 Charles Morris Ct. SE
  Washington, DC 20398-5540
  Tel: (202) 685-5055
  http://www.msc.navy.mil

SHIPBUILDERS COUNCIL OF AMERICA
  1455 F St. NW, Suite 225
  Washington, DC 20005
  Tel: (202) 347-5462

Fax: (202) 347-5464
http://www.shipbuilders.org

SOCIETY OF NAVAL ARCHITECTS AND MARINE
ENGINEERS
601 Pavonia Ave.
Jersey City, NJ 07306
Tel: (800) 798-2188
Fax: (201) 798-4975
http://www.sname.org

U.S. COAST GUARD NATIONAL MARITIME CENTER
100 Forbes Dr.
Martinsburg, WV 25404
Tel: (888) 427-5662
http://www.usgc.mil/stew

ABOUT THE AUTHOR

Victoria Breting-García is an independent scholar
who studies and writes on topics in the fields of environmental history, science and technology, urban development, and global systems. She is a
member of the North American Society for Oceanic History, the American Historical Association,
the American Society for Environmental History,
the American Chemical Society, and the American
Medical Writers Association. A graduate of the
University of Houston, she holds graduate degrees
in public administration and history.

FURTHER READING

Benamara, Hassiba. *Shipping and Global Trade: A
Review of Major Developments.* New York: United
Nations Conference on Trade and
Development, 2010.

Crowell, John Franklin. "Present Status and
Future Prospects of American Shipbuilding."
*Annals of the American Academy of Political and
Social Science* 19 (January, 1902): 46-60.

De la Pedraja Tomán, René. *A Historical Dictionary
of the U.S. Merchant Marine and Shipping
Industry: Since the Introduction of Steam.*
Westport, Conn.: Greenwood Press, 1994.

Dear, I. C. B., and Peter Kemp, eds. *The Oxford
Companion to Ships and the Sea.* 2d ed. New
York: Oxford University Press, 2005.

Finamore, Daniel. *America and the Sea: Treasures
from the Collections of Mystic Seaport.* New Haven,
Conn.: Yale University Press, 2005.

Fox, Nancy Ruth, and Lawrence J. White. "U.S.
Shipping Policy: Going Against the Tide."
*Annals of the American Academy of Political and
Social Science* 553 (September, 1997): 75-86.

Gardiner, Robert, and Arne Emil Christensen,
eds. *The Earliest Ships: The Evolution of Boats into
Ships.* Annapolis, Md.: Naval Institute Press,
1996.

Harley, C. K. "On the Persistence of Old
Techniques: The Case of North American
Wooden Shipbuilding." *The Journal of Economic
History* 33, no. 2 (June, 1973): 372-398.

Harris, Brayton. *The Navy Times Book of
Submarines: A Political, Social, and Military
History.* New York: Berkley Books, 1997.

Havighurst, Walter. *The Long Ships Passing: The
Story of the Great Lakes.* 1942. Reprint.
Minneapolis: University of Minnesota Press,
2002.

Heitzmann, William Ray. *Opportunities in Marine
Science and Maritime Careers.* New York:
McGraw-Hill, 2006.

Keeny, Sandy. "The Foundations of Government
Contracting." *Journal of Contract Management*
(Summer, 2007): 7-19.

Kennedy, Greg. *The Merchant Marine in
International Affairs, 1850-1950.* London: Frank
Cass, 2000.

Kotar, S. L., and J. E. Gessler. *The Steamboat Era: A
History of Fulton's Folly on American Rivers, 1807-
1860.* Jefferson, N.C.: McFarland, 2009.

Labaree, Benjamin W., et al. *America and the Sea:
A Maritime History.* Mystic, Conn.: Mystic
Seaport Museum, 1998.

Landström, Björn. *The Ship: An Illustrated History.*
Garden City, N.Y.: Doubleday, 1961.

Levinson, Marc. *The Box: How the Shipping
Container Made the World Smaller and the World
Economy Bigger.* Princeton, N.J.: Princeton
University Press, 2006.

National Academy of Sciences. *Shipbuilding
Technology and Education.* Washington, D.C.:
Author, 1996.

Roland, Alex, W. Jeffrey Bolster, and Alexander
Keyssar. *The Way of the Ship: America's Maritime
History Reenvisioned, 1600-2000.* Hoboken, N.J.:
John Wiley, 2008.

Stopford, Martin. *Maritime Economics*. 3d ed. New York: Routledge, 2009.

Talley, Wayne K. "Dockworker Earnings, Containerization, and Shipping Deregulation." *Journal of Transport Economics and Policy* 36, no. 3 (September, 2002): 447-467.

Thiesen, William H. *Industrializing American Shipbuilding: New Perspectives on Maritime History and Nautical Archaeology*. Gainesville: University Press of Florida, 2006.

U.S. Bureau of Labor Statistics. *Career Guide to Industries*, 2010-2011 ed. http://www.bls.gov/oco/cg.

U.S. Census Bureau. North American Industry Classification System (NAICS), 2007. http://www.census.gov/cgi-bin/sssd/naics/naicsrch?chart=2007.

Walters, William D. "American Naval Shipbuilding. 1890-1989." *Geographical Review* 90, no. 3 (July, 2000): 418-431.

Space Exploration and Space Science Industry

NASA

INDUSTRY SNAPSHOT

General Industry: Science, Technology, Engineering, and Math

Career Clusters: Government and Public Administration Occupations; Information Technology; Science, Technology, Engineering, and Math; Transportation, Distribution, and Logistics

Subcategory Industries: Computer Systems Design Services; Engineering Services; Geophysical Surveying and Mapping Services; Guided Missile and Space Vehicle Engine and Parts Research and Development; Guided Missile and Space Vehicle Manufacturing; Guided Missile and Space Vehicle Merchant Wholesalers; Guided Missile and Space Vehicle Propulsion Unit and Propulsion Unit Parts Manufacturing; Nonscheduled Space Freight Transportation; Satellite and Satellite Antenna Manufacturing; Space Research and Technology; Testing Laboratories

Related Industries: Alternative Power Industry; Defense Industry; Scientific and Technical Services; Scientific, Medical, and Health Equipment and Supplies Industry; Telecommunications Equipment Industry

Annual Domestic Revenues: $139 billion USD (The Space Report, 2009)

Annual International Revenues: $118 billion USD (The Space Report, 2009)

Annual Global Revenues: $257 billion USD (The Space Report, 2009)

NAICS Numbers: 334220, 336414-336419, 423860, 481212, 541330, 541360, 541380, 541512, 541712, 927110

INDUSTRY DEFINITION

Summary

The space exploration and space science industry creates piloted and unpiloted vehicles and devices that venture into space, study phenomena beyond Earth's atmosphere, and make use of extra-terrestrial resources, including extreme height—a resource used by satellites to study Earth itself and to enable mass communications, for example. The resources on Earth constitute only a tiny fraction of those available within an hour of light-travel time in the solar system. The space industry already reaches most technical and business sectors of in-

Space flight seemed a closer reality after the launch of the first rocket from Cape Canaveral, Florida, in 1950. (NASA)

dustry, and as it transitions from an industry primarily of scientific exploration and military uses to one primarily of commercial development, it has the potential for unlimited expansion. The industry's core sectors are launch, spacecraft, and ground operations. In the future, there may be large growth in a fourth sector, extraterrestrial operations. Communications, entertainment, and remote sensing are the industry's largest civilian market sectors. Though only nine organizations operate independent launch facilities, dozens of nations own and operate satellites, and most use data feeds or results obtained by satellites. Weather prediction and navigation of aircraft, ships, and automobiles all depend on the space industry.

History of the Industry

Although humanity has dreamed of cruising the heavens for thousands of years, it was only in June, 1944, that the first human-built object crossed the Kármán line, the traditional boundary between Earth's atmosphere and outer space (located 60 miles, or 100 kilometers, above sea level): A German V-2 missile reached 176 kilometers above Earth. In 1957, the Soviet Union's Sputnik satellite became the first controlled spacecraft to achieve the speed and altitude required to go into a stable orbit outside Earth's atmosphere; it transmitted radio signals back to Earth. The first man in space was Yuri Gagarin, and the first woman was Valentina Tereshkova, both of the Soviet Union.

The application of space satellites for reconnaissance and then for remote sensing of terrestrial resources followed. Space law evolved, first to allow overflights of national territory and thus avoid shoot-down incidents, then to ascribe national responsibility for damage caused by objects in or falling from space, to declare the resources beyond

Earth as the property of all humankind, and to ban weapons and nuclear explosions in space. Nations raced to place satellites in geostationary Earth orbit (GEO) above the equator. The Telstar satellite relayed telephone signals around the world in 1963. Launchers first developed for intercontinental ballistic missiles were turned into increasingly powerful boosters, placing heavy reconnaissance satellites and boosting equipment to build space stations, partly for military purposes.

President Dwight D. Eisenhower established the National Aeronautics and Space Administration (NASA) in 1958 to support the move toward human spaceflight. On May 25, 1961, President John F. Kennedy announced the objective of landing a human on the Moon before the end of the decade. The U.S. Mercury, Gemini, and Apollo programs and the Soviet Vostok, Voshkod, and Soyuz programs steadily increased the confidence of humans in space, building up to the landing of two men, Neil Armstrong and Buzz Aldrin, on the lunar surface in 1969. Five more successful human missions to the lunar surface followed. Before this, following several unsuccessful attempts, the Soviets' Luna 9 lunar lander had delivered the Lunokhod rover to the Moon's surface. Their Venera 7 spacecraft landed on Venus in 1970 and transmitted signals for fifty-eight minutes. The American Viking lander touched down on Mars in 1976. A total of nearly nine thousand space launches had occurred by 2010, the vast majority coming from the United States or the Soviet Union (later the Russian Federation).

Missions to the outer planets became feasible with very low energy levels after the invention of the "slingshot," or gravity-boost, maneuver, whereby a spacecraft would use the gravitational acceleration of a heavenly body to swing around it toward another destination. The Pioneer (launched in 1972) and Voyager (first launched in 1977) missions,

followed by the Galileo (1989) and Cassini-Huygens (1997) missions, sent back spectacular images of the planets and their moons. NASA's NEAR-Shoemaker mission touched down on the near-Earth object (NEO) Eros, an asteroid, in 2001, and the Japanese Hayabusa mission (launched 2003) landed on a NEO, lifted off from it, and returned to Earth, completing its mission in June of 2010.

NASA has landed and operated several solar-powered robotic rovers on Mars and, significantly, has proved the existence of water ice there. Missions to the Moon, including the Indian Chandrayaan mission (2008)—carrying a science payload cosponsored by the Indian Space Research Organization (ISRO) and NASA—and the NASA LCROSS mission (2009), helped prove the existence of

The Telstar satellite was designed by Bell Telephone Laboratories. (AP/ Wide World Photos)

significant amounts of water in the perpetually shaded regions of the Moon.

Orbiting obervatories including the Hubble Space Telescope (launched 1990), Compton Gamma Ray Observatory (launched 1991), Chandra X-Ray Observatory (launched 1999), Spitzer Space Telescope (launched 2003), and Kepler Planet-finder Telescope (launched 2010) have collected data in both the visible and some nonvisible portions of the electromagnetic spectrum, opening up deep space astronomy, reinforcing the Big Bang theory of the universe's origins, revealing cosmological phenomena such as dark matter and dark energy, and leading to the discovery of a growing number of planetary systems that could potentially support life. Between 1992 and 2010, astronomers using both earthbound and space-based telescopes discovered more than 450 planets outside the solar system, or "exo-planets." This number continues to rise, and the belief that conditions might exist for life—even intelligent life—beyond the solar system has gained increasing acceptance by scientists. On Earth, radio telescopes constantly collect radio emissions from distant parts of the Milky Way galaxy and beyond, downloading these data to computers that search for patterns that would suggest the presence of intelligent life.

An artist's rendering of a Mars Exploration Rover. (AP/Wide World Photos)

Closer to home, the GEO is now regulated by the United Nations to ensure that all nations can use this key region of Earth orbit. At GEO, satellites remain stationary above a particular point on Earth and are thus able to perform such important functions as relaying telecommunications and facilitating geopositioning. Specific parts of the GEO have been allotted to each nation. Large satellites at GEO enable tens of thousands of intercontinental telephone calls to be made simultaneously. The number of orbital slots at GEO is limited by the spread and interference of signal beams; as operating frequencies increase, beams get narrower and require less power, allowing closer spacing and hence more slots.

The Industry Today

Over seventy nations participate in the space industry. As of 2008, the U.S. space industry alone employed over 262,000 people in forty-one states. There are six major governmental or multinational space agencies today: NASA; the Russian federal space agency Federal'noye Kosmicheskoye Agentstvo Rossii (FKA), often known as Roscosmos (RKA); the European Space Agency (ESA); the National Space Agency of the People's Republic of China (CNSA); ISRO; and the Japan Aerospace Exploration Agency (JAXA). In addition, the French, Israeli, Iranian, and Ukrainian national space agencies are known to be capable of launching into space. A total of over seventy national and multinational space agencies exist. The total known annual budget of these agencies exceeds $44 billion.

The Cold War U.S.-Soviet "space race" has given way to more collaborative multinational efforts, with launch facilities in the United States, Russia, Kazakhstan, Guyana (owned by the ESA), the United Kingdom, China, India, Japan, and both the Korean republics. The Soviet Mir space station (which was destroyed in 2001) and the U.S.-led International Space Station (ISS) have hosted astronauts and cosmonauts from several nations, and the ISS has multinational scientific laboratories for microgravity research.

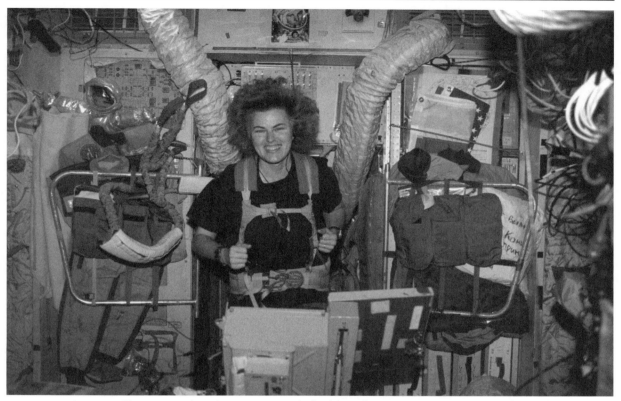

Astronaut Shannon Lucid works out on a treadmill while in the Russian Mir space station. (NASA)

The U.S.-owned Global Positioning System, the European Galileo, and the Russian GLONASS operate constellations of navigational satellites in middle-altitude orbits, providing global coverage. Earth observation satellites and weather satellites provide early warning of storms and fires, enable prediction of crop yields, and help locate natural resources.

Today, the space industry has three main components. The first is the launch enterprise. Space launchers are large vehicles consisting mainly of fuel tanks and rocket engines. These engines are chemical propulsion systems that use solid, liquid, or hybrid solid-liquid propellants. The payload to be delivered to space is placed near the top of a stack of two or three stages of such rockets, and each stage falls off sequentially as its propellant is exhausted. Liquid propellants include kerosene, nitric acid, liquid oxygen, and liquid hydrogen. Solid rocket boosters are cast from organic and inorganic chemicals into pressure vessels and transported as completed components to the launch

site. Launch facilities have the massive infrastructures necessary to assemble and handle such vehicles and to withstand the power of the launch process. Such facilities employ numerous technical and administrative personnel to conduct this process safely and efficiently. Payroll expenses greatly exceed fuel costs. The launch enterprise has much in common with chemical and mechanical heavy industries and power plants.

Spacecraft, the second component of the space industry, are highly sophisticated packages of instrumentation. They have solar panels that can be deployed once in space to provide the bulk of their power. Orbit correction fuel and thrusters are carried on board. Because every kilogram placed in low Earth orbit requires some 10 or more kilograms of launcher mass, spacecraft components must be designed for minimal mass. At the same time, packages must be able to survive the stresses experienced during launch and the harsh radiation and temperature extremes outside Earth's atmosphere. Typical large communications satellites

The space shuttle Atlantis *atop the shuttle carrier aircraft as it returns to the Kennedy Space Center.* (NASA)

placed in GEO are built to last more than seventeen years with no prospect of repair or maintenance, so components are produced and installed with extreme care to avoid contamination. Redundant systems are installed to provide safety margins. Solar panels for these spacecraft use the most efficient conversion technologies, albeit at high cost. Fuel cells are used to release energy.

The spacecraft industry strives to maximize the number of transmitter-responder units (transponders) that can be placed on a single satellite. The Space Systems-Loral Echostar 14 satellite—launched in March, 2010, to provide direct-to-home television services for the DISH network—has a mass of 6,384 kilograms (14,074 pounds), carries 103 Ku-band (11-18 GigaHertz) transponders, and is expected to reach over 13 million subscribers. This industry component has much in common with both the semiconductor electronic systems industry and the renewable power industry.

Other spacecraft are designed for long-duration missions to distant destinations. These are powered by electric-propulsion engines, typically ion rockets using xenon or other rare-gas thrusters.

Nuclear power is used in the form of thermoelectric conversion of the heat from radioisotope decay. Future craft may use enriched-fuel nuclear reactors for direct heating of propellants.

The third component of the space industry comprises the ground-based businesses that service mission operations, receiving data in the form of remote-sensing images or relayed radio, television, and telephone signals for sale in terrestrial markets. In addition to the communications industry, the entertainment industry is a major user of satellite services. With millions of customers as end users, this industry component includes telecommunication and entertainment distribution companies as well.

Efforts to find other commercial applications of spaceflight have led to the establishment of over twenty different NASA space commercialization centers and several spaceport organizations. In addition to NASA's centers, the U.S. Department of Commerce has an Office of Space Commercialization, based in facilities of the National Oceanic and Atmospheric Administration (NOAA), a major supplier of weather and resource data. The

ISS has been vigorously promoted by NASA as a multinational laboratory that could offer commercial product-development services in microgravity. These efforts have been limited by the delay in completing the ISS, which has also delayed ISS's relocation to an orbit high enough to achieve true microgravity. At a higher orbit, the station would no longer experience "g-jitter," a phenomenon caused by its proximity to the atmosphere and Earth's gravity gradients. The Moon-Mars Constellation program envisaged shutdown of the ISS to redirect funding, but in 2010, the Constellation program was canceled and ISS funding was revived. NASA announced contracts in 2010 to develop commercial transportation of supplies to the ISS.

Well-known U.S. corporate space entities around the world include Boeing, Lockheed-Martin, United Technologies, Northrop-Grumman, Orbital Sciences, Space Exploration Technologies Corporation (Space X), and Alliant Techsystems (ATK). International entities include the S. P. Korolev Rocket and Space Corporation (Energia) in Russia, European Aeronautic Defence and Space Company (EADS), China Aerospace Science and Industry Corporation (CASIC), Antrix in India, Japan Aerospace Corporation, and Mitsubishi International in Japan. Notable joint ventures include the United Space Alliance in the United States, the Arab Satellite Communications Organization (Arabsat), and the U.S.-Russia-Norway-Ukraine Sea Launch venture. Entities such as COMSAT and Globalstar are well known in the satellite communications industry.

INDUSTRY MARKET SEGMENTS

The space industry has three market segments. Beginning in 1998, commercial space expenditures have surpassed government space expenditures annually. The best-known market segment is still the government agencies that fund research and award operations contracts to advance their nations' space programs. The second is the remote-sensing market, which depends on the space industry for data to assist weather prediction, crop monitoring and prediction, disaster response, monitoring of demographic changes, and identifying

natural resources. The third and largest segment is the telecommunications and entertainment market, reaching billions of end users with products as diverse as television shows, telephone connections, and navigation data. Three more currently insignificant segments are held up as potentially very large future markets. The first is electrical power beamed from and through space to customers located on Earth and in space. The second is extraterrestrial natural resources and space-built products. (Space could become a limitless supplier of resources whose terrestrial supply is limited, and conditions in space may facilitate the construction of certain products at a level of quality beyond what could be achieved on Earth.) The third potential market is space tourism, which has so far sent only a few wealthy pioneers into orbit and sent several more on suborbital flights. If these three market segments are developed, each has the potential to become several times larger than today's space market.

Small Businesses

Small businesses in the space industry develop a wide array of products and services. Components for satellites and launch vehicles are specialized devices with small production runs and high costs due to stringent quality requirements. Most products require sophisticated technical analyses and computations to design and to ensure compatibility with the major systems on which they fit. Several small companies have been started under the U.S. Small Business Innovations Research (SBIR) program, which translates the requirements of agencies such as NASA or the Deparment of Defense (DoD) into projects suitable for small teams. When a project results in components or software products that are adopted by federal agencies or are bought by larger companies, the scale of operations grows rapidly.

Potential Annual Earnings Scale. According to the U.S. Bureau of Labor Statistics (BLS), in 2009 the average annual salary for an aerospace engineer was $87,730 and the average annual salary for an aerospace engineering and operations technician was $55,660. Software engineers in the aerospace field earned an average of around $97,000. Engineering managers earned $122,590 on average, while chief executives of aerospace companies earned $188,370. Many private companies in the industry pay bonuses and stock options in good years.

Clientele Interaction. Employees of small space-related businesses must expect to play several roles. Typically, a component will be designed to work with a much larger system that incorporates products developed by many suppliers. Thus, every project involves much planning, coordination, and integration. Companies hope to be working on several products and projects simultaneously, and business development functions are shared by all workers.

Amenities, Atmosphere, and Physical Grounds. Many space-related companies are located where opportunities for outdoor recreation are plentiful. Locations such as Washington State, California, Connecticut, the mountains of Utah, and the Florida coast are examples. Small companies that can offer their own recreational facilities are relatively rare. The physical amenities of the workplace are usually quite good, partly because small businesses are often in a nascent stage and occupy new buildings and partly because workplace organization and cleanliness are subject to regular inspection since they have significant implications for product safety and traceability of standards. The workforce is usually well educated and highly qualified. Employees generally work hard and are at comparable economic levels, making for good camaraderie. Many small companies strive for a collegiate environment.

Workers tend to dress informally, except when customer interaction calls for semicasual business attire. Actual internal dynamics vary widely from one workplace to another and depend on the policies of owners and immediate team leaders, whose own experience may come from military, government, large-company, venture-capital, or university backgrounds. Unlike in the computer or pharmaceutical industries, being bought out by a large company is not a common dream in the space industry.

Typical Number of Employees. A small space-related business may have anywhere from one employee to five hundred employees.

Traditional Geographic Locations. There is a heavy concentration of space-related workplaces near NASA centers, near the seat of federal agency headquarters in Washington, D.C., and all over the West Coast. The states of California, Maryland, Virginia, Texas, and Florida have high concentrations of such companies. Connecticut, Washington, New York, and Ohio also have several because of the proximity of aerospace manufacturers and research establishments, which implies a large supply of technically qualified workers and expertise.

Pros of Working for a Small Space-Related Business. Space-related businesses by definition work on the cutting edge of technological innovation. The environment in which their projects are assigned and executed is highly competitive and diverse, and employees who value such environments are likely to gain a sense of prestige simply by succeeding in the industry. They may find a level of fulfillment from seeing parts that they designed carried into space that is difficult to attain in other jobs. They will also be well compensated for their work.

Competitors must be highly adaptive and technically nimble to see potential for their skills and ideas in a number of opportunities that are of interest to the federal agencies. Typically, successful companies cite a success rate of one in eight proposals, which implies an intense proposal development effort at all times, in addition to the work required to develop and validate new ideas. Many smaller companies in the space industry have grown steadily and manage to retain workers for decades, operating with good profitability. Typically, space-related small companies grow through steady project successes on a number of different projects.

Cons of Working for a Small Space-Related Business. Since most space launches occur from government-affiliated facilities, even if the customer is not a government, employees and owners of space-related businesses are bound by detailed regulations and government oversight of all operations. Many jobs in the industry require U.S. citizenship because they involve working on government contracts that are themselves restricted to U.S. citizens.

The competitive atmosphere of the industry is not for everyone, and those who blanch at the thought of a one-in-eight success rate for proposals are probably not well suited to work in this industry.

Many space-related jobs involve some travel to collaborating companies; federal agencies; and product integration, launch, and test sites. Increasingly, the space industry involves international collaboration at the marketing, design integration, testing, launch, mission control, and data collection stages. Outdoor testing environments are exciting, especially to younger employees, but they can be quite stressful and involve long hours.

Costs

Payroll and Benefits: Small company compensation includes attractive pay packages and stock but typically lacks complex benefit plans. Biweekly pay periods and participation in a 401(k) plan are general expectations. Consultants may be employed to meet the diverse demands of specific projects; if so, they may be paid hourly, weekly, or on a per-project basis.

Supplies: Practically all space-related companies require advanced computer workstations and general office supplies. Those engaged in software development require relevant coding and engineering software as well, but little else. Those building hardware prototypes require specialized design software and equipment used to create and test such parts, which may be electrical, mechanical, materials-based, chemical, and so forth. Each type of development requires its own specialized raw materials and design and assembly equipment.

External Services: Since many spacecraft components are built of special materials to meet stringent demands of weight reduction and strength and radiation resistance, small companies must typically use external specialist services for several aspects of their production processes. Testing also requires instrumentation with large capital costs, best addressed by using external laboratories and consultants. In addition, small companies may contract traditional business support services, such as accounting and tax preparation, legal counsel, cleaning, maintenance, or security. They may also hire government-relations consultants to help secure contracts. If they produce hazardous materials as by-products of their work, businesses may contract disposal companies to remove them.

Utilities: Space-related companies must pay for electricity, heating, water, sewage, telephone, and Internet access.

Taxes: Space-related companies must pay corporate and property taxes, as well as payroll taxes.

Many items produced by such companies are covered under the International Traffic in Arms Regulations (ITAR) and require specific permission to export to other nations.

Midsize Businesses

Some jobs in the space enterprise are in university academic departments (schools) or in full-time research organizations. These are midsize employers, and, because of competitive aspects, there are many similarities between for-profit and nonprofit organizations, whether in academia or in other enterprises. There is considerable mobility between academic and commercial organizations because of similarities in types of work, working environments, and expectations to develop proposals and to "bring in" projects and customers.

Potential Annual Earnings Scale. According to the U.S. Bureau of Labor Statistics (BLS), in 2009 the average annual salary for an aerospace engineer was $87,730 and the average annual salary for an aerospace engineering and operations technician was $55,660. Software engineers in the aerospace field earned an average of around $97,000. Engineering managers earned $122,590 on average, while chief executives of aerospace companies earned $188,370. Many private companies in the industry pay bonuses and stock options in good years, while universities and nonprofits typically pay neither bonuses nor stock options.

Clientele Interaction. Midsize space-related companies tend to classify levels of clientele interaction more rigidly than do small companies, but less than do the mega-corporations. Workers are expected to interact with people who have similar work functions at other organizations—and probably with people a couple of organizational levels to either side. Clientele generally have highly technical education and training backgrounds. In the case of university and full-time research organizations, clientele interaction—writing proposals and making presentations—takes up a major portion of workers' time. The major products of university research consist of the education, skills, and experience imparted to talented individuals, as well as published ideas and methods. Several small businesses started on SBIR funding have spun off, usually to exploit patentable inventions.

One special sector of the space industry comprises midsize companies that are essentially clearinghouses for payroll and benefits for a large number of employees who work as contractors at government sites. Their workplaces are the same as those of federal agency employees. Many such employees hold doctoral degrees and must write proposals to fund their own positions and necessary support staff.

Amenities, Atmosphere, and Physical Grounds. Midsize companies have usually been located in established business parks or campuses for some years, so they provide good amenities. Many provide access to outdoor and indoor recreation facilities, as well as parklike campuses. However, this access may come at a substantial cost in commute times. Working from home may be possible, depending on the company and the type of project. Doing so comes with the responsibility for solving problems or developing proposals, so that many employees work much more than forty-hour weeks. Security regulations stemming from government requirements are more common in the space industry than are purely corporate proprietary concerns, and both types of requirments may be equally strict. Companies conduct thorough initial and periodic investigations of workers' credit solvency, personal habits, and other aspects of their lives, requiring employees to cede some level of privacy and possibly freedom. University environments pose fewer access restrictions, since they must be open to students and researchers who come from all over the world. They typically work on more open-literature, publishable work. However, workplace safety and access controls are becoming more uniform, even in nominally academic environments.

Typical Number of Employees. Midsize space-related businesses generally employ between five hundred and a few thousand people.

Traditional Geographic Locations. There is a heavy concentration of space-related workplaces near NASA centers, near the seat of federal agency headquarters in Washington, D.C., and all over the West Coast. The states of California, Maryland, Virginia, Texas, and Florida have high concentrations of such companies. Connecticut, Washington, New York, and Ohio also have several because of the proximity of aerospace manufacturers and research establishments, which implies a large supply of technically qualified workers and expertise. Midsize companies that produce physical prod-

ucts, and even some that produce only software, can take up a fair amount of space, so their campuses are likely to be located in suburban or rural areas near cities or other industrial centers, rather than in such cities proper.

Pros of Working for a Midsize Space-Related Business. It is a reality of the scientific and engineering workplace that there is a very large difference, equivalent to a factor of ten or more, between the actual worth of a top-notch employee and that of one whose resume looks nearly the same, when it comes to making progress. This is especially true in research and development. Large corporations and government organizations cannot recognize this difference easily, but midsize organizations can. Thus, such companies are less likely to employ "dead weight," improving both their own bottom lines and the work life of their employees.

Midsize space companies have usually been in business for over a decade and have established customer bases. Such a company's organizational structure is likely to be flatter than that of a large corporation, with project directors typically reporting straight to the top executive layer. One well-established midsize business shows over 50 percent of its employees as engineers and scientists; over 25 percent as manufacturing, testing, and quality assurance specialists; over 15 percent as business support specialists; 5 percent as program managers; and only 2 percent as general managers or marketing managers. Of the scientists and engineers, over half are mechanical or electrical engineers, over 10 percent are software engineers, and some 20 percent are from other specialties such as aerospace aerodynamics, aerostructures and aero propulsion, guidance, navigation and controls, optics, antenna engineering, and mission operations. Another 15 percent are systems engineers, and some 5 percent are designers. New graduates employed by midsize companies may be given the opportunity and responsibility to take on assignments that would be reserved for much more experienced, senior employees in large companies.

Cons of Working for a Midsize Space-Related Business. A midsize business is still dependent on a moderate number of projects, each of which comes with high risks. Because customers are likely to include government organizations and projects are likely to be at a level closer to flight systems, regulations on workplace conduct are likely to be as tight as in a large company.

The level of responsibility given to new employees may be exciting and fulfilling, but it may also make employees feel as if they are being thrown in the water, to sink or swim. This situation arises because midsize companies often cannot draw on deep resources of experienced specialists for every new problem that comes along. They thus have no choice but to expect their in-house staffs to take on difficult problems on short notice. Successful companies and employees use professional development opportunities, including lunchtime seminars, formal classroom training, online learning, and on-the-job learning—such as special task force assignments and some coaching where possible—to prepare employees for such contingencies.

Costs

Payroll and Benefits: Midsize companies usually pay employees salaries, although some may earn hourly wages. Universities and nonprofits regularly fund employees with grants—often grants written by the employees themselves. These grants may involve fixed-term contracts. Benefits are common among midsize companies in the space industry.

Supplies: Practically all space-related companies require advanced computer workstations and general office supplies. Those engaged in software development require relevant coding and engineering software as well, but little else. Those building hardware prototypes require specialized design software and equipment used to create and test such parts, which may be electrical, mechanical, materials-based, chemical, and so forth. Each type of development requires its own specialized raw materials and design and assembly equipment.

External Services: Since many spacecraft components are built of special materials to meet stringent demands of weight reduction and strength and radiation resistance, small companies must typically use external specialist services for several aspects of their production processes. Testing also requires instrumentation with large capital costs, best addressed by using external laboratories and consultants. In addition, small companies may contract traditional business support services, such as accounting and tax preparation, legal counsel, cleaning, maintenance, or security. They may also hire government-relations consultants to help secure contracts. If they produce hazardous materials as by-products of their work, businesses may contract disposal companies to remove them.

Utilities: Space-related companies must pay for electricity, heating, water, sewage, telephone, and Internet access.

Taxes: Space-related for-profit companies must pay corporate and property taxes, as well as payroll taxes. Many items produced by such companies are covered under the International Traffic in Arms Regulations (ITAR) and require specific permission to export to other nations. Nonprofit ventures may be exempt from property and income taxes, but they must still pay payroll taxes.

Large Businesses

Large space-related businesses include private (and publicly traded) corporations, as well as government space agencies. Since both types of entity work on the same projects, there is much similarity between their work environments. Unionized shop-floor labor is a special feature.

Potential Annual Earnings Scale. The difference in pay scales between private large corporations and government agencies is not seen as real any more, since competition based on cost per labor hour in project proposals drives these differences down, even as government pay scales have improved as a result of the high cost of living in the areas where many government jobs are located. Executive compensation at large corporations is reported to be around $2 million in salary and $4 million per year at the chairman level. The administrator of NASA earned $172,200 as of 2008.

Clientele Interaction. Large companies have formal protocols governing their employees' interactions with clients. Such clients often prominently include officials of the government, including military personnel. Companies must bid on contracts and then must deliver the products they have contracted to deliver in the time and for the amount of money specified.

Amenities, Atmosphere, and Physical Grounds. In the contemporary space business, even the largest companies typically try to organize their workforce into small teams operating with substantial autonomy, in an atmosphere approaching that of a small business. The physical grounds typically resemble campuses and are located in office parks, except for major final assembly and testing facilities. All have tight security requirements.

Typical Number of Employees. Large businesses in the space industry have more than one thousand employees. The largest ones have tens to hundreds of thousands of employees. These employees may be distributed among many different locations.

Traditional Geographic Locations. As with midsize companies, large corporations locate their operations centers near NASA centers and military facilities, and their headquarters are typically located in major metropolitan areas close to government agencies and financial institutions.

Pros of Working for a Large Space-Related Business or Agency. Unlike many other industries, large space corporations often organize themselves into smaller work groups, alleviating some of the cons typical of corporate employment. Large corporations are often much more financially stable and have signifant resources, enabling them to provide employees with more regular pay raises. Large companies also have well-organized programs through which employees can continue their education through distance learning or taking courses at local universities, and they reward employees for earning new degrees. They often have organized facilities for child day care and some medical care.

The "graying" of the U.S. workforce has had significant effects in large government organizations, where many long-term staff have chosen to take early retirement, while continuing to be available to work as part-time consultants. Thus, thoughtful young employees can draw on experienced advice while enjoying the freedom to implement new ideas.

Cons of Working for a Large Space-Related Business or Agency. There is significant movement of people between projects and groups within large space-related corporations. This mobility provides some freedom, but it also decreases the sense of stability usually imparted by working for a large company, especially given that entire groups may be expected to relocate geographically.

Large corporations often demonstrate a degree of inertia in recognizing employee effort and success, especially at the junior and middle levels. The ability to work in areas of one's choice is often more limited at such corporations because such moves must be approved through several layers of management. Moreover, corporate human resources divisions may prefer to hire new workers whose resumes suit them for the narrow job descriptions of new projects, rather than allowing employees without direct experience fitting such narrow descriptions the freedom to branch out from their most obvious areas of expertise.

Since the 1990's, the expectation of well-funded corporate retirement programs has changed drastically. The seismic changes in the industry through corporate mergers, break-offs, and "rightsizing" took away much of the pride of large-corporation identity. The sharp economic downturn of 2002 destroyed the secure comfort of company stock options and employee stock purchase programs. The crash in 2007-2008 has further damaged the prior model. Corporate cost-cutting ideas have severely reduced retirement benefits.

Costs

Payroll and Benefits: In the space industry, large companies do not appear to offer higher salaries for technical positions than smaller and midsize companies. In a reversal from the pre-1990 years, many employees switch from corporate to civil service (government) positions rather than the other way around, except at the executive level. Employee stock-purchase and retirement programs are no longer considered to be as secure and lucrative as they were in the days of steady government contracts. Against these considerations, the performance bonuses built into projects do offer good rewards when projects go well.

Supplies: Large space companies have dedicated purchasing departments with their own highly evolved processes and regulations. Space system components often require supplies of rare and precious commodities to manufacture alloys, photovoltaic cells, nuclear reactor components, and fuels. Thus, the forecasting and acquisition of supplies is a specialized occupation requiring very experienced and capable specialists.

External Services: Large companies often operate as prime contractors to the government and provide subcontracts for smaller companies and university researchers, as well as outsourcing some limited aspects of their routine operations. Proprietary concerns and the regulatory and financial implications of any information on the scale of their programs limit the outsourcing of key functions.

Utilities: Apart from the requirements of any large organizations with thousands of humans working on their premises, space companies often have specialized needs for large supplies of power and water to operate test facilities. Clean rooms, assembly lines, engine test stands, nuclear reactors, and fuel casting facilities all have special needs, and many have dedicated auxiliary power plants on their premises or located in close proximity.

Taxes: Large corporations and their employees pay large amounts of money as taxes, and are hence highly valued employers in the states where they are located. As a result, these corporations are often able to negotiate advantageous deals with local governments with regard to taxes, land occupancy, transportation, and utility infrastructure. Within the terms negotiated, however, they must still pay corporate and property taxes.

ORGANIZATIONAL STRUCTURE AND JOB ROLES

While the core of the space industry is highly technical, there are layers of business development, management, and support functions around and among the technical teams. Thus, space-related companies employ a wide range of job roles. At the largest corporations, employees average over fifteen years of industry experience.

The following umbrella categories apply to the organizational structure of businesses in the space exploration and space science industry:

- Executive Management
- Program Management
- Technology, Research, Design, and Development
- Engineering
- Manufacturing
- Support Professionals
- Human Resources
- External Services

Executive Management

The typical large space corporation is a subset of a larger aerospace enterprise. The space component is led by an executive vice president of the corporation, typically described as the executive vice president of space systems. Below this officer are a range of corporate managers who oversee all aspects of the space-related ventures of the corporation, ensuring that this division's activities match and contribute to the goals of the larger enterprise. Smaller companies are more likely to be self-contained ventures run by a president or chief executive officer.

The boardrooms of space businesses were populated some decades ago with people who rose through technology ranks or came with military and aviation experience. More recently, professional management talent has come from diverse corporations. A new generation of commercial space start-ups has also risen, led by aviation pioneers and successful entrepreneurs from venture-capital technology companies. These bring different approaches to technical and organizational barriers, often diverging from the traditional practices evolved from the military and governmental pedigree of the industry.

Executive management occupations may include the following:

- President/Chief Executive Officer (CEO)
- Chief Financial Officer (CFO)
- Chief Operating Officer (COO)
- Chief Technology Officer (CTO)
- Vice President of Space Systems
- Vice President of Human Resources
- General Counsel
- Comptroller
- Treasurer
- Vice President of Mergers and Acquisitions

Program Management

Managers and directors of programs and departments rank below the chief technology officer level. They are responsible for the overall progress of the development or manufacturing programs assigned to them. Directors are very experienced engineers and serve more technical functions than do managers. Program managers typically have bachelor's or master's degrees in science or engineering, and some have business management degrees. Directors may come from diverse backgrounds. The existence of a separate management track with higher financial rewards appears to be well-established even in some prominent midsize companies, though the rare experience of senior technical personnel is highly valued by knowledgeable directors and executives.

Program management occupations may include the following:

- Master Planner
- Senior Financial Analyst
- Proposal Analyst
- Senior Business Operations Manager
- Contracts Administrator
- Contracts Negotiator
- Business Operations Specialist
- Multifunction Financial Analyst
- Engineering Planner

Technology, Research, Design, and Development

The space industry is intensely immersed in science and technology. The term "rocket scientist" oversimplifies the vast array of technical disciplines and research areas but captures the essence of the mental makeup of people in these positions. In nonprofit research organizations, the research ranks may go from research engineer 1 to research engineer 2, senior research engineer, and principal research engineer, the latter being generally equivalent to the rank of a full professor in an academic institution. Many people in research departments hold doctoral degrees (Ph.D.s or D.Sc.s) in science and engineering disciplines, only a few of which deal with rockets or aircraft. Researchers in the space industry may come from the fields of electrical engineering, materials engineering, medicine, atmospheric sciences, chemistry, physics, astronomy, computer science, and economics, to name a few, in addition to aerospace and mechanical engineering.

Research and development jobs are exciting and provide nonstop challenges. People who go into such work enjoy solving technical problems. They enjoy a much greater degree of freedom to search for solutions than do systems engineers and others in more structured careers. Researchers are also expected to generate proposals for funding to pursue their ideas, a skill that is associated with businesspeople. Those interested in becoming researchers in the space enterprise should plan to acquire research education in a good university graduate research program before attempting to pursue such a career path.

The design function pervades the space industry at all levels. Each system is invariably designed to achieve better performance than was possible in prior systems, so every design requires innovation, risk taking, and problem solving. Design proceeds from analyzing market trends and from refining the definition of customer requirements. Trade studies are performed to arrive at a set of concepts for a system to be designed, followed by analyses to choose the best concept for that system. Modern design efforts are extremely complex and must go through several levels of risk assessment before any concept is chosen. Graphics and virtual-reality development skills are valuable in this line of work.

Mathematical optimization tools are used to arrive at optimal design solutions satisfying the constraints and weighting factors of various parameters. Detailed design follows, where different discipline groups take on analyses, computations, testing, and simulation activities covering the full life cycle of the system. As various test results come in, the design may have to go through several iterations, involving intense discussions and team activities to solve problems. Once the desired performance is shown to be achieved in simulations and testing, a detailed manufacturing process is organized, established, staffed, and implemented. The focus then shifts to efficient routine production, and the research and development teams move on to new opportunities.

Technology, research, design, and development occupations may include the following:

- Principal Research Engineer
- Senior Research Engineer
- Research Engineer
- Research Engineering Technician
- Principal Research Scientist
- Senior Research Scientist
- Research Scientist
- Research Technician

- Molecular Discovery/Development Analyst
- Scientific Systems Analyst
- Senior Staff Chemist
- Bioinformatics Software Developer

Engineering

Beyond research and development departments, engineering becomes somewhat more routine and involves a great deal of time spent in documentation and quality control using established operating procedures. For instance, the operations at Kennedy Space Center related to the space shuttle, carried out by industry teams with NASA oversight, depend on very detailed documentation to ensure the safety of the system. Senior engineer and senior systems analyst positions are below the director level. Below this level are systems engineers; test engineers; aerospace, mechanical, and electrical engineers; network engineers; logistics engineers; and other designations that vary from one organization to another. Integrating the massive number

OCCUPATION SPECIALTIES

Aerospace Engineers

Specialty	Responsibilities
Aerodynamists	Analyze the suitability and application of designs for aircraft and missiles. They also plan and evaluate the results of laboratory and flight-test programs.
Aeronautical design engineers	Develop basic design concepts used in the design, development, and production of aeronautical and aerospace products and systems.
Aeronautical drafters	Draft engineering drawings and other equipment and scale models of prototype aircraft that are planned by engineers.
Aeronautical engineers	Design, develop, and test aircraft, space vehicles, and missiles. They test models to study how they operate under a variety of conditions in order to make the equipment safe.
Aeronautical project engineers	Direct and coordinate activities of personnel who design systems and equipment for aeronautical and aerospace products.
Aeronautical research engineers	Conduct research in the field of aeronautics.
Aeronautical test engineers	Plan and supervise the performance testing of aerospace and aircraft products.
Field service engineers	Study performance reports on aircraft and recommend ways of eliminating the causes of flight and service problems in airplanes.
Stress analysts	Study the ability of airplanes, missiles, and components to withstand stress during flight.
Value engineers	Plan and coordinate engineering activities to develop and apply standardized production requirements for parts and equipment used in aircraft and aerospace vehicles.

of components of a space system and optimizing design and manufacturing to minimize life-cycle costs are the provinces of systems engineers, a title associated with a large number of positions. In addition to the reporting line of the engineering division, modern space companies also appoint technical fellows, who are engineers or scientists with doctoral degrees and distinguished records of achievement in the companies and the profession. Technical fellows are given large latitude in pursuing work of their choice in support of company objectives. They are expected to set new directions and develop methods to solve the difficult long-term technical challenges facing their companies.

Engineering occupations may include the following:

- Staff Aerospace Engineer
- Staff Electrical Engineer
- Staff Electronics Engineer
- Staff Mechanical Engineer
- Software Architect
- Project Engineer
- Staff Software Engineer
- Senior Staff Software Engineer
- Senior Programmer Analyst
- Staff Communications Systems Engineer
- Lead Engineering Staff Member
- Systems Engineer
- Chemical Engineer
- Construction Engineer
- Environmental Engineer
- Human Factors Engineer
- Materials Engineer
- Nuclear Engineer
- Reliability Engineer
- Safety Engineer
- System Safety Engineer
- Staff User Applications Analyst
- Integration Engineer

Manufacturing

A company's manufacturing operation is populated by production engineers, machinists, electri-

---

OCCUPATION PROFILE

Aerospace Engineer

Considerations	Qualifications
Description	Designs and develops spacecraft, satellites, and related equipment.
Career clusters	Manufacturing; Science, Technology, Engineering, and Math
Interests	Data; things
Working conditions	Work inside
Minimum education level	Bachelor's degree; master's degree; doctoral degree
Physical exertion	Light work
Physical abilities	Unexceptional/basic fitness
Opportunities for experience	Internship; apprenticeship; military service; part-time work
Licensure and certification	Required
Employment outlook	Average growth expected
Holland interest score	IRE

Note: See volume 1, "Publisher's Note," for an explanation of the Holland interest score.

cal technicians, materials engineers, and assembly-line technicians. Generally, manufacturing lot sizes are not large enough in the space industry to have fast-moving assembly lines. Thus, manufacturing assembly is performed by teams of technicians rather than by semiskilled assembly-line workers. In this process, many new problems are encountered that must be solved in collaboration between the technicians and the engineers present. Space industry components are expected to conform to an 80 percent learning curve, meaning that each time a product manufacture is implemented, the cost (mostly due to time spent) comes down to 80 percent of the previous cost.

Manufacturing occupations may include the following:

- Production Technician
- Quality Assurance Engineer/Analyst
- Manufacturing Engineer
- Engineering Planner
- Logistics Engineer/Analyst
- Industrial Engineer
- Multifunction Purchasing Manager
- Procurement Representative

Support Professionals

The diverse positions needed to keep the space industry moving are populated by staff systems integrators, information technology professionals, facilities/maintenance professionals, legal professionals, administrative and accounting associates, media contacts, graphics artists, machinist professionals, security officers, and custodial staff. Together they do everything from cleaning office spaces, to investigating and enforcing corporate intellectual property claims, to guarding entrances, to auditing corporate finances.

Support professionals may include the following:

- Graphic Artist
- Multimedia Design Engineer
- Training Representative
- Audiovisual Technician/Support Specialist
- Configuration Control Specialist
- Publication Coordinator
- Network Engineer
- Database Administrator
- Enterprise Architect

- Network Support Technician
- Security Officer

Human Resources

Success in recruiting, retaining, and nurturing some of the best innovators in the world takes a great deal of expertise. The space industry's workforce is very diverse, and the most talented workers come from all over the world and from different cultures. Barriers to competition from well-run foreign corporations and smaller and more nimble U.S. businesses are coming down. Thus, in the future, surviving large companies will likely devote more attention to the critical nature of human resources (HR) departments' leadership and policies, making it easier for new talent to come to the notice of knowledgeable company insiders and get recruited.

Human resources occupations may include the following:

- Human Resources Director
- Human Resources Manager
- Senior Life-Cycle Recruiter
- Administrative Representative
- Diversity Coordinator
- Employee Trainer
- Senior Training and Development Specialist
- Senior Labor Relations Representative
- Organization Development Analyst
- Senior Employment Representative
- Payroll Clerk
- Benefits Manager

External Services

Many interesting careers related to space are in organizations that monitor and analyze data. Examples are satellite ground monitoring stations, communications relay stations, astronomical observatories, ground-based radio telescope facilities, remote sensing data services, space debris monitoring, weather monitoring, and Global Positioning System satellite maintenance, as well as corresponding entities for the European Galileo system and the Russian Glonass systems. In the defense world, there are several areas of interest in satellite data analyses, early warning systems, and missile monitoring systems.

External service occupations may include the following:

- Remote Sensing Scientist
- Geographic Information System (GIS) Analyst
- Hydro and Ecological Management System Analyst
- Senior Imaging Scientist
- Hardware Engineer
- Software Developer
- Optical Engineer

INDUSTRY OUTLOOK

Overview

The outlook for this industry shows it to be on the rise. The space industry is still young and is undergoing a basic transformation from its military-dominated origins in the 1950's through the 1980's to a more open, global commercial industry. As recently as the late 1990's, there were optimistic projections of a "gold rush to orbit" based on demand for global positioning and satellite telephone constellations. However, with the collapse of the Iridium satellite telephone system and the economic decline following the September 11, 2001, terrorist attacks, commercial space-launch demand shrank. In 2002, the Walker Commission found that demand for commercial space launches was declining, partly because existing satellites were not failing and therefore did not need to be replaced and partly because new satellites could carry more transponders, so fewer satellites could perform more work. Launch costs per pound to Geostationary Transfer Orbit declined from $15,000 in 1990 to under $5,000 in 2002. The drastic reductions in workforce as military programs were reduced, combined with the failure of the early business models for commercial markets, resulted in reduced hiring and an increase in the average age of the technical workforce.

The Aldridge Commission of 2004 looked at human exploration and development of space, specifically at plans to return to the Moon, Mars, and beyond. The Constellation project, established in 2004, would have created new heavy-lift boosters, albeit with existing technology, enabling more satellites in low Earth orbit and heavier satellites in GEO, as well as possibly supporting lunar development opportunities. This project was essentially canceled in 2010. The new objectives being considered by NASA appear to emphasize commercial space-launch operations and increased science missions. Meanwhile, robotic and micro/nano space operations have continued to grow, boosted by the availability of a number of missile launchers that must be verifiably disposed of under nuclear arms reduction agreements.

The outlook for the global space industry is nonetheless bright, as capabilities improve around the world to access, inhabit, and develop resources in extraterrestrial environments. The newer space industries of China, India, Japan, and South America are investing heavily in both national and commercial space ventures. Whether this development leads to competition or collaboration, it bodes well for the future of the industry, as the resources and markets involved are potentially unlimited.

There are three distinct schools of thought regarding the future of the space economy. The first envisioned future is the closest to today's industry and involves incremental advances in propulsion systems, launch vehicles, and satellite-transponder technology as the growth path, constrained however by the difficulty of reducing launch costs. The second is born of the science enterprise and argues for investment in deep-space probes, observatories, and other exploration systems, including the mapping of asteroids and NEOs as generators of vital knowledge that can lead to many technological spin-offs. The third is born of the 1970's efforts to extract resources from beyond Earth, including solar power from space.

The quest to develop space solar power as a viable commodity has so far failed to break through the immense barriers in cost to create a working prototype, but international efforts by such entities as JAXA and the ESA continue to advance this dream. With evolutionary paths to space solar power being advanced, there is a real prospect of the barriers being circumvented, given international will and urgency.

Some breakthrough technologies are well within sight. "Reboost packages" developed under funding from the Defense Advanced Research Projects Agency (DARPA) have demonstrated the ability to rendezvous with GEO spacecraft nearing the end of their useful lives and renew their life spans by several years, reducing the insurance risk. As on-orbit-servicing technologies transition from the military to the commercial world, they will enable not only repair and refueling of satellites but also the creation of refuellable space-based orbit transfer vehicles. This will improve the payload fraction and reduce the need for redundant systems on many space launches. Thus, business models for the industry can improve substantially in the near future, driving demand for all sectors of the industry. Space tourism, while generating publicity, is likely to remain a niche market until costs come down and infrastructure in space expands greatly.

Current trends appear to involve NASA leaving the business of running routine space-access operations and instead focusing on science missions. Exploration missions to distant planets and asteroids appear destined to remain within the realm of government programs until there is a global move toward infrastructure development and collaborative planning of business ventures.

Employment Advantages

Space jobs are typically regarded as exciting, high-tech jobs that pay well and offer a good work environment. The prestige factor is high, starting from the Apollo program days and the public perception of "rocket scientists." This view was severely dented during the 1990's aerospace recession and simultaneous computer-industry boom. As the space industry shifts more toward commercial projects and the computer industry becomes more commoditized and outsourced, however, the trend may be reversed, returning prestige to the space industry. A good cross-disciplinary understanding of the demands of large space systems and of the intense quality demands of space products is a valuable by-product of working in the space industry. It can serve experienced workers well in founding their own businesses or transitioning to other technology businesses for advancement.

Annual Earnings

The civil and commercial portions of the space industry exceeded the government space establishment in expenditures for the first time in 1998, and since then nongovernment revenues have continued to climb. American space industry sales have grown from $29 billion in 1996 to an estimated $41 billion in 2010, though in real dollars they have stayed flat at $31 billion. Employment related to guided missiles, space vehicles, and parts dropped from approximately 76,500 in 2001 to a low of 70,000 in 2003, but it had climbed back up to 76,000 by the third quarter of 2009. The number of production workers in these areas climbed from below 19,000 in 2001 to over 47,000 in 2007. Sales of U.S. products related to space, excluding missiles, have remained relatively steady, near $40 billion per year, from 1994 to 2008. U.S. exports of civilian-sector spacecraft, satellites, and parts rose from $453 million in 2005 to a high of $811 million in 2007, then fell to $535 million in 2008. U.S. imports of such products ranged from $779 million in 2001 to a high of $960 million in 2007 to $668 million in 2009. With increasing global commercial space capabilities and competition, the earnings of this industry are poised for continued growth.

RELATED RESOURCES FOR FURTHER RESEARCH

AEROSPACE INDUSTRIES ASSOCIATION
  1000 Wilson Blvd., Suite 1700
  Arlington, VA 22209-3928
  Tel: (703) 358-1090
  Fax: (703) 358-1151
  http://www.aia-aerospace.org

AMERICAN INSTITUTE OF AERONAUTICS AND ASTRONAUTICS
  1801 Alexander Bell Dr., Suite 500
  Reston, VA 20191-4344
  Tel: (703) 264-7500
  Fax: (703) 264-7551
  http://www.aiaa.org

EIGHTH CONTINENT PROJECT
  Center for Space Resources
  Colorado School of Mines
  1310 Maple St.
  Golden, CO 80401
  Tel: (303) 384-2300
  Fax: (303) 384-2327
  http://www.8cproject.com

EUROPEAN SPACE AGENCY
  8/10 rue Mario Nikis
  75015 Paris
  France

Tel: 33-15-369-7654
Fax: 33-15-369-7560
http://www.esa.int

INSTITUTE OF ELECTRICAL AND ELECTRONICS
ENGINEERS
3 Park Ave., 17th Floor
New York, NY 10016-5997
Tel: (212) 419-7900
Fax: (212) 752-4929
http://www.ieee.org

NATIONAL AERONAUTICS AND SPACE
ADMINISTRATION
300 E St. SW
Washington, DC 20546-0001
Tel: (202) 358-1010
Fax: (202) 358-3469
http://www.nasa.gov

OFFICE OF SPACE COMMERCIALIZATION,
NATIONAL OCEANIC AND ATMOSPHERIC
ADMINISTRATION
6818 Herbert C. Hoover Bldg.
14th and Constitution Ave. NW
Washington, DC 20230
Tel: (202) 482-6125
Fax: (202) 482-4429
http://www.space.commerce.gov

SATELLITE INDUSTRY ASSOCIATION
1200 18th St. NW, Suite 1001
Washington, DC 20036
Tel: (202) 503-1560
Fax: (202) 503-1590
http://www.sia.org

SPACE STUDIES BOARD, THE NATIONAL
ACADEMIES
500 5th St. NW
Washington, DC 20001
Tel: (202) 334-3477
Fax: (202) 334-3701
http://sites.nationalacademies.org/SSB/
index.htm

SPACE.COM, SPACE LIBRARY
470 Park Ave. South, 9th Floor
New York, NY 10016
Tel: (212) 703-5801

Fax: (212) 703-5801
http://www.space.com/spacelibrary/

UNITED NATIONS OFFICE FOR OUTER SPACE
AFFAIRS
Wagramerstrasse 5
Vienna A-1220
Austria
Tel: 43-126-060 4950
Fax: 43-126-060 5830
http://www.oosa.unvienna.org

ABOUT THE AUTHOR

Narayanan M. Komerath is a professor of aerospace engineering at the Georgia Institute of Technology. He has taught aerospace engineering subjects, including aerodynamics and aerospace propulsion, for more than twenty-five years. He directs the John J. Harper wind tunnel and research programs in experimental aerodynamics, fluid mechanics, and advanced space concepts. He is an associate fellow of the American Institute of Aeronautics and Astronautics and a fellow of NASA's Institute of Advanced Concepts. In 2004, he served as a Boeing Welliver Summer Faculty Fellow and as an invited witness before the Presidential Commission on Implementation of United States Space Exploration Policy. He has also served as a senior fellow of the Sam Nunn Center for International Security, Technology, and Policy since 2004.

FURTHER READING

Aldridge, Edward C., et al. *A Journey to Inspire, Innovate, and Discover: Report of the President's Commission on Implementation of United States Space Exploration Policy.* Washington, D.C.: Government Printing Office, 2004.

Augustine, Norman R., et al. *Seeking a Human Spaceflight Program Worthy of a Great Nation.* Washington, D.C.: National Aeronautics and Space Administration, 2009.

Borrelli, Carmine, et al. *The Space Industry.* Ft. Belvoir, Va.: Defense Technical Information Center, 2007.

Collins, P., and A. Autino. "What the Growth of a Space Tourism Industry Could Contribute to

Employment, Economic Growth, Environmental Protection, Education, Culture, and World Peace." *Acta Astronautica* 66, nos. 11/12 (June/July, 2010): 1553-1562.

Commercial Space Transportation Study Alliance. *Commercial Space Transportation Study.* Washington, D.C.: National Aeronautics and Space Administration, 1997. Available at http://www.hq.nasa.gov/webaccess/CommSpaceTrans.

Federal Aviation Administration. Office of the Associate Administrator for Commercial Space Transportation. *The Economic Impact of Commercial Space Transportation on the U.S. Economy: 2002 Results and Outlook for 2010.* Springfield, Va.: National Technical Information Service, 2004.

Greenberg, Joel S., and Henry R. Hertzfeld, eds. *Space Economics.* Progress in Astronautics and Aeronautics 144. Washington, D.C.: American Institute of Aeronautics and Astronautics, 1992.

Gunther, Jocelyn S. *Commercial Space Transportation.* Hauppauge, N.Y.: Nova Science, 2010.

Jasentuliyana, Nandasiri, ed. *Space Law: Development and Scope.* Westport, Conn.: Praeger, 1992.

Komerath, N. M., J. Nally, and E. Taing. "Policy Model for Space Economy Infrastructure." *Acta Astronautica* 61, nos. 11/12 (December, 2007): 1066-1075.

Lamassoure, E., J. H. Saleh, and D. E. Hastings. "Space Systems Flexibility Provided by On-Orbit Servicing: Part 2." *Journal of Spacecraft and Rockets* 39, no. 4 (2002): 561-570.

Lewis, J. S., and R. A. Lewis. *Space Resources: Breaking the Bonds of Earth.* New York: Columbia University Press, 1987.

Longuski, Jim. *Advice to Rocket Scientists: A Career Survival Guide for Scientists and Engineers.* Reston, Va.: American Institute of Aeronautics and Astronautics, 2004.

National Research Council. *Defending Planet Earth: Near-Earth Object Surveys and Hazard Mitigation Strategies.* Washington, D.C.: National Academies Press, 2010.

_____. *An Enabling Foundation for NASA's Earth and Space Science Missions.* Washington, D.C.: National Academies Press, 2010.

Nicogaossian, Arnauld E., and Joseph H. Rothenburg. *Commercial Development Plan for the International Space Station: Final Draft.* Washington, D.C.: National Aeronautics and Space Administration, 1998.

U.S. Bureau of Labor Statistics. *Career Guide to Industries,* 2010-2011 ed. http://www.bls.gov/oco/cg.

U.S. Census Bureau. North American Industry Classification System (NAICS), 2007. http://www.census.gov/cgi-bin/sssd/naics/naicsrch?chart=2007.

U.S. Department of Commerce. International Trade Administration. Office of Trade and Industry Information. Industry Trade Data and Analysis. http://ita.doc.gov/td/industry/otea/OTII/OTII-index.html.

U.S. National Aeronautics and Space Administration. NASA History Office. "The Decision to Go to the Moon: President John F. Kennedy's May 25, 1961 Speech before a Joint Session of Congress." http://history.nasa.gov/moondec.html.

Walker, Robert Smith, et al. *Anyone, Anywhere, Anytime, Anything: Final Report of the Commission on the Future of the United States Aerospace Industry.* Arlington, Va.: Commission on the Future of the Aerospace Industry, 2002.

Zubrin, R. *Entering Space: Creating a Spacefaring Civilization.* New York: Tarcher, 1999.

Spectator Sports Industry

©Berlinfoto/Dreamstime.com

INDUSTRY SNAPSHOT

General Industry: Sports
Career Cluster: Business, Management, and Administration
Subcategory Industries: Independent Athletes; Racetracks; Sports Agents; Sports Promoters; Sports Teams and Clubs
Related Industries: Apparel and Fashion Industry; Broadcast Industry; Motion Picture and Television Industry; Sports Equipment Industry
Annual Domestic Revenues: $31.3 billion USD (U.S. Census Bureau, 2008)
NAICS Number: 7112-7114

INDUSTRY DEFINITION

Summary

The spectator sports industry comprises professional, semiprofessional, amateur, and tournament sports that are conducted live before a paying audience. It includes high-profile sports leagues such as the National Football League (NFL) and Major League Baseball (MLB), as well as horse, dog, and car racing. Participants in the industry include owners, athletes, trainers, managers, coaches, promoters, referees, and administrators, as well as groundskeepers and facility managers.

History of the Industry

The history of sports and games dates back to ancient times. Artifacts of an ancient Egyptian board game called enet have been extracted from pyramids, and the game's origin has been traced back to 3000 B.C.E. Likewise, Egyptians were fond of sporting competitions that involved running, jumping, and fighting. Egyptian wall paintings from around 1850 B.C.E. depict a wrestling competition that involves techniques still used by wrestlers today.

The ancient Greeks epitomized a culture obsessed with the human form and the pursuit of physical perfection. Competitive sport was a feature of many Greek religious and social ceremonies, and the Greeks constructed sporting arenas that were designed for spectator viewing. They also inaugurated the first sporting competition at Olympia in 776 B.C.E., founding a tradition that continued to be observed every four years for more than a millennium. The Olympic Games' schedule would eventually be expanded from a singular running race to include sports such as javelin, discus, chariot racing, wrestling, boxing, and the pentathlon (featuring five events). The Olympics were outlawed in 393 C.E. by the Romans, but after a fifteen-hundred-year hiatus the modern Olympic Games were founded in 1896, continuing the tradition of sporting competition among the world's elite athletes.

Horse racing also dates back to ancient times, when people held chariot races, jousted, and played a team game that was a predecessor of polo. The modern concept of horse racing, however, can be traced to England in the 1600's, when it found favor with King Charles II and the English aristocracy. The sport popularized gambling and formalized the concept of pedigree in animal breeding. In fact, some scholars contend that the fascination with genealogy in horse racing has roots in English aristocrats' obsession with their own lineage.

Modern sport, with standardized rules and regulations, began evolving in the 1800's in Europe as schools increasingly mandated sports in their curricula. At the same time, advances in transportation technology facilitated sporting competitions between villages and towns, and an increasing proportion of the population moved to large cities, where it became easier to form sporting leagues.

Over time, standardized rules and faster, cheaper travel made it possible to conduct national and international sporting competitions.

The development of spectator sports as an industry has been accelerated by communication technologies that make sports accessible to increasingly large audiences. Today, revenue generated from ticket sales and concession spending is dwarfed by the revenue generated from broadcasting rights, merchandising, advertising, and sponsorships. Consequently, sport in the United States and around the world has become big business. In fact, since the 1920's, when expenditures in the spectator sports industry were first tracked in the United States, the industry has seen rapid growth. From 1920 to 1930 alone, spending on spectator sports more than doubled, from $30 to $65 million. In the 1990's, spending was estimated at more than $11 billion.

The Industry Today

Sport cuts across national boundaries and demographics and is no less woven into the contemporary cultural fabric than it was woven into that of

Misters cool fans watching a baseball training game in Scottsdale, Arizona. (AP/Wide World Photos)

the ancient Greeks. Moreover, as a form of entertainment and recreation, sport is incredibly multifaceted. It accommodates players and managers from amateur to professional levels, and it offers a wide variety of allied pursuits, not least of which are gambling and spectating.

The 2004 Summer Olympics in Athens, Greece, made history when television broadcasts of the competition were viewed by 3.9 billion people worldwide. They generated over thirty-five thousand hours of broadcast viewing spread across thousands of stations. In the United States, 203 million people—nearly 70 percent of the population—watched at least some part of the games. The 2008 Summer Olympics in Beijing, China, comprised more than 302 events involving around ten thousand competitors, and they were covered by 24,500 media representatives from fifty-nine countries. Audience demand for the Olympics has grown strongly, if the increase in supply is any indication. Measured by the number of broadcast hours dedicated to Olympic events, there was a 27 percent increase in the supply of Olympic coverage between 1992 and 2004.

In the United States, the spectator sports industry employs roughly 138,700 people, of whom 9,380 are professional athletes. The other leading occupations in the industry include office and administrative support; service and guest attendance (ticket takers, ushers, and so on); food preparation and service; maintenance and repair; security services; transportation and freight; general and operations management; coaching and training; and business support (human resources, convention planning, accounting, auditing, and so on).

In 2009, the combined Big Four leagues—the NFL, the National Basketball Association (NBA), the National Hockey League (NHL), and MLB—accounted for an estimated annual revenue of $17.8 billion, according to Plunkett Research. Other significant spectator sporting leagues in the United States include the National Association for Stock Car Auto Racing (NASCAR), Indy Car, the Professional Golfers Association (PGA), the National Collegiate Athletic Association (NCAA), and Major League Soccer (MLS). Growing profes-

Horse racing is a popular sport, with well-attended events such as the Kentucky Derby. (©Dreamstime.com)

NASCAR fans often arrive before race day, camping in recreational vehicles in the parking lot. (AP/Wide World Photos)

sional sports subsectors include previously marginal sports such as motocross, skateboarding, monster trucks, aerobatics, and poker. Amateur and semiprofessional sports also create strong spectator demand. Some of these include cycling, poker, bowling, bodybuilding, beach volleyball, rodeo riding, figure skating, and rally-car racing.

Today, the majority of spectator sports revenue is generated from the sale of broadcasting and sponsorship rights. If a league engages in a profit-sharing business model, it distributes league-generated revenues among its franchisees. Coupled with salary caps that limit the earning potential of players, this arrangement can make franchise ownership incredibly profitable. However, statistics belie the vast scope of the disparity between the richest and the poorest sectors of the industry. In competitive leagues that do not engage in profit sharing, teams and individuals must privately fund their enterprises, and they must do so in an economy where consumer, sponsor, and investment spending can contract in response to economic downturns. As highlighted by the 2007-2009 global financial crisis and its economic impact on consumer spending, contracting spending in professional sports is a relatively new paradigm in an industry that has enjoyed decades of skyrocketing growth.

The spectator sports industry is undergoing a transformation in the early twenty-first century, as teams and their governing bodies diversify their business interests. Likewise, the industry is coming to terms with new technologies and how these may change the way in which spectators view and interact with sports and sporting events. Some examples include online fantasy leagues, video gaming, digital television, and Internet video streaming. The domestic spectator sports industry is also challenged by questions of how best to market its products to potential international and foreign audiences.

The sports agency field is dominated by IMG Worldwide, which manages professional athletes, coaches, celebrities, and events. Demonstrating the high value placed on sports managers and promoters in the industry, the career tournament earnings of Tiger Woods (the world's highest-paid athlete in the early twenty-first century) were overshadowed by the $500 million he earned from endorsements and other activities. Other leading sports agencies include Octagon Worldwide, BDA Sports Management, and the William Morris Agency.

INDUSTRY MARKET SEGMENTS

The spectator sports industry consists of organizations that range in size from individual athletes and agents operating as sole proprietors to multinational corporations. The following sections provide a more comprehensive breakdown of each of these segments. The average spectator sports organization employs only twenty-eight people. Such organizations often rely on a number of external business providers to coordinate and execute their complex operations. Individuals with career aspirations in the spectator sports industry should also not overlook opportunities in the amateur sports sector, which involves athletic associations and regulatory and governing bodies. The amateur sports sector offers participants valuable experience in sports administration, athletic talent identification and development, tournament and event coordination, and sports marketing.

Small Businesses

A small spectator sports business can have as few as one employee or as many as fifty. Annual revenues for small businesses range from $10,000 to $1 million or more, depending on the circumstances. While athletes in some sports are unionized, in other sports they operate as sole proprietors. Their earnings depend on their salary, competition winnings, and endorsements. Likewise, some agents, promoters, and event coordinators may operate as independent, sole proprietors. Some spectator sports also provide unique opportunities for small teams and individuals to compete alongside larger organizations. Sports such as racing are more accommodating of smaller teams than are leagues that require the acquisition of expensive franchises.

Small business opportunities in very high profile team sports such as the Big Four leagues tend to be limited, although independent opportunities may exist for highly experienced or qualified specialists, including coaches, trainers, agents, marketers, and event coordinators. Individuals seeking direct involvement in sports operations may find that horse, dog, and car racing represent some of the easier subsectors for small-business owners to gain entry. Horse racing syndicates, for example, work by grouping individual investors together to form small companies. The companies then purchase horses and pay to care for, maintain, and train the animals, as well as to enter them in competitions. The investors share any race winnings.

NASCAR is composed of a cluster of small teams whose sole desire is to qualify for races to receive a share of the winnings that are awarded to all competitors, including those in last place. These teams are colloquially known as "start-and-park" teams because, having qualified, they retire from qualifying races early so as to reduce their operating costs and to protect their vehicles from potential damage. These teams are very small. Such teams generally consist of one or two owner-operators, a hauler driver, a small team of mechanics, and a contract driver. In most cases, they do not employ a pit crew or any engineers. A start-and-park team can win over $1 million per season without ever finishing an entire race. The operation does, however, entail considerable risk and demand substantial working capital.

In some sports, small organizations can be very profitable, while in others small-business owners are considered hobbyists. They derive enjoyment from their business ventures but do not realize viable incomes from them. Sports memorabilia and collectibles trading, for example, attracts many small-business owners who utilize Web-based trading sites such as eBay to run full- or part-time businesses from home.

Potential Annual Earnings Scale. According to PayScale.com, the median annual salary for an athlete working as an amateur independent contractor in 2009 was $42,250, with a salary range of $25,000 to $73,500. The median salary for a business specialist in a small sports business was $35,500. This figure represents the aggregated salaries of team agents, account executives, athletic trainers, marketing managers and coordinators, administrative assistants, and event coordinators. Self-employed people in the spectator sports industry earn a median income of $53,500, while self-employed sports and celebrity agents earn a median income of $87,500. According to the U.S. Department of Labor, the average annual wage for sports teams and clubs in 2007 was $181,384.

Clientele Interaction. In the spectator sports industry, a company's clientele consists of a broader range of stakeholders than is associated with traditional businesses, in which customers exchange payment for products or services. In addition to direct paying customers (such as fans who buy game tickets and merchandise or athletes who pay agents for representation), the industry's clients can include any stakeholders with a direct or indirect interest in an organization's performance, including sponsors, investors, fans, and supporters.

Small-business owners and their employees are likely to be required to fulfill multiple roles within the business, including promotions, financial management and accounting, contract management, and administration. Many small sports businesses are also likely to require professional assistance from contractors, such as accountants, lawyers, and publicists, as well as specific technical specialists. A small horse-racing syndicate, for example, may outsource its training, jockeying, handling, and veterinary requirements, while a small NASCAR team may outsource its engineering needs. Interaction with investors, sponsors, owners, and other stakeholders is likely to be exceptionally high in the small business sector.

Amenities, Atmosphere, and Physical Grounds. Some small sports companies own or lease commercial space, while others are home based. Small sports businesses can avoid the expense of purchasing or renting real estate in high-traffic areas with street frontage because they do not generally market to consumers. Likewise, the overall quality of amenities offered by a business is predicated upon the organization's budget and its stakeholders' expectations. Where equipment, tools, or sensitive materials or information are involved, secure facilities are required. Small sports agencies and management firms are likely to require professional office space, although self-employed agents and consultants may elect to work from home. Their office arrangements need to present a professional and successful appearance, commensurate with the caliber of the athletes they represent.

One of the common issues facing small-business owners is the cost of overhead. While larger companies are able to defray their overhead costs across larger operations, small businesses' operating expenses can take up a significant proportion of their income. For this reason, small-business owners must attempt to minimize expenses by, for example, working from a home office, hiring the minimum number of employees, leasing affordable space, maximizing tax benefits, outsourcing nonessential services, and reducing energy and equipment costs. Sports that require expensive equipment and ongoing operating costs demand significant capital investment and financial resources.

Typical Number of Employees. Small spectator sports businesses consist of between one and approximately fifty employees.

Traditional Geographic Locations. With technological advances in transportation and communication, location is becoming less relevant to sports businesses. Small-business owners, however, need to establish their businesses in locations that reduce their overall running costs. For example, when the Team Valor International horse racing syndicate moved its administrative operations from California to Kentucky, it achieved closer contact with its horse handlers and trainers and was able to reduce the size of its administrative team and office space. This allowed Team Valor to reduce its costs and improve its client interactions. NASCAR is associated with North Carolina, and the vast majority of NASCAR teams are headquartered within a 40-mile radius of Charlotte. Independent athletes may be able to choose their locations, but many elect to base themselves where quality coaching and training facilities are readily available.

Sporting organizations that utilize Internet and other communication technologies, or those that have minimal face-to-face interaction with their clients or service providers, may find that their choice of location is much wider than those of companies that use dedicated sporting facilities. Online horse racing syndicates, for example, allow investors to influence training and management decisions through e-mail and online voting.

Pros of Working for a Small Spectator Sports Business. The owner of a spectator sports company or agency can experience a great deal of independence and autonomy. Such owners are literally their own bosses, so they can set their own work hours and conditions and formulate their own strategies for performance. This ability may especially appeal to seasoned professionals who have many years of experience coupled with the expertise to apply skills and methods learned at a larger organization to a leaner, more tightly focused operation. Small-business employees are also likely to gain well-rounded experience across all parts of an operation.

Cons of Working for a Small Spectator Sports Business. For small-business owners, autonomy and independence come with the vast responsibilities of running a small business. They are responsible for revenue generation, as well as for ensuring that their companies fulfill their legal and regulatory obligations. Where there is potential reward there is also potential risk, and owner-operators assume total responsibility for their organizations' financial performance and viability.

While these principles are true in any type of small business, the stakes are heightened in the spectator sports industry because both success and failure can occur in a much more public fashion than in other industries. Small organizations may often have to compete against bigger companies that have greater financial, human, and technical resources. Competitiveness in spectator sports does not stop at the end of the game. Businesses must also vie off the field for funding, sponsorship, talent, and other limited business resources.

Depending on the type of business, the initial capital investment of a sports organization may be considerable, especially when expensive equipment, technology, infrastructure, or frequent travel is required. While small-business owners are able to set their own work conditions, many find that they need to work long hours to realize profits. It is also likely that they will assume a very significant level of personal financial risk.

Costs

Payroll and Benefits: Small businesses pay an hourly wage or annual salary, depending on the position. Sports businesses customarily pay bonuses based on winnings or on specific performance benchmarks agreed to in advance. Benefits such as vacation and sick days, health insurance, and 401(k) plans are offered at the discretion of the business owner.

Supplies: Various types of sports businesses require office supplies and equipment, including computers, telephones, copiers, and so on; sporting equipment; training equipment, such as weights and gym machines; and mobile communications devices, such as smart phones or pagers.

External Services: Small sports businesses may contract computing support, equipment and tool maintenance, security, groundskeeping, or cleaning services, as well as renting post office boxes. They may also engage professional accountants, lawyers, tax professionals, or advertising and marketing services. Some companies may also elect to outsource technical services such as engineering, veterinary services, design, and logistics.

Utilities: Typical utilities include electricity, air-conditioning, heating, water, telephone, and Internet access.

Taxes: State and federal taxes are payable according to business revenue. Self-employed individuals must pay self-employment tax, and those who own office space may need to pay property taxes.

Midsize Businesses

A midsize business in the spectator sports industry can have as little as fifty or as many as five hundred employees. Annual revenues of such businesses generally range from $1 million to hundreds of millions of dollars.

Potential Annual Earnings Scale. According to the NFL Players Association, the average NFL player's annual salary is $1.1 million. The average nonathlete salary in midsize spectator sports organizations, however, ranges from $41,700 to $47,600. Most professional spectator sports teams fall in the midsize range, although most of these organizations rely heavily on external business support services, especially in areas such as grounds and facility maintenance, security, waste management, catering, and remediation services, as well as in professional areas concerning legal matters and advertising.

Clientele Interaction. With increasing size comes an opportunity for employees to specialize in certain organizational functions. Simultaneously, midsize businesses benefit from greater economies of scale that free up owners and managers to work as leaders of the business rather than as key producers. A professional spectator sports team, for example, employs around three hundred people, who are organized into professional categories such as athletes, coaches, administrators, sports operations staff, business operations staff, and stadium operations staff. This structure affords employees strong opportunities for specialization, while the manageable size of these organizations allows management to remain in contact with daily business operations.

Amenities, Atmosphere, and Physical Grounds. Sporting organizations require facilities appropriate to their specific activities. They generally own or lease dedicated space that also forms their headquarters or home. An increasing number of teams and leagues own or control their own stadiums as well, but many lease stadiums, racetracks, or other venues from independent or public owners. The leasing arrangement dictates how revenue from ticket sales is distributed.

With increasing professionalism in spectator sports over the last few decades, sports organizations have built and developed increasingly state-of-the-art training, playing, and administration facilities, usually in prime locations. Many organizations design their facilities with the experience of fans and supporters in mind. Many provide supporters with opportunities to tour their facilities and to feel a sense of interaction with the team. The facilities and amenities demanded of spectator sports often make industry entry extremely expensive. Many leagues also operate on a franchise system, which severely limits entry opportunities and increases the cost of the few that exist.

Typical Numbers of Employees. Midsize spectator sports businesses consist of between approximately fifty and five hundred employees.

Traditional Geographic Locations. In professional spectator sporting leagues, location is often defined by a team franchise agreement. Sporting teams are generally tied to a specific city, town, or state. In other sports—such as motor racing, for example—location may be more flexible because audience loyalties tend to be tied to team or driver identities that are not necessarily linked to specific geographic locations.

Pros of Working for a Midsize Spectator Sports Business. Employees of a midsize spectator sports organization may enjoy greater career advancement opportunities than their peers working in a small business, depending on the sport. The midsize sector offers opportunities to gain supervisory and management experience and to work in a very professional environment that provides exposure to a range of sports management areas. In fact, many midsize sporting businesses are world-class organizations.

Employees in this sector may also benefit from receiving exposure to other functional areas of the operation, as well as formal training. Employees

motivated to seek social recognition may find satisfaction and pride in working in an industry that has a high public profile. For people who thrive on fast-paced, high-pressure work, the midsize spectator sports sector may provide relentless daily and weekly deadlines, constant pressures, and unyielding performance scrutiny. In certain careers within the industry, remuneration can be extremely lucrative.

Cons of Working for a Midsize Spectator Sports Business. In keeping with the competitive nature of sports generally, the administrative and operational environments within sporting organizations can be extremely competitive. This atmosphere often fosters a work culture that expects higher-than-usual levels of company loyalty, including evening and weekend work. Employees may find that success hinges on working long hours and making themselves highly accessible to their companies. This lifestyle may not suit employees who value work-life balance or who have other commitments. The competitive nature of professional sports can also manifest as job insecurity. While remuneration for some jobs may be extremely lucrative, one must keep in mind that careers in professional spectator sports (both athlete and nonathlete jobs) can be demanding and short.

Costs

Payroll and Benefits: Midsize businesses pay an hourly wage or a salary depending on the type of work. As is customary with competitive sports environments, positions in this industry are likely to provide bonuses and commissions. Benefits such as vacation and sick days, health insurance, and 401(k) plans are offered at the discretion of the business owner, although most employees receive comprehensive compensation and benefits packages.

Supplies: Various types of sports businesses require office supplies and equipment, including computers, telephones, copiers, and so on; sporting equipment; training equipment, such as weights and gym machines; and mobile communications devices, such as smart phones or pagers. In addition, stadium-based teams require supplies related to operation and upkeep of their stadiums, including tickets, food-related supplies, and equipment necessary for field upkeep.

External Services: Midsize sports businesses may engage business support services such as computing, bookkeeping, equipment and tool maintenance, security, groundskeeping, and janitorial services. They may also engage external professional experts such as accountants and tax professionals, as well as advertising and marketing companies (including merchandise design and manufacturing). Some companies may also elect to outsource technical services such as engineering, veterinary services, design, and logistics.

Utilities: Typical utilities include electricity, air-conditioning, heating, water, telephone, and Internet access. For teams with stadiums, these expenses can be significant.

Taxes: State and federal taxes are payable according to business revenue. Businesses also need to pay applicable property and other taxes. A sports team, however, may be exempt from paying property taxes on its stadium as a condition of its contract with a city or state. Franchises often negotiate such contracts with governments that benefit from their presence.

Large Businesses

A large spectator sports business has between approximately five hundred and five thousand employees, with annual revenues of up to hundreds of millions of dollars. Some of the largest spectator sporting organizations in the world, such as McLaren Formula One and Manchester City Football Club (both in the United Kingdom), employ around six hundred people each.

The largest organizations in the spectator sports sector are mainly global sports promotion and management agencies. IMG Worldwide employs around three thousand people globally, while Octagon Worldwide employs around one thousand people in sixty countries. Octagon claims to represent over one thousand athletes, personalities, sporting franchises, and corporate sponsors and to organize around five thousand sporting events annually. Octagon athletes earned twenty-two gold medals at the 2008 Olympic Games in Beijing, and Octagon managed many of the Olympics' largest corporate sponsors. Octagon is owned by the publicly listed company Interpublic Group of Companies, which also owns other leading marketing and advertising agencies, such as Jack Morton Worldwide. Jack Morton produced the 2004 Olympic Games' opening and closing ceremonies. Interpublic's combined advertising and marketing businesses employ more than ten thousand people and have annual revenues of more than $6 billion.

Potential Annual Earnings Scale. Players and managers lead the earnings in this industry. The average nonathlete salary in large spectator sports organizations ranges from $42,500 to $64,000 per year. In the sports agency sector, the average nonathlete salary range is $51,400 to $65,000. According to the U.S. Department of Labor, the average annual wage for sports teams and clubs in 2007 was $181,384.

Clientele Interaction. Employees' level of client interaction in large businesses very much depends on their role. One of the advantages of large businesses is that those who seek career advancement without sacrificing client interaction have an opportunity to advance into key operations, account management, or senior relationship-management roles. Those who prefer less client interaction have an opportunity to advance into other management and executive positions. The large size of such businesses, however, makes it generally likely that senior and executive employees will experience less client interaction than do associate-level staff.

Owners and managers of large companies are not expected to be key producers. Their role is to provide strategic direction that maintains company performance and shareholder favor and to ensure that the company adheres to its legal and fiduciary obligations. Employees of large businesses experience less pressure to fulfill multiple job roles, and they have greater opportunities to specialize in niche areas. They are required, however, to adhere strictly to company policies and procedures. Corporate culture is also likely to entail committee-based decision making, as well as complex organizational hierarchies.

Amenities, Atmosphere, and Physical Grounds. Sporting organizations require facilities appropriate to their specific activities. Generally speaking, very large sporting organizations have world-class facilities. McLaren Formula One's facility in the United Kingdom, for example, mirrors the high level of engineering mastery found in the design of its race cars. Large sports agencies operate mainly from high-quality office spaces. These environments are highly professional and aligned with well-developed corporate cultures. Firms such as IMG and Octagon are also becoming increasingly involved in athletic talent identification, testing, and development, which demand dedicated athletic and sporting facilities.

Typical Numbers of Employees. Large spectator sports businesses consist of between approximately five hundred and five thousand employees.

Traditional Geographic Locations. In professional spectator sporting leagues, location is often defined by a team franchise agreement. Sporting teams are generally tied to specifics cities, towns, or states. Sports management and promotional agencies tend to be located in large cities from which they can service large numbers of clients and stakeholders.

Pros of Working for a Large Spectator Sports Corporation. Employees of large companies enjoy significant career-advancement opportunities that come from working within a highly structured organization. Such opportunities may include promotion into management, horizontal career progression into a different field or area of operations, national and overseas relocation, and professional specialism. Working for a large company is also likely to ensure exposure to leading-edge technologies, access to thought leaders in the industry, formal and on-the-job training, professional certifications, and other education opportunities. Job stability may also be greater at a larger company than at a smaller one.

Corporate culture can be highly appealing to some people. While corporate culture is often associated with long work hours, employees may experience fewer work and performance pressures in large spectator sports organizations than at midsize ones because their involvement with the company's core operations may be more peripheral. A design engineer working at McLaren Formula One, for example, is one of around 150 engineers working in a highly structured, hierarchical environment. An engineer on a midsize NASCAR team, on the other hand, is one of approximately 20 engineers in a much flatter organizational structure.

Cons of Working for a Large Spectator Sports Corporation. While layers of management and highly developed corporate culture may serve to alleviate some of the work pressures experienced in the small and midsize sectors, employees of large companies can become stuck in peripheral jobs that do not satisfy their desire for close involvement with a wide variety of team operations and clients. By comparison, smaller organizations provide employees with better opportunities to gain experience in a wider array of functions.

People who prefer high levels of personal contact with their clients or in operations—or who like to work autonomously, make their own decisions, do things their own way, express their individuality, and become involved across an entire organization—may find highly structured corporate environments stifling. The complexity of large business, moreover, can be vexing for individuals who are frustrated by committee-style decision making and authority structures. Those who rise to senior management positions are likely to spend an increasing amount of their time involved in business strategy, people management, and administration and less time working on the technical specifics of the sport.

Costs

Payroll and Benefits: Large businesses pay an hourly wage or a salary depending on the type of work. As is customary with competitive sports environments, positions in this industry are likely to provide bonuses and commissions. Large companies are more likely than smaller ones to offer above-average compensation and benefits packages, including vacation and sick days, health insurance, and 401(k) plans.

Supplies: Various types of sports businesses require office supplies and equipment, including computers, telephones, copiers, and so on; sporting equipment; training equipment, such as weights and gym machines; and mobile communications devices, such as smart phones or pagers. In addition, stadium-based teams require supplies related to operation and upkeep of their stadiums, including tickets, food-related supplies, and equipment necessary for field upkeep.

External Services: Large sports businesses may engage business support services such as computing, bookkeeping, equipment and tool maintenance, security, groundskeeping, and janitorial services. They may also engage external professional experts such as accountants and tax professionals, as well as advertising and marketing companies (including merchandise design and

OCCUPATION SPECIALTIES

Sports Instructors/Coaches

Specialty	Responsibilities
Coaches of professional athletes	Work with groups of paid professional athletes and paid assistant coaches. Their duties often include not only game preparation and game coaching but also recruiting, assessing, and selecting new professional talent.
Head coaches	Work with groups of athletes through subordinate assistant coaches.
Physical instructors	Work with individuals and small groups in beginning or advanced exercises for reducing weight or improving health.

manufacturing). Some companies may also elect to outsource technical services such as engineering, veterinary services, design, and logistics.

Utilities: Typical utilities include electricity, airconditioning, heating, water, telephone, and Internet access.

Taxes: State and federal taxes are payable according to business revenue. Businesses also need to pay applicable property and other taxes. A sports team, however, may be exempt from paying property taxes on its stadium as a condition of its contract with a city or state. Franchises often negotiate such contracts with governments that benefit from their presence. International companies may face complex taxation structures, as they need to pay applicable taxes in multiple countries.

ORGANIZATIONAL STRUCTURE AND JOB ROLES

Any company in the spectator sports industry must account for activities in the following areas. In smaller companies, one person often holds several roles within several groups. In larger companies, specialists fulfill unique requirements in specific groups. Regardless of size and scope, the functions must be fulfilled. The spectator sports industry also demands a wide range of different technical specialties.

The following umbrella categories apply to the organizational structure of businesses in the spectator sports industry:

- Athletes and Coaches
- Referees and Officials
- Business Management
- Team Operations
- Event Operations
- Sales and Marketing
- Administration
- Information Technology
- Facilities and Grounds
- Security
- Human Resources
- Health Care and Medical
- Entertainment
- Transportation and Logistics
- Professional Services

Athletes and Coaches

Athletes, coaches, and trainers fulfill a sports organization's core function. Coaches are responsible for managing a team or athlete's performance, while athletes are responsible for executing the strategies and tactics developed by (or in consultation with) their coaching staff. While these jobs may appear glamorous, they are regularly characterized by grueling physical, mental, and emotional demands. Professional coaching and player salaries are extremely attractive (the average NFL player earns $1.1 million a season), but these are high-pressure, highly competitive jobs, and relatively few are available for the number of people competing for them. Playing and coaching careers are subject to the vagaries of success and loss, as well as uncontrollable factors such as injury. The average NFL player's career, for example, is only three years long.

Athletes and coaches must also manage the pressures of dealing with the public and media. Players and coaches are the public face of their organizations, and they have the potential to become public figures in their own right. Invasion of privacy and public scrutiny can create additional psychological and emotional pressures.

Athlete positions do not generally require formal education, although many professional athletes develop their playing ability through collegiate sports. Coaching staff are increasingly required to possess formal coaching and physical training qualifications.

Athlete and coaching occupations may include the following:

- Athlete
- Player
- Driver
- Jockey
- Pit Crew Member
- Coach
- Trainer
- Personal Trainer

Referees and Officials

Referees and officials oversee, or officiate, the conduct of play according to the rules and codes of their sports. Officiating is an increasingly high pressure role, given the large amounts of money and the high stakes riding on sports results—not only for the vying teams, their fans, and their sponsors but also for gamblers and the gambling industry. As a

---

OCCUPATION PROFILE

Athletic Trainer

Considerations	Qualifications
Description	Works with amateur and professional athletes to help prevent, evaluate, and treat injuries, as well as ensure that formerly injured athletes are ready to play.
Career cluster	Health Science
Interests	People; things
Working conditions	Work outside; work both inside and outside
Minimum education level	Bachelor's degree
Physical exertion	Medium work
Physical abilities	Unexceptional/basic fitness
Opportunities for experience	Internship; apprenticeship; volunteer work
Licensure and certification	Required
Employment outlook	Faster-than-average growth expected
Holland interest score	SRE

Note: See volume 1, "Publisher's Note," for an explanation of the Holland interest score.

result, many sports have introduced off-field media referees, video reviewing, and other technologies that assist referees to make accurate rulings.

In some sports, referees and officials are contracted as full-time employees, while in other sports they are part time. This difference in status is generally reflected in their remuneration. The NBA, the NHL, and MLB offer their full-time referees salaries of more than $100,000 per year, whereas part-time professional referees may expect payments ranging between $25,000 and $70,000 per season. The national average annual salary for early-career referees and officials, including amateur and professional sports, is $23,500 to $50,800. Entry into this career is extremely competitive.

Referee and official occupations may include the following:

- Referee
- Umpire
- Line Judge
- Field Judge
- Official

Business Management

Managers are responsible for an organization's financial performance and for ensuring that it runs smoothly and efficiently. Responsibilities include establishing the company's financial and operational objectives, as well as formulating its strategic direction. Day-to-day duties may include hiring, firing, and managing employees; managing finances and other resources; providing leadership, coaching, and direction; making high-level business decisions; and ensuring that the company fulfills its legal and fiduciary obligations. Business managers also coordinate key relationships with business partners and may be involved with important clients at an executive, nonoperational level. Where a business has a board of directors, the business manager reports to and follows direction from the board.

Specialist business roles within the spectator sports industry include agents and promoters, who are responsible for assisting athletes and sporting organizations in managing their careers. They may, for example, secure endorsements and

OCCUPATION PROFILE

Professional Athlete

Considerations	Qualifications
Description	Performs athletic feats at the professional level.
Career cluster	Hospitality and Tourism
Interests	Data; people
Working conditions	Work outside; work both inside and outside
Minimum education level	On-the-job training; high school diploma or GED
Physical exertion	Medium work
Physical abilities	Excellent fitness
Opportunities for experience	Internship; military service; volunteer work; part-time work
Licensure and certification	Usually not required
Employment outlook	Faster-than-average growth expected
Holland interest score	SRC

Note: See volume 1, "Publisher's Note," for an explanation of the Holland interest score.

sponsorships, book speaking engagements and public appearances, manage their clients' public image, negotiate contracts, or advise clients on their investments and tax preparation. Agents are playing an increasingly important role in the spectator sports industry, as athletes derive smaller portions of their income from competition and greater portions from commercial endorsements. Agents generally work on a commission of 3 to 5 percent of their clients' earnings. Some agents specialize in managing events rather than individuals.

Increasingly, typical business managers possess advanced degrees in business administration, management, accounting, or other specialist areas. Extensive practical work experience at a senior level is also usually a prerequisite, and it may substitute for formal qualifications. Commensurate with the level of responsibility, typical salaries for business managers are higher than are the salaries received by employees performing other functions within the company.

Business management occupations may include the following:

- Chief Executive Officer (CEO)
- Chief Financial Officer (CFO)
- Chief Operating Officer (COO)
- General Manager
- Business Manager
- Accountant
- Business Development Director
- President
- Vice President
- Sports Agent
- Promoter

Team Operations

Team operations comprise the sorts of functions that are specific to a business that supports sporting performance. Team operations positions are differentiated from business operations positions because their outcome is focused on team and athletic performance, as opposed to financial performance. Salary, working conditions, and prerequisite qualifications vary according to the type of job and type of sport. In field sports, for example, team operations include equipment management, player coordination, team and competition administration, and talent scouting.

Some professional teams have dedicated audio-visual personnel who assist coaches and scouts by preparing visuals for analysis and training purposes. Computing, communications, and other technical positions may belong to team operations when those roles are dedicated to supporting team or athletic performance. For example, most teams have a traveling information technology group to ensure that their computing and radio communications are working properly. They also have specialist administrative employees such as travel and competition coordinators.

In the motor sports arena, engineers require a minimum bachelor's degree in engineering, and experience in motor racing, even at the hobby level, is highly regarded. Specialist fields within engineering include aerodynamics, vehicle dynamics, research and testing, design, and simulation programming. Some engineering positions are shop based, while race engineers and crew chiefs attend race meetings where they manage their teams' race strategies and car setups. Sponsor manufacturers (such as Toyota, Ford Bridgestone, and Goodyear) provide alternative job opportunities for engineers and technicians seeking nonteam-based careers in motor sports. Mechanics may be shop based or members of a travelling race team. Fabricators, machinists, and engine tuners and assemblers tend to be shop based, as they prepare cars before races. Other operational positions in motor sports include competition coordinators, who oversee and manage key personnel at races, and spotters, who relay information to drivers during the race.

In horse racing, operational roles include breeding managers, who manage equine reproduction; horse trainers, who develop and execute training programs to prepare horses for competition; grooms (stablehands), who provide hands-on care for horses and maintain their accommodations; exercise riders, who implement trainers' exercise instructions during training sessions; farriers (also known as blacksmiths), who shoe horses; bloodstock agents, who are experts in pedigree; and veterinarians, who provide medical care to horses. While many of these positions do not require formal qualifications, increasing competition for employment in the industry makes it difficult for candidates without any formal training to find entry-level positions. Operational employees may expect to work long hours, including weekends, and to start at the bottom of the career ladder. Promotion and career advancement opportunities in this industry are based on proven abilities, as opposed to standardized progression, but successful employees can realize significant financial and personal rewards.

Team operations occupations may include the following:

- Competition Coordinator
- Team Coordinator/Administrator
- Equipment Manager
- Talent Scout
- Engineer
- Crew Chief
- Mechanic
- Horse Trainer
- Veterinarian
- Groom/Stablemaster
- Bloodstock Agent

Event Operations

Event operations staff are responsible for managing and coordinating tournaments, competitions, and other events. These events may be held in public venues (as is the case for marathons and triathlons) or in purpose-built sporting venues. Event operations subfunctions include food service and preparation; client services staff (including cashiers, ticket takers, ushers, and so forth); and stadium, race course, or event management personnel. Food and client services staff are likely to be engaged on an hourly basis.

Stadium, course, and event managers coordinate event support personnel, as well as manage the financial, promotional, administrative, and physical requirements of venues. Some universities offer specialist degrees in sporting venue and track management. According to PayScale.com, the average annual salary for event coordinators in the spectator sports industry in 2009 was $37,000.

Event operations occupations may include the following:

- Event Coordinator
- Event Manager
- Stadium/Track/Race Course Manager
- Catering Manager
- Catering Assistant
- Food Server
- Cashier
- Usher
- Ticket Collector

Sales and Marketing

Sales and marketing personnel manage the solicitation, acquisition, and expansion of revenue. They generate revenue by designing and executing campaigns that drive the sale of tickets, subscriptions, merchandise, broadcasting rights, advertising, and sponsorships. They usually possess undergraduate degrees in business, marketing, communications, or related disciplines, although practical experience is highly regarded.

Marketing is usually an office-based function requiring incumbents creatively to synthesize market data into promotional and public-relations campaigns. The sales function, on the other hand, often demands face-to-face meetings, telephone conversations, and networking with prospects. In addition to traditional sales and marketing functions, the spectator sports sector includes specialist roles in public relations, community relations, broadcasting, new media, merchandising, image management, and cheerleader and mascot programs. According to PayScale.com, the average annual salary range in 2009 for a sales manager in the spectator sports industry was between $38,000 and $88,000. Marketing manager salaries averaged between $35,000 and $75,000.

Sales and marketing occupations may include the following:

- Sales Manager
- Salesperson
- Sales Administrator
- Account Executive
- Territory Manager
- Marketing Manager
- Marketing Administrator
- Marketing Officer
- Sponsorship Manager
- Merchandising Director

Administration

Administrative personnel support the general running of a company. They help with accounting and purchasing, provide secretarial and executive assistance, work in reception, staff switchboards, and provide business support within other departments. Experience and qualifications vary. Transactional accounting personnel (for example, accounts payable and receivable clerks) may not have formal qualifications, while accounting managers who assume financial management and reporting responsibilities are likely to have undergraduate or advanced degrees. Secretarial and clerical roles may have special prerequisites depending on the type of company. Positions range from full to part time.

Administrative remuneration varies significantly according to one's area of administrative specialty. According to data from PayScale.com, average administration specialist salaries in 2009 ranged from $36,700 to $48,200 per year, while administrative management salaries ranged from $37,400 to $61,200 per year.

Administrative occupations may include the following:

- Accounting or Finance Manager
- Accounts Payable Clerk
- Accounts Receivable Clerk
- Financial Clerk
- Secretary
- Executive Assistant
- Administrator
- Administrative Support Manager
- Administrative Assistant
- Payroll Administrator
- Purchasing Manager
- Contracts Manager

Information Technology

While some companies may outsource some of their information technology (IT) requirements, most retain internal IT groups. An IT department maintains computer hardware and software, as well as a company's overall technology infrastructure. Specialist IT roles in the spectator sports industry include audiovisual, communications, broadcasting, and Internet media technicians.

IT personnel typically have degrees or industry certifications in fields such as computer science, computer networking, and software engineering. Some business services companies may also develop proprietary software. The average salary for an IT manager ranges from $59,000 to $99,400 per year.

IT occupations may include the following:

- Information Technology Manager
- Information Technologist
- Computer Support Specialist
- Network Administrator
- Webmaster

Facilities and Grounds

Maintenance personnel are charged with the responsibility of maintaining an organization's office, training, stadium, track, or course facilities. The facilities and grounds department includes, for example, janitorial duties, carpet cleaning, building maintenance and repair, building engineering, remediation services, landscaping, and groundskeeping. For most organizations, it also includes vehicle, equipment, and fleet maintenance. Maintenance, janitorial, and landscaping personnel are rarely required to possess postsecondary degrees. Depending on the facility, they may be hired on a full-time, part-time, or contract basis. They are likely to be paid an hourly wage.

Groundskeeping and turf maintenance is becoming an increasingly specialized profession. Positions responsible for maintaining stadium and track surfaces tend to require associate's or bachelor's degrees in fields that have taught candidates the principles of horticulture, handling fertilizers and pesticides, and maintaining high-usage surfaces. Salaries in sports turf management commence at $28,000 per year, with the average salary being $44,000 per year. Job opportunities at world-class venues are extremely competitive, but allied opportunities exist at universities and other educational institutions, tennis centers, city parks, golf courses, minor stadiums, and race courses.

Facilities and grounds occupations may include the following:

- Maintenance Manager
- Facility Manager
- Maintenance Officer
- Custodian/Janitor
- Landscaping Worker
- Building Engineer
- Groundskeeper
- Turf Manager

Security

A security department is responsible for protecting an organization's facilities, equipment, and personnel. Given the high level of public interest and involvement in spectator sports, security services in this industry include surveillance, crowd management, personal security, and bodyguard services. Security personnel must have training in public safety, which may be obtained via undergraduate programs, vocational training, or a security certification program. Some companies may require their security staff to be trained in emergency response and first-aid techniques. Because security is highly specialized and demanding, organizations often elect to outsource their security needs to external experts. The average salary for security managers ranges from $41,700 to $72,500 per year.

Security occupations may include the following:

- Security Manager
- Security Officer
- Security Guard
- Investigator
- Bodyguard
- Crowd Controller

Human Resources

Human resources staff manage an organization's personnel and employment requirements. They recruit, hire, and fire employees; administer compensation and benefits (including salaries, insurance, and retirement plans); and ensure that their company adheres to appropriate labor laws. In large organizations, human resources departments may include training and development, relocation, labor relations, and compensation specialists. Human resources specialists usually possess undergraduate or postgraduate degrees in human resources management. The national annual salary for a human resources manager averages between $46,900 and $73,300.

Human resources occupations may include the following:

- Human Resources Manager
- Human Resources Coordinator
- Personnel Administrator
- Employee Services Officer

Health Care and Medical

Health care and medical professionals provide remedial and preventative medical services to athletes and other team members. Medical and first-aid personnel in this industry are usually purpose-trained and experienced in dealing with sports injuries and with health needs that are peculiar to athletes. Some of the specialist health care areas in the spectator sports industry include sports medicine, physical therapy, chiropractics, nutrition, dietetics, psychology, massage, orthopedics, and alternative medicine (such as acupuncture and herbal remedies). Candidates seeking a health care or medical role with a spectator sports team must undertake formal university studies or vocational training appropriate to their area of specialization.

The median salary for a medical doctor specializing in sports medicine is $235,000 per year, while dieticians and sports nutritionists attract annual average salaries of $45,000. The average salary for team physical therapists ranges from $62,990 to $73,400; chiropractors earn an average of $40,000 to $78,600. The median salary for full-time massage therapists is $45,900.

Health care and medical occupations may include the following:

- Physician
- Physical Therapist
- Dietician
- Sports Nutritionist
- Chiropractor
- Massage Therapist
- Nurse
- Medical Assistant
- Sports Psychologist

Entertainment

Entertainment is a significant factor in spectator sports, so some spectator sporting organizations provide sundry entertainment services that can include musicians, mascots, cheerleaders, announcers, and comperes. No particular formal qualifications are required for these positions. Cheerleader salaries range between $200 and $1,000 per month, and some cheerleaders may receive payments for corporate appearances, as well as sharing in revenues from special merchandise sales. Salaries for full-time professional mascots begin at around

$25,000 per year. Entertainment positions in the spectator sports industry are highly competitive.

Entertainment occupations may include the following:

- Cheerleading and Mascot Programs Director
- Cheerleader
- Mascot
- Musician
- Announcer

Transportation and Logistics

Transportation and logistics are key functions in spectator sports organizations because of the large volumes of equipment involved and the fact that teams regularly travel to compete. Logistics administrators oversee operational personnel such as drivers, loaders, movers, and fabricator workers, who pack, assemble, and install equipment. Truck driver's average salaries range from $11.00 to $21.50 per hour, depending on location and experience. Logistics manager salaries range from approximately $46,000 to $75,000 per year.

Transportation and logistics occupations may include the following:

- Truck Driver
- Transport Assistant
- Logistics Manager
- Transport Administrator
- Logistics Administrator

Professional Services

Spectator sports organizations require professional services in areas such as accounting and auditing, legal counsel, and advertising. Some may also demand consulting services or speciality business and technical services, such as occupational health and safety advice. These roles require undergraduate or advanced degrees.

Professional services occupations may include the following:

- Attorney
- General Counsel
- Accountant
- Auditor
- Consultant
- Public Relations Manager

INDUSTRY OUTLOOK

Overview

The outlook for the spectator sports industry shows it to be stable. Between 1998 and 2005, revenue in the spectator sports sector skyrocketed by 32 percent, and that of the agency and promotion sector increased by 36 percent. Experts agree, however, that the meteoric growth of spectator sports will not be matched in the wake of the global economic recession of 2007-2009. High unemployment and reduced consumer spending is slowing the industry. For example, many more internships are transitioning to unpaid positions, and the NFL and NBA both cut jobs, by nearly 20 and 10 percent of overall staff, respectively, in response to the recession. As well as reduced revenues from game attendances, concession, and merchandise sales, reduced consumer spending results in decreased advertising and sponsorship revenues, on which many sporting organizations rely.

While overall the industry is still expected to grow, observers can expect to witness corrections in overvalued salaries and company stocks. These pricing corrections follow decades of unfettered growth that resulted in ticket, merchandise, salary, and company values that cannot be sustained in the postrecession economy. In keeping with general employment trends, spectator sports organizations are working toward smaller, leaner workforces. While wage and salaried jobs in the arts, entertainment, and recreation industry are expected to grow generally, job competition in the spectator sports sector will tighten and intensify. This trend is likely to result in keener competition in the amateur and semiprofessional sectors as well.

These economic factors are forcing sports businesses to look beyond their traditional markets and means of distribution. Foreign markets, especially in Asia, are proving particularly attractive. The key to opening these foreign markets, however, is to develop awareness and appreciation for new sports within them. Such initiatives demand long-term investment. The NFL, for example, has established a youth flag-football league in China. In 2007, the NFL also scheduled a regular season game at Wembley Stadium in the England, in an attempt to generate European interest in American football. NASCAR, meanwhile, is attempting to broaden its audience demographic by broadcasting in Spanish.

Sporting organizations are also competing in the new media space, as consumer demand for instant and interactive services increases. The rising demand for Web-based services challenges traditional marketing paradigms, as the industry grapples with expanding its audience and cementing viewer loyalties beyond traditional broadcast technologies. The challenges of leveraging new communication technologies and media methods cannot be understated, given increased competition among various sports in a saturated domestic market.

Revenue in the spectator sports industry is expected to grow generally, but many businesses (especially those competing in nonfranchise leagues) will experience lower profit margins resulting from increased competition. While revenue from consumer sales is likely to plateau, income from the sale of long-term broadcasting and sponsorship agreements assures financial security for most high-profile leagues. Business survival will be more cutthroat in sports whose officiating bodies do not share profits from broadcasting or event sponsorship with teams or athletes. NASCAR, a privately owned, family-operated business, is a good case in point: Sponsorship and broadcasting revenues earned by NASCAR remain solely with NASCAR. This situation can lead to tension when competing teams accuse NASCAR of stealing their sponsors and of pocketing huge broadcasting revenues that leverage the teams' participation without providing any reimbursement. In 2005, NASCAR signed a $4.5-billion broadcasting deal that expires in 2014. Meanwhile, many teams are reducing their workforces, cutting salaries, and scrabbling for sponsorship dollars.

Employment Advantages

Despite slowing growth and increased employment competition in the spectator sports industry, opportunities will continue to exist for talented, motivated, and qualified individuals. Practical experience is highly regarded in this industry, so candidates are encouraged to seek relevant experience through volunteering, community involvement at local schools and clubs, amateur leagues, and hobby activities. Candidates who combine relevant practical experience with high levels of academic achievement or athletic talent will be best positioned for opportunities, as will those who can apply their skills in new and high-demand areas. Although employment entry may be difficult, competition keen, and the work demanding, those who do become successful are likely to be remunerated generously.

Annual Earnings

The total sports industry in the United States is valued at $410 billion annually: This figure includes the spectator sports, sporting equipment and apparel, health, fitness and recreation, and promotions industries. The spectator sports industry specifically (including sports promoters, managers, and agents) contributes around $50 billion per year to these revenues. In 2007, the NFL was responsible for more than 10 percent of the industry's earnings, which break down as follows:

- NFL: $5.86 billion
- MLB: $5.2 billion
- NBA: $3.13 billion
- NHL: $2.2 billion
- Other sporting leagues: $3 billion
- Horse racing: $15 billion
- Promotion: $16.1 billion

The NFL is one of the world's most profitable sporting leagues, with the average team valued at $957 million. Second place goes to MLB, with an average value of $295 million per team. The NFL's value can be attributed mainly to broadcasting rights valued at $17.6 billion over eight years, and a player-salary cap that ensures that franchise teams realize strong profits. The top teams also own or control their own stadiums, which garner strong income from ticket and concession sales, as well as multimillion-dollar naming deals. The NFL has also identified unique business opportunities by entering into preferred supplier arrangements with relatively small, burgeoning organizations in return for stock options in these companies. This tactic has paid large dividends, as these partnerships drive up sales and company stock values. The NFL also owns its own broadcasting network.

These domestic statistics are dwarfed by the potential revenues offered by burgeoning sports markets overseas. In China, for example, increasing professionalism in sports, coupled with wider media coverage, is resulting in massive growth in the sports industry. As of 2010, the Chinese sports industry was valued at about 1.5 percent of China's gross domestic product ($4.5 trillion), which equates to industry earnings of $66 billion per year—a number that is expected to increase rapidly as the Chinese consumer market continues to develop.

RELATED RESOURCES FOR FURTHER RESEARCH

AMATEUR ATHLETIC UNION
P.O. Box 22409
Lake Buena Vista, FL 32830
Tel: (407) 934-7200
Fax: (407) 934-7242
http://www.aausports.org

INTERNATIONAL OLYMPIC COMMITTEE
Château de Vidy
Case postale 356
1001 Lausanne
Switzerland
Tel: 41-21-621-6111
Fax: 41-21-621-6216
http://www.olympic.org

NATIONAL ATHLETIC TRAINER'S ASSOCIATION
2952 Stemmons Fwy., Suite 200
Dallas, TX 75247
Tel: (214) 637-6282
Fax: (214) 637-2206
http://www.nata.org

NORTH AMERICAN SOCIETY FOR SPORT MANAGEMENT
NASSM Business Office, West Gym 014
Slippery Rock University
Slippery Rock, PA 16057
Tel: (724) 738-4812
Fax: (724) 739-4858
http://www.nassm.com

SPORTS TURF MANAGERS ASSOCIATION
805 New Hampshire, Suite E
Lawrence, KS 66044
Tel: (800) 323-3875
Fax: (785) 843-2977
http://www.stma.org

U.S. OLYMPIC COMMITTEE
1 Olympic Plaza
Colorado Springs, CO 80909
Tel: (719) 632-5551
http://www.olympic-usa.org

ABOUT THE AUTHOR

Kylie Grimshaw Hughes has had a fifteen-year professional career that includes experience with industry leaders such as Parker Hannifin, Honeywell, and the Hanover Finance group. She has a bachelor of arts degree with honors in labor studies and politics from the University of Adelaide and a master of arts degree in communication studies from the University of South Australia, as well as professional certifications in adult education and financial services. Hughes lives in the United States, where she works as a consultant and freelance writer.

FURTHER READING

Bowles, Tom. "As NASCAR Money Gap Widens, Start and Parkers Soldier On." *Sports Illustrated*, June 11, 2009. http://sportsillustrated.cnn .com/2009/writers/tom_bowles/06/11/Start-and-park/index.html.

Fowler, Elizabeth M. "Careers: Learning to Manage a Race Track." *The New York Times*, May 1, 1990. http://www.nytimes.com/1990/ 05/01/business/careers-learning-to-manage-a-race-track.html.

Funk, Daniel C. *Consumer Behaviour in Sport and Events: Marketing Action*. Boston: Butterworth-Heinemann/Elsevier, 2008.

Hart, Chris J., Corinne M. Daprano, and Peter J. Titlebaum. "Rules of the Game: Ethics in Sports Marketing." *Sports Media* 33 (March, 2005). http://www.sports-media.org/ newpedimension7.htm.

Horrow, Richard B., and Karla Swatek. *Beyond the Box Score: An Insider's Guide to the $750 Billion Business of Sports*. New York: Morgan James, 2010.

Jozsa, Frank P. *Global Sports: Cultures, Markets, and Organizations*. Hackensack, N.J.: World Scientific, 2009.

López-Egea, Sandalio Gómez, Kimio Kase, and Ignacio Urrutia. *Value Creation and Sport Management.* New York: Cambridge University Press, 2010.

Mather, Victor. "Two Horse-Racing Syndicates Flourish on Line. *The New York Times,* June 4, 1998. http://www.nytimes.com/1998/06/04/technology/2-horse-racing-syndicates-flourish-on-line.html.

PayScale.com. "Salary Survey for Industry: Spectator Sports." http://www.payscale.com/research/US/Industry=Spectator_Sports/Salary.

_____. "Salary Survey for Industry: Sports Agency." http://www.payscale.com/research/US/Industry=Sports_Agency/Salary/by_Company_Size.

_____. "Salary Survey for Job: Referee, Umpire, or Other Sports Official." http://www.payscale.com/research/US/Job=Umpire%2c_Referee%2c_or_Other_Sports_Official/Salary.

Plunkett, Jack W. *Plunkett's Sports Industry Almanac, 2010.* Houston, Tex.: Plunkett Research, 2009.

Quinn, Kevin G. *Sports and Their Fans: The History, Economics, and Culture of the Relationship Between Spectator and Sport.* Jefferson, N.C.: McFarland, 2009.

Szymanski, Stefan. *The Comparative Economics of Sport.* New York: Palgrave Macmillan, 2010.

U.S. Bureau of Labor Statistics. *Career Guide to Industries,* 2010-2011 ed. http://www.bls.gov/oco/cg.

U.S. Census Bureau. North American Industry Classification System (NAICS), 2007. http://www.census.gov/cgi-bin/sssd/naics/naicsrch?chart=2007.

U.S. Department of Commerce. International Trade Administration. Office of Trade and Industry Information. Industry Trade Data and Analysis. http://ita.doc.gov/td/industry/otea/OTII/OTII-index.html.

Van Riper, Tom. "The Most Valuable Teams in Sports." *Forbes,* January 13, 2009. http://www.forbes.com/2009/01/13/nfl-cowboys-yankees-biz-media-cx_tvr_0113values.html.

Zimbalist, Andrew S. *The Bottom Line: Observations and Arguments on the Sports Business.* Philadelphia: Temple University Press, 2006.

_____. *Circling the Bases: Essays on the Challenges and Prospects of the Sports Industry.* Philadelphia: Temple University Press, 2011.

Sports Equipment Industry

INDUSTRY SNAPSHOT

General Industry: Manufacturing

Career Cluster: Manufacturing

Subcategory Industries: Archery Equipment Manufacturing; Athletic Shoes Manufacturing; Badminton, Squash, and Tennis Equipment Manufacturing; Ball Manufacturing; Boxing Equipment Manufacturing; Exercise Equipment Manufacturing; Fishing Supplies and Equipment Manufacturing; Golf Equipment Manufacturing; Golf Shoes Manufacturing; Gymnasium and Playground Equipment Manufacturing; Ice Skate Manufacturing; Roller Skate Manufacturing; Ski Equipment Manufacturing; Sporting Goods Stores; Sports Apparel Manufacturing; Team Sports Equipment Manufacturing; Track and Field Equipment Manufacturing; Wet Suit and Scuba Diving Equipment Manufacturing

Related Industries: Apparel and Fashion Industry; Health and Fitness Industry; Retail Trade and Service Industry; Spectator Sports Industry; Toys and Games Industry

Annual Domestic Revenues: $68.4 billion USD (Sporting Goods Manufacturers Association, 2008)

Annual International Revenues: $44.28 billion USD (Global Industry Guide: Sports Equipment, 2008)

Annual Global Revenues: $73.8 billion USD (Sporting Goods Manufacturers Association, 2008)

NAICS Numbers: 315, 33992, 45111, 316219

INDUSTRY DEFINITION

Summary

The sports equipment industry designs, produces, and distributes equipment for a wide range of sports and recreation activities. Products include balls, protective and other equipment, and apparel for team sports such as baseball, basketball, football, soccer, and hockey; adventure equipment for camping, hunting, and fishing; fitness equipment, including exercise bikes, resistance training machines, and treadmills; rackets, apparel, and other supplies for sports such as tennis and badminton; scuba gear, surfboards, and other water-related sporting goods; golf equipment and apparel; ice skates, skis, snowboards, and related equipment; roller skates, skateboards, and related equipment; and so on. The industry is present throughout the world and provides a wide range of employment options, from the initial design of

The exercise and fitness equipment sector of the industry supplies both consumers and such institutions as health clubs, schools, and hotels. (©Andres Rodriguez/Dreamstime.com)

equipment down through the sale of products to consumers.

History of the Industry

Some experts in the industry trace it to the ancient chariot races and gladiatorial contests that entertained people of ancient Rome. In retrospect, the suppliers of chariots and swords can be seen as having produced sports equipment. In this period of history, sport and leisure was a reward for wealth and nobility and was not part of the common person's life.

Early sports such as golf, tennis, and even fishing began to demand specialized products. In the 1800's, specialized companies began to form that concentrated solely on the production of leisure activity products. Some of those early companies have grown into today's industry giants.

In the early 1900's, several companies banded together to form the Sporting Goods Manufacturers Association (SGMA). The goal of this organization was to encourage participation in sports and to serve the interests of its member companies. The sports equipment industry experienced a surge in growth and recognition shortly after World War I, when organized team sports began to grow in popularity. The origin and early history of nearly every major sporting activity can be traced to this period.

In 1957, the Sporting Goods Fair was started by the SGMA; it became the Super Show in 1986 and eventually became the single largest sporting goods product show in the world. Today, the SGMA also has a political presence, as was seen in 1997, when the organization was instrumental in eliminating the use of child labor to produce soccer balls in Pakistan.

The main impetus for the industry's rapid growth was the revolutionary growth in technology that took place during the twentieth century. Labor-saving devices and machines in the workplace and the home increased the average amount of leisure time, so there was a corresponding increase in leisure activities. The SGMA became the leading organization representing manufacturers' interest in the creation of standards for protective equipment. The National Operating Committee on Standards for Athletic Equipment (NOCSAE) was created in 1969. NOCSAE was required by sport governing bodies to establish standards for protective athletic equipment. The SGMA was very active in the creation and development of NOCSAE.

In the last half century, sporting and recreational activities of all types have grown substantially. The sports equipment industry has profited from this growth by supplying sporting goods, and it has also helped spur further growth by making high-quality, safe, and ever-better products available to the public. Regardless of how much elite athletes and weekend recreationalists train, the quality of their equipment will always be a factor influencing the quality of their performance.

The Industry Today

Despite the economic downturn of 2007-2009, the sports equipment industry remains steady, as Americans continue to participate in around one hundred different athletic, recreational, and exercise pursuits that use or rely on the industry's products. People of a wide range of ages purchase sports equipment, including many retired baby boomers, who are buying and using fitness equipment to enhance their quality of life. Also, over the past two decades, the number of boys and girls participating in high school varsity sports teams has risen by 27 percent and 60 percent, respectively. Increases in the popularity of specific sports also affects the industry. Mixed martial arts styles, such as so-called extreme fighting, represent one example of an increasingly popular sector of the sports industry; snowboarding is another. Sales of martial arts equipment of all sorts, including boxing, have continued to grow, as have sales of tennis equipment.

Sports equipment manufacturers have kept pace with consumer demand for high-quality and high-performance equipment by advanc-ing design and materials technologies. Indeed, the materials used to manufacture sports equipment have constantly improved as a result of sustained research and technological advances. The main raw materials used in much of the production of sports equipment are steel, various plastics products, resins, carbon fiber, rubber, and leather. In recent years, advances in materials have enabled the development of new types of equipment with enhanced properties, improving overall product design and safety.

Sports equipment manufacturers are continually redesigning their products to enhance performance and to keep pace with ongoing media exposure to many organized sports. More young athletes are motivated to perform more aggressively to obtain recognition and school scholarships. This increase in the performance of sports equipment and the intensity of youth competition leads to potential increases in sports-related injuries as well. NOCSAE continues to monitor the safety of sports equipment and to develop and enforce standards. The committee funds research on sports equipment and helps distribute findings pertaining to injury data, as well as closely related areas of sports medicine. For example, it may fund studies of the effectiveness of protective headgear when exposed to different levels of impact. Foot-

Game balls for Super Bowl XLV were made at the Ada, Ohio, factory of Wilson Sporting Goods, the official Super Bowl football manufacturer. (AP/Wide World Photos)

ball helmets in particular have already been targeted as the subjects of one such study.

Once it is designed, manufactured, and tested, sports equipment is distributed through several channels. Approximately 50 percent of all sports equipment is sold through sporting goods stores, while 35 percent is sold by discount chains, department stores, and other such general-purpose merchants. The last 15 percent is sold through other channels, including the Internet. Some of the larger sports equipment companies sell directly to consumers through company-owned retail outlets.

Sports equipment specialty shops that focus on select product lines have become increasingly popular. These stores are generally smaller in size and attempt to recruit knowledgeable staff to offer quality service. They cater to such specific sports and activities as skateboarding, ice skating, and bicycling. Similar to these shops are multisport specialty shops, which are not as narrowly defined and which often originate from one-sport specialty shops that have broadened their product lines. Such stores often find that they need to expand to generate income throughout the year by providing equipment for both cold-weather and warm-weather sports. For example, multisport specialty shops may operate chains of stores focusing on five sports: camping, climbing, cycling, paddling, and skiing.

Equipment stores called pro shops are similar to specialty shops, with the biggest difference being their location. Rather than stand-alone venues, pro shops are generally connected to and operate within or alongside sports facilities such as golf courses, tennis clubs, and ice rinks. They get their name from the fact that they provide not only equipment but also advice and instruction from professional athletes/trainers. Because they are highly specialized and sell merchandise to supplement and support instruction, pro shops are small and carry relatively few product lines. Rental shops are another venue for product sales by manufacturers. Rental shops buy equipment to rent out, and they also often sell accessory items, such as golf or tennis balls.

Big-box stores are large, carrying thousands of equipment items. Manufacturer outlets represent another avenue of distribution, and some manufacturers have established chains of retail stores that sell their own brands and little else. To gain more publicity and promotion, rather than volume, some manufacturers establish concept stores that portray themes to help display products in exciting and entertaining settings.

Many manufacturers open outlet stores to dispose of overstocked items. Such outlet stores can be near manufacturing factories or in outlet centers, which are often located in suburbs or near tourist destinations. To promote good locations and decrease competition, many outlet stores are located in areas at least thirty minutes away from metropolitan shopping malls.

Many manufacturers establish mass merchandising channels through discount stores. These stores carry selected sporting goods at relatively low price points. Smaller full-line sporting goods stores may find it difficult to compete with discount stores because they generally cannot match their prices. They attempt instead to compete by offering greater selections and by cultivating reputations as experts in sports equipment who can provide consumers with better advice than can general-purpose, low-service discount stores. Some department stores also carry sports equipment. For example, Sears has become the largest retailer of fitness equipment.

The exercise and fitness equipment sector of the industry remains stable.

Two-piece golf balls have a solid rubber core with a plastic or urethane cover. (©Gualberto Becerra/Dreamstime.com)

Rock climbing requires dependable equipment. (©Paulo Resende/Dreamstime.com)

This sector supplies both consumers and such institutions as health clubs, schools, and hotels. Today, over 44.1 million Americans are members of health clubs. This number increased by 21 percent over the first decade of the twenty-first century, and the sports equipment industry offers a huge variety of the exercise machines that help sustain the fitness industry. Free weights remain the most universal form of fitness equipment found in the home, yet more money is now being spent on treadmills.

According to the SGMA, the sports experiencing the greatest sales growth in the early twenty-first century were fitness walking, lacrosse, running, and strength training. Challenges lie on the horizon for the industry, which will need to adapt to slower consumer spending and decreased availability of skilled labor. The availability and cost of materials will be another concern. The SGMA is an active voice for the industry in Washington, D.C., and advocates for government policies that are fa-vorable to its members. For example, it is working to build congressional support for legislation to encourage fitness activities to improve Americans' health. It also supports the Personal Health Investment Today (PHIT) bill, which would encourage physical activity by easing the financial burden to participate in health and fitness-related activities: The bill would allow workers to pay for expenses related to physical activity—including sports equipment—out of their pretax incomes.

INDUSTRY MARKET SEGMENTS

Sports equipment businesses range in sizes from privately owned small specialized companies to major manufacturers. The following sections provide a comprehensive breakdown of each segment.

Small Businesses

While some manufacturers of sports equipment establish brands used across many different sports, smaller specialist companies still account for a significant portion of the industry. New companies in particular may find it easier to gain entry to the industry by specializing in a specific product or sport. Such companies can produce successful products without needing to invest in large-scale manufacturing plants, and they can often sustain higher profit margins than can larger businesses by cultivating reputations for the high quality and relative rarity of their products. A good example of this phenomenon is a high-end pool cue made almost entirely by hand and with extreme precision.

Potential Annual Earnings Scale. According to the U.S. Bureau of Labor Statistics (BLS), in the class of manufacturing to which the sports equipment industry belongs, the average annual salary of a commercial or industrial designer in 2009 was $54,630 and the average annual salary of a materials engineer was $87,020. Sales representatives earned an average of $61,260, product assemblers and fabricators earned $30,220, inspectors and testers earned $34,390, and general and operations managers earned $118,550. Employees of small businesses may earn considerably less than these averages.

Clientele Interaction. Small businesses in general rely on repeat business from previous customers. Some small sports equipment producers may sell their own equipment, as is the case with a shop specializing in custom-designed surfboards, and they go out of their way to emphasize not only the uniqueness of each product but also the personal relationship between producer and consumer. Other businesses may sell to retailers and have little direct consumer contact. Such businesses nonetheless seek to develop mystiques around their products, which often rely on the cache of unique qualities or features to drive sales. An owner or sales representative may cultivate personal relationships with retailers, seeking to convince them that they will enhance the reputations of their stores by carrying the manufacturer's products.

Amenities, Atmosphere, and Physical Grounds. Small sports equipment businesses may be small manufacturing concerns or they may be artisan shops hand-crafting a limited number of items. In either case, work areas are generally functional, including all tools and resources necessary to create products. Businesses may also feature showrooms or attached retail outlets where customers can view samples of and purchase products. Sales representatives and managers work in standard office settings, often decorated with images taken from the particular sport to which their companies cater.

Typical Number of Employees. Small sports equipment businesses generally employ between one and fifty people.

Traditional Geographic Locations. Small sports equipment businesses can be located nearly anywhere. Manufacturing concerns that sell only at wholesale generally seek to locate themselves near transportation infrastructure to facilitate shipping of their products to retail outlets. Small manufacturers and artisans that sell directly to consumers may locate themselves near the appropriate types of sporting venues. For example, surfboard shops are likely to be located near beaches popular among surfers, while skiing equipment manufacturers may locate themselves near ski slopes. Good locations for small businesses are also dependent upon the economic environment and local competition. Sports equipment outlet stores are often located near related manufacturing factories and within outlet centers to reduce the cost of transportation. To decrease potential competition, many sports equipment outlet stores are also located in areas at least a half hour away from metropolitan shopping malls.

Pros of Working for a Small Sports Equipment Business. Small sporting equipment businesses can often be started at low cost and on a part-time basis. A business of this size is well suited to Internet marketing, as it can easily serve specialized equipment niches that once were dependent upon direct mail. Change is inevitable in business, and small businesses tend to respond more easily to shifts in the marketplace. Small-business owners and employees tend to have more personal relationships with their customers and clients. These relationships can be fulfilling in themselves, improve business-customer communication, and lead to increased sales.

Independence is one of the more popular rewards and advantages of owning a small sports equipment business. Many people prefer to make their own decisions within the constraints of economic and other environmental factors. Franchising may allow small-business owners to benefit from the scale of a big corporation yet work in a small-business environment. Franchises allow their owners to have greater physical presences in their stores, enabling each franchise to capitalize both on its brand name and on its identification with a particular owner.

Cons of Working for a Small Sports Equipment Business. Small businesses in general often face a variety of problems related to their size. Not having enough capital is a common cause of financial and mental stress. Finding and retaining good employees is difficult for small-business owners, yet it is critical to the success of many small businesses. If a small business is located near a major brand-name store in the same industry, it may have difficulty competing with the larger store's name recognition and national reputation. In the United States, insurance costs are some of the largest concerns of small businesses. Larger businesses are better equipped to bear these costs, as they are to bear the costs of doing business in general. Small businesses generally have far smaller cash reserves on which to draw in times of financial difficulty.

Costs

Payroll and Benefits: Small sports equipment businesses may hire staff on an hourly or salaried basis. Seasonal businesses may hire temporary staff for only part of each year. Self-employed business owners must pay themselves out of their companies' profits, only after all other financial obligations and employee salaries are paid. If there are no profits, owners may draw no pay. Benefits are rarer at small businesses than at larger companies and are offered at the discretion of owners or management.

Supplies: Small sports equipment manufacturers require artisanal tools, industrial production equipment, or both, as well as raw materials and standard office supplies.

External Services: Small sports equipment businesses may contract external vendors to provide cleaning and maintenance services, security, landscaping, accounting, and marketing and advertising. Legal services may also be required, especially to develop and protect intellectual property rights.

Utilities: Small businesses typically require water, sewage, electricity, telephone, and Internet access.

Taxes: Small businesses must pay applicable local, state, and federal income and property taxes. Sole proprietorships and some other small business partnerships pay no corporate taxes; instead, owners and partners must pay self-employment taxes and pay taxes related to their businesses on their personal returns.

Midsize Businesses

Midsize sports equipment businesses typically create more types and even brands of equipment than small businesses and compete across more sports. They enjoy significantly lower profit margins, on average, than small businesses. Entering the market with less of a specific and specialized product increases the need to invest in production, as profits are driven not by high quality or rarity but rather by volume of product.

Potential Annual Earnings Scale. According to the BLS, in the class of manufacturing to which the sports equipment industry belongs, the average annual salary of a commercial or industrial designer in 2009 was $54,630 and the average annual salary of a materials engineer was $87,020. Sales representatives earned an average of $61,260, product assemblers and fabricators earned $30,220, inspectors and testers earned $34,390, and general and operations managers earned $118,550. Employees of midsize sports businesses may earn salaries equal to or somewhat less than these averages.

Clientele Interaction. Repeat business from previous customers is important to any size business. Midsize businesses need managers and sales representatives knowledgeable about their products, about the sports and recreation activities supported by those products, and about their competitors. Managers and sales representatives must be able to cultivate relationships with purchasers and other decision makers at retail outlets in order to drive and maintain sales.

Amenities, Atmosphere, and Physical Grounds. Midsize sports equipment manufacturers are generally located in industrial plants that include assembly lines and other production areas. Research and development facilities may include engineering stations and offices, as well as small athletic fields and other venues for testing new equipment in real-world conditions. Management offices and reception areas may be decorated in a style related to sports and fitness.

Typical Number of Employees. Midsize sports equipment businesses typically employ between fifty and five hundred people.

Traditional Geographic Locations. Midsize sports equipment businesses can be located nearly anywhere, but they tend to be close to metropolitan and industrial regions that have the infrastructure to support them. Production and distribution facilities are usually located near major transportation hubs where truck, rail, air, or water transportation is readily available. Corporate offices, if separate, are often located in urban business centers. Retail outlets tend to be located near areas where their products will be used. For example, outlets offering camping, hunting, and fishing supplies are often located near open, publicly accessible outdoor areas where such equipment can be used.

Pros of Working for a Midsize Sports Equipment Business. While midsize sports equipment businesses require more capital than small businesses, they require much less capital than large businesses. They are well positioned to take advantage of Internet marketing because they can easily serve more generalized sports equipment needs. Change is inevitable in business, and small and midsize businesses tend to respond more easily to shifts in the marketplace than large businesses. Midsize businesses are often small enough that owners and employees are still able to develop personal relationships with their customers and clients, encouraging good word-of-mouth and repeat business. They also retain a certain degree of independence and lack of bureaucracy as compared to large corporations, but they are often able to realize greater earnings and profits than small businesses.

Cons of Working for a Midsize Sports Equipment Business. Midsize businesses, like small businesses, often face a variety of problems related to their size. While they often have greater capital than small businesses, they usually have significantly lower capital than large businesses, and the capital advantage they enjoy over small businesses may well be overwhelmed by higher overhead costs from research and development, production, and distribution. They may also have trouble competing with large businesses for the best employees. In this and other ways, the success of midsize businesses may be disproportionately affected by competition from larger concerns, with which they are more direct competitors than are small, specialized companies.

Costs

Payroll and Benefits: Midsize sports equipment businesses may hire staff on an hourly or a salaried basis, and they sometimes hire other workers on an as-needed basis as well. However, they tend to need more full-time, permanent employees than small businesses. Benefits are more common at midsize businesses, especially those competing with large businesses for workers.

Supplies: Midsize sports equipment manufacturers require industrial production machinery, as well as the tools necessary to maintain it and the raw materials that it manipulates into finished products. They also need standard office supplies, as well as computer workstations, laboratory equipment, and other supplies necessary to test and develop new products.

External Services: Midsize sports equipment businesses may contract external vendors to provide cleaning and maintenance services, security, landscaping, accounting, computer networking and systems support, and marketing and advertising. Legal services may also be required, especially to develop and protect intellectual property rights.

Utilities: Midsize businesses typically require water, sewage, electricity, telephone, and Internet access.

Taxes: Midsize businesses are required to pay local, state, and federal corporate taxes, as well as property taxes if applicable.

Large Businesses

Large sports equipment businesses are often well-diversified concerns that manufacture products for a wide range of sports and recreation activities. Some, by contrast, specialize in particular sports and seek to become the brand of choice for most enthusiasts of that sport. Both types of business often expend significant sums on advertising campaigns that incorporate professional sports figures, and their reputations and popularity derive in part from the popularity of the celebrities endorsing them, as well as from the quality of their products. In addition to marketing their products through sporting goods chains and other third-party channels, large manufacturers often have their own retail presence. Their retail stores generally sell only a small fraction of their total inventories, but their presence in shopping malls and elsewhere increases brand visibility and name recognition.

Potential Annual Earnings Scale. According to the BLS, in the class of manufacturing to which the sports equipment industry belongs, the average annual salary of a commercial or industrial designer in 2009 was $54,630 and the average annual salary of a materials engineer was $87,020. Sales representatives earned an average of $61,260, product assemblers and fabricators earned $30,220, inspectors and testers earned $34,390, and general and operations managers earned $118,550. Chief executives earned an average of $187,780.

Clientele Interaction. Repeat business from previous customers is important to any size business. Large businesses continue to need managers, sale representatives, and retail salespersons who are knowledgeable about the sports equipment within a particular department and about the athletes who require that equipment. In management and sales, employees should enjoy working with people, have the ability to communicate with customers clearly, have a pleasant personality, and present a neat professional appearance. Sales representatives at large corporations must understand the place of their companies within the industry and the nature of the competition they face in various sectors, and they must be able to communicate effectively with purchasers and other decision makers at various retail corporations, sometimes playing competing retailers off against each other to ensure the widest possible market penetration of their products. Indeed, large corporations seek not only shelf space but also display space at significant retailers, and marketing staff must attempt to ensure that patrons of discount stores and sporting goods chains will see prominent displays featuring their companies' products. Such displays not only drive immediate sales but also reinforce corporate branding and prestige among consumers who are in stores seeking unrelated products, laying the foundation for future sales.

Amenities, Atmosphere, and Physical Grounds. Most employees in sports equipment and accessories retailing work in clean, well-lit conditions. Retail salespeople and cashiers often stand for long periods, and stock clerks may perform strenuous tasks, such as moving heavy, awkward boxes. Sales representatives and buyers frequently travel to visit clients and may be away from home for several days or weeks at a time. Those who work for large retailers may need to travel outside of the country on a relatively regular basis.

Manufacturing employees work at large industrial plants that may occupy one building or several buildings. Production areas may contain heavy machinery, requiring safety equipment and precautions, and may be quite noisy. Research and development staff work in engineering and sports science laboratories designed to study both materials and the human body to facilitate the development of new products.

Typical Number of Employees. Large sports equipment businesses typically employ more than five hundred people.

Traditional Geographic Locations. Large businesses within the sports equipment industry can be located practically anywhere but are usually in highly populated areas for manufacturing and sales reasons. If the business actively manufactures its own products, the plant facility is usually closer to metropolitan and industrial areas that supply necessary labor. In terms of distribution, large businesses seek close proximity to appropriate transportation infrastructure, such as highways, railroads, ports, and airports. In terms of sales, visibility is important, especially for retail outlets designed to enhance brand at least as much as to sell product. Being near areas where their products will be used can be beneficial for sales. Outlets sports equipment stores of large parent operations are often located near those operations' manufacturing factories or in outlet centers.

Pros of Working for a Large Sports Equipment Company. Large sports equipment businesses generally have large amounts of capital and are publicly traded. Such companies can afford state-of-the-art research and manufacturing facilities. Larger businesses may offer the opportunity for managers and employees to share challenges and concerns. They are usually well established and have significant marketing and advertising departments that study how best to capitalize on brand recognition to drive sales. Their financial resources make it possible for them to purchase major sports celebrity endorsements, further enhancing their brands. Employees of large companies generally receive full benefits, including paid vacation, sick time, maternity leave, corporate education and training, and health insurance. They also receive better pay and more regular raises and enjoy greater opportunities for advancement and more well defined job titles and roles. Potential financial rewards in the way of salaries are often better in the larger businesses for most personnel.

Cons of Working for a Large Sports Equipment Company. Large-business owners and employees may have less time to interact personally with customers and clients, and there may be no direct communication between consumers and the vast majority of company employees. Many large businesses outsource certain aspects of their labor, which can harm local and regional economies. Employees must follow more rigid corporate protocols and deal with company bureaucracies that afford less room for creativity. Finding good, knowledgeable employees often remains a difficult task for large businesses, which face significant competition for this valuable resource. Insurance and related costs are required for more employees, along with workers' compensation claims and employee unemployment benefits that can potentially be more frequent and costly because of the size of the operation.

Costs

Payroll and Benefits: Large businesses usually hire staff on an hourly or annual salary basis. Because many of the employees work full time, benefits are required by government regulations. Benefits such as vacation and sick time are available and, to a certain degree, the amounts of each are at the discretion of the management.

Supplies: Large sports equipment manufacturers require industrial production machinery, as well as the tools necessary to maintain it and the raw materials that it manipulates into finished products. They also need standard office supplies and equipment, as well as computer workstations, laboratory equipment, and other supplies necessary to test and develop new products.

External Services: Large sports equipment businesses may contract external vendors to provide cleaning and maintenance services, security, landscaping, auditing, and computer networking and systems support. They generally have their own marketing and legal departments, but they may contract additional services in these disciplines, especially to develop major advertising campaigns and to lobby the government regarding proposed changes in regulations that could affect the industry.

Utilities: Large businesses typically require water, sewage, electricity, telephone, and Internet access.

Taxes: Large businesses are required to pay local, state, and federal corporate taxes, as well as property taxes if applicable. Multinational corporations and those with an international presence must pay taxes in multiple countries and may need to pay tariffs and other import fees and taxes.

ORGANIZATIONAL STRUCTURE AND JOB ROLES

The organization and distribution of tasks within the sports equipment industry are based upon the type and size of each business. In a small business, where one individual has manufactured a single specialized product, very few positions are needed to encompass the various tasks necessary to run the business. In contrast, a large company may rely on

engineers to research and develop sports equipment, a production unit to manufacture it, and a sophisticated distribution chain to ship products to retail stores—all in addition to the management staff that oversees operations and the various support positions that ensure things run smoothly.

The following umbrella categories apply to the organizational structure of businesses in the sports equipment industry:

- Technology, Research, Design, and Development
- Business Management
- Production
- Customer Service
- Sales and Marketing
- Human Resources
- Security

Technology, Research, Design, and Development

Engineers employed in the sports equipment industry develop and design new products and evaluate the effectiveness of existing products. They analyze the human body's motion and performance to better understand the equipment and training needs of athletes and sports enthusiasts, and they study the properties of materials and devices to evaluate their ability to augment or facilitate human motion. Engineers also study how environmental factors such as temperature, rain, wind, and terrain affect the body, as well as how different surfaces act on skin and muscles. These studies allow them to increase equipment's performance in a range of conditions and to help prevent injury.

Sports equipment must comply with a specific set of standards and regulations before it is made available to the public. Mechanical and electrical engineers design instrumentation and testing procedures that measure, calculate, and assess each product's specifications. For example, mechanical engineers can predict the levels and location of specific stress points on bicycle parts. This knowledge helps increase the performance and life span of bicycles.

Testing and prototyping by industry engineers verifies the work done in the design phase. In some projects, physical models are constructed before actual prototypes are attempted. However, designers are beginning to employ virtual prototyping technology, using computer-assisted design (CAD) programs to create three-dimensional models of proposed equipment. Such software may be helpful to establish a new product's correct proportions, overall dimensions, or material specifications, among other properties.

Technology, research, design, and development occupations may include the following:

- Vice President of Research and Development
- Lead Designer
- Product Tester
- Compliance Specialist
- Mechanical/Electrical/Materials Engineer
- Mechanical/Electrical/Materials Engineering Technician
- Mechanical Drafter
- Metals Scientist
- Biomedical/Biomechanical Engineer

Business Management

Business managers oversee overall companies and specific departments, ensuring that they remain efficient and profitable, setting goals, and evaluating success in meeting those goals. They approve new products, assign employees roles in producing, distributing, and marketing those products, and bear ultimate responsibility for product quality, regulatory compliance, and success or failure in the marketplace. Business managers are often involved in marketing, organizing sales and promotion events, and ensuring that merchandise is displayed effectively.

Business managers oversee employees, implement work schedules, and supervise employee performance, and they are responsible for the overall sales and profitability of their departments. In small to midsize businesses, they may be responsible for all of these areas within a department or even within the entire business. In a small business, it is not uncommon for one person, such as the

Trek is a best-selling bicycle manufacturer. (AP/Wide World Photos)

owner, to bear responsibility for all areas of management.

Business management occupations may include the following:

- President/Chief Executive Officer (CEO)
- Owner
- Chief Financial Officer (CFO)
- Chief Technology Officer (CTO)
- Chief Operating Officer (COO)
- General and Operations Manager
- General Counsel
- Engineering Manager
- Sales and Marketing Director

Production

Production staff create the products that have been designed by research and development engineers and that will be sold by the sales and marketing staff. In small businesses, owners may both design and manufacture their companies' products. Large corporations employ dedicated production crews, which often incorporate a mix of skilled and unskilled laborers working on production lines to fabricate and assemble finished products.

Production occupations may include the following:

- Owner/Craftsperson
- Production Manager
- Production Supervisor
- Assembly Team Member
- Machine Operator

Customer Service

Customer service personnel ensure proper communication between equipment manufacturers and retail outlets, as well as handling inquiries, feedback, and complaints directly from consumers. Some of these inquiries and complaints they handle themselves; others, they forward to personnel or departments that are better equipped to resolve particular issues. Most customer service representatives in this industry perform their work by telephone from an office; in larger businesses, they may work in call centers. Most other interaction is done by e-mail, fax, or face to face.

A large portion of customer service inquiries involves general questions about sports equipment. Thus, customer service representatives must know a fair amount about the sports they serve in general and the culture of those sports, in addition to understanding the proper use of their companies' products and anticipating common problems in their use. They may also receive many requests to provide purchasers with the current status of their orders or to update business records. Representatives employed by large companies are often required to follow company polices and take specific steps to resolve customer issues. They may have the authority to reverse fees that have been wrongly applied to customers and to send replacement equipment parts. Although selling sports equipment is not the role of customer service representatives, some may provide information to assist customers with their purchasing decisions. Thus, it may be necessary for each member of the department to have a good knowledge base of the industry, their companies' products, and their competitors' products.

Customer service occupations may include the following:

- Customer Service Manager
- Customer Service Representative
- Call Center Staff

Sales and Marketing

Sales and marketing personnel develop and execute strategies to sell products. They include development managers, market research managers, and general sales personnel. Together, these employees evaluate current markets, identify potential new markets, and seek to ensure that their companies' products achieve the greatest possible penetration into those markets. Important to the sports equipment industry is the task of monitoring trends that affect consumer demand. For example, winter sports equipment can be in higher demand and of more interest around the time of the winter Olympics. Marketing managers are involved in overseeing sports equipment development and help promote a company's products and general image.

The success of large sports equipment companies—and even of smaller ones, to a certain extent—is closely related to corporate branding. High-ranking marketing personnel have the important task of shepherding their companies' brands, ensuring that all advertising, including store displays, reinforces and capitalizes upon overall brand strategies.

OCCUPATION PROFILE

Quality Control Inspector

Considerations	Qualifications
Description	Inspects manufactured products, such as sports equipment, machinery, or furniture, to ensure compliance with contract specifications and consumer protection regulations.
Career clusters	Government and Public Administration; Manufacturing; Transportation, Distribution, and Logistics
Interests	Data; things
Working conditions	Work inside
Minimum education level	On-the-job training; high school diploma or GED; junior/technical/community college
Physical exertion	Light work
Physical abilities	Unexceptional/basic fitness
Opportunities for experience	Apprenticeship
Licensure and certification	Required
Employment outlook	Decline expected
Holland interest score	REI

Note: See volume 1, "Publisher's Note," for an explanation of the Holland interest score.

Marketing managers for an international sports equipment company are likely to be required to do some travel. Sales and marketing staff may also be responsible for arranging media coverage of product introductions. Good communication skills are essential for this position, since marketing managers need to interact with different departments in the company, along with various media contacts in television, radio, print journalism, and so on. Sales personnel convince stores to carry their companies' products. They thus must be able to explain both the benefits of a product to a consumer and the benefits of carrying that product to a retailer.

Sales and marketing occupations may include the following:

- Vice President of Sales and Marketing
- Branding Expert
- Marketing Manager
- Market Research Analyst
- Sales Manager
- Sales Representative
- Retail Sales Director
- Media Buyer

Human Resources

Human resources personnel recruit and hire employees. In doing so, they seek to maximize a company's return on investment in its workforce and to minimize its financial risk. They place each employee, aligning skilled and qualified individuals with an organization's business plans. They develop policies, standards, systems, and processes to manage employees; train and develop employees; respond to grievances; enforce corporate discipline; and administer payrolls and benefits.

Human resources occupations may include the following:

- Human Resources Director
- Human Resources Generalist
- Benefits Specialist
- Payroll Clerk
- Quality Assurance Director
- Recruitment Director
- Director of Employee Drug Testing
- Safety Council Manager

Security

Small and large sports equipment businesses rely on security to protect their assets against fire and illegal activity such as theft, vandalism, and terrorism. Security personnel protect corporate property, including intellectual property, enforce company protocols, and discourage illegal activity. Security services may be contracted by small businesses, but large businesses often employ their own security personnel.

Security personnel set up security systems, including alarms and surveillance systems. They establish procedures and protocols for using these systems, and they write reports outlining their observations and activities during their assigned shifts. One of the most important attributes a security officer can demonstrate is good judgment and common sense. Officers need to follow company policy and guidelines in the event of an emergency, and they need to be comfortable taking charge in stressful situations, such as when directing others to safety during emergencies. In large businesses, a security manager might oversee a group of security officers.

Security guards are often assigned to one location for a specific length of time. Guards must be acquainted with the property they are monitoring and with employees and other people associated with the business. Guards of large facilities may be assigned to mobile patrols to cover the grounds and conduct security checks. They must be trained to detain or arrest criminal violators, and many have backgrounds in law enforcement or military service. In some cases, security personnel are qualified to issue traffic violation warnings on or around business properties.

Security occupations may include the following:

- Security Manager
- Armored Car Guard
- Security Guard
- Security System Technician

INDUSTRY OUTLOOK

Overview

The outlook for the sports equipment industry shows it to be on the rise. According to Datamonitor, the industry grew by 2.9 percent between 2006 and 2008, and it is forecast to grow by 6.6 percent between 2008 and 2013. The greatest factor influencing industry growth is the amount of disposable income among consumers. Between 2006 and 2008, despite a slowing economy, personal consumer spending for sporting goods increased by 6 percent. This trend is expected to continue for at least five to ten years.

PROJECTED EMPLOYMENT FOR SELECTED OCCUPATIONS

Sporting Goods, Hobby, Book, and Music Stores

Employment		
2009	Projected 2018	Occupation
103,690	111,800	Cashiers
55,120	55,400	First-line supervisors/ managers of retail sales workers
335,760	353,400	Retail salespersons
9,840	9,100	Shipping, receiving, and traffic clerks
21,420	20,700	Stock clerks and order fillers

Source: U.S. Bureau of Labor Statistics, Industries at a Glance, Occupational Employment Statistics and Employment Projections Program.

Steady growth in the industry was seen in the 1970's and continued throughout the rest of the twentieth century, driven largely by sales to members of the baby boom generation. Beginning in the 1990's, as the baby boomers aged, they shifted their purchases from higher-impact sports to lower-impact sports and fitness activities, resulting in a shift in markets.

Sales of exercise equipment to consumers remain steady at around $3.5 billion. Sales of exercise equipment to institutions such as clubs, schools, and hotels increased in 2007 by 2.7 percent. The exercise equipment sector remains very large and strong, with $4.7 billion sales in 2007 according to the SGMA. The market is thought to be driven by the availability of an ever-increasing variety of user-friendly machines. While the United States has the largest consumer market for athletic consumer goods, China's impact on the consumer goods industry has been increasing for many years as companies send manufacturing operations overseas in an attempt to be more competitive.

Employment Advantages

According to a 2007 report of the SGMA, general sports merchandise stores (including sports equipment) will have numerous job openings over the 2008 to 2018 period. These openings will include many caused by worker transfers and turnover. The sports equipment industry is an extremely exciting and growing segment of the consumer goods industry and of the economy as a whole. Employment growth in the industry will be steady and determined primarily by the global and local economy and consumer spending. Consumer preference for the latest sports equipment is driven by increasing participation in recreational sports, awareness and interest in physical fitness, and the popularity of the athletes associated with particular sports equipment brands.

Annual Earnings

Today, the sports equipment industry is strongly influenced by the challenges of slower consumer spending and the availability and cost of skilled labor, quality materials, and energy. In 2013, the global sports equipment market is expected to reach a value of $81.7 billion, representing an increase of 10.7 percent since 2008. According to a survey conducted by the SGMA in 2008, the five fastest-growing sales sectors in the industry are products related to yoga and Pilates, fitness walking, lacrosse, running, and strength training.

RELATED RESOURCES FOR FURTHER RESEARCH

AMERICAN SOCIETY FOR TESTING AND MATERIALS
100 Barr Harbor Dr.
P.O. Box C700
West Conshohocken, PA 19428-2959
Tel: (610) 832-9500
Fax: (610) 832-9555
http://www.astm.org

NATIONAL OPERATING COMMITTEE ON STANDARDS FOR ATHLETIC EQUIPMENT
Executive Director/Legal Counsel
11020 King St., Suite 215
Overland Park, KS 66210
Tel: (913) 888-1340
Fax: (913) 498-8817
http://www.nocsae.org

NATIONAL SPORTING GOODS ASSOCIATION
1601 Feehanville Dr., Suite 300
Mount Prospect, IL 60056
Tel: (800) 815-5422
Fax: (847) 391-9827
http://www.nsga.org

SPORTING GOODS MANUFACTURERS ASSOCIATION
8505 Fenton St., Suite 211
Silver Spring, MD 20910
Tel: (301) 495-6321
Fax: (301) 495-6322
http://www.sgma.com

WORLD FEDERATION OF SPORTING GOODS INDUSTRY/MAISON DU SPORT INTERNATIONAL
Building C, 3d Floor
Ave. de Rhodanie 54
1007 Lausanne
Switzerland
Tel: 41-21-612-6161
Fax: 41-21-612-6169
http://www.wfsgi.org

ABOUT THE AUTHOR

Jeffrey Larson is the director of physical therapy at the Tioga Medical Center in Tioga, North Dakota. He is a graduate of North Dakota State University and the University of Utah. He holds degrees in both athletic training and physical therapy. He has been evaluating and treating the rehabilitative needs of athletes of all ages and sports for more than twenty years. He is also a medical writer and founder of Northern Medical Informatics, a medical communications business that he operates with a focus on continuing education for allied health care professionals, as well as consumer health education. He is a member of the American Physical Therapy Association and the American Medical Writers Association.

FURTHER READING

Carbasho, Tracy. *Nike*. Santa Barbara, Calif.: Greenwood Press, 2010.

Fenn, Dominic. *Sports Clothing and Footwear.* Hampton, Middlesex, England: Key Note, 2009.

Fuss, F. K., A. J. Subic, and S. Ujihashi, eds. *The Impact of Technology on Sport II.* London: Taylor & Francis, 2008.

Lipsey, Richard A. *The Sporting Goods Industry: History, Practices, and Products.* Jefferson, N.C.: McFarland, 2006.

Museo Del Tessuto. *Superhuman Performance: The Evolution of Textiles for Sports/L'evoluzione del tessuto per lo sport.* Prato, Italy: Author, 2008.

Plunkett, Jack W. *Plunkett's Sports Industry Almanac, 2010: The Only Comprehensive Guide to the Sports Industry.* Houston, Tex.: Plunkett Research, 2009.

Ross, Stewart. *Higher, Further, Faster: Is Technology Improving Sport?* Hoboken, N.J.: Wiley, 2008.

Smit, Barbara. *Sneaker Wars: The Enemy Brothers Who Founded Adidas and Puma and the Family Feud That Forever Changed the Business of Sport.* New York: Ecco, 2008.

Sporting Goods Manufacturers Association. *The State of the Industry, 2009: SGMA's Annual Report on the U.S. Sporting Goods Market.* Washington, D.C.: Author, 2009.

"The Sports Industry." *BERA: Business and Economics Research Advisor* 3/4 (Summer, 2005). http://www.loc.gov/rr/business/BERA/issue3/issue3_main.html.

U.S. Bureau of Labor Statistics. *Career Guide to Industries,* 2010-2011 ed. http://www.bls.gov/oco/cg.

_____. "Sporting Goods Sales by Product Category, 1990 to 2003." In *Statistical Abstract of the United States, 2004-2005.* Washington, D.C.: Author, 2004.

U.S. Census Bureau. North American Industry Classification System (NAICS), 2007. http://www.census.gov/cgi-bin/sssd/naics/naicsrch?chart=2007.

U.S. Department of Commerce. International Trade Administration. Office of Trade and Industry Information. Industry Trade Data and Analysis. http://ita.doc.gov/td/industry/otea/OTII/OTII-index.html.

Telecommunications Equipment Industry

©Danil Chepko/Dreamstime.com

INDUSTRY SNAPSHOT

General Industry: Manufacturing

Career Cluster: Manufacturing

Subcategory Industries: Alarm System Monitoring Equipment Manufacturing; Data Communications Equipment Manufacturing; Global Positioning System Equipment Manufacturing; Mobile Communications Equipment Manufacturing; Radio and Television Broadcasting and Wireless Communications Equipment Manufacturing; Telephone Apparatus Manufacturing; Telephone Central Office and Switching Equipment Manufacturing; Traffic and Railroad Monitoring and Signaling Equipment Manufacturing

Related Industries: Computer Hardware and Peripherals Industry; Internet and Cyber Communications Industry

Annual Domestic Revenues: $70 billion USD (Research and Markets, 2006)

Annual International Revenues: $197 billion USD (Research and Markets, 2006)

Annual Global Revenues: $267 billion USD (Research and Markets, 2006)

NAICS Number: 3342

INDUSTRY DEFINITION

Summary

The telecommunications equipment industry manufactures devices that facilitate the exchange of information across distances. It provides hardware and systems for voice, video, data, image, media, Internet, financial services, and process control through wired, wireless, fiber, cable, and satellite services across the planet. Products include radio and television broadcasting equipment, antennas, cable television equipment, telephone handset and switching equipment, and data communications equipment. The infrastructure that the industry plugs into is often a combination of wire lines, fiber cables, and wireless and satellite link equipment. Customers range from government-owned telecommunications service providers to large public or privately held companies to individual consumers.

History of the Industry

Optical telegraphy in the late 1700's used a telescope to make possible transmission of information across long distances. A person with flags sent information by semaphore. Equipment started with basic telescopes and then included light signaling devices, which heralded the age of optical telegraphy. This then progressed to mechanical semaphore and light towers used to send

1799

A Verizon lineman installs fiber optic cable on a telephone pole in Massapequa Park, New York, in 2006. (AP/Wide World Photos)

coded information. These forms of telecommunications depended on line-of-sight to see, record, and decode the message being sent. Electrical telegraphy was made possible by the growth of the science of magnetism and electrical signaling. Electrical technology replaced the optical (eyesight-based) forms of telecommunications by sending coded electrical impulses to mechanical devices which read the code and could record marks on paper. The use of copper and insulation gave rise to hardwired connections between continents, countries, and people in order to connect electronic forms of transmission with reception of the coded information. The speed of transmission and reception increased many times over the limited forms of optical telegraphy. Distances surpassed those available by optical means and the speed of transmission increased.

The science of electromagnetic radiation enabled a change to wireless methods of transmission, eliminating the limitations of a hardwired connection. The use of fiber optics enabled the development of optical transmission via glass fiber. This opened up high-speed communications for multimedia in an "always on" world of information exchange.

Telecommunications services were often initiated to meet the needs of governments to govern, wage war, defend themselves, and communicate with other governments. The emergence of services for citizens and businesses was an extension of the postal systems of many countries. Government was the customer for large purchases of telephone communications equipment. Data services were added as technology allowed. In the United States in the 1920's, American Telephone and Telegraph (AT&T) operated as a virtual monopoly. One of its divisions, Western Electric, was a primary manufacturer of telecommunications equipment. Until the breakup of the many AT&T Bell system entities in 1974, equipment manufacturing in the United States was dominated by Western Electric, while in

Europe each country had a dominant supplier like Alcatel, Nortel, Siemens, Marconi, or L. M. Ericsson. In Asia, European companies had licensee manufacture arrangements or European equipment was imported by government entities to deploy their systems. Japan started its own companies and had its own standards for telecommunication equipment.

Equipment during the Industrial Revolution was characterized by large manual switchboards with many operators connecting calls to the wired network as requested by callers. Electromechanical switch bays replaced this type of equipment. Many jobs were created to manufacture, install, and maintain large clickety-clack bays of equipment in central office locations. Third-generation equipment before the age of computers employed electronic switches: complex bays of electronic modules created connections in unattended buildings with high requirements for environmental conditioning and maintenance. For equipment manufacturers around the world, this was the heyday of design, manufacture, installation, and maintenance. Rolling out this infrastructure to Asia and the developing world created the illusion of an industry that would just keep growing.

Wireless transmission technology in the twentieth century forever changed telecommunication equipment. Radio and then television broadcasting demonstrated the ability to transmit traditional voice and data traffic wirelessly over microwave links, then up and down to satellites across continents. This technology set the stage for the contemporary evolution of the industry. The construction of terrestrial microwave link stations and interface gear to the wired network created a rapid growth in manufacturing in the 1950's and 1960's. Then, it was found possible to connect satellite communications not only to microwave links but also through an underground cable network, connecting people across the world like never before. A communications signal would traverse many forms of equipment and over a com-

bination of wired and wireless technology to its destination.

The environment for telecommunications service providers of the twenty-first century continues to evolve rapidly while providing simpler and more comprehensive solutions to customers than before. Equipment reliability and flexibility requirements for wireless communications are escalating to provide quality services anywhere and all the time.

The Industry Today

Today, the profile of companies in the industry is changing quickly. In 2005, British Telecom announced the replacement of its traditional public switched telephone network with a next-generation multimedia infrastructure. Four of the ten suppliers named in that announcement are better known as computer companies. (One of the selected ten telecommunications equipment suppliers declared bankruptcy after the announcement). In the United States, there is an ongoing shift by consumers to abandon services from traditional telephone companies and depend solely on cell phones. However, with the introduction of the Internet phone in wireless and cable networks, a huge change is taking place in the way media, data, music, video, and information are received by consumers. Information technology merging with telecommunications technology is enabling a new world of always-on and always-connected devices

Optical fiber. (©Danil Chepko/Dreamstime.com)

and consumers. Equipment is becoming more computer-like and less telecommunications-like.

Equipment, therefore, has a completely new complexion. Television station transmission and signaling is now moving to all-digital, managed by computer-based programming. Unattended radio stations are the norm. Cable television systems provide telephone, Internet, and television services. Pay-per-view is a combination of wired telephone service to order and pay for the event being watched. Music, publishing, and video conferencing are increasing requirements for equipment performance in both the wired and the wireless world.

The old design and manufacturing model was a large company decentralized into the countries it served. This met needs for distribution and design for the unique requirements of standards for that market. National pride and provision of jobs locally were the standard in the twentieth century. Many countries had their own unique telecommunication equipment manufacturers. In the late 1990's, technological advancements, Internet protocol technology, privatization away from government monopolies, and opening of markets to competition caused the globalization of equipment vendors. In addition, vendors have become telecommunication carriers themselves by becoming integrators of end-to-end solutions.

Old line equipment manufacturers have become shadows of themselves. The financial crisis of 2007-2009 has added to the downfall of established firms, and the environment for start-ups has also been dismal. Suppliers have had to favor standards-based solutions (as opposed to proprietary ones) through loosely defined partnerships. The term "next generation" is used widely. That is a transitory term, as 3G networks compete with 4G networks and the lifetime of technology nomenclature can be a year or less. The demanding economic environment is forcing a rapid decline in what infrastructure providers can charge per minute for services. Aggressive pricing requirements are forcing a restructuring of core business definitions for equipment suppliers. Technology shifts are forcing traditional manufacturers to adapt their own technology or acquire new technology companies.

An equipment supplier under siege today must deal with the necessity of finding core competencies, create least-cost operations, provide professional services, and demonstrate the ability to integrate products and manage network operations. Surprising to many in the business was the demise in 2009 of a traditionally excellent supplier, Nortel. Consolidations and mergers of traditional players will lead to the emergence of many new competitors, many of them from the computer industry.

Increased use of the wired environment through compression techniques and encryption requires equipment more common to the computer equipment industry. Network management today is akin to the structure of computer networks more than the telecommunication network topologies of the past. Requirements for redundancy, network monitoring, and high-speed data reliability are increasing the use of traditional incumbent local exchange carriers (land based and undersea). Incumbent local exchange equipment is changing to a new world of information technology.

In parallel to wire lines, there now exist cross-country, undersea, and cross-continent fiber-optic networks for telecommunications. Equipment is structured around a new language of en-

Converter boxes eased the transition from analog to digital television. (©Richie Lomba/Dreamstime.com)

coders, optical cable splicing, computer information encryption techniques, and standards. Existing networks, both over land and undersea, have a lot of unused capacity to be exploited with new technology.

Wireless can be used over land and via satellite. Already enjoying the evolution of the use of cellular technology, WiFi and the coming WiMax technology will provide customers with telecommunications service virtually anywhere and anytime. Wireless equipment and information encryption use techniques from the field of computer information network technology.

The need for equipment providing the key components for transmission paths, network management and monitoring, automated traffic management, and billing is creating opportunities for new entrants, as well as traditional network and computer equipment companies. Global equipment suppliers, therefore, are changing from build-it-yourself companies to integrators of multivendor systems. Their advantage is their traditional presence and penetration of existing markets, along with staying power and financial strength to implement systems. Cisco Systems is an example of taking this to a new level. It is now a systems supplier creating infrastructure for new cities in China. Equipment not only for telecommunications but also for process control, video conferencing, and energy management for sustainable environmental monitoring are part of the new age for a computer component supplier of the twenty-first century.

The fast buildup of wireless Internet is changing the profile of revenue streams from traditionally defined equipment suppliers to suppliers recording revenues in the information technology sector. Two suppliers in China, Huawei and ZTE, have emerged quickly with help from capital supplied by the Chinese government for large projects. Their emergence has changed the landscape for European and American companies. China Telecom could itself become a primary bidder in countries around the world, especially developing countries, as has been seen in their participation in major steel, mining, and seaport projects in the twentieth century. There is an opportunity for technology start-ups to gain traction and attention quickly, and be acquired. Cisco has had a history of acquiring up to twenty-five companies per year. Midsize equipment companies are those with a

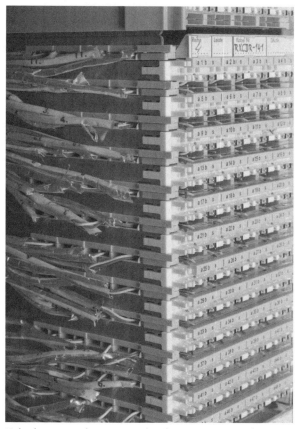

Telephone switching equipment. (©Sergei Butorin/Dreamstime.com)

critical technology that is publicly held; they are always a target for acquisition. Required skills will include being able to work with the large companies with market presence, providing end-to-end solutions and financing.

INDUSTRY MARKET SEGMENTS

Many manufacturers specialize in either wired or wireless technology. Wired telecommunications equipment includes PBX equipment, LAN communications equipment, cable television equipment, and central office switching equipment. Wireless telecommunications equipment includes television broadcasting equipment, antennas, Global Positioning System technology, and cellular telephone and mobile communications equipment. Most manufacturers are midsize-to-large, publicly held companies. In other countries, government manufacturers have moved to co-owned entities or have transitioned to publicly held companies.

Small Businesses

Small businesses in the telecommunications equipment sector operate in niche markets. They may sell base stations for WiFi or WiMax installations; specialized devices for interface to undersea cables; system components such as terminals, interfaces, or bridges; or specialized fiber optic hardware.

Potential Annual Earnings Scale. According to the U.S. Bureau of Labor Statistics (BLS), the average annual salary of all employees of the communications equipment industry was $66,390 in 2009. Industry engineering managers earned an average of $135,730, general managers earned an average of $143,160, and chief executives earned an average of $209,220. Systems software engineers earned an average of $93,960, application software engineers earned an average of $96,590, electrical engineers earned an average of $89,060, and electrical engineering technicians earned an average of $50,070. Sales representatives earned an average of $80,800, customer service representatives earned an average of $40,170, and electronic equipment assemblers on the production floor earned an average of $30,220. For all these occupations, salaries at small businesses are likely to be lower than these industry averages.

Clientele Interaction. Small telecommunications equipment companies sell to private companies, systems integrators, and large companies. Internet marketing, trade shows, and conferences are primary ways to get noticed. To get new business there is a cycle of providing samples, an evaluation period including systems testing, and a final pricing proposal before a purchase is made. Small companies become candidates for acquisition if their technology is superior and priced right. The difficulty is that the price being negotiated for the acquisition is never enough for the owners of the start-up. Success for a small equipment manufacturer is to become a qualified vendor to an end user or larger company doing system integration.

Amenities, Atmosphere, and Physical Grounds. Facilities are typically on one site. There is a fast-paced environment with few employees. Engineers and technicians act as jack-of-all-trades, including client interaction to get the piece of equipment qualified for purchase. Available capital is always related to the amount of orders on the books or the entity supplying capital. Financing from venture capitalists or large telecommunications companies fronting money to small companies has waned.

During the introductory phase of new product development, the atmosphere is one of applying technical people to complete the designs, reaching out to potential customers and working with the customer to get the item accepted for future purchase. Upon getting a purchase agreement, the emphasis shifts to manufacturing, electronic, and environmental testing. Contracts, order management, purchase of components, and assembly personnel will be required. The atmosphere then becomes closer to that of a fully functional manufacturer. The facility is most likely a laboratory environment, in leased space, with manufacturing in close proximity to where the design work is being done. The most significant requirement is security. Protection of proprietary designs is crucial to a small company.

Typical Number of Employees. One of the largest issues facing a small telecommunications equipment company is money. Therefore, the employee count includes people working full time as well as those employed on a temporary, part-time, or contract basis. Often students from work-study programs will be working on various stages of design or manufacture. The combination of all of these categories can range from ten to one hundred, with the count at any time determined by the order book.

Traditional Geographic Locations. Small telecommunications equipment companies are often created by people who leave a larger supplier or computer company in large metropolitan areas. They often occupy new business incubator locations, and are located near universities. They enjoy the benefits of access to technology, potential customers, and employees by being near technical universities and existing larger companies.

Pros of Working for a Small Manufacturer. Because they are often owner-founded, small companies offer quicker decision making. It is possible to have a future stake in the company through stock ownership. The environment can be creative and entrepreneurial. As a jack-of-all-trades, the opportunity to use a combination of skills and contribute innovative solutions is high and satisfying. Working on a temporary or contractor basis also allows time to work at more than one venture. The opportunity to contribute to various technical subjects is much greater. The opportunity to work with customers in order to have the equipment accepted and then to manufacture it as well gives an overview of the complete design-to-delivery process that does not happen in larger work environments.

Cons of Working for a Small Manufacturer. Money is always an issue at small companies, for the product and for the employees. There are highs and lows dependent on a limited product line, the achievement of working on designs, producing of samples, and acceptance or rejection by prospective customers. Responsibility for technical training and growth rests solely with the employee. There will always be a background strain on cash flow, which puts pressure on the longevity of employees; it takes a certain type of person to continue to work through the highs and lows. Variations in worldwide economics will flow back through the large telecommunication system manufacturers who quickly respond by adding or reducing orders to the midsize and small manufacturers, thus creating a whiplash effect. Highs become very high and lows can become disastrous. Company size is also a factor in whether a potential customer will have confidence in the ability of a smaller size supplier to produce adequate production quantities. Forced mergers and acquisitions are ways for a company to complete the adoption of a contributing piece of technology into the market.

A communications tower. (©Dreamstime.com)

Costs

Payroll and Benefits: Small telecommunications equipment manufacturers are caught in a squeeze by the necessity to pay for technical expertise while requiring highly paid skills. Benefits such as vacation and sick time are offered at the discretion of the owner and are usually lacking. Compensation is often a combination of low wages in the short term with a promise of future stock or performance bonuses in the future.

Supplies: Site requirements for cleaning, office, and information technology supplies (ink, discs, paper) are sourced locally.

External Services: Services for a small manufacturing company include security and cleaning.

Utilities: Typical utilities include water, electricity, telephone, and alarm connections.

Taxes: Small properties are required to pay local, state, and federal income taxes, as well as applicable property taxes.

Midsize Businesses

Midsize telecommunications manufacturers range in size from two hundred employees to five thousand. Many are technology-specific businesses concentrating on an interface to fiber or wireless technology networks. Some have created technology to extend the life of wired networks by increasing speed through compression technologies.

Potential Annual Earnings Scale. According to the BLS, the average annual salary of all employees of the communications equipment industry was $66,390 in 2009. Industry engineering managers earned an average of $135,730, general managers earned an average of $143,160, and chief executives earned an average of $209,220. Systems software engineers earned an average of $93,960, application software engineers earned an average of $96,590, electrical engineers earned an average of $89,060, and electrical engineering technicians earned an average of $50,070. Sales representatives earned an average of $80,800, customer service representatives earned an average of $40,170, and electronic equipment assemblers on the production floor earned an average of $30,220. For all these occupations, salaries at midsize businesses are likely to be in line with these industry averages.

Clientele Interaction. Midsize companies with specific products face the challenge of catching the attention of larger system manufacturers. They usually provide samples and engineering support to have their products evaluated for acceptance. The time required to reach production level depends on their customer rolling out their systems and then getting paid. Cash flow cycles in this business are lengthy, so investment up front is often required by investors or other stakeholders.

Interaction is characteristically of business to business. This means all levels of management in the midsize manufacturer are involved with corresponding levels of their customer. Midsize companies have limited marketing and sales personnel. Often, engineering and technician resources are required for applying the product long before production quantities are achieved. The need to approach many prospects simultaneously stretches a midsize company's management focus on its own needs.

Amenities, Atmosphere, and Physical Grounds. A midsize manufacturer is under pressure to provide the amenities of a large one. The competition for skills is more acute for management, engineering, and technical skill levels. Amenities at those levels therefore are similar to those of large manufacturers. At other levels in the organization, such as administration and manufacturing, amenities and benefits are provided relative to those available from competitors in the geographical area where the manufacturer resides.

The atmosphere at a midsize manufacturer is dependent on the product life cycle of their technology. Early introductions are characterized by high involvement with potential customers and technical application to get the product accepted. Once a purchase contract is received, the momentum changes to manufacturing, materials, and final test of the product.

A midsize manufacturer is highly likely to be producing mature and new products simultaneously. Technical and engineering workers are stretched to meet the needs of an ongoing product life cycle while putting attention on a product not yet released for production.

The physical plant is usually a single site. This size manufacturer needs economy of scale so as not to have duplications caused by more than one site. Leases are more common than purchased property to direct capital toward product development and introduction.

Typical Number of Employees. Midsize telecommunications manufacturers employ two hundred to five thousand people. The trend is to outsource manufacturing, so the profile of employees is weighted toward engineering, technical expertise, and marketing.

Traditional Geographic Locations. A midsize manufacturer is likely to be close to potential customers or technology centers in the United States. This is because a combination of needs, including a nearby university, available sources of capital, and ready sources of key employees in technology niches, are likely to be met here. An example is the concentration of fiber-optic work in Petaluma, California, or the storage technology area around Denver, Colorado.

Pros of Working for a Midsize Manufacturer. Midsize companies have attributes similar to large providers, with a defined management structure, and possibilities for advancement and training. Technical employees are likely to gain experience in development, introductions to customers, application of the product, and introduction to manufacturing in a short space of time. Finance and administrative skills can be broadly developed because a midsize manufacturer is always under pressure to keep overhead costs low. Human resources and legal work often are outsourced in an effort to keep ongoing overhead costs down.

Cons of Working for a Midsize Manufacturer. Midsize in this industry is a transitory stage. Constant pressures for economies of scale create pressure to grow. A few large customers put pressure on to modify the product to meet just their needs, thereby inhibiting growth as a large-scale manufacturer. The employee must be flexible to bear the pressure of a boom or bust environment.

Technologies move at a pace that puts pressure on product investment dollars for midsize companies who need to maintain their technical edge. Skill sets of existing employees are also under pressure as technology changes rapidly. Training and skills development are made possible by associating with local community colleges or universities. New technology training may rest on the shoulders of the employee, sometimes with the company paying for it. For employees, it is a fast-paced environment but the pressures on revenue and expenses might truncate spending on training. There is attendant stress that comes from working in environments that change while constantly requiring doing more with less.

Costs

Payroll and Benefits: Midsize telecommunications companies hire staff on a salary, hourly, or on-call basis. Benefits such as vacation and sick time are provided based on industry practices or requirements of the geography in which they operate. Geography and local competitors dictate levels of pay and benefits. Scarce technical skills in an emerging field can create bubbles of wages, beyond the norm.

Supplies: The biggest expense-related items are laboratories, development, and high-technology equipment. In addition, costs related to land (either owned or leased) and access for their facilities is large. Site requirements for cleaning, office, and information technology supplies (ink, discs, paper) are sourced locally or based on purchase agreements.

External Services: Security services, alarm monitoring, utilities, and backup power supply are the types of services required.

Utilities: Water, power, and communication links are usually needed at a single location, whether owned or leased.

Taxes: Taxes are corporate in structure to meet local, state, and federal requirements.

Large Businesses

Large telecommunications manufacturers employ thousands of employees and may have joint manufacturing agreements with other midsize or large manufacturers. With the growth in computer, software, and networking technology coming from the computer industry, it is becoming more difficult to identify a pure telecommunications equipment manufacturer. There are products within large computer companies that are solely telecommunications systems and devices.

Potential Annual Earnings Scale. According to the BLS, the average annual salary of all employees of the communications equipment industry was $66,390 in 2009. Industry engineering managers earned an average of $135,730, general managers earned an average of $143,160, and chief executives earned an average of $209,220. Systems software engineers earned an average of $93,960, application software engineers earned an average of $96,590, electrical engineers earned an average of $89,060, and electrical engineering technicians earned an average of $50,070. Sales representatives earned an average of $80,800, customer service representatives earned an average of $40,170, and electronic equipment assemblers on the production floor earned an average of $30,220. For all these occupations, salaries at large businesses are likely to be equal to or higher than these industry averages.

Clientele Interaction. Large telecommunications equipment providers often provide systems integration and operations management and finance services to their customers. Client interaction is very much business to business, with complex proposal and contracting stages in the sales and business development cycle.

Interactions occur across all levels of management in the company, typically orchestrated by marketing and sales. A client decision to select a telecommunications provider often comes through a proposal stage of several competitors narrowed down to a final selection of a provider. Many governments and large customers have a preferred supplier list in order to reduce technical conflicts, adopt standards, and shorten acquisition processes for new solutions.

Interaction is also required to stay current with regulations, industry standards, minority-owned sourcing, and government agencies concerned about monopolistic practices. Ignoring this area can often result in costs for fines and legal actions for noncompliance.

Amenities, Atmosphere, and Physical Grounds. A large company has combined space for a large number of employees, proper laboratory facilities for engineers, and an attractive atmosphere for close employee interaction in the layout of the workspace. More hierarchy is involved in creating departments with specialties to operate in the enterprise. There are standards for documentation, specifications of equipment, and processes for purchasing in a large project management environment. The working culture is one where the tone is set by management and there is a history to be learned of how that culture works in both formal and informal organization links.

A large company location can become a small city unto itself. Recreation and fitness facilities are often provided for employees. Multiple sites may exist, but there is always the pressure of economy of scale, even for a large manufacturer, to reduce duplication of costs. Many elements of the manufacture or design may be in offshore facilities or achieved through the use of contracted software and hardware development as is seen with Indian companies such as Wipro.

Typical Number of Employees. A large telecommunications service provider employs tens of thousands of employees. Sites can be large and spread out. AT&T has approximately 126,000 employees worldwide, supporting a $51 billion revenue stream. Within that employee complement are manufacturing sites that supplement outside manufacture from other sources. Sites of several hundred employees are common, and the character of each site can be different within a large company according to the main business or engineering functions of that site.

Traditional Geographic Locations. Headquarters operations and operating sites are chosen carefully for availability of employees, tax incentives, and quality of life profiles for their employees. Suboperations are specifically chosen for reaching their market, located within high technology areas or near a university.

Pros of Working for a Large Manufacturer. Large telecommunications equipment providers offer a career that uses and grows skill sets inside its functions of engineering, administration, marketing, and manufacturing. The financial backdrop of a publicly held company takes away some of the highs and lows of employment as the existing lines of telecommunications equipment need to be supported in the telecommunications infrastructure. There is a chance to learn from longer-term employees, apply for new and challenging positions inside the company, and with experience, become a part of the emerging new technology areas.

Because so much of the work is done in partnerships with outside companies, in offshore locations, and with suppliers, it is easier than in midsize companies to gain experience in managing contracts, overseeing quality, and building relationships with peers in business-to-business transactions. There are careers with an external focus like this in addition to careers which exist inside major entities of the company.

With good performance and personal technical growth, there are more inside opportunities for change and trying a different application of one's skill sets. If the company is making acquisitions, there are chances to work in the successful merger of a new acquisition. In large companies, there is a wider panorama of opportunities.

Cons of Working for a Large Manufacturer. In recent times with large shifts of the economy, manufacturers have experienced declines in revenue of 25 percent. This has resulted in massive shifts and layoffs in this sector. This once-stable industry has joined the ranks of a cyclical industry with a subsequent reduction of employment at any single company. The impetus is on the employee to be flexible and plot a path through an industry experiencing turbulence.

Installed base technology can mire a large company in the need to support old technologies and stagnate its employees in old technology. The rapid change from wired to wireless technology creates pressure on a large manufacturer to grow if it can or to acquire the technology. Employment in large companies has become far less certain than in the past.

Costs

Payroll and Benefits: The salary structure of a large telecommunications manufacturer includes hourly, annual, and contract employees. The overall compensation profile is designed to be competitive with others in the industry and the geography of the location. With economic upheavals causing disruption, all benefit areas are under scrutiny for reduction. It is possible in large companies to have health insurance, benefits, and pension-matching schemes that enhance the overall earnings picture for employees. A stock purchase plan for companies in this sector could be quite a wealth builder over a long period of time. Seminars and outside lectures on broad topics are often available for employee enrichment. Training to keep up on and introduce new technologies is a major benefit. On-site university extension course work through video links can be offered.

Supplies: Large telecommunications providers require a wide range of items for running large sites. Besides cleaning and office supplies, there are also requirements for inside cafeteria-like food courts. Information technology is an inside function that requires supplies of paper, discs, ink, and hardware items for employees. Most purchases are done via national negotiated annual contracts.

External Services: There is a trend to outsource functions to meet the needs of the company. Examples are: inside and outside maintenance, food service employees, and even computer help desks for office systems used by the employees at large sites. Certain human resource functions, and benefits for employee assistance, are contracted with outside specialist providers in the areas of legal assistance and psychological counseling.

Utilities: Typical utilities for a large company site include water and sewage, electricity, backup power provision, and oil. As significant users in their community, they work with local sources to negotiate annual rates where possible.

Taxes: Large telecommunications manufacturers are required to pay local, state, and federal income taxes, as well as applicable property taxes.

ORGANIZATIONAL STRUCTURE AND JOB ROLES

Telecommunications firms combine traditional engineering, marketing, and manufacturing with chief executive, financial, human resources, and administrative functions. In addition, a large manufacturer may have divisions of wireless, wired, Internet, and networks within its engineering, manufacturing, and sales and marketing functions. In smaller or midsize companies, where one or two businesses are served, the functions are more directly described with their direct titles, such as wireless services or Internet services. The human resources function is often nested under an administrative function.

The following umbrella categories apply to the organizational structure of businesses in the telecommunications equipment industry:

- Executive Management
- Marketing and Sales
- Engineering
- Manufacturing
- Administration, Finance, and Purchasing
- Human Resources
- Information Technology
- Public Affairs, Policy, and Government Relations

Executive Management

Executive management handles the overall direction and operations of the company. Responsibilities for profit and loss, goal setting, direction of the company, and regulatory compliance rest in these functions in large telecommunications providers. In large providers, a vice president or director title is used for major functions. Since the telecommunications industry is highly technology driven in an environment where quality of service is paramount, executives require strong leadership skills and backgrounds in both business and technology. They are responsible for a large span of subjects within each heading in large companies and therefore have large support staffs and departments within their functions. Their purpose is to assure customers, employees, and stockholders of a viable, healthy, and growing presence in their chosen areas of the telecommunications industry.

Executive management occupations may include the following:

- Chief Executive Officer (CEO)
- Chief Financial Officer (CFO)
- Vice President of Public Affairs, Policy, and Government Relations
- General Counsel
- Marketing and Sales Director
- Engineering Director
- Manufacturing Director
- Administration, Finance, and Purchasing Director
- Human Resources Director
- Information Technology Director

Marketing and Sales

Sales and marketing personnel solicit and acquire revenue streams for the various types of businesses that use telecommunications equipment. Large equipment and systems sales require complex proposal and contracting processes to win the business. Remuneration for marketing is on a salary basis, while sales functions are compensated with a low base salary upon which commission and bonus schemes are applied for meeting sales targets.

The primary task of marketing personnel is to create an awareness of and desire for the company's equipment. The primary task of sales personnel is to turn the prospect into a sale. Both use customer calls, trade shows, conferences, and other events to retain current clients as well as develop new ones for future business.

People serving in these functions must have a high level of knowledge of the equipment they are promoting. Technical staff are often used as a backup as the discussions with the customer dig deeper into the technical details of equipment and systems performance. Contracting and proposal staff also support the business relationship that is achieved. Contact between business units is essential for marketing personnel to develop proposals for large sales.

Sales and marketing occupations may include the following:

- Corporate Sales Manager
- Government Sales Manager
- Consumer Sales Manager
- Corporate Sales Representative
- Government Sales Representative
- Consumer Sales Representative
- Marketing Manager
- Market Research Analyst
- Proposal Writer
- Contract Writer
- Technical Support Specialist
- After-Sales Support Staff

Engineering

Engineering is central to the core technologies of the telecommunications enterprise. Engineers design equipment for the market. For equipment already released to manufacturing, they issue change orders to fix or improve existing equipment. Research and development of new equipment and technologies is the most prominent engineering function. Often, engineers specialize in voice, video, data, compression, or systems integration. Testing, regulatory compliance, documentation, and release to manufacturing are other components of the engineering function.

The range of skills needed by engineers has to match the existing and proposed technologies of the business. Engineers work on advanced technologies for future needs, while maintaining and upgrading existing products. Reliability analysts report on installed base equipment so that engineering can provide solutions to improve the quality and performance of equipment already in use.

Engineers utilize computer-aided modeling, schematics, simulation, design, and layout systems in order to turn their work into reality. Often, the manuals and designs for installation, commissioning, and maintenance of equipment are developed and produced in engineering. Technicians and technical writing specialists are employed at early stages of equipment design to create a release of the product to manufacturing. Members of the staff are commonly university and technical school graduates.

Engineering occupations may include the following:

- Electrical Engineer
- Electronics Engineer
- Electrical Engineering Technician
- Electronics Engineering Technician

OCCUPATION PROFILE

Stationary Engineer

Considerations	Qualifications
Description	Operates and maintains stationary engines and mechanical equipment to provide utilities or power for buildings and industrial processes.
Career cluster	Manufacturing
Interests	Data; things
Working conditions	Work inside
Minimum education level	On-the-job training; high school diploma or GED; high school diploma/technical training; apprenticeship
Physical exertion	Medium work
Physical abilities	Unexceptional/basic fitness
Opportunities for experience	Apprenticeship; military service
Licensure and certification	Required
Employment outlook	Slower-than-average growth expected
Holland interest score	REI

Note: See volume 1, "Publisher's Note," for an explanation of the Holland interest score.

- Industrial Engineer
- Industrial Engineering Technician
- Wired, Wireless, and New Technology Engineer
- Telecommunication Standards Specialist
- Network Interface Engineer
- Equipment Design and Layout Technician
- Technical Writer
- Regulatory Compliance Specialist

Manufacturing

Manufacturing personnel build and ship equipment to meet a monthly plan that is developed by manufacturing managers, as well as marketing and sales personnel. Manufacturing operates from a bill of materials for each product, a manufacturing cycle time (time on the line to produce and test the piece of equipment), and a strategy for raw materials and finished goods inventory. This job requires forecasts from marketing, planners, materials sourcing specialists, and supplier quality specialists to ensure 100 percent availability of components and materials in order to produce the equipment on time for shipment.

Manufacturing systems, supporting equipment, and electronic test personnel (including automated assembly and test specialists) create and manage the manufacturing environment. If offshore manufacturing is employed, then selection of the manufacturing vendor is the responsibility of manufacturing engineers. Infrastructure requirements for a manufacturing line, such as gases and utilities, are designed and implemented working with the facilities group.

Testing and quality assurance are vested within this function. Engineers and technicians ensure the production of the equipment to the original design. There often is a test engineering function, which develops automated testing to ensure lower

OCCUPATION PROFILE

Production Coordinator

Considerations	Qualifications
Description	Prepares production schedules and coordinates and expedites the flow of work within or between departments of manufacturing plants.
Career clusters	Architecture and Construction; Manufacturing; Marketing, Sales, and Service; Transportation, Distribution, and Logistics
Interests	Data; people
Working conditions	Work inside
Minimum education level	Junior/technical/community college
Physical exertion	Light work
Physical abilities	Unexceptional/basic fitness
Opportunities for experience	Part-time work
Licensure and certification	Usually not required
Employment outlook	Slower-than-average growth expected
Holland interest score	ESR

Note: See volume 1, "Publisher's Note," for an explanation of the Holland interest score.

cost, more thorough quality testing, and shorter production times.

Personnel in manufacturing range from the hourly employees for assembly and test through degreed engineers. By employee count it is the largest function within the company, unless all manufacturing is outsourced. Administrative positions in materials, supplier management, and quality assurance are also part of the manufacturing staff.

Manufacturing occupations may include the following:

- Production Manager
- Test Technician
- Production Operator
- Manufacturing Engineer
- Documentation Specialist
- Packaging and Shipping Specialist
- Industrial Engineer

- Manufacturing Information System Specialist

Administration, Finance, and Purchasing

Telecommunications manufacturers depend heavily on the finance staff to balance and manage the company's balance sheet and income statement. Cycles of economic forces can affect the cost of capital and the business cycles of shipments to customers. Analysts provide forecasts and economic scenarios to the executive team. Predictive models are often required for monthly and quarterly reporting of financials and future results.

For electronics manufacturers, not unlike the pharmaceutical industry, there is a long delay between expenditures for research of a product, its development for production, and receipt of purchase orders for the market-ready product. In the middle, a lot of money is expended in wages, equipment, facilities, and material. Administrative staff manage the details during these cycles and into the manufacturing phase. Therefore, purchasing and the material requirements planning systems are essential inputs for finance to have the cash available to the enterprise.

Jobs in these functions include clerical staff (who enter data into computer databases), analysts (who constantly identify trends and opportunities to stretch scarce capital monies), and business professionals (who lead the strategy for the company's cash flow and uses of funds). Financial software or enterprise management systems are heavily used to keep overhead costs low while speeding up the month and year-end financial closing cycles.

Administration, finance, and purchasing occupations may include the following:

- Accountant/Auditor
- Cost Analyst
- Contracts Manager
- Materials Manager
- Supply Manager
- Shipping and Receiving Clerk
- Purchasing Agent
- Contracts Attorney
- Facility, Property, and Services Manager

Human Resources

Human resources personnel handle employee hiring and dismissal processes, employee relations, and employee payroll and benefit administration (including insurance, retirement programs, and other employee benefit programs). Relocation expertise, training, and leadership development are often functions residing within human resources departments. In a union environment, it is important to have specific expertise and a talent for working with union representatives.

In a large company, with over 100,000 employees, this function has the substantial responsibility

---

OCCUPATION PROFILE

Telephone Installer and Repairer

Considerations	Qualifications
Description	Installs, maintains, and repairs telephones and related equipment in homes, businesses, or central offices of telephone companies.
Career cluster	Manufacturing
Interests	Data; things
Working conditions	Work inside; work both inside and outside
Minimum education level	On-the-job training; high school diploma or GED; high school diploma/technical training; apprenticeship
Physical exertion	Light work; medium work
Physical abilities	Unexceptional/basic fitness
Opportunities for experience	Internship; apprenticeship; military service
Licensure and certification	Usually not required
Employment outlook	Slower-than-average growth expected
Holland interest score	RCI

Note: See volume 1, "Publisher's Note," for an explanation of the Holland interest score.

for responding to changes in personnel needs, adding new locations, closing locations, responding to employment issues, and operating within various state or national laws. Payroll and benefits are subject to operations in various locales, requiring human resources to comply with hiring, payroll, and benefit issues by state or country.

Training at all levels is a function of this unit. Employee growth, retention, and leadership training for supervisors and managers are specialties that are crucial to the involvement of human resources in the total business.

Companies often contract through human resources with outside providers for services such as legal assistance, counseling services, and a health insurance service center. Online services, both from kiosks within the company information network and through access by Internet, require expertise in human resources to ensure security and privacy of personal information.

Human resources occupations may include the following:

- Human Resources Director
- Human Resources Coordinator
- Training Manager
- Administrative Assistant
- Benefits Manager
- Benefits Specialist
- Union Liaison
- Employee Information Specialist

Information Technology

Telecommunications equipment manufacturers have extensive needs for manufacturing resource planning systems, sales tracking, market forecasting, financial systems, and design and modeling systems. Information technology (IT) is the service function that ensures the selection and operation of information systems for those jobs. The IT environment also provides computer services; voice, video, and data links; conferencing; hardware; software; computer design workstations; and networks for the company.

IT generates recommendations for privacy, internal usage, Internet usage, standards, new technology adoption, retirement of old technology tools, and software. Projects can involve upgrades, new site start-ups or old site closures, and merging of the IT environment with that of a newly acquired company. Outside providers, national computer supply contracts, network capacity planning and usage, disaster recovery, archival data, and systems software backups are some of the many responsibilities for IT.

A new area is the use of social networking solutions in the conduct of daily business. Policies regarding privacy and protection of company data are new areas requiring IT to respond to the always-on, always-connected world of work. Social networking solutions put a strain on the security and data protection needs of the company.

IT occupations may include the following:

- Software Engineer
- Hardware Technician
- Response Center Specialist
- Network Administrator
- Manufacturing Systems Specialist
- Disaster Recovery Specialist
- Office Systems Specialist
- Design and Modeling Systems Specialist

Public Affairs, Policy, and Government Relations

The telecommunications equipment industry is heavily affected by external requirements set by local, state, federal, and international legislative and regulatory bodies. The environment changes quickly, and there are always recommendations for changes that arise from government and the industry. Telecommunications standards are often in the purview of engineering. However, with such far-reaching implications to the viability of a telecommunications manufacturer, a company often has a specialist in government affairs.

Government entities often request industry input, and members of this function supply individuals for working on task forces or for giving testimony to commissions. Areas of public policy, competition, regulation, and standards are constantly under discussion. The larger the company, the more subject it is to questions about becoming a monopoly. Expertise in this area is relied upon to be the interface to government on behalf of the executive committee. Smaller and midsize companies often rely on the chief executive officer or their managers for this function; a midsize company might use one or two persons. Engagement of an outside lobbying firm would be managed out of this function. Large industry associations conduct lobbying on behalf of the industry, but often depend on input from people working in this area. Decisions on corporate monetary support for outside associations, alliances and lobbyists are led by this function.

Public affairs, policy, and government relations occupations may include the following:

- Telecommunications Attorney
- Policy Analyst
- Regulatory Specialist
- International Telecommunications Attorney
- Trade Association Liaison
- Lobbyist
- Communications Director
- Corporate Relations Specialist
- Vice President of Public Affairs

INDUSTRY OUTLOOK

Overview

The outlook for telecommunications equipment manufacturers is one of turbulence in the second decade of the twenty-first century. The worldwide economic crisis of 2007-2009 is changing the rules for investment and capital availability for infrastructure projects. Moreover, the rapid shift to broadband and wireless technologies has leveled demand for traditional wire- and fiber-based transmission equipment.

The use of handheld and mobile devices instead of wire line-based services has experienced an exponential growth rate. Broadband access spending has tripled over four years at the expense of spending in the dial-up market. The introduction of Internet-connected phones and other devices will only exacerbate the spending shift to Internet-based infrastructure. Subscribers shifting exclusively to their cell phones and abandoning their land line phones are increasing. The opportunity for the traditional plain old telephone service providers and equipment manufacturers is to shift the usage of that installed infrastructure to higher-speed services. Using higher-speed interfaces to their wire line structure as well as coded information devices will open new markets to them for data transmission.

In 2009, precipitous drops in shipments of telecommunications equipment were in the range of 24 percent. Looking inside that overall number, it is clear that the wireless and broadband increase in shipments helped to keep that number from being even larger. The rapid expansion of broadband wireless network equipment has come from the computer equipment sector. Many of the standard names shipping this equipment are Cisco, Juniper Networks, Huawei, ZTE, IBM, and Hewlett-Packard. Smaller equipment manufacturers are classified in the electronic component and network device sector of NAICS reporting.

Therefore, the outlook for the telecommunications equipment industry is changing for three reasons: response by industry and governments to economic upheaval and shifting investments in telecommunications infrastructure; rapid shift to wireless broadband technologies; and shift in technology to chip integration, software, and network data management technology. What lies ahead in terms of applications in the way people of the world interact, conduct business transactions, and communicate with their governments is very exciting. Therein lies the very definition of telecommunications. Equipment and software providers of the future will be defined by new entrants, shifts in business by existing companies, and the adaptability of traditional telecommunications equipment providers to add new capabilities.

Use of video and voice over Internet protocol (VOIP) will grow dramatically and offer opportunities for telecommunications equipment providers. The twentieth century saw early failures as the quality of the voice and video suffered from conflicts for use of Internet paths. With that period behind us, providers of video teleconferencing (Cisco and Hewlett-Packard), subscriber video telephony (Skype), and very low cost telephony (Vonage) all emerged, shifting the consumer away from cellular telephone companies and traditional land line service providers. Selling to consumers through business transactions coupled to video (real estate, travel destinations, or automobiles) with high-definition quality of video available twenty-four hours a day, seven days a week is a high growth area. Video technology for telecommunications providers is another niche for growth or acquisitions.

Consumers expect wireless hot spot access to their portable devices (Internet phones, netbooks,

PDAs) now. Wireless data available through the implementation of WiMax wider range coverage over many miles, instead of over a few feet (wireless hot spots) will set expectations of pervasive computing available anytime and anywhere. Because this allows simultaneous connection to multiple networks, the horizon will open up to collaboration amongst systems and users on common topics or commercial transactions that are currently limited by distance and technology. High definition for images (digital cameras), full-flow video, and text will allow us to be right next to the person to whom we are connected. What a distance the industry has come from peering into the optical telescope on a clear day to communicate over a few miles. Telecommunications equipment providers for today's market will include technologies of computing, software, 4G network wireless technology, and applications not yet seen. Will this equipment come from innovators, existing equipment manufacturers, or businesses not yet defined in this business (Google, Yahoo, or You Tube)?

In summary, the industry outlook for telecommunications equipment by the Telecommunications Industry Association over five years projects that broadband-wire line equipment will grow 6.7 percent as wireless equipment grows at nearly 80 percent. Wire line shipments are essentially flat during this period. One can expect that the top ten telecommunication providers of the twentieth century will be replaced by a top ten of new and surprising names.

Employment Advantages

With a projection of a nearly 80 percent expansion of wireless services over the next five years, new employees entering the telecommunications equipment manufacturing sector can expect exciting challenges and rewards. It is important to search within the computer manufacturing sector for divisions which supply telecommunication network and interface device infrastructure, as well. The challenges will be to hone technical skill sets and adapt business skill sets as the form of manufacturing continues to change to a combination of outsourced and in-house manufacture. Marketing and sales skill sets will be needed to work with nontraditional customers where an application, not just technology, is important.

The spread of applications is keeping intense pressure on the telecommunications manufacturing industry to respond and grow. It is also an industry that is international in nature as manufacturing will be subcontracted to other countries. Technical schools, colleges, and universities are adding course work in the fields of transmission and as a result draw new students to where they know their graduates can find employment. Graphics, video, television, live meetings, voice and image transmission, information compression on wire and wireless networks are all subjects of study leading to entry into the field of leading applications and technologies.

There are exciting prospects for expansion now, such as increased usage of the satellite, wired, and wireless infrastructure for large-area coverage of wireless connections (WiMax). These will likely be eclipsed with new terminology in periods of three years or less. The environment is a constantly moving window of change, and the challenge will be to renew one's skills to stay at the crest of the wave.

Annual Earnings

The Telecommunications Industry Association report for global revenue in 2008 for telecommunications service providers is $1.7 trillion, with the portion from the United States providers being $518.3 billion. The compounded growth rate is just over 10 percent. Revenue for the telecommunications equipment sector has typically been 16 percent of the total revenues for services. The growth rate for equipment is expected to also be just over 10 percent. The startling change for the equipment industry is flat growth for wire line and nearly 80 percent growth in wireless.

The technologies in play are VOIP, WiMax, and Internet television, as well as higher-speed systems on both wireless and wire lines. A lot of this growth will occur as a shift from wire line services and utilizing existing overcapacity in wire and fiber routes. Technologies allowing for greater speed and compression of information will use the same service paths without adding employment.

Computer hardware, semiconductor, and software companies will also be participating in this growth. The network infrastructure is heavily served by divisions of existing large companies, as well as small and midsize manufacturers. The revenues are not separated out in the statistics, neither are many of the company's revenues reported in the traditional telecommunications equipment sector.

RELATED RESOURCES FOR FURTHER RESEARCH

BROADBAND FOR AMERICA
P.O. Box 57244
Washington, DC 20037
Tel: (866) 646-8668
http://www.broadbandforamerica.com

CTIA-THE WIRELESS ASSOCIATION
1400 16th St. NW, Suite 600
Washington, DC 20036
Tel: (202) 736-3200
Fax: (202) 785-0721
http://www.ctia.org

INSTITUTE OF ELECTRICAL AND ELECTRONICS ENGINEERS
3 Park Ave., 17th Floor
New York, NY 10016-5997
Tel: (212) 419-7900
Fax: (212) 752-4929
http://www.ieee.org

INTERNATIONAL TELECOMMUNICATION UNION
Place des Nations
1211 Geneva 20
Switzerland
Tel: 41-22-730-5111
Fax: 41-22-733-7256
http://www.itu.int

JOURNAL OF TELECOMMUNICATIONS AND INFORMATION TECHNOLOGY, NATIONAL INSTITUTE OF TELECOMMUNICATIONS
Szachowa St. 1
04-894 Warsaw
Poland
Tel: 48-22-5128-183
Fax: 48-22-5128-400
http://www.nit.eu

MICROWAVE JOURNAL
685 Canton St.
Norwood, MA 02062
Tel: (781) 769-9750
Fax: (781) 769-5037
http://www.mwjournal.com

TELECOMMUNICATIONS INDUSTRY ASSOCIATION
2500 Wilson Blvd., Suite 300
Arlington, VA 22201
Tel: (703) 907-7700
Fax: (703) 907-7727
http://www.tiaonline.org

ABOUT THE AUTHOR

Charles L. Bonza has thirty years of experience in general management and CEO positions at Hewlett-Packard, Acterna, Sypris Electronics, and BSW South Africa in electronics equipment, telecommunications instrumentation and software, computers, and telecommunications software development, management, and systems implementation. He worked for fifteen years in international environments and engaged in career counseling and change coaching in working with employees during hiring, development, and layoff situations. His technical training in career coaching includes both course work and practical experience at the Hudson Institute for coaching.

FURTHER READING

Buehler, Kevin S., Lee Scoggins, and Mark D. Shapiro. "Caveat Vendor." *McKinsey Quarterly*, August, 2001.

Business Communications Review. *New World Telecom: A Survival Guide for Global Equipment Suppliers*, September, 2005.

Columbia School of International and Public Affairs. *Career Opportunities in Telecommunications.* http://sipa.columbia .edu/resources_services/career_services/ current_students/career_resources/ opportunities/CareerOpp _Telecommunications.pdf.

Courcoubetis, Costas. *Pricing Communication Networks: Economics, Technology, and Modelling.* Hoboken, N.J.: John Wiley & Sons, 2003.

Gruber, Harold. *The Economics of Mobile*

Telecommunications. New York: Cambridge University Press, 2008.

Huurdeman, Anton A. *The Worldwide History of Telecommunications.* Hoboken, N.J.: John Wiley & Sons, 2003.

Laffont, Jean Jacques. *Competition in Telecommunications.* Cambridge, Mass.: MIT Press, 2001.

Plunkett, Jack W. *Plunkett's Telecommunications Industry Almanac Statistics, 2010.* Houston, Tex.: Plunkett Research, 2009.

Rosenberg, Robert. *The 2008 Telecommunications Industry Review: An Anthology of Market Facts and Forecasts.* Boonton, N.J.: Insight Research, 2007. http://www.insight-corp.com/ ExecSummaries/review08ExecSum.pdf.

U.S. Bureau of Labor Statistics. *Career Guide to Industries,* 2010-2011 ed. http://www.bls.gov/ oco/cg.

_____. *A New Approach to Classifying Industries in the Information Sector.* http://www.bls.gov/ opub/ils/pdf/opbils75.pdf.

U.S. Census Bureau. North American Industry Classification System (NAICS), 2007. http:// www.census.gov/cgi-bin/sssd/naics/ naicsrch?chart=2007.

U.S. Department of Commerce. International Trade Administration. Office of Trade and Industry Information. Industry Trade Data and Analysis. http://ita.doc.gov/td/industry/ otea/OTII/OTII-index.html.

Telecommunications Infrastructure Industry

©Eimantas Buzas/Dreamstime.com

INDUSTRY SNAPSHOT

General Industry: Communications
Career Cluster: Arts, A/V Technology, and Communication
Subcategory Industries: Satellite Telecommunications; Wired Telecommunications Carriers; Wireless Telecommunications Carriers
Related Industries: Computer Systems Industry; Internet and Cyber Communications Industry
Annual Domestic Revenues: $518.3 billion USD (Plunkett Research, 2008)
Annual International Revenues: $1.2 trillion USD (Plunkett Research, 2008)
Annual Global Revenues: $1.7 trillion USD (Plunkett Research, 2008)
NAICS Number: 5171-5174

INDUSTRY DEFINITION

Summary

The telecommunications infrastructure facilitates the transmission of voice, video, data, images, media, Internet, financial services, and medical data through wired, wireless, satellite, cable, and fiber connections throughout the world. Transmission methodologies may be based on a single technology or a combination of technologies. Customers range from individual subscribers to companies and governments throughout the world.

History of the Industry

Optical telegraphy in the late 1700's through the use of the telescope enabled the first practice of transmitting information across long distances by mechanical forms of signaling from a sender to a receiver: the telescope. Electrical telegraphy was enabled by the growth of the science of magnetism and electrical principles. This replaced the optical (sight-based) forms of telecommunications with forms of coded marks or sounds sent over a wire. The use of copper and insulation gave rise to hardwired connections between continents, countries, and people in order to connect transmission equipment to receivers of coded information. The speed of transmission and reception increased many times beyond the limitations of optical telegraphy.

The science of electromagnetic radiation enabled the change to wireless methods of transmission, emulating and then surpassing the forms used in the copper wire era. Fiber optics enabled

Wired technologies include cable television, broadband Internet, and traditional telephone lines. (©Kalina Vova/Dreamstime.com)

the development of optical transmission in glass fiber, opening up higher-speed communications for multimedia in an "always on" world of information exchange. Voice, data, and images sent over fiber are of higher quality, with no delays evident in the sound or picture.

Telecommunications services were used to meet the needs of governments to govern, wage war, defend themselves, and communicate with other governments. Over time, services were made available to traders, companies, and individuals. Finally, both wired and wireless telecommunications became the veins and arteries for the Internet. Thus, services have become available to all without borders. From individuals to large entities, the need for instant information in all forms of data, voice, video, and images is changing the divisions within the wired and wireless industry segments. Divisions are becoming multifaceted, encompassing computing, software, networking, protocols, encoding, electronics, materials science, and transmission technologies that are all coming together to provide the infrastructure.

Business parameters involving cost and revenue accounting are being challenged. Revenues could in the future be based on the amount of data transmitted or the time required for transmission. Costs and where they are assigned to the transmission become an issue in traditional business income state-

ments. Communication activity is a flow involving speed, time, and crossing of technology-provider barriers among wireless, wired, and satellite technologies such that the value of a piece of transmitted information is a dynamic one within the reporting of revenue apportioning. The cost across these participants in the transmission pipeline becomes a complex equation, much more complicated than the situation when a single person looking through a telescope at a sender in the distance could figure out the cost to further transmit the sender's message. Cloud computing and cloud telecommunications challenge not only technologists in the telecommunications world but also business professionals to keep up with changes.

With parallel developments in computing, computing chips, communications, and Internet protocols, the world stands at the precipice of a new explosion of information at very high speeds and low costs. At the same time, people excluded from the benefits of telecommunications are poised to become directly connected to the cloud, bypassing the intermediate stages of development that started with optical telegraphy. Latest-technology installations of wireless, cellular, and Internet will speed connections in developing countries. The environment for telecommunications service providers of the twenty-first century will evolve rapidly while providing simpler and more comprehensive solutions to customers than ever before.

The Industry Today

Today, wired and wireless service providers range from small, regional providers to large multinationals doing business in vast regions or across the country. A small provider can be a single rancher with a cell tower providing services in a rural area, a wireless Internet service provider inside a small town or section of a large city, or a small cable franchise providing media, Internet, and phone service to a defined area. Midsize providers are members of the same set but sell their services over wider geographical areas. Some have absorbed smaller providers into larger franchises. Large providers are publicly held corporations or large international corporations with branches in the United States. They may have grown to their present state through mergers and acquisitions, spurred by the breakup of AT&T by the Department of Justice in 1974.

Services provided by smaller and midsize businesses fit the definition of wired and wireless market sectors. The large entities participate in wired and wireless provision of services or partner with others like the large satellite television companies to provide a complete package of services to their customers (examples being large telephone or cable companies providing a trio of services of voice, Internet, and television). Large national voice and cell phone companies, national cable television providers, and Internet service providers with voice over Internet protocol (VOIP) capabilities provide telecommunications in various packages

to their customers. Small and midsize businesses compete by providing advantages to their customers with technology or region- specific coverage. Larger companies may create partnerships or have their eyes on smaller companies for future acquisitions.

A combination of forces is driving opportunities in the telecommunications industry. Advances are being made in computing and software technology, in semiconductor technology, and in communications protocols and encoding methods. Fiber-optic cable is being installed more broadly and reaching more consumers. Satellite technologies, including the satellites themselves and applications exploiting them, continue to expand. New applications are being developed to leverage mobile technology, such as those enabling consumers to make vending machine purchases through their cell phones, for example. Increased speed and reliability alongside cost reductions are leading to a society that is "always on."

Wireless technologies include paging, cellular, and other mobile technologies, including wireless wide-area network systems. (©Wayne Ruston/Dreamstime.com)

There is an exponentially increasing opportunity for small and midsize businesses to start and emerge while larger providers meet the challenges of serving their existing customers. Can large providers move fast enough? Traditional computer equipment companies are becoming sole source providers for delivering telecommunication and information infrastructure to cities of the future under construction now. This is an example of one industry becoming a principal contributor to the old definition of telecommunications service providers. Large providers are learning to grow through mergers and acquisitions as well as by innovation. Companies previously categorized as computer or networking companies are morphing into wired and wireless telecommunications providers through subdivision or acquisition. Companies that never thought of themselves as telecommunications service providers have opportunities, as the cable companies did in 2010, to provide a trio of services. Cable companies are now providing phone and Internet services, in addition to tele-vision. Satellite television companies will add capabilities that expand into the telecommunications world.

Subindustries are springing up to provide wireless hot spots in buildings, towns, and businesses wherever people congregate with their handheld devices to gain access to information. The sector called "other" by the North American Industry Classification System is the fastest-growing in revenues over the other two main categories, wired and wireless. Traditional revenue models for the large traditional players are being threatened by the change in delivery over the telecommunications infrastructure. One example is the decline in the number of land lines as customers go to a wireless-only method of access. In some regions of the country, a third of voice customers have decided to use their cell phone as their only telephone. The impact on large infrastructure providers of wired land line connections is immense.

One of the challenges facing companies will be conflicts over access to the infrastructure. Once a

A telecommunications engineer at work. (©Eimantas Buzas/Dreamstime.com)

A remote GPS antenna station on a mountain peak, with a communications tower. (©Dreamstime.com)

provider allows access of one type of business on top of their existing channels, problems of filtering, delaying, or barring of content may arise. This provides a demand for new solutions of both technology and business model acumen to these industries. An example is when owners of "dark" fiber (unused capacity in existing fiber cables) contract with content providers and find that the content is in competition with their own. One solution is to control the speed or quality of their competitor. VOIP transmissions on telecommunications infrastructure owned by traditional companies is an example of where complaints of this type have arisen.

Common partnerships early in the twenty-first century are traditional phone companies providing packages that include satellite television and Internet service. Emerging partnerships might include commercial enterprises partnering backwards into the traditional telecommunications sector in order to provide phone contact, images, commercial sales, and process control information

to customers. A simple example is the use of a network to control power usage in peak consumption times of homes and buildings. VOIP companies could well become a part of traditional land line companies in order to preserve the revenue streams and usage of the fiber optic infrastructure installed both in ground and under the ocean in the twentieth century. Media companies (newspapers and magazines) are threatened by the emergence of the application of telecommunications technology; they might well become telecommunications providers of their own content or be merged into existing providers.

A look at the state of the industry opens up exciting new possibilities for combinations and permutations of technologies as demands upon the telecommunications infrastructure escalate. Innovations do not necessarily occur just in the domestic U.S. arena. The United States is twenty-fourth out of the top thirty countries in broadband connections. Applications that use the telecommunications infrastructure in Scandinavian countries, Japan, and European countries often exceed what is available in the United States.

This situation leads to a massive pent-up demand for services in the United States. Once maps and music are on one device such as a cell phone, the pressures are even higher to implement applications across the network. More strain on existing telecommunications infrastructure exists, opening new opportunities for growth for new alliances and new providers.

The result is a massive parallelism of growth and opportunity to participate in this industry sector. Required skills and accompanying job titles in business processing, engineering, customer service, sales, marketing, maintenance, and deployment of infrastructure are changing. This is increasing demand for an accelerated rate of growth in this sector. Other factors involving training, certification, and renewal of skills will follow the curve of application of a broader and more complex world of telecommunications providers. Entry into these industries will be available in all sizes of businesses and in captive applications (such as telecommunications infrastructure within a company or law office). Provision of services in a defined area (such as wireless services to a town or airport space) is growing daily. National and international growth occurs as developing countries race to the future and the digital divide is crossed. Developing countries benefit at the same time as the developed countries.

INDUSTRY MARKET SEGMENTS

Telecommunications infrastructure companies often specialize in wired or wireless technologies. Wired technologies include cable television, broadband Internet, and traditional telephone lines. Wireless technologies include paging, cellular, and other mobile technologies, including wireless wide-area network (WAN) systems. Other companies provide satellite telecommunications services, which are categorized separately.

The telecommunications infrastructure industry ranges from small companies and start-ups to large government entities (especially outside the United States) to quasi-governmental entities (companies owned by the government but outsourced to public companies) to publicly and privately held companies. Within these divisions, the lines can blur, as wired and wireless services along with Internet service are often provided within one entity.

Small Businesses

Telecommunications service providers typically serve small, defined regions or territories. They are privately owned and were started as adjuncts to other interests. A cell phone tower put up by a local businessperson along an interstate, a wireless service to cover an area in a region not served by other alternatives, or an Internet service provider all derive revenues either from the customers they serve or from pass-through revenues of larger partners. Small telecommunications infrastructure businesses earn less than $25 million in annual revenues.

Potential Annual Earnings Scale. According to the U.S. Bureau of Labor Statistics (BLS), the average annual salary of all telecommunications industry employees was $57,760 in 2009. Computer and information systems managers earned an average of $127,720, general and operations managers earned an average of $127,180, and chief executives earned an average of $189,920. Systems software engineers earned an average of $90,830, network systems and data communications analysts earned an average of $79,030, network administrators earned an average of $72,100, and computer support specialists earned an average of $45,350. Electronics engineers earned an average of $84,950, while electronics engineering technicians earned an average of $57,420. Service sales representatives earned an average of $57,150, while product sales representatives earned an average of $79,660. Customer service representatives earned an average of $36,640, telecommunications equipment installers and repairers earned an average of $55,280, and line installers and repairers earned an average of $52,660. For all these occupations, salaries at small businesses are likely to be lower than these industry averages.

Clientele Interaction. Small telecommunications providers rely on direct customers or may themselves be the customers of larger companies for which they provide an extension of coverage. The success of these businesses is primarily based

Many residents of this apartment building have satellite dishes. (©Dreamstime.com)

on the quality of service they provide and the cost basis for their business. In some cases, they may have title or exclusive local relationships or property holdings that keep out outside competition. They become candidates for acquisition either because of their exclusive coverage or the loyalty of their customer base. This type of business is in a position to provide local content or identity to their customers, which gives them a marketing advantage in their region.

Amenities, Atmosphere, and Physical Grounds. Facilities to provide services are typically on one site. They are required to provide coverage twenty-four hours per day, seven days per week. A facility has to be secure and temperature controlled through all seasons. Customer expectations for cell phone coverage and Internet services are high. Reliability factors determine the basic costs for the facility, which are higher than for usual commercial or retail space. If the company is providing services to a national provider, such as roaming for a cell phone company, it will have to comply with requirements that are specified to get the fran-

chise for their area. In the case of Internet service providers, their customers may have quality requirements for the space into which they put their equipment. Environmental hardening of the facility, and security needs are examples of these cost factors for this industry.

The most rigid requirement is for security. These facilities are usually unattended for long periods of time. External hardening to secure the area, locked cages in the case of Internet providers for each occupant of their facility, a backup power supply, and alarm systems are all attributes of an unattended high-quality space for telecommunication Internet service providers.

Typical Number of Employees. One of the largest issues facing a telecommunication service provider is expense. The fact that facility costs are high creates a built-in base expense coupled to the high cost of the equipment, cell phone tower, and electronic equipment. These costs make entry into this business expensive. Thus, the number of employees, especially direct hires, is small. The preference is to hire contract workers in technical or facilities specialties to minimize full-time wages and benefits. For an individual employee, lacking benefits and sometimes only paid on a per-job basis, there is the opportunity to spread the work over a combination of technologies. Experience in multiple technologies such as Internet service provision, networking, and cell phone services provides well-rounded experience not available in larger companies where specialization is the norm.

Traditional Geographic Locations. Small service providers usually have one facility or location. A cell phone provider could have several towers and an attendant support facility in a county. Since the area of coverage is operating in an underserved area, the location may often be remote or rural. In the case of satellite television services, the locations will be on the customer's sites, such as hotel properties. A small Internet service provider has one location.

Pros of Working for a Small Provider. Because small providers are owner-founded, there is quicker decision making and the opportunity to spread oneself over many technologies is great. The opportunity to gain wide experience, therefore, is unmatched. The opportunity to grow into the operations management area depends on the owner's involvement in the business, other business interests of that owner, and their age and family involvement in the business. For entrepreneurs, there exists the opportunity to start from scratch, but the initial entry investment is high as a result of the demand for a high-quality facility and expensive equipment. If one works as a contractor, then the opportunity to work with multiple telecommunications providers exists, allowing workers to apply their talents over a wide range of technologies.

Cons of Working for a Small Provider. In many ways, the positive aspects of working for a small telecommunications provider are the same as the negative elements. For example, the fact that there is such a stringent requirement for quality of service means an employee or contractor is on call twenty-four hours per day. The owner also would be expected to respond and can be quite demanding of others. The knowledge requirement for the technologies of the whole operation is much higher as there is no one else to ask in case of problems. Some training may come from the equipment suppliers, but much will be self-taught. Seasonality will be a factor, if the facility is subject to

weather-related outages or variation in service. In the case of cell phone and cable television service providers, the outdoor elements can be a factor in work environment in responding to outages.

Costs
Payroll and Benefits: Small telecommunications providers are caught in a squeeze, needing to pay for technical expertise while usually operating in areas of lower wages. Benefits such as vacation and sick time are therefore offered at the discretion of the owner.

Supplies: Providers are subject to high parts-replacement rates when operating cell phone services, Internet service hosting, satellite television downlinks, and wireless networks.

External Services: Security services, alarm monitoring, utilities, and backup power supply maintenance contracts are the types of services required. Annual audits and inspections are sometimes outsourced.

Utilities: Typical utilities include water, electricity, gas or oil, telephone, and alarm connections.

Taxes: Small properties are required to pay local, state, and federal income taxes, as well as applicable property taxes. They must also collect state and local taxes if they have direct customers for their services.

Midsize Businesses
Midsize telecommunications providers range in size from one thousand to almost fifty thousand employees. A business of this type could have more than one technology service, such as wireless and satellite television, or Internet service provision along with telephone service. They operate over wider territories and regions and have revenues of over $25 million annually.

Potential Annual Earnings Scale. According to the BLS, the average annual salary of all telecommunications industry employees was $57,760 in 2009. Computer and information systems managers earned an average of $127,720, general and operations managers earned an average of $127,180, and chief executives earned an average of $189,920. Systems software engineers earned an average of $90,830, network systems and data communications analysts earned an average of $79,030, network administrators earned an average of $72,100, and computer support specialists earned an average of $45,350. Electronics engineers earned an average of $84,950, while electronics engineering technicians earned an average of $57,420. Service sales representatives earned an average of $57,150, while product sales representatives earned an average of $79,660. Customer service representatives earned an average of $36,640, telecommunications equipment installers and repairers earned an average of $55,280, and line installers and repairers earned an average of $52,660. For all these occupations, salaries at midsize businesses are likely to be in line with these industry averages. Benefits, stock purchase, and pension-matching are provided only on a competitive basis and depend on the city or region where a given firm is located in order to attract and retain employees.

Clientele Interaction. Service providers have direct customers or their customers are national companies for which they provide service. In the case of Internet service providers, their customer is the content or media provider for which they provide space and hosting in their facility. Service providers with direct customers must have the patience and customer service skills of a retail environment including having call center access in case of problems with service on a twenty-four-hour basis. Service providers whose customer is a larger corporation will have to manage relationships on a business-to-business basis and create technical linkages into national operation centers for quality of service monitoring and response.

Amenities, Atmosphere, and Physical Grounds. Multiple facilities with network linkages are normal for midsize service providers. They may operate in multiple cities or states, such that the operations and facility skills for telecommunications are required in their employee complement. Depending on the company, an employee may get to know and work with people outside of the employee's main skill set. Over time there will be the opportunity to work on projects which require personal interactions and mixing of skill sets for different lines of the company's business. Physical grounds are composed of midsize sites involving several hundred employees or sublocations that easily fit leased spaces in larger office parks. These will be located to accommodate the needs and competitiveness of the company and to recruit and retain their employees for business functions in that area.

Typical Number of Employees. Midsize providers employ from one thousand to fifty thousand people.

Traditional Geographic Locations. Locations are multipoint within a city, a county, or a state, or over several states. In the case of cable or satellite television, the locations are dictated by the customers' properties where services are provided. A midsize Internet service provider might have different hosting locations dictated by profiles of their customer base's home locations.

Pros of Working for a Midsize Provider. Midsize companies have similar attributes to large providers, with a defined management structure, and possibilities for advancement and training. Staying current with technology is important as the field is moving so quickly, so this aspect as part of a working environment is key to progress in the telecommunications field. At the same time, for those on the administrative side, regulations, partnerships, and contracting are also challenges which provide career opportunities. Constant pressure to provide more with less money and fewer people creates an environment of growth and possibility for pursuing skill sets around the enterprise in an environment of rapid change.

Cons of Working for a Midsize Provider. Midsize in this industry is a transitory stage. Constant pressures for economies of scale create pressure to grow, add more services, or merge just to stay even in the industry. Technologies move at a pace that puts pressure on capital dollars for midsize companies to maintain their existing base while moving on. Training and skills development are possible where the equipment vendors offer training, while more generic skills and new technology training rest on the shoulders of the employee, sometimes with the company paying for it. For those working there, it is a fast-paced environment but the pressures on revenue and expenses might truncate spending on training. There is attendant stress that comes from working in environments that change while constantly requiring doing more with less.

Costs

Payroll and Benefits: Midsize telecommunications companies hire staffs on a salary, hourly, or on-call basis. Contractors also are used to respond to projects and variation in loads. Benefits such as vacation and sick time are provided based on industry practices or requirements of the geographical area in which they operate. Some may also have union contracts operating for their hourly workers.

Supplies: The biggest related expense items are plant and high-technology equipment. In addition, costs related to land (either owned or leased) and access for their facilities are large. Site requirements for cleaning, office, and information technology supplies (ink, discs, paper) are sourced locally or based on national purchase agreements.

External Services: Security services, alarm monitoring, utilities, and backup power supply maintenance contracts are the types of services required. Annual audits and inspections can be subcontracted to specialists.

Utilities: Water and power needs are typical for large companies, but they have the added burden of high reliability requirements. They need to be supplemented by backup generators in case of outages from the supplier or that are due to weather.

Taxes: Taxes are corporate in structure to local, state, and federal requirements. In addition, direct customers for voice and data services are taxed according to local, state, and federal requirements and reported and paid accordingly.

Large Businesses

Large telecommunications providers employ tens of thousands of employees and their scope of operations is usually both in the United States and abroad. The range of business activities is matched by the range of job titles available. Jobs exist beyond typical engineering and business titles in such areas as disaster recovery, right-of-way agents, and government relations.

Potential Annual Earnings Scale. According to the BLS, the average annual salary of all telecommunications industry employees was $57,760 in 2009. Computer and information systems managers earned an average of $127,720, general and operations managers earned an average of $127,180, and chief executives earned an average of $189,920. Systems software engineers earned an average of $90,830, network systems and data communications analysts earned an average of $79,030, network administrators earned an average of

$72,100, and computer support specialists earned an average of $45,350. Electronics engineers earned an average of $84,950, while electronics engineering technicians earned an average of $57,420. Service sales representatives earned an average of $57,150, while product sales representatives earned an average of $79,660. Customer service representatives earned an average of $36,640, telecommunications equipment installers and repairers earned an average of $55,280, and line installers and repairers earned an average of $52,660. For all these occupations, salaries at large businesses are likely to be equal to or greater than these industry averages. Large companies often offer health insurance, pension-matching schemes, and other benefits, including stock options or stock purchasing plans. Seminars and outside lectures on broad topics are often available for employee enrichment. Training to keep up on and introduce new technologies is a major benefit.

Clientele Interaction. Large service providers have direct customers for which they provide their service and a combination of resellers, partners, alliances, and governments as well. In the case of the Internet service operation, the customer is the content or media provider for which they provide space and hosting in their facility. Interactions occur through customer service centers and network operation centers; these are employed to maintain quality of service of the delivered product as well as personal contact to respond to customer needs. All of this is required on a full twenty-four-hour basis, seven days a week.

Interaction occurs also on a large scale involving multiple points of contact with states, government entities, and regulators in order to maintain and grow coverage. Ignoring this area can often result in costs for fines and legal actions for noncompliance or poor customer service.

Amenities, Atmosphere, and Physical Grounds. A large company has combined space for a large number of employees, proper laboratory facilities for engineers, and creates an atmosphere in which there is a lot of employee interaction due to the layout of the workspace. More hierarchy is involved in creating departments with specialties to operate in the enterprise. Competition for space and status symbols can be a part of large company environments. The working culture is one where the tone is set by management and there is a history of how that culture works in both formal and informal organization links.

Large companies provide parking, eating facilities, kiosks such as automated teller machines, and break areas inside or out of doors. Because of concern for productivity, often there is on-site contact with the surrounding community businesses and commerce. A large company location can become a small city unto itself. Recreation and fitness facilities are often provided for employees.

Typical Number of Employees. A large telecommunications service provider employs tens of thousands of employees. Sites can be large and spread out. AT&T has approximately 126,000 employees, supporting a $51-billion revenue stream. Sites of several hundred employees are common and the character of each site can be different within a large company, according to the main business or engineering functions of that site.

Traditional Geographic Locations. Headquarters operations and operating sites are chosen carefully for availability of employees, tax incentives, and quality of life profiles for their employees. Suboperations are specifically chosen for reaching their market and even for engineering reasons. For example, they may need to be located next to major communications and Internet-connect points in the Defense Advanced Research Projects Agency (DARPA) network.

Pros of Working for a Large Provider. More so than smaller and midsize telecommunications service providers, large companies depend on interaction of their major functions (business, marketing, service delivery) to deliver quality of service and respond to market changes. Employee career paths are often in a major area of expertise. Careers will ascend along with earnings within an area and will be challenged by the growth in the telecommunications industry. For hourly employees, a benefit is the relative stability of pay, due in large part to collective bargaining for several of the job categories involving maintenance, installation, and operation center personnel. Economic downturns have resulted in major layoffs so there are cycles of ups and downs to which the companies respond. Technologies are essential to responding to the market, so training and exposure to new technologies is a key strategy to maintaining the expertise of their employees in addition to outside hires.

Cons of Working for a Large Provider. For many companies the sheer complexity of the telecommunications environment, the entry of new technologies, and the need to maintain a large installed technology is proving to be difficult financially and management-wise for large companies. This creates a turbulent environment for the employees as the company responds. Also, it is possible for a career in what was a new technology to become cornered. While seeming to move slowly, employees and managers in large telecommunications companies face myriad changes every week that can seem bewildering; the need to learn one new operational policy after another requires a lot of flexibility on an employee's part.

Costs

Payroll and Benefits: The salary structure of large telecommunications providers can be complex, owing to the many positions and job types. Service personnel (such as installers and maintenance) are generally paid on an hourly basis. Many are subject to union contracts. Those in administrative positions (managers, administrative assistants, and salespersons, for example) are paid on a yearly basis with some performance incentives. Benefits such as stock purchase, pension matching, vacation time, and sick time are offered on a competitive basis with others in the industry and through union contracts.

Supplies: Large telecommunications providers require a wide range of items for running large sites. Besides cleaning and office supplies, and facilities needs, there can also be requirements for inside cafeteria-like food courts. Information technology is an inside function that requires supplies of paper, discs, ink, and hardware items for the IT environment for employees. Most purchases are generally under annual contracts.

External Services: There is a trend to outsource functions in order to avoid the demand for benefits of full-time employees. Examples of outsourced jobs are inside and outside maintenance functions, food service employees, and even computer help desks for office systems used by the employees at large sites. Certain human resource functions, and counselors for employee assistance are contracted with outside providers specializing in areas of legal assistance and personal counseling.

Utilities: Typical utilities for a large company site include water and sewage, electricity, and backup power provision. As significant users in their community, they work with local sources to negotiate annual rates where possible.

Taxes: Large telecommunications infrastructure companies are required to pay local, state, and federal income taxes as well as applicable property taxes. They must also collect federal, state, and local taxes from their individual subscribers for voice and data services through their wired and wireless business units.

ORGANIZATIONAL STRUCTURE AND JOB ROLES

Telecommunications infrastructure companies base their organizational structures on their operational, market, technological, employment, and regulatory needs. From the largest companies, where these functions have their own vice presidents or directorships under the chief executive officer, to the smallest, where the functions are grouped together, all elements are found in the structure of a company.

With the multiplicity of business functions and relationships that a large entity covers, areas such as marketing, operations, service delivery, and engineering might be so large as to require specialties in wireless, wired, Internet, networks, and perhaps a global executive as well. These are very often business units in themselves tapping into the expertise in the other functions.

Functional titles might include mobile markets, consumer markets, business solutions, and diversified businesses (a catchall where very often emerging businesses and alliances reside).

In smaller or midsize companies, where one or two businesses are served, the functions are more directly described with their direct titles, such as wireless services, or Internet services. The human resources function is often nested under an administrative function in small companies.

The following umbrella categories apply to the organizational structure of businesses in the telecommunications infrastructure industry:

- Executive Management
- Development and Planning
- Marketing and Sales
- Public Affairs, Policy, and Government Relations
- Operations
- Engineering
- Human Resources
- Information Technology

Executive Management

Executive management handles the overall direction and operations of the company. Responsibilities for profit and loss, goal setting, direction of the company, and regulatory compliance rest in these functions in large telecommunications providers. In large providers, each of these often has a vice president or director title. Since the telecommunications industry is highly technology driven in an environment where quality of service is paramount, the requirement for strong leadership with a background in both business and technology is optimal. These individuals cover a large span of subjects within each heading in large companies and therefore have a large supporting staff and departments within their function. Their purpose is to assure customers, employees, and stockholders of a viable, healthy, and growing presence in their chosen areas of the telecommunications industry.

Executive management occupations may include the following:

- Chief Executive Officer (CEO)
- General Counsel
- Chief Financial Officer (CFO)
- Marketing and Sales Director
- Operations Director
- Engineering Director
- Development and Planning Director
- Public Affairs, Policy, and Government Relations Director
- Human Resources Director
- Information Technology Director

Development and Planning

Development and planning departments provide corporations with plans to address changes in technology, customer revenue patterns, and the competitive environment. This function works closely with marketing to constantly assess the current direction of provision of service, international trends, new entrants, and technical advances; it makes recommendations for existing as well as new directions for the company.

The current and future reach of the telecommunications network is constantly being reviewed. Current capacity, weighed against customer demand, is a constant topic for development and planning to put forth recommendations and models for the future. Since there is high pressure on revenue per customer, the cost structure is always in review with a view to increasing productivity or making decisions on economies of scale. This group is always at the center of those discussions, especially when it comes to the budgeting process for the years ahead.

Often development and planning will create small teams drawn from engineering, operations, and marketing to address specific challenges put forth by the executive team to address both threats and opportunities. This group can package alternatives into recommendations in short periods of time and assure cross-functional input.

Development and planning occupations may include the following:

- Network Analyst
- Financial Analyst
- Technology Analyst
- Right-of-Way/Easement Specialist
- Mergers and Acquisitions Specialist
- Market Analyst
- International Analyst
- Computer Modeling Specialist

Marketing and Sales

Marketing and sales personnel solicit and acquire revenue streams for the various types of businesses of the telecommunications provider. Customers range from individual customers, such as Internet service for a small local provider, to large businesses and government departments. The services required by these customers have to be described by marketing for fulfillment by salespeople in the form of direct contact through complex proposal and contracting processes to win the business. Remuneration for marketing is on a salary basis while sales functions are compensated with a base salary upon which commission and bonus schemes are applied for meeting sales targets.

The primary task of marketing personnel is to create awareness and desire for the company's services. The primary task of sales personnel is to turn the prospect into a sale. Both marketing and sales personnel work at trade shows and conference events to maintain current clients as well as develop new ones for future business.

People serving in these functions must have a high level of knowledge of the services they are promoting. Technical staff are often used as a backup as the discussions with the customer dig deeper into the services. Contracting and proposal staff also support and lead to fulfillment the business relationship that is achieved.

Marketing and sales occupations may include the following:

- Corporate Sales Manager
- Corporate Sales Representative
- Government Sales Manager
- Government Sales Representative
- Consumer Sales Manager
- Consumer Sales Representative
- Proposal Writer
- Contracts Attorney
- Technical Support Specialist
- After-Sales Support Specialist

Public Affairs, Policy, and Government Relations

Telecommunications are greatly affected by external requirements set by local, state, federal, and international legislatures and regulatory bodies. The environment changes quickly, and there are always recommendations for changes that arise from government and the industry. Telecommunications standards are often in the purview of engineering. However, with such far-reaching implications for the viability of a telecommunications provider, a company often has a specialist in government affairs.

Government entities often request industry input, and members of this function supply individuals to task forces or for giving testimony to commissions. Areas of public policy, competition, regulation, and standards are constantly under discussion. The larger the company, the more subject it is to questions about becoming a monopoly. Expertise in this area is relied upon to be the interface to government on behalf of the executive committee. Smaller and midsize companies often rely on the chief executive officer or their managers for this function; a midsize company might use one or two persons. Engagement of an outside lobbying firm would be managed out of this function. Large industry associations conduct lobbying on behalf of the industry, but often depend on input from people working in this area. Decisions on corporate monetary support for outside associations, alliances, and lobbyists are led by this function.

Public affairs, policy, and government relations occupations may include the following:

- Telecommunications Attorney
- Policy Analyst
- Regulatory Specialist
- International Telecommunications Attorney
- Trade Association Liaison
- Lobbyist
- Vice President of Public Affairs
- Corporate Relations Specialist
- Communications Director

Operations

Operations is the customer-interface portion of the telecommunications infrastructure business. It has the largest employee count of a typical company. It can be divided along major customer lines (business, voice subscriber) or base technology lines (wired, wireless, Internet).

Closest to the customers are installation, maintenance, and repair jobs. The industry at large has union representation in these occupations. Installers, optical and copper splicers, switching and routers repair personnel, customer premises repair employees, outdoor installers, and outdoor maintenance people are examples of this job category.

PROJECTED EMPLOYMENT FOR SELECTED OCCUPATIONS

Telecommunications Industry

Employment		Occupation
2009	Projected 2018	
124,930	132,200	Customer service representatives
25,090	22,300	Electronics engineers, except computer
17,030	16,400	First-line supervisors/managers of office and administrative support workers
130,520	118,100	Telecommunications equipment installers and repairers, except line installers
95,130	86,000	Telecommunications line installers and repairers
13,910	13,300	Telephone operators

Source: U.S. Bureau of Labor Statistics, Industries at a Glance, Occupational Employment Statistics and Employment Projections Program.

Operations employees include first-line supervisors and managers of office and administrative support workers for customer-interfacing tasks such as billing, customer service, call center, and network operations centers. The management of customer engagement through an order, contract, or other form of service requires specialists in tune with the business detail required for each customer covering a range of customer categories (government, business, and consumer).

The operations function includes the installation, monitoring, tuning, calibrating, and running of the in-line delivery of the telecommunications infrastructure, whether through wireless or wired/fiber optic connections. These are typically advanced technician skills, and part of a career path that can follow experience in installation and repair functions.

In addition, project management, asset deployment, and tracking are areas that deal with the facility, plant, layout, and deployment in the area of coverage. Provision and deployment of specialized vehicles are other functions that often come within the purview of operations.

Quality of service involves network operations center personnel, disaster recovery planners and specialists, customer service representatives, and performance analysts.

Operations occupations may include the following:

- Network Management and Monitoring Technician
- Disaster Recovery Specialist
- Project Manager
- Plant Support Engineer
- Service/Quality of Delivery Analyst
- Administrative Assistant
- Customer Service Representative

- Telecommunications Installer/Repairer
- Asset Management and Tracking Specialist
- In-Line Equipment Operator

Engineering

Engineering is at the heart of telecommunications infrastructure enterprises. Engineers design and issue plans for projects, as well as specifications and expansions for existing routes, design fixes, and improvements for quality of service. They also research and develop new equipment and technologies. Often, this function divides itself into specialties for voice, video, data, compression, and systems integration. Studies are often undertaken to find new applications using existing or new technology. Testing of sophisticated communication systems is a major part of their responsibility to the company.

OCCUPATION SPECIALTIES

Telecommunications Equipment Installers/Repairers

Specialty	Responsibilities
Central office repairers	Test, analyze defects in, and repair telephone circuits and equipment in central telephone company offices.
Central-office installers	Install equipment used to select, connect, and disconnect telephone lines in the telephone company central office.
Central-office repairer supervisors	Supervise and coordinate workers who construct, install, test, maintain, and repair electric power equipment.
Frame wirers	Connect wires from telephone lines and cables to distributing frames in telephone company central offices.
Instrument repairers	Repair, test, and modify telephone and telegraphic equipment.
Office electricians	Adjust submarine cable and terminal circuits and rearrange connections in cables.
PBX installers	Install telephone switchboards, telephoto circuits, mobile radiotelephones, and teletypewriters.
PBX repairers	Analyze and repair defects in telephone switchboards, teletypewriters, and mobile radiophones.
Trouble locators	Locate malfunctions in telephone and telegraph lines and coordinate corrective work of maintenance crews.

OCCUPATION PROFILE

Telecommunications Installer and Repairer

Considerations	Qualifications
Description	Sets up and maintains telecommunications equipment to transmit communication signals via computer, television, radio, and telephone.
Career cluster	Manufacturing
Interests	Data; people; things
Working conditions	Work inside
Minimum education level	Bachelor's degree
Physical exertion	Light work
Physical abilities	Unexceptional/basic fitness
Opportunities for experience	Internship; apprenticeship; military service; part-time work
Licensure and certification	Usually not required
Employment outlook	Slower-than-average growth expected
Holland interest score	RSE

Note: See volume 1, "Publisher's Note," for an explanation of the Holland interest score.

The range of skills has to match the existing technologies for the business and includes people working in advanced technologies for future needs. Installed base technology for older voice systems requires engineering change orders and improvements along with other current and newer wired or wireless systems. Input from the quality of service analysts needs to be passed through engineering for solutions to improve system quality and performance.

Within engineering is the need for computer-aided modeling, schematics, computer simulation, design, and layout systems in order to turn the work into reality. Often the manuals and design for installation, commissioning, and maintenance of the systems is written and produced in engineering. Specialists in technical writing are often employed at early stages of a system design.

Engineering occupations may include the following:

- Wireless and New Technology Engineer
- Systems Engineer
- Telecommunication Standards Specialist
- Transmission Methods Engineer
- Compression and Traffic Engineer
- Systems Design and Layout Technician
- Systems Installation Technician
- Technical Writer
- Regulatory Compliance Specialist

Human Resources

Human resources personnel handle employee hiring and dismissal processes, employee relations, and employee payroll and benefit administration (including insurance, retirement programs, and other employee benefit programs). Relocation expertise, training, and leadership development are often functions residing within human resources. In a union environment, it is important to have specific expertise and a talent for working with union counterparts.

In a large company, which can be 100,000 employees or more, this function has the substantial responsibility for responding to changes in personnel needs, adding new locations, closing locations, responding to employment issues, and operating within various state or national laws. Payroll and benefits are subject to operations in various locales, requiring human resources to comply with hiring, payroll, and benefit issues by state or country.

Companies often contract with outside providers for legal assistance, counseling services, and health insurance service. Online services, both from kiosks within the company information network and through access by Internet, require expertise in human resources to ensure security and privacy of personal information.

Human resources occupations may include the following:

- Human Resources Director
- Human Resources Coordinator
- Human Resources Manager
- Administrative Assistant
- Benefits Manager
- Benefits Specialist
- Union Liaison
- Employee Information Specialist

Information Technology

Telecommunications providers are information technology (IT) providers through their network services. They also have their own needs for computer services; voice, video, and data links; conferencing; hardware; software; computer design and modeling workstations; and networks. The IT group is inward-facing to meet its own company's needs, while the telecommunications provider is outward-facing, often providing similar services to its external customers.

The IT department generates recommendations for privacy, internal usage, Internet usage, standards, new technology adoption, retirement of old technology tools, and software. Projects can involve upgrades, new site requirements, old site closures, and merging of the IT environment of a newly acquired company. Outside providers, national computer supply contracts, network capacity planning and usage, disaster recovery, archival data, and systems backups are some of the many responsibilities of IT.

A new area is the usage of social networking applications as a part of the business environment. Policies regarding privacy and safeguarding of company data are new areas requiring IT to respond to the always-on, always-connected world of work.

IT occupations may include the following:

- Software Applications Specialist
- Hardware Specialist
- Response Center Specialist
- Network Specialist
- Network Services Specialist
- Disaster Recovery Specialist
- Office Systems Specialist
- Design and Modeling Systems Specialist

INDUSTRY OUTLOOK

Overview

Even in a period of financial crisis and upheaval, telecommunications is going through an accelerating transformation. During the second decade of the twenty-first century, environments will be driven by applications, which are rapidly being adopted by media, government, and traditional corporations. Social networking, television everywhere, texting, phoning, GPS combined with images, high-speed technologies, commercial transactions processed through handheld devices, and video conferencing or meetings are all factors changing the landscape of the telecommunications infrastructure.

Telecommunications service providers are the spine, veins, and arteries of the international information revolution. It is a revolution far beyond the imagination of an individual who peered through a telescope across a land mass at a person signaling back. It is the continuation of an evolution, not a revolution, of technology and human interaction with information. Driven by individuals, commerce, governments, and technology, the evolution will happen at increasing rates of speed.

There is a digital divide. A vast distance exists between the developed world that is enjoying this technology, and the developing world which will be able to install and use this information to their advantage without having to work through the stages that occurred from the late sixteenth century to the present. The progress being experienced now will continue unabated and provide the connection between people in the developing world in the areas of basic voice, data, and text, while setting the stage for adoption of advanced services for economic development as the nation progresses.

Finance, technology, and deregulation (as in the United States market) and privatization of government monopolies in Europe, have served to restructure the environment of competition. Especially with the momentum provided by wireless technology, telecommunications infrastructure providers have to grow at rates faster than their own forecasts. In 2009, the introduction of the Internet connected phone from Apple brought the network bandwidth of the telecommunications provider to its knees and negatively impacted its net profit. At the same time, the door was opened to other providers to fill the void created by such rapid demand for this technology.

According to projections by the BLS, despite increased demand for telecommunications services, industry jobs are expected to decline by 9 percent between 2008 and 2018. Reasons for this include workers due to retire; the shift in technologies from wired to wireless, which reduces the number of people needed in the traditional wired sector; and increased reliability, which reduces the occupational groups required for repairing the infrastructure. In addition, network monitoring and automated forms of service provision reduce the need for manned network operation centers as operations are combined amongst fewer workers.

Hardest hit is the sector of wired infrastructure (including the installed base of fiber optic trunks across the land and under the sea). Decline is projected at 11 percent. Growth of the expanding wireless infrastructure will not replace the employment base that the wired sector is losing. The decline in wireless is projected at 1 percent. Technology is also being implemented to allow higher traffic rates over the existing wired and wireless infrastructure. That fact will not increase the number of employees required to implement higher speed, higher density traffic on existing trunks.

Within the wireless sector, there will be an increasing need for customer service, automated support of customer service representatives, and personnel to implement, install, and support the new combinations of technology. Computer design and application skills will grow to support this sector because of the automation that is central to this sector.

Changes in the service offerings of cell phone, cable television, and Internet companies will change the skill set for new employees. Voice, video, and meeting services over the Internet will increase usage for cable television providers, Internet service providers (including wireless companies), and, in the future, wireless service provided over larger geographic areas (referred to as Wi-Max). This change to wider coverage of wireless will either create revenue streams for existing large providers or allow new entrants to provide wireless services.

A battle is waging between technologies. Will the cell phone become the ubiquitous communications, music, and computing device, or will the netbook or the Internet phone become a personal digital assistant? Vehicles are starting to have capabilities of roving computers connected to telecommunications infrastructure providers. Services provided in public environments, planes, trains, and automobiles will be in demand from telecommunications infrastructure providers as WiFi hotpots are now.

Over the long term, movements by government to deregulate, demonopolize their existing providers, and implement telecommunications-friendly regulations and taxation will create the environment for the emergence or contraction of various forms of delivery of telecommunications services. In addition, the economy on a national and international basis is a determining factor in providing capital for the design and implementation of infrastructure and technology.

Existing small and midsize companies will constantly face cost pressures where economies of scale are the norm. They will be targets for merger and acquisition if they provide high quality and serve a niche in their business. Large providers face pressures of cost because as they grow larger they have to bring along their installed base of current services and customers. That can cause a drain on their capital as they go into new technologies, make strategic acquisitions, and make decisions quickly as the market is moving.

Thus, employment prospects are bright in most levels and stages of the industry. It is up to the individual to be knowledgeable of these trends and factors that affect skill sets in order to navigate one's career. Because of the speed of change, personal responsibility for upgrading skills is a key factor for enjoying a long career in telecommunications.

Employment Advantages

The availability of many new applications in Internet phones is keeping intense pressure on the industry to respond and grow. The industry has moved beyond games and music to essential applications for daily lives, especially social networking. It is also an industry that is international in nature as these applications work across borders and connect people in real time to each other. Technical schools, colleges, and universities are adding course work in this field. They draw new students in fields where they know their graduates can find employment. Graphics, video, television, live meetings, voice and image transmission, information compression on wire and wireless networks are all subjects of study enabling students to enter the field of leading applications and technologies.

Basic subjects of transmission, magnetic field theory, antennas, information compression, and wired and wireless transmission standards are excellent places to enter and replace retiring traditional employees. Subjects such as transmitting light signals along glass strands, using existing up and down link satellite frequencies, voice and data compression techniques, and wireless technology are strong entry technologies for a career.

Current exciting prospects for expansion, such as increased usage of the satellite, wired, and wireless infrastructure for large-area coverage of wireless connections (WiMax), will rapidly be eclipsed with new technology not yet named. The environment is a constantly moving window of change and the challenge will be to renew one's skills in order to stay at the crest of the wave.

Annual Earnings

The Telecommunications Industry Association reported global revenues in 2008 of $1.7 trillion and U.S. revenues of $518.3 billion. The compounded growth rate was just over 10 percent. Wireless will be the largest growth area as the market is expected to grow at a rate faster than that of wire line broadband services. The technologies in play are VOIP, WiMax, and Internet television;

higher speeds are becoming available on both wireless and wire line. A lot of this growth will occur as both a shift from wire line services as well as by using some of the overcapacity in wire and fiber routes. However, technologies allowing for greater speed and compression of the information use the same service paths without adding employment.

Since telecom providers are constantly addressing profitability issues as the landscape changes beneath their feet, they will be looking to outsource many of the services that now exist within the enterprise. Customer care centers and network operations centers are two examples. As such, there will be opportunities for midsize companies to enter businesses associated with the telecommunications services sector. Small companies, especially wireless services, will be threatened by the introduction of WiMax, which will provide services blanketing the areas they currently serve on a niche basis.

RELATED RESOURCES FOR FURTHER RESEARCH

BROADBAND FOR AMERICA
P.O. Box 57244
Washington, DC 20037
Tel: (866) 646-8668
http://www.broadbandforamerica.com

CTIA-THE WIRELESS ASSOCIATION
1400 16th St. NW, Suite 600
Washington, DC 20036
Tel: (202) 736-3200
Fax: (202) 785-0721
http://www.ctia.org

INSTITUTE OF ELECTRICAL AND ELECTRONICS ENGINEERS
3 Park Ave., 17th Floor
New York, NY 10016-5997
Tel: (212) 419-7900
Fax: (212) 752-4929
http://www.ieee.org

INTERNATIONAL COMMUNICATION ASSOCIATION
1500 21st St. NW
Washington, DC 20036
Tel: (202) 955-1444

Fax: (202) 955-1448
http://www.icahdq.org

INTERNATIONAL TELECOMMUNICATION UNION
Place des Nations
1211 Geneva 20
Switzerland
Tel: 41-22-730-5111
Fax: 41-22-733-7256
http://www.itu.int

JOURNAL OF TELECOMMUNICATIONS AND INFORMATION
TECHNOLOGY, NATIONAL INSTITUTE OF
TELECOMMUNICATIONS
Szachowa St. 1
04-894 Warsaw
Poland
Tel: 48-22-5128-183
Fax: 48-22-5128-400
http://www.nit.eu

MICROWAVE JOURNAL
685 Canton St.
Norwood, MA 02062
Tel: (781) 769-9750
Fax: (781) 769-5037
http://www.mwjournal.com

TELECOMMUNICATIONS INDUSTRY ASSOCIATION
2500 Wilson Blvd., Suite 300
Arlington, VA 22201
Tel: (703) 907-7700
Fax: (703) 907-7727
http://www.tiaonline.org

ABOUT THE AUTHOR

Charles L. Bonza has thirty years of experience in general management and CEO positions at Hewlett-Packard, Acterna, Sypris Electronics, and BSW South Africa in electronics equipment, telecommunications instrumentation and software, computers, and telecommunications software development, management, and systems implementation. He worked for fifteen years in international environments and engaged in career counseling and change coaching in working with employees during hiring, development, and layoff situations.

His technical training in career coaching includes both course work and practical experience at the Hudson Institute for coaching.

FURTHER READING

Columbia School of International and Public Affairs. *Career Opportunities in Telecommunications.* http://sipa.columbia.edu/resources_services/career_services/current_students/career_resources/opportunities/CareerOpp_Telecommunications.pdf.

Harte, Lawrence. *Voice over Data Networks for Managers.* Fuquay Varina, N.C.: Althos, 2007.

Huurdeman, Anton A. *The Worldwide History of Telecommunications.* Hoboken, N.J.: John Wiley & Sons, 2003.

International Telecommunications Union. *ICT Statistics Database.* http://www.itu.int/ITU-D/ICTEYE/Indicators/Indicators.aspx.

Lee, Beong Gi. *Broadband Wireless Access and Local Networks: Mobile Wimax and Wifi.* Fitchburg, Mass.: Artech House, 2008.

Plunkett, Jack W. *Plunkett's Telecommunications Industry Almanac Statistics, 2010.* Houston, Tex.: Plunkett Research, 2009. http://www.plunkettresearch.com/Industries/Telecommunications/Telecommunications Statistics/tabid/96/Default.aspx.

Simpson, Wes. *Video Over IP: IPTV, Internet Video, H.264, P2P, Web TV, and Streaming.* 2d ed. Burlington, Mass.: Focal Press, 2008.

U.S. Bureau of Labor Statistics. *Career Guide to Industries,* 2010-2011 ed. http://www.bls.gov/oco/cg.

_____. *A New Approach to Classifying Industries in the Information Sector.* http://www.bls.gov/opub/ils/pdf/opbils75.pdf.

U.S. Census Bureau. North American Industry Classification System (NAICS), 2007. http://www.census.gov/cgi-bin/sssd/naics/naicsrch?chart=2007.

U.S. Department of Commerce. International Trade Administration. Office of Trade and Industry Information. Industry Trade Data and Analysis. http://ita.doc.gov/td/industry/otea/OTII/OTII-index.html.